W9-CZU-188

Studies in Jewish Culture and Society

A SERIES OF THE

CENTER FOR ADVANCED JUDAIC STUDIES

UNIVERSITY OF PENNSYLVANIA

CONTRIBUTORS

GULIE NE'EMAN ARAD Ben-Gurion University in the Negev

ARNOLD J. BAND University of California, Los Angeles

YORAM BILU Hebrew University of Jerusalem

DANIEL J. ELAZAR Temple University and Bar Ilan University

MICHAEL FEIGE Ben-Gurion University in the Negev

NURITH GERTZ Open University in Israel

ARTHUR ARYEH GOREN Columbia University

TRESA GRAUER Ben-Gurion University in the Negev

JENNA WEISSMAN JOSELIT historian of American Jews

IRA KATZNELSON Columbia University

BARBARA KIRSHENBLATT-GIMBLETT New York University

DEBORAH DASH MOORE Vassar College

EWA MORAWSKA University of Pennsylvania

JEFFREY SHANDLER Rutgers University

S. ILAN TROEN Ben-Gurion University in the Negev

BETH S. WENGER University of Pennsylvania

EDITED BY DEBORAH DASH MOORE

AND S. ILAN TROEN

Divergent Jewish Cultures

Israel and America

Yale University Press/New Haven & London

For Ione Strauss

Set in Galliard type by Keystone Typesetting, Inc.
Printed in the United States of America.

Library of Congress Cataloging-in-Publication Data

Divergent Jewish cultures : Israel and America / edited by Deborah Dash Moore and S. Ilan Troen.
p. cm. — (Studies in Jewish culture and society)
Includes bibliographical references and index.
ISBN 0-300-08426-9
1. Jews—United States—Identity. 2. Jews—United States—Attitudes toward Israel. 3. Jews—United States—Social life and customs. 4. Jews—Israel—Identity. 5. Israel and the diaspora. 6. Israel—Civilization. I. Moore, Deborah Dash, 1946– II. Troen, S. Ilan (Selwyn Ilan), 1940– III. Title. IV. Series.
E184.J5 D55 2001
956.9405—dc21

2001002536

A catalogue record for this book is available from the British Library.

The paper in this book meets the guidelines for permanence and durability of the Committee on Production Guidelines for Book Longevity of the Council on Library Resources.

10 9 8 7 6 5 4 3 2 1

Contents

Preface

This book is the third in the series Studies in Jewish Culture and Society, published by the Center for Advanced Judaic Studies of the University of Pennsylvania. It constitutes part of the written record of the regular weekly seminars, intense ongoing conversations, and culminating academic conference (The Martin Gruss Colloquium) that took place during the academic year 1996–97.

In that year, the center initially created two distinct research groups: the first on Israeli culture and society during the early years of Israeli statehood, and the second on American Jewish culture and society in the twentieth century. The seminars were scheduled at different times in the day, and members of each research group were encouraged to cross boundaries and participate in one another's seminars. What emerged in the end, to the delight of all, was a unified research group that examined the commonalities and divergences of Jewish social and cultural life in the twentieth century in the two major centers, Israel and the United States, particularly after the Nazi Holocaust.

In the main, the Israeli group was made up of Israeli scholars, most of them male. On the American side, most of the scholars were American and female. On many levels, the seminars on Israeli and American Jewish culture became a unique experiment in communication. The participating scholars brought to the table their particular cultural and methodological perspectives. The Israeli scholars were divided ideologically and methodologically. Adding the American mix, with an oft-stated feminist bent, created remarkably lively and even contentious discussions. For Israeli scholars to be exposed to American Jewish history, sociology, and literature was also a major breakthrough in their cultural awareness of fields generally not part of their education. And the same was true for most of the American scholars, who found themselves delving into the intricacies of Israeli sociology, literature, and politics. The result was most exciting, unanticipated, and deeply rewarding—a kind of mini–summit conference extending through an entire year between intellectuals of the two communities, each attempting to understand and communicate with the other. This book represents the partial result of this invaluable human encounter.

One of the most cherished members of both groups was the late professor Daniel Elazar. He was clearly "the swing man," a product of both American and Israeli cultures and a distinguished scholar of both societies. His astute comments at both seminars added immensely to the success of the groups' deliberations. He was more than a scholar of American and Israeli cultures; he had been a full-fledged participant in the shaping of both societies during the past forty years. For all members of the research groups, it was a unique privilege to learn from him. His presence is surely felt in the creation of this volume, and in many respects it represents a memorial to his scholarly career and his passionate and energetic life. May his memory be a blessing to all of us who as teachers and scholars continue his life work.

I would like to thank all those who have had a hand in shaping this book, beginning with its two conscientious and thoughtful editors, professors Deborah Dash Moore of Vassar College and Ilan Troen of Ben Gurion University. All the members of the seminar, both those whose contributions appear below and those not represented, added immensely to the intellectual ambience of the center. My thanks to the center's able and devoted staff for their critical work in preparing this volume, especially Etty Lassman. Charles Grench of Yale University Press served ably in seeing this volume through to publication.

In dedicating this book to Ione Strauss, the center honors one of the great friends and supporters of higher Jewish learning and the University of Pennsylvania. Virtually from its inception, Ms. Strauss has served faithfully and energetically as a member of the Board of Overseers of the Center for Advanced Judaic Studies. Her deep understanding and commitment to the shaping of a literate Jewish culture in the United States is reflected in her unfailing support for the center's programs and intellectual achievements. We hope that she will enjoy the exciting learning presented in this volume and view it as the fruit of a collaboration between scholars and individuals like herself who have helped build the environment from which this scholarship has emerged.

David B. Ruderman
Director, Center for Advanced Judaic Studies
University of Pennsylvania

Introduction

DEBORAH DASH MOORE AND S. ILAN TROEN

Two creative centers of Jewish life emerged in the twentieth century. These divergent centers in Israel and in the United States claimed self-sufficiency, authority, and competence. Jews living in the United States established an alternative mode of cultural expression to that of Jewish citizens in the sovereign state of Israel, instead of yet another classic Jewish diaspora linked to other peripheries by trade in commerce, religion, and culture. Despite their common claims to centrality, Israeli and American Jews recognize shared Jewish concerns and connections. Ironically, these two diverse communities developed out of similar European roots. Eastern European Jews pursued very different visions as they settled in American cities and the land of Israel. Yet common crises confronting both centers as well as ties of kinship and history until recently have obscured their divergent paths. Complicating perceptions of their distinct trajectories, Jews in the United States often projected their own image upon Israeli society while

Israelis fashioned versions of America that spoke to the needs of a new nation struggling to define its values and secure its existence.

Jewish population statistics drawn from both ends of the century register its dramatic changes. In 1900, more than 80 percent of world Jewry lived in Europe. Yet immigration and upheaval relentlessly redistributed European Jews. At the outbreak of World War II, only about 60 percent remained. In the aftermath of the Holocaust, the decimated communities of European Jewry contracted even further as a result of mass emigration and rapid assimilation, so that at the end of the twentieth century fewer than 20 percent of the world Jewish population lived in Europe. European Jews progressed in the course of the century from the dominant center to a diasporic periphery. In a radical reversal, former peripheries, notably American Jewry and Israel, became the centers. By the end of the first decade of the twenty-first century America and Israel will likely share more or less equally close to 80 percent of world Jewry.[1]

The impact of European Jews on both societies extends beyond their demography to social solidarity. European Jews and their descendants form the majority of both the American and Israeli Jewish populations. Family ties endure between relatives whose kin made alternate choices, though their extent has never been calculated. Both centers share memories and heritage. These common vestiges help account for intense connections between the two communities. A sense of mutual responsibility and fate deeply rooted in Jewish historical experience and religious culture animates American and Israeli Jews. Indeed, a keen sense of Jewish solidarity probably remains the salient characteristic binding Jews who reside in distant places, speak different languages, and live in diverse political and social contexts.[2]

Nevertheless, awareness grows of the attenuation of bonds that connect both communities. Manifest and active kinship has been diminished if not forgotten. Yiddish is no longer a common language, and with its loss as a lingua franca, a moral vocabulary disappears from currency among Jews. English is the mother tongue (and often the only language) of American Jewry, and Hebrew is the language of Israeli Jews. While knowledge of English is surely greater in Israel than Hebrew is in America, most American and Israeli Jews do not share a language that expresses common experiences and concerns or a cultural and group identity that transcends both time and place. Although American Jews resort often to translation, turning the works of Israeli writers into English, Israeli and American Jews lack intimate knowledge of one another. They tend to hold stereotypes rather than real people in mind when they think of each other, despite their similar origins.[3] The pervasiveness of American popular culture enthusiastically embraced by Israelis often substitutes for knowledge and makes many indifferent to American Jews as a distinctive social group. Impressed by the power of the United States on the world scene, most Israelis ignore the individuality of the American Jewish community. Different social realities, historical experience, and political needs have generated distinctive cultures.

In the United States, Jews have accommodated to a Christian culture and a society that prizes individualism and self-reliance; in Israel, they have created, in the midst of the Moslem Middle East, an ethnic Jewish sovereignty in which personal status is defined in terms of communal membership. In the United States, Jews have entered and contributed to building the world's wealthiest society where they enjoy great physical security. In Israel, they have reclaimed a semi-arid and resource-poor land and struggled to maintain a state in which widespread prosperity is recent and security not yet fully assured. Such distinctions have necessitated fundamental ecological adaptations and have produced differential patterns of cultural development.

Yet this divergence between American and Israeli Jewry actually predates emigration from Europe, finding its roots in Jewish responses to the Enlightenment and modernization. The Enlightenment repelled traditional sectors of Jewish society, which responded by creating traditional versions of Judaism, ranging from Hasidim and *haredim,* or pietist movements, to modern orthodoxy. Each sector claimed to be the authentic guardian of Judaism. The pietists often denied opportunities for significant cultural interaction with the non-Jewish world. Other Jews discovered in Enlightenment ideals new ways of thinking and sought to integrate into emerging democratic, national states in Western Europe. These liberal Jews articulated alternative forms of Judaism that contributed to the shaping of Reform and Conservative Judaism.

European Jews also posited collective responses to modernity. Defined in their host societies, the Russian and Austro-Hungarian empires, as a nation with distinctive linguistic, cultural, religious, and ethnic characteristics, Jews from these regions sought a national solution to the Jewish problem. Ranging from the socialist Jewish Workers Bund, which sought to retain distinctive collective characteristics as a discrete nation within Europe, to Zionism, which promoted a national homeland in Palestine, the solutions championed by Eastern European Jews aimed for a goal of national autonomy. In contrast, most Western European Jews desired integration as a religious community or acculturation on an individual basis.[4]

Thus, in responding to conditions that obtained in the United States and possibilities created by Jewish sovereignty in Israel, European Jews were implementing choices that antedated the emergence of these two centers. Both locales afforded the prospect of constructing new identities that had already been posited by different sectors of European Jewry. Immigration patterns reinforced these opportunities, drawing ideologically committed Eastern European Jews to Palestine in two waves constituting the second and third aliyas before and after World War I. Family ties, chain migration, and dreams of economic opportunity motivated most other Eastern European Jews to look across the Atlantic Ocean to the United States. The former migration dynamic stimulated an elite eager to build a new Jewish society; the latter encouraged masses of working-class Jews to seek a better future for themselves and their children.

An evolving secular Israeli culture expresses conceptions of national autonomy championed by Eastern European Jews. This model diminishes the authority and centrality of Jewish law even as it affirms a collective Jewish civic consciousness. The large majority of Israeli Jews, perhaps 80 percent, are avowedly secular—*hiloni*—an identity that may include spirituality and does not require affirmation of atheism or agnosticism. Such secularism encourages cultural innovation that speaks directly to Israelis in Hebrew. Although many secular Israeli Jews retain vestiges of religious culture, most have embraced a civil religion that has programmatically and creatively borrowed from traditional Judaism. As a result, native-born Israelis differ significantly from their immigrant parents or grandparents.[5]

Descendants of those who emigrated to America similarly negotiate with their past. In the United States, only a minority of fewer than 10 percent choose forms of orthodoxy. Most prefer Reform and Conservative religious orientations, which have only a slight representation in Israel. With roots in Western Europe, both movements reflect Jewish willingness to enter modern, democratic societies. The Reform and Conservative Jewish communities have flourished in the fertile soil of an open American society where the absence of an established church encourages voluntarist religious activity. Although both Jewish patterns reflect an understanding that religion is but one of the elements that command the attention and constitute the identity of American Jews, Jewish cultural creativity in the United States as often occurs outside of religious frameworks as within them. American Jews share an American civil religion that emphasizes ideals of tolerance, pluralism, consensus, and individualism, and enshrines democracy as an ultimate ideal.[6]

These American and Israeli descendants of European Jewry have developed divergent solutions to living in their distinctive societies. Israelis have accommodated themselves and are apparently at ease in the ancient homeland. Their American counterparts are "at home" in America. Despite differences, real commonalities precipitate expressions of unity and shared destiny.[7]

"As we approach the 21st century, we pause to celebrate and rededicate ourselves to the enduring ties that bind us together as one people." So begins "A Covenant Between The Jewish People of North America and Israel," a document circulated when the 1998 General Assembly of North American Jews convened in Jerusalem. Signed by members of the Knesset and leaders of American Jewry, this statement elaborately reiterates a popular slogan articulated at similar meetings for more than a generation: "We are one." The intensity and frequency with which such declarations are made indicate a growing need to counter a contrary reality.[8]

These affirmations differ substantially from rhetoric characterizing Jews living outside of Israel shortly after the state was established in 1948. Both David Ben-Gurion, Israel's first prime minister, and Jacob Blaustein, president of the American Jewish Committee, had agreed that Israel and American Jews were not one. In 1952 they signed a document designed to articulate that position and define the relations between the new Jewish state and the largest Jewish society in the aftermath of the Holocaust. Yet neither leader questioned the vitality of the bonds between these branches of the

Jewish people. With the exception of fringe groups in both countries, the majority shared a commitment to the concept of a world Jewish community encompassing Jews in Israel and throughout the diaspora. The sense of a common fate, made so painfully real by the Holocaust, permeated their generation's consciousness as did a host of shared memories. Both Ben-Gurion (born in 1886) and Blaustein (born in 1892) had risen to lead communities located on the periphery of a Jewish world that had been overwhelmingly European at the time of their birth.

This book seeks to understand how divergent cultures have emerged from shared origins. In locating the nature of and reasons for continuities with Europe, it examines as well the source of distinctive characteristics. This is not and could not be a comprehensive study. Rather, it explores phenomena that have parallel expression in both societies. Similar studies have focused on the distinctiveness of Judaism as experienced in America and Israel.[9] The emphasis here on political and social cultures grounds discussion in examples of literature, art, history, and politics.

ESTABLISHING NEW IDENTITIES

We begin by addressing the question of identity. The first six chapters analyze cultural and social phenomena to trace how European Jews and their descendants assumed new identities as American and Israeli Jews.

S. Ilan Troen introduces the construction of new identities by examining how European Jews understood the purposes and meanings of Zionism in Zion. Pioneers built Zionism on a rejection of Europe and an anticipation of creating an alternative modern Jewish personality. His analysis rests on a study of the largest social institution established by Zionist society: a secular, public school system. Through it, Zionist ideologues, public officials, and educators attempted to transform European Jewry. Willing to preserve what they admired in the culture of the shtetl, they rejected its passivity in the face of physical threats and actual violence. These educators insisted on a new national educational cultural ideal. In turning away from the traditional orthodox schooling of the shtetl, Zionists developed a new curriculum to produce modern, secularized Jews capable of defending themselves and their homeland.

Zionist educators provided secularized Hebrew instruction that revolutionized the Jewish relationship to sacred literature to approximately 80 percent of Jewish youth from the 1920s to the present. They supplanted such traditional texts as the Talmud and prayer book (*Siddur*) with the Bible, particularly its historical sections. This revolutionary emphasis is expressed in the opening paragraph of Israel's Declaration of Independence, which begins: "The Land of Israel was the birthplace of the Jewish people," and concludes with the radical claim: "Here they wrote and gave the Bible to the world." Zionism excised Divine authorship of the Bible and made Jews the prime actors in shaping their own destiny as a people. Zionists urged that Jews should no longer rely on salvation or redemption by the Almighty. The radical intent is captured in the words of a classic Zionist song: "We have come to the land to build it and to be rebuilt by it." This contrasts vividly with the traditional prayer for Redemption recited daily: "When the Lord brought back those who returned to Zion we were like dreamers. . . . The Lord will do great things for us; We shall rejoice" (Psalms cxxvi).

The new secular curriculum had unwanted consequences. It devalued Jewish life abroad and, by focusing on the national renaissance in the homeland, threatened to sever connections with the diaspora and Jewish past. Moreover, such continuities have been reinforced over the past generation by the penetration of American values that emphasize individualism at the expense of community, that is, an ethnic nationality. The pursuit of personal growth and self-satisfaction may be eroding a collective commitment to shared objects.

One could argue that in this sense, Jewish identities as constructed in Israel and the United States now confront similar forces that threaten to undermine their otherness. Nevertheless, American culture challenges American Jews with a more immediate and acute alternative. Living in a Jewish state affords a buffer to outside influences and enables Israeli Jews to exploit possibilities not available to Jews who live as a minority.

Watching the process of settling the land from afar, American Jews saw an utterly different reality, one made in their own image. As Jeffrey Shandler vividly describes, European Jews who immigrated to the United States Americanized their images of Israel. Adopting the posture of impresarios, they celebrated pioneers and the settlement of the land in terms that gave meaning to their own choice of America. In this way, American Zionism invited Jews to partake of a performance that affirmed Americanism as much as Jewishness. Far from obliging Jews to leave their new Promised Land for the ancestral homeland, American Zionism became one of the building blocks in the identity of American Jews.

Shandler shows how Zionism was domesticated for American Jews who were invited to consume the agricultural products of Zionist pioneers, especially wines and olives and even cigarettes. The impresarios Shandler investigates incorporated Zionist songs and dances into pageants based on Zionist pioneering. The producers of these representations of Zionist society expected their shows to anchor European-born Jews in America rather than induce them to emigrate to Palestine. They clearly assumed that support for Zionism was an American value. From Louis Brandeis around World War I to Abba Hillel Silver after World War II, Zionism has been defined as a form of American liberalism. Loyalty to Zionist goals has been viewed as consistent with devotion to American ideals. If Europe was the increasingly distant past that led to a tragic end, Israel represented a future in which American Jews had a stake and which reflected a blend of American and Jewish virtues.

The Israeli reality differed significantly from American imaginings of it. Settled in their homeland, Israelis, particularly recent immigrants from North Africa, reversed the process described by Shandler. Immigrants in poor settlement towns far from the centers of Israeli politics turned to explore and reclaim their connections with their communities of origin in the diaspora. Scholars, including Alex Weingrod and André Levi, have found that Jewish immigrants from North Africa and the Middle East invented rituals to assert their prior identity and rebel against the Ashkenazi (i.e., European) version of the New Israel.[10] Like American Zionists, they staged their own rituals and projected identities.

Yoram Bilu points out that by the 1970s immigrants from North Africa had inaugurated pilgrimages to sites on the Israeli periphery where they venerated religious figures, many of whom hailed from outside Israel. This phenomenon has grown to become a recognized and accepted feature of Israeli life. Scholars interpret such pilgrimages as a firm rejection of the culture and manners of the new Israeli as defined by European-born intellectuals, politicians, and educators. Not only do the ornate shrines and elaborate ceremonies create religious meaning but they also become instruments of cultural and political self-assertion and defiance. Simultaneously this form of hagiolatry, disinterring the remains of spiritual leaders who died abroad and reinterring them in Israeli soil, indicates a commitment to bonding with the new country.

Although Bilu focuses on North African Jews, similar practices exist among formerly European Jews, particularly among the ultra-Orthodox. Numerous Hasidic courts, whose origins are Eastern European, have reconstituted themselves in Israel. The Lubavitcher Hasidim who actively proselytize other Jews, for example, have built an exact replica in Israel of the residence and headquarters of their spiritual leader (*rebbe*) on Eastern Parkway in Brooklyn. Much of the Yeshiva world of Lithuanian Jewry has been reconstituted in sections of B'nai Brak, near Tel Aviv, and in numerous neighborhoods in Jerusalem. A distinctly European ambience animates these areas, readily observable in their residents' dress and in the pervasive use of Yiddish. Thus, while Israeli society has insisted on the transformation of the large mass of diaspora Jewry who became citizens, it has at the same time preserved unyielding minorities.

European Jews who came to Palestine did not think of themselves as entering a society where they had to adapt to externally imposed social patterns. Ottoman authorities possessed political power and Palestinian Arabs established the rhythms of daily life, but most Jews had no intention of becoming like the Arab majority or assimilating into their culture. Jews also denied that they were settling in a place that belonged to others. Rather, they understood themselves as returning home to the "homeland"—their *molede,* or birthplace.

Their ideological intentions notwithstanding, Jews still found themselves in a totally unfamiliar environment, where they had to cultivate knowledge of a strange land and nurture a sense of their new home. European Jewish immigrants were familiar with the country as an imagined land rooted in religious texts and collective memory, not as a place they had personally experienced. To provide first-hand experience, Jews invented a process of discovery termed *yediat ha'aretz,* or "knowing the land." The ways of doing this included youth movement field trips, learning songs, and reading modern Hebrew literature. Jews in Israel turned to Hebrew as part of the process of returning to the land. Aware that naming asserts authority and control, they identified sections of the country with biblical nomenclature, and designated settlements and streets with the names of events and personalities derived from ancient Hebrew and modern Jewish history.

Archaeology acquired a significant place in the process of taking possession of the country and in reshaping European Jews into authentic natives in a land they had known only in their imagination prior to emigration. Michael Feige demonstrates how archaeology achieved such influence and explains why this academic discipline enjoyed a large following among citizens of the new Jewish state. He observes that archaeology was explicitly geared to enable a preponderantly immigrant society to discover its ancient roots in the land and to use these in the shaping of a national identity. Jews took symbolic possession of the land and its history. The annual meetings of the Israeli Exploration Society became a form of secular pilgrimage, with mass, public meetings taking place not only at such major centers as Jerusalem and Tel Aviv during the time of the traditional autumnal holiday of Succoth (Tabernacles) but also in peripheral communities from the Galilee in the north to the Negev and Eilat in the south. Scholars and government officials including the prime minister, the president, and leading military officers addressed the thousands who attended the three-day meetings. Indeed, Yigael Yadin and Moshe Dayan were both archaeologists and chiefs of staff.

Not surprisingly the Ministry of Education funded archaeology because it was not only a scientific discipline but also a means for inculcating a sense of belonging, yet another form of yediat ha'aretz. Immigrants encountered the history of their ancestors through these pilgrimages and public assemblies and were invited to see themselves as legitimate successors. Immigrants living in peripheral sites, particularly newly established development towns where they constituted the overwhelming proportion of the population, were publicly and officially endowed with the status of pioneers reclaiming the ancestral homeland. In this fashion, even the newest immigrant in the most isolated and unpromising location received membership in both an ancient and contemporary narrative. Perhaps the most popular site—Masada—remained uninhabited. Nevertheless, as the site of the rebellion of the last defenders of Jewish autonomy in the face of the mighty Roman Empire, Masada came to represent a spirit of bravery and self-sacrifice that had shriveled in the diaspora. As a heroic site, it attracted legions of volunteers who assisted in excavations and visitors who made the early morning climb to see the sun rising over the desert and the Dead Sea. These rituals invested immigrants with the grandeur of the past and ushered them into their new Israeli identities.

The popularity of archaeology began to subside by the end of the second decade of independence. Perhaps the meetings became too scientific and thereby lost their mass appeal. Alternatively, archaeology itself may have assumed less relevance in constructing a national identity.

As newcomers to the land of Israel labeled sites throughout the countryside as Jewish, so did American Jews identify certain clothes as "Jewish." However, for European Jews in Palestine, such naming affirmed a positive collective identity while for Jewish immigrants in the United States, labeling clothing involved rejecting an undesirable, gendered identity. Jenna Weissman Joselit tackles the problem of building identity through American Jews' obsession with their sartorial appearance in gentile eyes. Joselit focuses on controversies over clothing, jewelry, and fashion to uncover the gendered dimensions of Jewish concerns with integration. Her analysis demonstrates that ostensibly superficial details of dress reflect deep concerns about identity in a society in which Jews were still newcomers and unsure of their acceptance. This topic often appears in literature written by American Jews. From Abraham Cahan's *The Rise of David Levinsky* (1917) through Norman Podhoretz's *Making It* (1967), the clothes and behavior of Jews in public places have concerned American Jewish authors. Cahan describes at length the garments Levinsky dons as a new American in a scene that symbolizes his shedding of European appearance and identity. Podhoretz recounts in detail lessons in dining and fashion he received from his gentile high school teacher. These incidents metaphorically appreciate the difficult and sometimes painful transit from poor immigrant to commercial success. They reveal the social costs of acceptance in the case of Cahan's hero, or in Podhoretz's account of himself, the price of moving from working-class status to an Ivy League university and the center of American intellectual society. As DeTocqueville observed about Americans, so Jewish immigrants and their children have realized about themselves: in a democratic society, correct manners and fashions are needed to find one's place in America.

The setting for Joselit's analysis is the synagogue, and the actors are rabbis and their congregants, particularly women. In Mel Brooks's film *The Producers* (1968), Zero Mostel views from his office window a flashy woman entering an obviously expensive car and calls out: "If you got it, flaunt it!" Rabbis preaching from the pulpit demurred. They worried about the "de-orientalization" of Jewish women. Weaning them from gaudy taste was a step in their westernization or Americanization. Indeed, Joselit traces rabbinic sermons into the 1960s and 1970s, when rabbis still commented on dress as indicators of the difference between European-Jewish and American culture. This analysis of the discussion of fashion in the synagogue illustrates a pervasive anxiety with what should be retained from the old world and what should be adopted in the new. That European Jews and their children engaged in such calculations reveals that they were aware of the price of entering a society not of their own making and sensitive to demands that they conform to American gendered social norms.

Beth Wenger enlists the history of Haym Salomon, the Jewish financier of the American Revolution, as a barometer of tensions within the American Jewish community. Wenger uncovers Salomon as he emerged from fragments of historical evidence as a hero and patriot worthy of the honored place Jews sought as integrated and authentic members of American society. Toward the end of the nineteenth century, when the Daughters of the American Revolution were staking out their role in American history, some Jews saw in the glorification of Haym Salomon an opportunity to participate in the founding moment of their adopted country. They proposed his commemoration in monuments and medals. Others opposed this. They worried lest Jews appear too visible in their wealth, thereby giving rise to anti-Semitism as experienced in Europe. It would have been better had Salomon been a general in the Revolutionary War. A Jewish banker was not, in their view, a cause for public celebration.

In the 1920s Polish-Jewish immigrants adopted the cause of Haym Salomon as an immigrant hero, a Polish Jew, with as much success as their predecessors. Not until the growing Nazi threat during the Depression heightened concern for a monument to democracy and tolerance did Salomon receive public veneration, albeit initially as part of a triumvirate with George Washington and the patriot Robert Morris. After World War II, when American Jews were sufficiently secure in themselves and in their place in American society, popular books transformed Haym Salomon, the banker, into an unalloyed patriot. The act of sculpting an icon reveals as much about Jewish cultural struggles over memory and place within American society as it does about the figure himself.

CONTESTED IDENTITIES

Both centers saw acute struggles over the meaning of Jewish identity in a post-Holocaust world. Only during the 1960s were Israeli schoolchildren introduced in a sympathetic manner to the world of Sholom Aleichem—that is, the shtetl. It required the Eichmann trial to introduce a new sensibility to European Jewry and their way of life. At least a generation earlier, a sympathetic, if not patently nostalgic, perception of this shared past flourished among American Jews. For both American and Israeli Jews, however, the crucial event that prompted a reconsideration of that lost world was the Holocaust.

Barbara Kirshenblatt-Gimblett reminds us of a tradition of popular ethnography that would be mobilized to interpret the lost world of Eastern European Jewry after the Holocaust. These included literary studies, memoirs, and religious eulogies as well as festivals, exhibits, and performances. In choosing to focus on texts remote from standard anthropological accounts, Kirshenblatt-Gimblett retrieves a hidden intellectual history informing what became the standard American Jewish text describing Eastern Europe, *Life Is With People*.

Behind this history lies a moral vision not only to salvage what had been lost through violence by invoking memory but also to reclaim the cultural authority of the shtetl and thus to enhance Jewish and American life. The moral world of Eastern European Jews gains its most authoritative articulation in Abraham Joshua Heschel's extended eulogy, "The Earth is the Lord's."[11] Heschel translates Eastern European Jewish life into a timeless religious language, utterly contemporary for American Jews. He endows the very landscape of the shtetl with democratic aspiration and its denizens with a daily routine of divine encounter. Bella Chagall, wife of artist Marc Chagall, writes a memoir of her childhood in a timeless present that resembles the ethnographic present.[12] Structured not according to Western chronology but following the cycle of the Jewish year, Chagall dissolves her own story into an account of Jewish girlhood. Finally, the Zionist writer Maurice Samuel introduces through his biography of Sholom Aleichem the concept of a Jewish world, providing the trope to synthesize the popular ethnographic arts.[13] These inscribe a particular Jewish sensibility into American culture at a moment of Jewish loss and devastation.

As Israelis looked toward their own future they not only distanced themselves from Europe, they disassociated themselves from it in diverse ways. Israelis viewed Europe as a negative experience from which Jews should escape. As Anita Shapira has demonstrated in *Land and Power: The Zionist Resort to Force, 1881–1948*,[14] Zionism's embrace of the ethos of power and its search for heroes has related directly to the growing tide of violence against Europe's Jews since the end of the nineteenth century. Forced to recognize that Europe was not a possible home for Jews, Zionist thinkers concluded that only in a land of their own could Jews be freed from persecution and transformed into a normal people. The experience of impotence in the face of persecutors shaped Zionism's concept of the "new Jew" and of a reformed national character.

However severe the crisis of powerlessness at Zionism's inception more than a century ago, the Shoah escalated the problem to unprecedented dimensions. The proximity of this enormous tragedy to the establishment of Israel verified Zionist claims about the meaning of the European past and the necessity for a Jewish state. As a consequence, Zionism glorified Jews who actively resisted the Nazis. It exalted the heroic as the ultimate response while at the same time castigating European Jews for their failure to prevent the tragedy.

Gulie Arad examines how changes in Israeli society resulted in an evolving attitude toward the Shoah. She observes that the continuing conflict between Jews and Arabs has given cause for maintaining heroism as an essential national quality. During the first decade of independence, the state inaugurated a national holiday in enacting the Holocaust and Heroism

Remembrance Law (1953), established Yad Vashem as the museum and memorial of the Holocaust, and introduced materials into the school curriculum in praise of ghetto fighters and partisans. However, after the 1967 Six-Day War convincingly demonstrated Israeli military supremacy and provided Israelis with a heightened sense of security, cracks began to appear in the national consensus about how to interpret the Shoah. As criticism mounted over national policy in the territories and relations with Palestinian Arabs from the 1970s through the present, it became impossible to maintain a unitary canonical view of what the Holocaust meant. At the same time, other peoples appropriated the Holocaust as metaphor, deliberately eroding the Jewish/Zionist monopoly. With the ascension of Menachem Begin and the Likud party to power in 1977, the invocation of the Holocaust to justify political policies engendered confusion and debate. Some Israelis came to regard the Palestinians as victims of Israeli policy. These critics publicly and vigorously questioned the notion of the unerring, heroic virtue of Jews and criticized the martial affinity of Zionism's new Jew. This debate highlights the centrality of the Holocaust to the construction of national identity.

Nurith Gertz introduces a woman's perspective in order to unravel the gendered dimensions of the process of creating a national identity. She uncovers a profound ambivalence animating Yehudit Hendel's writing on Holocaust survivors. Hendel managed to shatter the hegemonic Zionist mold that depicted partisans and participants in ghetto uprisings as having a faster and easier transition than those who survived the camps. Nevertheless, all European Jews inexorably had to be reconstructed into Israelis in the fictional texts of postwar decades. Hendel disrupts such a view by inserting the voice of a survivor into her narrative and letting us hear it speak with authority. Thus competing accounts vie with each other, reflecting Hendel's own ambivalence and anticipating trends in Israeli culture that ultimately gave primacy to survivors in the 1970s and 1980s. As Gertz argues, Hendel challenges the articulation of Zionist as male and Jew as female that dominated the early decades of statehood. She breaks up the elision of nationality and gender effected by Zionist writers and filmmakers. But she also discourages the elimination of nationality championed by recent writers as a blanket response to earlier trends.

Zionist responses to the powerlessness of European Jewry also entered the consciousness and art of American Jews, who shared the idea that building a Jewish state reflected courage and symbolized a will to live. Expressions of this conviction can be found in the writings of Meyer Levin and Leon Uris. Both wrote from a perspective of the Jewish people's need for security, a deep sense of the injustice visited on Jews, and an appreciation for the virtue and courage of those who established Israel as an appropriate and necessary response to the Holocaust.[15] Even as Arad and Gertz illustrate how this view waned in Israel, Tresa Grauer traces and analyzes its decline in the American Jewish experience.

Grauer concentrates on the work of Philip Roth, particularly *The Counterlife* (1986) and *Operation Shylock* (1993). The distance from earlier days of a simple Israeli-centered idealism is apparent in these novels, though Roth never championed a Zionist interpretation as Levin and Uris did. The corruption Roth finds in the use of power by Israelis, particularly in their relationship to Palestinians, tarnishes the moral superiority that had been Zionism's claim. The demystification of Israel may be observed as early as Saul Bellow's *Mr. Sammler's Planet* (1970), which deals with the psychological and moral costs of Israeli militarism, but Roth extends this observation further in his novels written after the Israeli invasion of Lebanon and the Intifada of the 1980s. He characterizes Israelis as conquerors and Palestinians as refugees. In a reversal of roles that invites a change of sympathies, Jews no longer are refugees as in Uris's *Exodus,* but rather Palestinian Arabs occupy the position of underdog worthy of universal support. Moreover, Israel is no longer the promised, safe haven for world Jewry rooted in virtue and justice.

Roth's work echoes criticism rife in contemporary Israel where filmmakers, novelists, artists, and intellectuals have debunked myths of the past. In the American context his writing challenges the popular postwar construction of American Jewish identity. Roth would have his American Jewish heroes live out their lives in the American diaspora free of any sense of inferiority or insecurity. In his writings, Israel cannot challenge America as the legitimate and preferred home for the descendants of Europe's Jews.

Roth observes Israel from a distance, yet the Israeli writer Haim Hazaz knows from first-hand experience the triumphs and tragedies of the new state. The creation of a Jewish state obviously looms large for those like Hazaz who write in Hebrew and live in Israel. Arnold Band explores how Hebrew writers coped with Israel's establishment through an analysis of Haim Hazaz, one of the most celebrated writers of modern Hebrew. Born in Eastern Europe in 1898, Hazaz experienced pogroms and the Russian Revolution and spent eight years in Paris before moving to Palestine in 1931. Like many of his generation, he viewed art as an instrument for furthering national ends. His characters are often framed against the historic events which he himself experienced, including the Russian Revolution, the struggle for the state, the ingathering of exiles, and settlement of the land.

With Israel's creation, a new generation of writers, many of whom served as fighters in elite units during the War of Independence, took the place of immigrant Europeans like Hazaz. Yet Band finds precisely Hazaz's relative maturity captivating. Long a dreamer of the state, Hazaz was well positioned to comment on its realization. Above all, the possibility of a return to "normalcy" fascinated him, and he investigated its many meanings. With the anomaly of Jewish life in Europe apparently terminated by a return to the land in an independent state, Hazaz maintained, the Hebrew writer would have to engage universal human questions. Band points out that by the end of the first decade of independence, Hazaz was in transition between the traditional rhetoric of his generation, which tended to the messianic, and the mundane realities of life in a Jewish state. The main characters of his stories struggle between the heroic missions of Zionist ideology and the actuality, paradoxes, and ironies of building their lives in a society overburdened with utopian expectations. In this way, Hazaz prefigured the work of contemporary scholars, intellectuals, and artists who question what Israel actually is and what it has accomplished.

POLITICAL CULTURES

Literary texts provide one window into the tensions surrounding statehood. Political theory offers another mode of analysis. The entry into statehood and history dramatically changed Jewish political culture in Israel. With the exercise of sovereign power came efforts to reconfigure Jewish interpretations of political possibilities and the relation between means and ends. These unprecedented opportunities reverberated across the ocean to the United States, where Jews, energized by their participation as fighters in the military during World War II, sought to secure their status as equal citizens. Yet the politics of statehood and civil rights had roots in prewar Jewish cultures, shaped by the interaction of Jews as a minority with a majority Gentile society.

Ewa Morawska deftly defines the relationship of historical experience with ethnic norms in her wide-ranging comparison of alternative modes of assimilation adopted by Eastern European Jews in the United States. She develops several models of American Jewish political culture. Each integrates a collective ethnic identity with incorporation into mainstream economic, political, and social institutions set within specific historical circumstances. By rescuing the assimilationist interpretation from its ahistorical context, Morawska shows how ethnic identity emerged out of circumstances rather than following a linear progression from strong to weak. Perhaps more significantly, Jewish ethnicity assumed various characteristics depending upon characteristics of the surrounding environment and local Jewish groups. Among the latter, Morawska identifies internal divisions between German and Eastern European Jews as well as between immigrant and second generations.

Thus at one extreme stands New York, and also Boston and San Francisco, representing situations that enhance ethnic identity and strengthen assertive political postures. In San Francisco, Jews pursued a politics of resentment, sharpened by conflicts between Eastern European immigrants and native-born Jews of German descent. In Boston, Jews created a defensive political culture in an overwhelmingly Catholic city. Zionism, eschewed by many Jews in San Francisco, enhanced Jewish identity in Boston. At the other extreme can be found such southern communities as Greensboro, North Carolina, and Charleston, South Carolina. There assimilation did take hold, caused by an absence of conflict with the liberal Christian majority. Morawska locates a city like Cleveland, Ohio, midway between the two extremes because it sustained an inclusive politics of ethnicity, without resentment or defensiveness. She concludes that the variety of "differently 'textured' group ethnic identities" reveals a rich array of political cultures that implicitly challenge efforts to paint American Jews into a political corner (usually one labeled "liberal").

Distinctions and tensions existed among American Jews. Morawska observes how older communities of Central European Jews and the more recent Eastern European arrivals usually occupied different places geographically and economically, as well as within American culture. Yet, these distinctions gradually attenuated, especially during World War II. Even as the war experience contributed to a sense of brotherhood among Jews and, indeed, among most American citizens, the general prosperity of the postwar period enabled the children and grandchildren of Eastern European immigrants to close the gap with earlier arrivals from Western and Central Europe. In the postwar decades, a far more homogeneous and cohesive Jewry emerged in the United States than in Israel.

Zionism changed Israel's demographics by vastly increasing the Jewish community of Palestine—from around 25,000 in 1880, most of whom were native-born, to 650,000 at independence in 1948, most of whom were immigrants—and by making it overwhelmingly European, with Eastern European Jews as the critical element. The political leadership of the Yishuv (the pre-state Jewish settlement in Palestine) came from Russia and Poland. Most arrived prior to the mid-1920s. The mass immigration of the immediate post-Independence period, 1948–52, doubled the country's population to more than a million. Most immigrants were still European, largely Holocaust survivors. The expectation that Israel would emerge as a cohesive society built on foundations imagined and established by Eastern European Jews appeared likely. The massive immigration of North African Jews, of whom the largest group were Moroccan, shattered this illusion. Their entry into Israeli society provoked friction and conflict. Muted in the early years of the state, antagonism grew in intensity and by 1977 helped Menachem Begin's Likud coalition overturn Labor's hegemony. In marked contrast to the American Jewish experience, Jews in Israel had to sort out social, cultural, and political issues among themselves without the mitigating effect of living as a minority that had to confront a shared challenge of adapting to a host culture.

American Jews met this challenge in the postwar years with particular aplomb, benefiting from the rapid decline of discrimination and anti-Semitism. Ira Katznelson argues that the orientation of Jews to the entry rules of the West shifted in the United States from a strategy of "city niches" of "cautious, edgy vigilance" to a wider array of political cultures. The latter included everything from individual choices to pass, usually through intermarriage and conversion, to frontal assaults on ethnic discrimination, to ethnic mobilization to secure a collective foothold in society. Katznelson explores the social shifts modifying Jewish political culture. Although he credits the mobilization of World War II as a watershed in the process of change, he emphasizes the roots of transformation in the interwar years, specifically in changing residential patterns that disrupted earlier linkages between work and living. As Jews distanced their homes from their workplaces, they redefined their ethnicity along more homogeneous class and religious lines. In such settings, ethnic identity could be cast in symbolic terms. Jews felt free to fly the blue-and-white flag of Zionism and Israel alongside the Stars and Stripes in their synagogues and community centers.

Katznelson concludes that "the establishment of the State of Israel in 1948 effectively normalized Jewish ethnicity, making it comparable to Catholic ethnicities." Like other white Americans, Jews possessed a homeland and nation-state. The transformation of Jews into "whites" allowed them political choices previously unavailable.[16] With the establishment of Israel securing their identity as an American ethnic group, American Jews could explore the many possibilities of a democratic political culture and even contribute to its development.

By the end of World War II, being Jewish in the United States became a recognized and accepted identity that opened doors to opportunity and integration. What Western European Jewry had posited for itself, only to be disappointed by the course of twentieth-century European history, became a reality for American Jewry. As Will Herberg noted, American society included Protestants, Catholics, and Jews.[17] This inclusively universalist formula permitted distinctions based on association with a particular religious community which, in any case, was viewed as compatible and similar to the other religions. Thus, as Daniel Elazar observes in the concluding chapter, Jews may have sought cultural pluralism, but they found acceptance within the context of religious pluralism. In the ease and tolerance of this environment, association with a recognized religion was consistent with personal mobility. Assimilation or affirmation of collective identity coexisted in a society that encouraged permeable and fluid borders. Such an outcome was unimaginable for Jews emigrating to Palestine.

Elazar places the possibility of forming a distinctive American Jewish identity within a discrete historical framework and contrasts it with the historical possibilities that obtained in the Yishuv and Israel. His analysis illuminates why the choice of destination was critical to the growing divergence between the two centers. European Jews who came to the United States entered a society that had evolved a universalist, inclusive culture resting on individualism. Pluralism, articulated by the American Jewish social philosopher Horace Kallen became an accepted social and political principle. Jews in Israel came to a society based on varieties of parochialism and collective identities. Rights and recognition in the Ottoman Empire were not possible for Jews or anyone else as individuals. Everyone was categorized by membership into groups classified according to Moslem law. Jews were therefore accorded a place as an inferior but protected people. Such religiously linked classifications extended into the totality of non-religious matters. The collective character of identity was reaffirmed by the terms of reference of the British Mandate, which dealt with Arab and Jewish communities as discrete entities. Individuals belonged to either of these communities or their recognized subdivisions, and their affairs were attended to by communal institutions. The establishment of the State of Israel reaffirmed communal identities. Jews were citizens of a Jewish state even as the place of Arabs was confirmed by tradition, custom, and law. There was no experience or intention or desire to seek an alternative form of social organization. The individualistic civil society that evolved out of the American experience was beyond the ken or need of Israelis, unless one was an American Jew, a committed Zionist, who made aliyah to Israel.

Arthur Aryeh Goren is one such Jew. His epilogue takes a personal look at what it meant to move from the individualistic civil society of the United States to the collective, ethnic society of Israel. His memoir articulates the twin demands that socialism and democracy made upon Zionists of the generation of World War II. Within the American youth movement *Habonim* (the builders), Goren championed the values of socialist idealism, tempered by sensitivity to democratic individual aspirations. Arriving in the new state, he found himself speaking out for similar values, albeit with a different emphasis. Throughout his narrative, Goren weaves specific stories that illuminate the tensions of the era and how a representative American Jewish Zionist negotiated the complex reality of transforming oneself and one's society. Living in two different Jewish cultures involved flexibility and courage, imagination and resourcefulness, idealism and pragmatism.

A pattern of cultural divergence emerges from weaving back and forth across the Israeli and American Jewish experience that highlights how immigrant European Jews and their descendants constructed new identities. The outlines of these variants of accommodation, posited prior to emigration from Europe, became actualized in the distinctive political, historical, and social ecologies European immigrants encountered in America and Israel and found expression in an array of cultural, political, and social forms.

We have not addressed how far divergence might evolve. The processes examined do not necessarily indicate separation although, particularly in Israel, some view such a result as inevitable and even claim it already exits.[18] Rather, we find that the intensity and depth of the ties that bind American and Israeli Jews suggest the Jewish people may now conform to what has long been a normal condition among other nations. After nearly two millennia solely as a diaspora nation, Jews have finally become a people with a diaspora *and* a homeland. The fact that Israel is a Western-oriented society and that a large proportion of its Jewish citizens have shared roots with American Jews bodes well for maintaining vital connections despite unmistakable differences required by adaptations to different environments. A new stage of "normalcy" is evolving out of Europe's demise as the paramount center of Jewish history under conditions more benign than could have been imagined a mere century ago. The Jewish people will continue their journey through history as a world community enjoying the diversity afforded by having successfully rooted itself in two new centers.

NOTES

1. Bernard Wasserstein, *The Vanishing Diaspora: The Jews in Europe since 1945* (Cambridge, MA, 1995); S. Ilan Troen, "Introduction: The Post-Holocaust Dynamics of Jewish Centers and Peripheries," in S. Elan Troen, ed., *Jewish Centers & Peripheries: Europe between America and Israel Fifty Years After World War II* (New Brunswick, NJ, 1999), pp. 1–26.

2. S. Ilan Troen, "Organizing the Rescue of Jews in the Modern Period," in S. Ilan Troen and Benjamin Pinkus, eds., *Organizing Rescue: Jewish Solidarity in the Modern Period* (London, 1992), pp. 3–19.

3. Joyce R. Starr, *Kissing Through Glass: The Invisible Shield Between Americans and Israelis* (Chicago, 1990); Peter Grose, *Israel in the Mind of America* (New York, 1984).

4. Ezra Mendelsohn, *On Modern Jewish Politics* (New York, 1995).

5. Charles S. Liebman and Eliezer Don-Yehiya, *Civil Religion in Israel: Traditional Judaism and Political Culture in the Jewish State* (Berkeley, 1983) and Charles S. Liebman and Elihu Katz, eds., *The Jewishness of Israelis: Responses to the Guttman Report* (Albany, 1997).

6. Barry A. Kosmin and Seymour P. Lachman, *One Nation Under God; Religion in Contemporary American Society* (New York, 1993); Jack Wertheimer, *A People Divided: Judaism in Contemporary America* (New York, 1994).

7. Deborah Dash Moore, *At Home in America: Second Generation New York Jews* (New York, 1981); Jacob Neusner, *Strangers at Home: 'The Holocaust,' Zionism and American Judaism* (Atlanta, 1996); Robert M. Seltzer and Norman J. Cohen, eds. *The Americanization of the Jews* (New York, 1995); Charles Silberman, *A Certain People: American Jews and Their Lives Today* (New York, 1985); Gerald Sorin, *Tradition Transformed: The Jewish Experience in America* (Baltimore, 1997).

8. "A Covenant Between The Jewish People of North America and Israel," September 15, 1998, Jerusalem, in preparation for the meeting of the General Assembly of North American Jews (Jerusalem, 1998).

9. Charles Liebman and Stephen M. Cohen, *Two Worlds of Judaism: The Israeli and American Experiences* (New Haven, 1990).

10. Alex Weingrod, *Reluctant Pioneers: Village Development in Israel* (Port Washington, NY, 1972); Alex Weingrod, *The Saint of Beersheva* (New York, 1990); André Levi, *Le-Maroko vue-hazarah: hebetim etniyim shel nesi'ot yots'e Maroko le'erets huladetam* (Jerusalem, 1989).

11. Abraham Joshua Heschel, *The Earth Is the Lord's: The Inner World of the Jew in Eastern Europe* (New York, 1950).

12. Bella Chagall, *Burning Lights Burning Lights,* Norbert Guterman, trans. (New York, 1946).

13. Maurice Samuel, *The World of Sholom Aleichem* (New York, 1943).

14. Anita Shapira, *Land and Power: The Zionist Resort to Force, 1881–1948* (New York, 1992).

15. Andrew Furman, *Israel Through the Jewish-American Imagination: A Survey of Jewish-American Literature on Israel 1928–1995* (Albany, 1997). See, too, Grose, *Israel in the Mind of America.*

16. Karen Brodkin, *How Jews Became White Folks and What That Says about Race in America* (New Brunswick, NJ, 1999); Matthew Frye Jacobson, *Whiteness of a Different Color: European Immigrants and the Alchemy of Race* (Cambridge, MA, 1998).

17. Will Herberg, *Protestant Catholic Jew: An Essay in American Religious Sociology* (Garden City, NY, 1960).

18. For negative perspectives on future relations see Avraham Avi-Hai, *Danger! Three Jewish People* (New York, 1993) and Boas Evron, *Jewish State or Israeli Nation?* (Bloomington, IN, 1995).

PART I

Establishing New Identities

ONE

The Construction of a Secular Jewish Identity: European and American Influences in Israeli Education

S. ILAN TROEN

The curriculum of Zionist schools during the half century from the Yishuv (the pre-state Jewish settlement in Palestine) through the early years of statehood was a reaction to Jewish life as most educators experienced and remembered it in Europe. It reflected their impatience with the passive religiosity they identified as a prime target for reform. At the same time, it was rooted in what they admired and wished to retain from the culture of their birthplace. In debates over the content and structure of the new curriculum, educators openly expressed misgivings over their success in selectively rejecting and preserving the cultural heritage of European Jewry. I will argue that the ambivalent response to European origins remains a principal factor in the present crisis of secular Zionist education. The encounter with another model, drawn largely from the American experience, clearly influenced Israeli education after independence. But what Israelis perceived as useful or troubling in the American model only exacerbated a long-term crisis; it did not give rise to it.

The central problem for Zionist educators in the twentieth century was how to provide Jewish children in an avowedly Jewish state with a secular "Jewish" education. Immigrants and native-born had to be loyal citizens, committed to the new state and deeply rooted in the land. At the same time, they had to see themselves as responsible members of the Jewish people, maintaining ties to a common culture which, increasingly, they did not share. Israeli educators were acutely aware of the contradictions inherent in their endeavors. The statement made by Zalman Aranne, minister of education and culture for most of the period between 1955 and 1970, at a session of the Knesset in 1959 is a concise and lucid formulation of the dilemma which echoes throughout the vast educational literature of that generation: "The national school in this country has had to contend with a number of educational contradictions since its very beginning. How to educate youngsters here for loyalty to the Jewish people when the overwhelming majority of the Jews are in other places? How to implant in youngsters here a feeling of being part of Jewish history when half of that history took place outside the land of Israel? How to inculcate Jewish Consciousness in Israeli youth when Israeli consciousness and the revolution it demanded denies the legitimacy of exile and dispersion? How to educate Israeli youth who receive their education in a non-religious school to appreciate the cultural heritage of the Jewish people which for most of its time has been suffused with religion?"[1]

Aranne was more successful in defining the problems than in gaining assent for proposed solutions. He established the Center for Fostering Jewish Consciousness of the Ministry of Education to deal with them, and successor agencies continue to wrestle with the issues he raised. At the root of the difficulty is that Zionist educators like Aranne tried to square a circle. How does one create a new secular national culture for citizens of a modern state that must remain connected to a religious national culture developed over centuries by a dispersed people? The questions Aranne posed have bedeviled Zionist educators since the beginning of the twentieth century, and remained unresolved at its end. Increasingly, these questions confront Jewish educators in the Diaspora as well. They, too, are seeking ways to convey a shared culture rooted in religion to secular Jews, citizens of modern states who no longer yearn to return to Zion and who see Israel as a potential tourist site, at best.

This dilemma and the crisis it poses for education in Israel grew out of Zionism's relation to Europe. At least until around 1970, or twenty years after the establishment of the state, nearly all who had authority in shaping Israel's schools had been born and educated in Europe, and their traditional Jewish schooling as well as their secular learning had been European. Both Ben-Zion Dinur and Zalman Aranne, the ministers of education who presided over and contributed most to the character of education during Israel's first two decades, acquired their traditional Jewish schooling in yeshivot and their professional training in universities. They are representative of the generation that emigrated to Palestine primarily from Eastern Europe in the decades before and after World War I. When they left Europe they were in their twenties and steeped in ideologies highly critical of the traditional Jewish society in which they had been raised. Unlike immigrants who had to contend with the problems of adjustment and assimilation to a host culture, they had become leaders and innovators in a new land where the traditional authorities such as parents, rabbis, and even community were absent. Their avowed purpose was to create a new and independent society, and they imagined a revolutionary *Bildung* as a part of their program. Thus, by explicit declaration and actual practice, Zionism was a revolutionary educational movement.[2]

Yet, in their deliberations and debates, the men and women responsible for planning a curriculum for the new state shied away from a total rejection of Jewish life in Europe. Something had to be retrieved from the culture they had known, something of value, which could and should be mixed with new elements in order to create the new individual and a new society. There was, as Aranne's statement indicates, a large measure of contradiction and even paradox in their efforts. The chemistry for achieving the appropriate formula of revolt and preservation was complex and often experimental. More than fifty years after the establishment of the state, contemporary educators are still racked by doubt and dissension as they debate what can be salvaged from the European past and how it can be refashioned for use in Israel's schools.

The record of negotiations over the curriculum is extraordinarily rich. Zionists were engaged in the institutionalization of educational ideas from the earliest years in Palestine. By independence, schooling accounted for the largest segment of the Yishuv's budget except for colonization and defense, and it continued to receive a large part of the budget in the new state. The financial investment was paralleled by public interest, and schooling commanded the attention of the political and intellectual leadership as well as the powerful lobby of two prestigious unions, those of the teachers and of the writers. The schools were mandated to accomplish Zionism's primary social and cultural objective of transforming the young into capable citizens of the new society.

The greatest effort was expended in the liberal or bourgeois schools and in those sponsored by labor Zionism during the Yishuv, two streams that amalgamated after independence. From at least the 1920s through the present, these schools have instructed no fewer than three-fourths of the children in Zionist society, becoming the largest school system ever established for Jews. Yet the divides described by Aranne in 1959 still plague Israeli education today. A curriculum that will, at the same time, define and transmit an agreed Israeli secular Jewish culture, engender loyalty to the state, and provide a firm basis for cohesion with world Jewry remains elusive.

REACTION AGAINST THE RELIGIOUS CULTURE OF EUROPEAN JEWRY

In Europe, the United States, and other Diaspora communities, secular Jewish education has been a minority phenomenon and generally of limited duration. There Jewish education remains largely in the hands of rabbis, whether ultra-Orthodox, Orthodox, Reform, Conservative, or Reconstructionist. While many of those who support and attend Jewish schools are not themselves religious, the Jewish education framework is typically provided by a religious establishment. Consequently, even significant alterations of traditional schooling within such religious frameworks do not approximate the radicalism found in secular Zionist schools.

A fundamental difference between Jewish education in the Diaspora and in Israel stems from the fact that, whether implicitly or explicitly, secular

Zionism denies that the connection between the Jewish people and Divine authority is the operative modality for interpreting Jewish experience. While acknowledging that Jews believed in this connection in the past, secular Zionists have reinterpreted the history of the Jewish nation, substituting a secular national culture for the religious national tradition. This substitution is manifest in curricula as a reinterpretation or suppression of traditional texts and the invention of new ones. The place of the central text of traditional Jewish life throughout the European Diaspora—the oral law as expressed in the Talmud and rabbinic literature—was diminished. Instead the Bible was made the central text of modern secular Jewish culture, and it is read as a historical and ethical document with a humanistic rather than a theological orientation.

The substitution of Hebrew for Yiddish as the language of instruction throughout the entire curriculum changed the status of what had been *lashon hakodesh* (the sacred language). The use of modern Hebrew literature and Jewish history as moral and political instruments reinforced the view that people have shaped Jewish culture. Historicism similarly influenced the approach to the study of the Bible and of Jewish history in a radical reassessment of human affairs. The immanence of God was excised from Jewish history even as the Divine was removed from the Bible and all other writings previously considered sacred. The direction was humanistic in the fundamental sense of that term, that is, oriented toward humanity.

Although it has obvious roots in European culture, this Zionist humanism was also a direct response to a dangerous reality. Secular Zionists claimed that in the absence of Divine intervention Jews had to reinsert themselves as actors in history by confronting rising anti-Semitism. Leaving Europe for Palestine was essential, but it was only a first step toward forging a new national character.

The Israeli national curriculum of "Jewish consciousness" as initiated by Aranne's ministry at the end of the first decade of independence provides numerous illustrations of the new *Bildung* secular Zionism invented. A comparative analysis of public school curricula for the *Mamlachti* (secular Zionist) and the *Mamlachti Dati* (religious Zionist) schools indicates the character and direction of the proposed change. Both offered courses in the sciences and modern languages. Both systems (*zeramim*, or "streams") offered the same Jewish subjects—Talmud, Bible, Hebrew language and literature, and Jewish history—but in markedly different proportions. The degree of radicalism in the secular Zionist approach to the past and the future is clearly exposed by its revolutionary treatment of ostensibly similar subject matter.

CURRICULA IN SECULAR AND RELIGIOUS SCHOOLS

The gulf between secular Zionist and religious Zionist education is especially striking in the treatment of the oral law, the essential core of Jewish education for centuries. The 1957 curriculum for Zionist religious high schools retained the traditional rationale: to "deeply involve the student with the appreciation that the Oral Law is an integral part of the Torah which has been given by G-d so that the student may perceive it as a base for practical *mitzvoth* [commandments] to strengthen his faith and further the fulfillment of *mitzvoth* and to ensure that he will see in the life of the Jewish people a reflection of the Oral Law and will have an appreciation for the Rabbis and their work through the generations." In addition to civil jurisprudence, the tractates selected deal with religious law, regulations, and ritual. That is, they provided information vital to the conduct of holidays, prayers, family life, and public affairs.[3]

In the secular high schools the Talmud was treated solely as a historical document. "Typical portions" of the text were presented "in the context of the continuity of original Jewish creativity." Those portions selected for study were largely related to civil jurisprudence, particularly laws concerning liability and workers' rights. Seen in this light, the Talmud was a source of universal ethics that were accepted by contemporary humanism, liberalism, and Labor Zionism. Moreover, the text was divorced from Divine revelation. Students were directed to appreciate the cultural, economic, political, and social experience of Jews who lived when the Talmud was composed—that is, "especially within the framework of Babylonian autonomy." The Talmud was thus effectively disassociated from the European Jewish world—the ghetto, shtetl, heder, and yeshiva—where for nearly two millennia it had been the central text. In the secular Zionist schools it reverted to being a historical artifact, a creation of the proud and autonomous communities of Babylon. The measured doses of talmudic texts had an additional benefit in a secular curriculum. They could contribute to the revival of Hebrew, enriching the student's vocabulary with phrases and concepts that had been part of the speech of educated Jews.

The Bible, too, came to be treated as a historical and ethical text, and not the Law given by God. This perspective was enshrined in the opening paragraph of Israel's Declaration of Independence, perhaps the most important single document created by secular Zionism. The first sentence proclaimed a widely accepted understanding that "The Land of Israel was the birthplace of the Jewish people." The last sentence was revolutionary: "Here they wrote and gave the Bible to the world." This claim to authorship dramatically and decisively overturns the principle, adhered to for more than three millennia, that God gave the Torah to Moses at Sinai and through him to the Jewish people.

Children in secular schools studied "the world of the Bible," delving into the economic, cultural, and social life of their people in the ancient period. There was also a patent attempt to employ such study to advance contemporary Zionist ideology. The ancient Hebrew "kingdoms" were referred to as "*ha-medinah*"—the "state." The idea of "the state" rather than "kingdoms," of course, was not a construct that existed in the ancient past. The anachronism takes the biblical period as a precedent for contemporary events. Similarly, the Book of Joshua, in which an earlier generation reclaimed the Promised Land after the long sojourn in Egypt, could be seen to presage the Jews' taking possession of the homeland in the twentieth century. Biblical texts validated the present and served as a guide for future action.[4]

Instruction in the Bible was also intended to highlight the unique place of Israel among the nations; to enhance the students' knowledge of the Hebrew language; to acquaint Israeli children with the fauna, flora, and landscape of the country; and to induce a sense of rootedness in the old/new homeland. However, the study of rabbinic commentaries as aids to understanding the text, a tradition of the more recent past, was pointedly bypassed. If commentaries were used at all, it was only for their linguistic value.

Even as the Talmud was taught by culling useful texts, the Bible, too, was taught selectively. Portions dealing with rituals and ceremonies associated with religious worship were removed, and the Book of Leviticus, traditionally the first book to be studied, was nearly excised from the secular curriculum. Only a few sections that deal with the sabbatical and jubilee years and similar topics, and that could be interpreted as pertaining to ethical legislation protecting the rights of workers, were retained.

Questions over what to include and what to exclude from the secular curriculum were not merely academic. There was a heated and extensive discussion among educators and in the Knesset subcommittee on education at the end of the 1950s about whether to include the *Siddur*, or prayer book. Perhaps the most universal and ubiquitous text in the history of the Jewish people aside from the Bible, it was also the most controversial. Opinion was divided over whether it could be a part of the Hebrew literature curriculum. Some urged its incorporation for its aesthetic, linguistic, and historic value, arguing that it could be presented without theological reference and without imposing or even implying worship, the obvious purpose of a prayer book. Others, who found the book too closely associated with the traditions of the world they had rejected, denied the possibility of making such fine distinctions. Apparently, while God could be successfully removed from the Bible, He could not be removed from the Siddur. Although it was often part of the curriculum in the pre-state schools, the prayer book was no longer taught by the end of the first decade of independence. The fact that generations of Israeli youth are currently educated in avowedly Jewish schools without experience with or knowledge of the Siddur still occasions expressions of misgivings, even among some secular Israelis. However, a satisfactory way of divorcing prayer from theology has not been found.[5]

There was also debate over new topics that were not part of the traditional curriculum in Europe: Hebrew literature and history. Often expressions of ferment and major sources of radical opinions and criticism of contemporary Jewish society, these subjects were usually read independently and outside a formal educational setting in Europe. In the Yishuv and Israel, Zionist educators institutionalized them as central and essential components of the curriculum. Jewish history and Hebrew literature depicted both the shortcomings of Jewish life in Europe and the possibilities for renewal in the Land of Israel. By transmitting the nation's experiences, it was hoped, the national literature and history would imbue youth with loyalty to the nation, a commitment to its goals, and the determination to participate in its reformation.

The guidelines for Hebrew literature typically began by indicating what the study of literature was not to include. It was not to engage in literary analysis or teach aesthetics and theory. Like the study of the Talmud and the Bible, the study of literature was to focus on the historical, social, and linguistic value of texts. It was, in effect, a complement to the study of history. The literary curriculum comprised a "canon" designed to realize national goals. Although it began with the Hebrew literature of the Middle Ages, it was heavily invested in the present, and even included poetry, fiction, and essays by living authors such as Agnon, Ben-Zion Dinur, and David Ben-Gurion. The line between art and politics was thin and permeable.

Students also read translated texts from world literature, which actually meant European literature. There was no work from the neighboring Arabic culture or more distant non-European cultures. The list contains readings found in the familiar humanities courses before the advent of multiculturalism—from Greek classics to Russian, French, and German literature of the past two centuries. English classics were read in English. It was the curriculum for the enlightenment of a European. This portion of the emigrants' European heritage was transferred intact. Throughout, there was a keen appreciation that literature served culture by reflecting its ideals, exposing its problems, and offering correctives. The study of non-Hebrew literature was intended to nurture social and political sensibilities. Finally, there was the manifest message that great literature—Hebrew and European—should reflect the cultural experiences and possibilities of the nation.

The history curriculum had similar objectives.[6] As many scholars have noted, history became the handmaiden of modern secular nationalism during the nineteenth century. Zionist historiography emerged from this context but nevertheless reflected the ambivalence of secularists toward the traditional past. The conflicting pulls of modern secular nationalism and religious tradition are clearly attested to in the introductions to texts and curricular guides. For example, in the guide for Jewish history produced by Aranne's ministry, the stated purpose of teaching history was:

- To instill in the heart of youth a national Jewish recognition, to strengthen in them a sense for the common fate and destiny of all Jews, and to plant in their heart a love of the Jewish people in their land and throughout the world and make firm their bonds to Jews everywhere.
- To place in the heart of students a recognition for the importance of the State of Israel so that they may ensure its biological continuity and the continued historic existence of the Jewish people, to develop in them the feeling of personal responsibility for establishing the state and developing it, to place in their heart the desire to fill its needs and a willingness to serve the state.

Some versions include inculcating a willingness to sacrifice oneself for the state. For religious Zionists, this exclusive emphasis on the role of the people in shaping their own destiny distorted the meaning of history. Guides to history texts in religious Zionist schools pointed out that the object of the study of Jewish history was "To nurture the point of view that, at the root of human history and especially the history of the Jewish people, the hand of Divine Providence is at work and that He provides special guidance to the path of national life." Moreover, they maintained that historical study must be suffused with a sense of the Divine Presence in all human affairs.

Whereas the religious curriculum represented centuries of Jewish survival and creative endeavor as evidence of exemplary faith in Divine intervention, the secular curriculum emphasized and criticized Jewish passivity in the face of hostility. The European Middle Ages were subject to particularly negative attention, as were modern anti-Semitism and the Holocaust, which were described with great thoroughness. Only the celebratory history of Zionist pioneering surpassed this section in detail and in extent. In effect, secular Zionism created a sustained and comprehensive *weltanschauung* (world view) in which its leaders and adherents were the central actors. It was this insistence on the active role of modern Jews in shaping the nation's destiny that constituted the central discontinuity with the world of their ancestors. They repudiated its religiosity, its understanding of itself and its place in history, its language, its rituals, and many of its values and customs. And they tried to replace all these by refocusing Jewish life in a secular national mode. Ultimately, there is a message of hope in this view of history. Jewish creativity did not end with the creation of the Bible. National cultural creativity was renewable.

THE PARADOX OF SUCCESS

The irony of secular Zionist education is that it may have succeeded too well in disseminating criticism of European Jewry and its culture. The minutes of the meetings during Aranne's ministry are replete with criticism and expressions of unease. There were worrying signs that the new secular curriculum might have already engendered alienation and that Israeli youth had already internalized conscious separation from essential cultural resources and had distanced themselves from the Diaspora.

Zionist educators were indeed in a double bind, and one that was already apparent in the work of Zionist theoreticians in Europe at Zionism's beginnings. Ahad Ha'am, the leading proponent of a secular Jewish nationalism, sensed these problems at the turn of the century. The concerns voiced in his essay *Umwertung aller Werte* (The transvaluation of values) (1898) —a study of the dangerous attractions of Nietzsche's philosophy to rebellious Jewish youth—appear prophetic. In it he urges youth not to abandon the moral traditions of the Jewish people, and he warns that a search for mastery and power over circumstances and an embrace of the unrestrained activism of the *Ubermensch* (Superman) would be disastrous. For example, the "call for the strong arm and the power and value of force . . . as opposed to the power of morality and righteousness" would result in emulating *"die blonde Bestie"* (the fair beast). He exhorts against a flight from inherited culture, even as he advocates its transformation through secularization. This concern is echoed in the writings of his disciples in the Yishuv. Inappropriate alien models could result in the corruption of Jewish youth. Indiscriminate change from known paths could produce unpredictable trajectories.[7]

Using new methods to study familiar texts could also be dangerous. When he visited the new Herzliah Gymnasium shortly after its founding, Ahad Ha'am was appalled by the extent to which Mossensohn's new methodology for Bible instruction distorted the traditional reading of the text. Here and elsewhere, he expostulated on the need to secularize and modernize but, at the same time, to respect received texts. Once the authority of traditional methods and interpretations was questioned, there was no assurance that new authorities with agreed goals and predictable results could be established.

The concern for the unexpected and uncontrolled is found throughout the interwar period and through the post-independence period. During the 1930s, for example, Jewish youth in the Yishuv were described as "speaking *dugri*," according to the recent analysis of anthropologist Tamar Katriel. The term *dugri*, an Arabic word meaning "straight" and "direct," emphasizes linguistically the distance between preconceptions forged in Europe and the actuality of the Middle Eastern setting.[8]

That is, the sabra was perceived by "the elders" as direct and without the pretenses, fashions, mores, values, and book-learning of European ancestors and as acting from pragmatism rather than idealism. As far as leading secular educators were concerned—and they were largely identified as followers of Ahad Ha'am—sabras had distanced themselves too far from the culture of their parents.

Already in the generation prior to independence, the youthful "products" of Zionist education caused doubt, regret, and concern. Hayyim Nachman Bialik, the Yishuv's unofficial poet laureate, stood at the head of the Writers Association in 1932 in the presence of politicians, intellectuals, and hundreds of Tel Aviv's citizens in a staged "Trial of the Youth." On this public occasion, the Yishuv's intellectuals and educators expressed both pride in the youth who had grown up with the new Hebrew curriculum and distress at their indifference to cherished aspects of traditional Jewish culture. The event brought to public attention the hopes and the shortcomings of Zionist education. Similar doubts aggravated educators during the 1950s. Israeli youth were only minimally connected to Diaspora Jewry and appeared indifferent to and ignorant of their common cultural heritage.[9]

It is interesting to compare these mixed reactions to the emergence of the *dugri* sabra with the attitude toward the new American described in Ralph Waldo Emerson's famous essay "The American Scholar."[10] In both cases the children of European colonists had developed into a cultural type that was distinct from European origins. Both the new Americans and the new Jews had freed themselves from the culture of their ancestors to become authentically rooted in a new land while acquiring new national characteristics. However, unlike Bialik, Emerson was born an American and his forebears had resided in America for nearly two centuries. It was perhaps natural for him to identify with and extol the local product of a new, national culture. For Emerson, Europe was a distant memory and foreign reality whose authority had undergone a long process of erosion. For Ahad Ha'am and Bialik, Dinur and Aranne, the European experience was still an integral part of their being. They were discomfited when they saw sabras dismiss as irrelevant a heritage they still believed contained a "usable past."

Reconnecting youth became the centerpiece of the national program designated "Jewish Consciousness" and its curriculum. Zionist educators analyzed the deficiencies of the past and posited what they wanted in its place: good, loyal, knowledgeable, and committed citizens of Israel and members of a world Jewish community. The effectiveness of this reform, in turn, came to be questioned by the 1980s. This resulted in yet another call for revision articulated in the Shenhar Report of 1994. Frustration with the results of earlier curricular changes led to proposals for new programs. Their formulations reflect the post-independence reorientation of Israeli intellectuals and educators away from Europe and toward the United States as the frame of reference for ideas and values that could contribute to shaping Israeli society.[11]

"AMERICA" IN THE EDUCATION OF ZIONIST YOUTH

With the destruction of most of European Jewry during World War II, American Jewry became the largest and most important contemporary Diaspora. At the time of Israel's independence it was only about half the size of European Jewry prior to the Holocaust. Nevertheless, the American Jewish population was nearly ten times larger than the Yishuv. It has required fifty years of natural increase since statehood and significant immigration for Israeli Jewry to approach the size of the American Jewish community. The extent, wealth, and power of the American Diaspora as well as its location within the preeminent seat of world power required Israelis to take note of America and its Jews.

Yet the American Jewish experience has never found a significant place in the Israeli curriculum. Despite ties of kinship and shared beginnings, deep knowledge of the experience of American Jewry has remained well beyond the ken and outside the concerns of Zionist leaders and educators. Indeed, the nature and prospects of American Jewry were so unlike anything they had experienced or observed in Europe that in some ways it was unintelligible. The problem of persuading secular Israeli youth that they had an underlying commitment to the Jewish people in all their dispersions was in some ways comparable to the challenge of linking secular American Jews to Israel. The notion of a universal people bound by a covenant to God and to one another was easier to communicate to traditional, religious Jews wherever they resided.

The difficulty of secular Zionist leaders to imagine the world of American Jewry can be illustrated by an anecdote. In July 1950 Ben-Gurion created a private two-day seminar of key leaders familiar with America to analyze the desired attitude toward American Jews. Among those in attendance were Moshe Sharett, Golda Myerson (soon to become Meir), Abba Eban, Eliahu Elath, Levi Eshkol, and Teddy Kollek. Ben-Gurion titled the meeting *Gishateynu le-Yahadut Amerika* (Our attitude towards American Jewry). He observed that America and its Jews did not fit Zionist stereotypes; America did not threaten Jews, and the Jews would not make aliyah. The seminar was an unsuccessful attempt to discover an operative ideology that would fit this anomaly to a Zionist ideology rooted in the negative experience of European Jewry.

Teddy Kollek's suggestions as to what a Zionist recruiter—the *shaliach*—should never say to an American Jew reflect the challenge of understanding American Jewry:

- Don't try to scare American Jews; there will be no pogroms in America.
- Don't try to tell them they should not love and admire America.
- Never mention Marx. Berl Katznelson, the grand-teacher of Labor Zionism, is okay; the Bible and Hebrew language are better.
- Only the misfits are likely to come; immigrants and perhaps their children who have not yet adjusted to the United States can be talked to in traditional terms: that is, as if one were in a *hachsharah* or pioneering camp in Poland or Germany.

- Don't try to inculcate the dream of the kibbutz; it is a romantic idea but it does not have the same resonance in bourgeois, individualistic America.
- Do not try to communicate to them the angry revolution some of us have undergone in relation to Jewish religion, Jewish ritual and the synagogue. Treat Judaism and Jewish traditions with respect.[12]

Kollek concluded with an appeal for a new approach based on commonalities, particularly the notion of the "shared fate" and "common destiny" of the Jewish people. Even had his advice been heeded, it is doubtful it would have had much impact. Few American Jews ever made aliyah. Some of those who did could have been classified as "misfits"; others emigrated for religious reasons that were not shared by this gathering of largely secular Jews.

Little of the American Jewish experience had entered the consciousness of Israelis, nor had it become part of the secular curriculum. America at large did not fare better. The American Revolution was explored, but merely as a precursor to the French; the Civil War, slavery, and Lincoln were a fragment in the history of the nineteenth century; and something of the New Deal was imparted in the context of the interwar crisis in the West. In English classes the schools offered "The Devil and Daniel Webster," a bit of Poe and Whitman, and little else as samplings of American literature. There was little or nothing here which resonated with the Zionist experience. The teaching of America imparted a modest amount of information devoid of moral or ideological moment.

While America did not penetrate the curriculum directly, however, knowledge of America began to proliferate after World War II. Its impact on Israeli society and thereby on Israeli education was often indirect but profound. It affected the structure and purpose of the schools and the values they engendered.

Prior to World War II, American literature had hardly existed in the Hebrew language. A few works of fiction had been translated into Hebrew, and one history text. Then, during the 1950s, there was a flood of translations from American literature, history, and the American academy.[13] The reasons for this sudden interest are conveniently stated in the geography textbook expressly written for Israeli schools in 1959. Its introduction states: "[This is] the first full-fledged text on the United States [in Hebrew] — the great nation on the other side of the Atlantic Ocean. . . . It is remarkable that there have not yet appeared amongst us comprehensive monographs on the United States. There are many ties that bind the State of Israel with this Power, whether economic or political and even national. In America about half of our nation [i.e., the Jewish people] is concentrated. The Jews of America take a very active part in the building of this country and are involved in all that transpires here. The Israeli public is also interested in all that is done in the United States, witness the many articles and essays published in our press."[14]

The message is clear. With European power diminished by the destruction of war, and its long-admired civilization exposed as the scene of one of the greatest tragedies in Jewish history, America emerged as the great and benevolent world power. Moreover, half the Jews remaining in the world lived there. The point is that a fundamental shift had taken place. America replaced Europe as the society against which Israel measured itself and on which, in many ways, it consciously tried to model itself.

The issue of modeling is central to understanding both the European and American influences on Zionist education. At the beginning of the twentieth century, European society was at its apogee and exerted a powerful attraction on European Jews who were emerging from centuries of isolation in the shtetl or urban ghettoes. European thought supplied the terms by which Jews criticized their own society and sought to remake it. Secular nationalism, for example, is but one of a host of concepts which had been borrowed by European Jews and applied to their own condition and needs. When European civilization was discredited and contact with the continent was diminished in the aftermath of World War II — particularly in the Soviet East and vanquished Nazi Central Europe — Israelis turned westward, largely to America.

What could be found in America and what it might mean for Israelis was the subject of much dispute in divergent interpretations of the American historical experience. One small but articulate group, identified as Canaanites, thought that America provided a suitable analogy for understanding their own experience. Indeed, Canaanites were so anxious to share the

American experience that they initiated the vast translation enterprise described above. They saw America as a new nation which, in the course of nation-building, produced a new people by means of a melting pot. They considered this model very relevant to Israel. Within the space of its first four years of independence, Israel's population had doubled through a massive immigration of Holocaust survivors from Europe and refugees from Arab lands throughout the Middle East and North Africa. Like America's immigrants, they came from a multitude of cultures, spoke a Babel of languages, and, indeed, could be understood as having come from a variety of centuries. If the size and diversity of immigration provided a close parallel, it was most important that out of these human materials a new people would emerge, even as it had in the American experience. Indeed, the Canaanites believed that Israel could become "the America of the Middle East."[15]

In essence, this movement denied that there were any continuities between Jewish life in Israel and in the Diaspora. Canaanites interpreted the melting pot experience as one in which the cultures of Europe and all other countries of origin were cast off and eliminated. Here was a complete break with the immediate past. The only connections that mattered were with the new country, its landscapes, and the peoples resident there. Thus, the study of America was valued as an instrument that would separate Jews from the experience of the exile; encourage them to be transformed in their ancient/ new frontier in the Middle East; and persuade them to embrace their new identity as modern Hebrews rooted in, and part of, a historic landscape.

The American model also seemed to support their vision of the new Hebrew nation. Territory, rather than racial or religious ties, was the basis for defining community. In this, Canaanites carried to an extreme conclusion the idea of "the denial of the exile" found throughout Zionist thought in the past century. It was against such total separation that Aranne protested. Indeed, the debate over "Jewish Consciousness" echoes with the voices of particularly the religious Zionists who recognized the imprint of Canaanite influence in the evolving secularism of the curriculum.

An alternative interpretation of America was articulated by Yehoshua Arieli, the first professor of American history at the Hebrew University. He accepted the Canaanite use of the United States as a model for understanding Israel's search for national identity. Referring to Seymour Martin Lipset's concept of "the first new nation," he also noted that early Americans had had to sever themselves from Europe, particularly Britain, so as to establish their own discrete and unique identity. Nevertheless, as a Zionist who himself had left the Diaspora for Israel, Arieli did not extend the analogy to the crucial issue of the relationship between Israeli Jewry and Diaspora Jewry. For him, there was no question that the Zionist state had deep and legitimate roots in the part of the nation still outside the borders of the new state. The state provided the territory and security necessary for national self-renewal. Whatever the shape of Israeli nationality, it was unlikely to be disconnected from the past. The creation of Israel represented an opportunity for change, not discontinuity.[16] Much the same view was held by Oscar Handlin, Arieli's mentor at Harvard. Based on his study of immigration, he thought that in Israel, as in America itself, the end result of the process of transplanting Europeans would be adaptation, evolution, and synthesis. Something would be lost, something maintained, and something new discovered. The process was rich and complicated. It was not merely one of severance.[17]

Models drawn from the American experience were employed by Israeli scholars in other disciplines. Shmuel Eisenstadt, the founder of Israeli sociology, organized his department with an explicitly American orientation. Its manifesto proposed to establish an Israeli sociology that was nonparochial, whose methods would be historical and comparative, and whose research would be judged by "universalistic" criteria, in particular the procedures of the established, mainly English-speaking sociological community. In practice, this meant largely the United States. This was appropriate, since the manifesto proposed to study Israeli immigration in the context of other immigrant societies, especially the United States. His own work in the decade and a half after independence, which at the time had won widespread acclaim, was devoted to analyzing in appreciative terms the transit of immigrants from one culture to another. Later sociologists have uncovered much to criticize in the American assimilation model of absorbing immigrants. Nevertheless, whether the scholarship was conceived as praise or censure, the frame of reference was generally American.[18] American-generated concepts such as assimilation, melting pot, conformity, and pluralism have shaped the debate of what ought to take place in Israeli society. This includes education.

Perhaps the prime examples of American influence on Israeli education were the movements to measure equality in Israeli schools and to foster *integratzia* (integration). James Coleman, an American expert in these areas, was directly involved in transmitting American models and methods through extensive visits to Israel beginning in the 1960s, as well as through his writings.[19] Israeli education, especially in terms of its avowed social functions, became Americanized, though here, too, issues of group unity and peoplehood over individual interests could be understood in terms of established Jewish/Zionist values. The paramount concern was how to forge a cohesive and democratic Zionist society.

In subsequent decades what was drawn from the American experience changed. It became increasingly focused on individualistic values. As numerous observers of Israel have noted, the past few decades have witnessed an erosion of collective principles. The traditional Zionist value was the primacy of group needs; in contemporary Israel many fault Zionist collectivism. There is presently a rising tide of writing that criticizes the national, group, and collective traditions in Israeli society and espouses their replacement with an explicitly American-inspired individualism. The attempt to enhance individualism, based on what is perceived as an American model, can be found in many academic disciplines including "critical" sociology, the "revisionist" history, and "post-modern," and "deconstructionist" critiques; in recent decisions in Israeli courts; in literature, theater, and film; in the movement to privatize government or Histadrut-controlled companies and institutions; and in the Americanization of the political system through the direct election of the prime minister, the head of Israel's representative government. In much of this, Israelis are urged to emulate the United States as the model of the ideal society. They are urged to repudiate their collectivist past and to replace it with the American version of an individualistic civil society rather than the Zionist ethnic nation-state.[20]

This phenomenon finds echoes in the contemporary version of "Jewish Consciousness." In the Ministry of Education's 1994 Shenhar Report the key concepts are pluralism and identity. Both are light-years distant from the secular, collective Jewish identity Aranne and his generation attempted to instill, and reflect new tensions in Israeli education. As employed by contemporary educators, "identity" and "pluralism" suggest choice. It is the child and youth who decides what he or she is to become from a range of choices provided by the schools. This includes the Jewishness of his or her choice or even no Jewishness at all. This possibility stands in contrast, if not contradiction, to the way "Jewish Consciousness" as a collective phenomenon was originally conceived.[21]

Zionist educators traditionally thought in group terms. Not only in the kibbutz but in urban schools, great value was placed on the *hevra*—the social group that schools were charged to nurture. This was a microcosm of a larger pattern of association. Aranne, for example, did not speak of individual children. The secular curriculum he called for grew out of the Jewish nation, Jewish values, and Jewish culture. The operating assumption was that the individual should be molded by the national culture to serve national purposes. This belief in Jewish peoplehood was deeply rooted in his understanding of Zionism as a movement of national rescue and collective rejuvenation. As such, Aranne's views accurately reflected the prevailing understandings and ideologies of the generations of Jews born and educated in Europe who had shaped Israeli society through its early decades.[22]

Contemporary educators draw inspiration from American education models and practices rooted in historical conditions that did not exist in Europe. Like so many throughout the world, they are attracted to currents, fashions, and principles produced by the unique conditions and needs of a powerful, wealthy, individualistic, civil society. In the case of Israel this can lead to a deprecation of values conceived in ethnic/national terms. In an American-influenced scenario, the opportunities for individualism are given at least parity with the demands for continuity of the ethnic collective.

The contemporary debate over content and process in education, itself an American import, reflects these conflicting attitudes toward the individual and the nation. On the side of process are those who believe that equipping children with skills has priority over transmitting a determined quantum of knowledge whose definition may be subject to dispute. Cultural literacy and a content-based curriculum contend with an emphasis on analytic skills which, some would argue, puts the established secular Jewish curriculum at risk. For example, authors and teachers of Hebrew literature warn that the assured place the national literature enjoyed during the twentieth century could be a casualty if the curriculum is "liberalized" with a view to emphasizing critical skills. They argue that it is essential to maintain a body of knowledge that should be the inheritance of every Israeli Jew. The debate over this issue resonates with arguments first articulated at the beginning of the twentieth century by advocates of a secular Zionist culture and pits them against foreign methodologies, values, and paradigms.[23] Much the same debate has occurred in the teaching of history. Those who argue that Jewish history should be taught in the context of general (i.e., largely Western) history typically prefer a universalistic humanism to what they regard as a sectarian nationalism, if not outright chauvinism.[24]

CONCLUSION

The kinds of questions posed by an education theory originating in America intensify the anxieties and dilemmas Aranne faced more than four decades ago. The primary problem for Aranne stemmed from a conscious decision to deviate from a religiously anchored culture and polity endowed with transcendent authority and sanctity. The rationale for making this choice was first formulated in Europe and then elaborated and implemented in the Yishuv.

However, educating children for a secular Jewish nationhood was more complicated in the Yishuv than it had seemed in Europe because the nation did not and would not live in the same territorial polity. While it was obvious that those living in open multiethnic and multiracial democracies, such as America, would be subject to the forces of assimilation, it was not initially recognized that even children growing up in Israel would be free to abandon the historic, transnational community that had spawned their society. This possibility was already in evidence when Aranne addressed Israel's "educational contradictions" in remarks to the Knesset quoted at the beginning of this chapter. The continuous infiltration of American ideas and models has further complicated and deepened the problem of designing a curriculum that would bring about a commitment to Jewish community and continuity.

It is likely that both the force of individualism and the declension of community as well as the commitment to a collective heritage and peoplehood will continue to compete in Israeli society, and that the terms of contention will continue to be debated in discourses imported from foreign models. It would be an oversimplification to imagine that Europe represents the rejected or outmoded past and that reforms in Israeli education lead consistently and irrevocably in the direction of a model made in America in which individuals tend to take precedence over the community. Attitudes toward both the European past and the American present continue to influence Israeli education and the construction of a secular Jewish identity. After a century of attempting to reformulate an age-old tradition of schooling, Zionist educators are still beset by uncertainty and tension over the consequences of inculcating new forms of "Jewish Consciousness" and the implications of failing to do so. "Educational contradictions" remain inherent in the Zionist attempt to replant the roots of a transnational people, identified as a religious community throughout a long history, in the soil of a secular state.

NOTES

This chapter is the outgrowth of a series of conversations conducted with Professor Walter Ackerman during 1995–1996 on the problems of educating Israelis as Jews. I am deeply indebted to his insights and guidance. For a recent example of Ackerman's own interpretation of similar problems see, "Making Jews," *Israel Studies* 2:1 (Fall 1997). I am also grateful for the opportunity provided by David Ruderman for reflection and interaction among wise, knowledgeable, and critical colleagues at the Center for Judaic Studies at the University of Pennsylvania.

1. The Aranne quote is found in *Deepening Jewish Consciousness* (Jerusalem, 1959), p. 40 (in Hebrew). This paragraph was originally presented in a speech to the Knesset in a discussion on Jewish consciousness on June 15, 1959. See, too, *Speech to the Knesseth by the Minister of Education and Culture Zalman Aranne Concerning the Ministry's Budget for the Fiscal Year 1965/66,* (Jerusalem, Mar. 22,

1965) (in Hebrew). For an appreciation of Zalman Aranne as well as a collection of his writings see *Zalman Aranne: A Memorial Volume* (Jerusalem, 1973) (in Hebrew).

2. For a very useful analysis see Mark Rosenstein, "The New Jew: The Approach to Jewish Tradition in the High Schools of the General School Trend from Its Inception until the Establishment of the State" (unpublished Ph.D. diss.), Hebrew University, Jerusalem, 1985 (in Hebrew). Essential for understanding the resonance of traditional religion in Israeli society are Charles S. Liebman and Eliezer Don-Yehiya, *Civil Religion in Israel: Traditional Judaism and Political Culture in the Jewish State* (Berkeley, 1983), and Charles S. Liebman and Elihu Katz, eds., *The Jewishness of Israelis: Responses to the Guttman Report* (Albany, 1997).

3. See the Preface to *Curriculum for the Public and Religious Public School: The Oral Law* (Jerusalem, 1968) (in Hebrew).

4. J. Schoenvald, *The Bible in Israeli Education: A Study of Approaches to the Hebrew Bible and Its Teaching in Israeli Educational Literature* (Amsterdam, 1976). For an indication of a radical, early attempt at reform of the Bible curriculum see Ben-Tzion Mossinsohn, "The Bible in the School," *Ha-Chinnukh,* 1 (1910), 23–32, 110–19 (in Hebrew). See, too, Shlomo Dov Goitein, "Regarding the Philosophical Foundations of Teaching Bible in the Hebrew School," in Chaim Roth, ed., *Hebrew Secondary Education in Eretz Yisrael* (Jerusalem, 1939).

5. A. Shmueli, M. Talmy, and Y. Yager to Ami Asaf, undersecretary of education, "Report on Teaching the Siddur," *Ramatayim,* Jan. 10, 1957. See, too, Ministry of Education and Culture, *Deepening Jewish Consciousness in the Secular Public Schools: Guidelines and Curricula* (Jerusalem, 1959], pp. 9–10, for the assumption that the Siddur and the Machzor (High Holiday prayer book) would be taught. The siddur was described as "the most popular [*ammami*] book in the spiritual heritage [of the Jews] and which contain[s] many sublime creations, of deep feeling and thought, which have not found their worthy place in the public secular schools, and there is no justification for this situation; neither education nor principled. One must therefore provide instruction in the siddur in the public schools and the same holds true for the 'machzor.'" The Siddur actually had a greater and more prominent place in the curriculum in secular Zionist education prior to independence. See, for example, *The Curriculum Together with a General Overview of the Institution and the Student House* (Tel Aviv, 1937) (in Hebrew).

6. See the Preface to *History Curriculum in the Elementary Schools* (Tel Aviv, 1957). See, too, *Recommendations for the High School Curriculum* (Tel Aviv, 1957).

7. Ahad Ha'am, "The Transvaluation of Values," in Leon Simon, ed. and trans., *Selected Essays of Ahad Ha'am* (Philadelphia, 1962), pp. 218–41.

8. Tamar Katriel, *Talking Straight: Dugri Speech in Israeli Sabra Culture* (New York, 1986).

9. Rachel Elboim-Dror, "From the Land of the Fathers to the Land of the Sons," in *Hebrew Education in Eretz Yisrael, 1914–1920,* vol. 2 (Jerusalem, 1990), pp. 375–82. On the trial see Ya'acov Fichman, "On the Hebrew School," *Moznayim,* 3 (12 Sivan, Tart"zav [1932]): 1–2; Y. Azaryahu, "The Problems with Our Education," 3 (12 Sivan, Tart"zav [1932]): 8–10; Y. Azaryahu, "The Trial of Palestinian Youth," 19 (12 Sivan, Tart"zav [1932]): 8–9, 13–15.

10. Ralph Waldo Emerson, "The American Scholar," in *The Portable Emerson* (New York, 1946), pp. 23–46.

11. For a variety of opinions on Jewish consciousness including the confessions of leading personalities over the inability to realize initial expectations, see *Protocol of the Meeting of the Committee for Jewish-Israeli Consciousness* (Jerusalem), July 24, 1956 (in Hebrew). Present were Natan Rotenstreich, Hugo Bergman, Eliezer Rimalt, Yitzhak Ziv, Shmuel Goitein, Israel Yeshayahu, Dov Sedan, David Shimoni, Zalman Aranne, and others. This theme is repeated in other meetings through 1959. Copies of these proceedings can be found in the Ben-Gurion Archives in Sede Boker as well as in the Israel State Archives in Jerusalem.

12. See the protocol of a meeting held under the auspices of Ben-Gurion on July 25, 1950, entitled "Our Attitude towards American Jewry," Ben-Gurion Archives, Sede Boker (in Hebrew).

13. For a discussion of this phenomenon see S. Ilan Troen, "The Discovery of America in the Israeli University: Historical, Cultural and Methodological Perspectives," *Journal of American History* 81:1 (June 1994), 164–82.

14. Y. Paporich, *The United States; Physical, Economic and Settlement Geography* (Tel Aviv, 1959), p. 1.

15. On the Canaanite movement see James S. Diamond, *Homeland or Holyland? The "Canaanite" Critique of Israel* (Bloomington, IN, 1986); and Yaacov Shavit, *The New Hebrew Nation: A Study in Israeli History and Fantasy* (London, 1987).

16. "Dimyon ve'shoni beyn ha-chavayah ha-leumit ha-amerikayit ve-hechavayah ha-leumit ha-yisraelit—simpozion" (Similarities and differences between the American national experience and the Israeli national experience—a symposium), *Bitfutzot Hagola* 15 (1973), 14–29. Among the participants were Aharon Amir, Yehoshua Arieli and Arthur Goren.

17. "Shock of Alienation" (from Oscar Handlin's *The Uprooted*), Aharon Amir,

trans., *Keshet* 13 (1970–1971), 126–40. In the same issue, Amir selectively emphasized the uniqueness of America by publishing translations of Turner and Crevecoeur.

18. Baruch Kimmerling, "Sociology, Ideology, and Nation-Building: The Palestinian in Israeli Sociology," *American Sociological Review* 57:4 (August 1992), 446–60.

19. For a review of the diverse European traditions that could be found in the Jewish community of pre-independence Palestine see S. Ilan Troen and Walter Ackerman, "Childhood in Israel," in J. Hawes and N. Hiner, eds., *Children in Comparative and Historical Perspective: An International Handbook and Research Guide* (Greenwich, CT, 1991), pp. 333–60. In addition to frequent visits, James Coleman's study immediately became standard reading and directly shaped Israeli educational policy. See James Coleman, et al., *Equality of Educational Opportunity* (Washington, DC, 1966).

20. The critiques are ubiquitous in the very large contemporary literature on Israeli society. See, for example, Yaron Ezrahi, *Rubber Bullets: Power and Conscience in Modern Israel* (New York, 1997). For one convenient source that consistently publishes critical literature as well as rejoinders consult *Israel Studies,* especially the section entitled "Zionist Dialectics." A key essay is Eliezer Schweid, "'Beyond' All That—Modernism, Zionism, Judaism," *Israel Studies,* 1:1 (Spring 1996), 224–46.

21. See *Summary of the Shenhar Report,* a one-page English bulletin prepared and distributed by the Ministry of Education and Culture. The report itself is entitled *A People and the World: Jewish Culture in a Changing World* (Jerusalem, 1994), p. 1 (in Hebrew). In the Ministry of Education's central offices in Jerusalem, the complete if disorganized files of the Shenhar Committee can be found.

Considerable disagreements were apparent from the discussion of the members of the committee who signed the report. Their interpretations were various and often contradictory. Mooki Tzur, for example, doubted the report would ever be implemented unless there were significant financial support as well as substantial testing of programs. Dr. Eliezer Marcus reflected on the internal dissension among committee members and compared their work unfavorably with that of the Harari Committee, which had reported at the same time on technological and scientific education. He argued for a more interdisciplinary approach, innovations in teaching, and the proper preparation of teachers. Professor Eliezer Schweid responded that "interdisciplinary" was too ill-defined a notion, and that the many Jewish humanistic disciplines were by themselves interdisciplinary such as history, literature, and Jewish thought. He thought the value of the committee's work was in making a clarion call to pay attention to a severe crisis in the nation's culture, which he identified as the disappearance of the nation's cultural heritage and historical memory. A contrary view was held by Professor Uri Rappaport, who claimed that the committee placed too much emphasis on Jewish values at the expense of humanistic ones. Professor Avi Ravitsky thought the report was the best that could have been achieved given the composition of the committee. The director general of the ministry, Dr. Shimshon Shoshani, praised the "rhetoric" of the report and thought it would take a lot of work, time, and money to produce results through the ministry's bureaucracy. There were clearly divisions among committee members over what was to be done and a lack of confidence that anything would ever be accomplished. Still, this is a watershed report that reflects deep concerns and significant changes in Israeli society.

22. Gideon Shimoni discusses how the national orientation of Zionism grew out of European ideas. Particularly valuable is the description of the Jewish ethnic-religious collectivity as an *ethnie*. See Gideon Shimoni, *The Zionist Ideology* (Hanover, NH, 1995), pp. 3–28.

23. For an example of recent arguments regarding the literary canon versus skills, see Ziva Shamir, "The End of Teaching Literature in the Schools?" *Ha-Aretz,* Mar. 22, 1996 (in Hebrew).

24. A widely reported public controversy erupted just prior to the opening of the 1999/2000 school year over the introduction of a history text for the ninth grade in the secular schools. The dispute found its way into Israeli radio, television, newspapers, and even the international press. All viewed the issues in terms of a *kulturkampf* between traditional and new values. The first article that set the frame for the dispute was actually published abroad. See Ethan Bronner, "Israel's History Textbooks Replace Myths with Fact," *New York Times,* Aug. 14, 1999, and Nimrod Aloni, "Gentlemen, History Is Stormy," *Ha-Aretz,* Oct. 12, 1999 (in Hebrew: *Rabotay, Ha-Historia Soereth*).

TWO

Producing the Future: The Impresario Culture of American Zionism before 1948

JEFFREY SHANDLER

Among the wealth of images featured in an exhibition catalog on Zionist visual culture in the pre-state era, published by Beth Hatefutsoth on the occasion of the State of Israel's fiftieth anniversary, a 1937 poster for the U.S. Central Shekel Board in New York stands out. In some respects it is typical of Zionist propaganda during the years between the two world wars. This appeal to American Jews to purchase *shekalim* (nominal contributions to the World Zionist Organization, which entitle purchasers to vote in Zionist Congress elections) features a sunlit Palestinian landscape, one of the most familiar images in Zionist iconography. A line of new arrivals streams from a boat onto the shore, passing through an oriental olive arch to ascend a hill studded with palms and cypresses. Overhead the oft-cited verse from Psalm 137 states, *Im-eshkohekh Yerushalaim tishkah y'mini* ("If I forget you, O Jerusalem, may my right hand wither"). All of this conforms to the aesthetic agenda of mass-produced Zionist iconography, as characterized by Michael Berkowitz, to "construe . . . a national landscape" in the minds of

European and American Jews and "recast traditional Jewish images in a national context."[1]

But this is only one scene depicted on the poster. To its left is a parallel image of the destruction of Jewish culture, both at the hands of European anti-Semites (a building labeled "Universities—Discriminations"; a pile of burning books, including titles by Emil Ludwig, Heine, and Einstein) and by Palestinian Arabs (a bearded figure in a *kefiyah* [Arab headdress] chops down a tree that a kneeling woman—presumably a *halutzah* [pioneer]—is planting). Above this image a caption (in English) reads, "500,000 shekolim from American Jewry will combat this."

Yet this is not all that appears on the poster, nor is this what distinguishes it from other appeals and exhortations that were so important to the Zionist movement in the first half of the twentieth century. At the center of the poster stands a figure, much larger than any other depicted, of a middle-aged man with a trim mustache, wearing a three-piece suit, tie, and fedora, who holds aloft an oversized shekel coupon. As the exhibition catalog editor Rachel Arbel notes, "The poster is unique in that its central figure is neither the pioneer nor the refugee but the 'bourgeois' Zionist in the Diaspora."[2]

This rare presentation of the American Zionist suggests a distinctive approach to reading other American-made images promoting Palestine as a future Jewish national homeland and, by extension, to understanding American Zionist culture. Rather than situating American Jewry at the periphery or behind the scenes of the Zionist enterprise, as it is typically viewed from the perspective of the *Yishuv* (the pre-state Jewish settlement in Palestine), here the American Jew is positioned according to his own vantage point in the United States. This one time, at least, he comes on stage to "stand up and be counted"—as the poster's main caption proclaims.

This image offers rare direct acknowledgment of the distinctive role in which American Jews were cast during the years between the two world wars, by others as well as by themselves, as "impresarios" of Zionism. Although this is not a term that most American Zionists are likely to have used to describe themselves, the theatrical analogy is appropriate. Like theatrical producers, American Zionists have engaged in activities centered around making financial and other material arrangements for an enterprise realized by others. Their tasks also involve making choices about the nature of the productions they underwrite; both theatrical producers and American Zionists are discoverers, promoters, and nurturers of talents and, moreover, shapers of audience opinions, tastes, and sensibilities. In each case their power is at some remove from the ultimate result of their efforts yet is vitally linked to it. For the impresario and the American Zionist, the measure of the production's success is not merely financial; public appreciation of its merit — on aesthetic, political, or moral grounds — is key.

While the impresario mode may seem at odds with classic Zionist ideology, which champions Jewish self-sufficiency and active participation in creating a productive Jewish polity, it does conform to an American sensibility, especially with regard to promoting matters of ideology and taste during the Progressive Era. In his chronicle of publicists, managers, and producers in America's performing arts from P. T. Barnum to Sol Hurok, Milton Goldin observes that, "brimful of enterprise," the impresario "was in many ways a representative American," epitomizing an entrepreneurial spirit among confident and ambitious figures "who made business into a kind of religion. Nobody was sure that they would not produce wonders."[3]

Viewing American Zionism as an impresario culture not only helps us understand it from the perspective of the diaspora community in which it has functioned, as opposed to the Jewish state that it has served. This model also provides an approach for exploring the links between the fundraising and performative modes that are, in both the past and the present, so prominent in American Zionist and Jewish culture.

The end of World War I was a watershed for American Zionism; following the Balfour Declaration and the Armistice, support for the movement increased rapidly in the United States. Then, as now, this growth was measured quantitatively, in the rising membership rolls of Zionist organizations and the increase in contributions to the cause. American Jews — who generally enjoyed greater economic stability and prosperity in the immediate postwar years than did most of their fellow Jews in Central and Eastern Europe — quickly assumed a prominent role in financing the Zionist enterprise, as they did in other areas of international Jewish philanthropy. In his history of American Zionism before 1948, Melvin Urofsky cites Chaim Weizmann's founding of Keren Hayesod in the United States in 1921 as an important first response to "the exigencies of the situation" following World

War I, which made raising money for the purchase of land in Palestine and the construction of settlements a priority. Weizmann "anticipated that [Keren Hayesod] would become the chief financial instrument in the rebuilding of the homeland, and that the bulk of the money would come from American Jewry." Urofsky notes that the Twelfth Zionist Congress, held in Carlsbad in 1921, approved a budget of $6 million, of which it was expected that "at least 75 percent . . . would come from America."[4]

American Zionists developed a distinct approach to participating in the effort to establish a Jewish state in Palestine. Zionists on the other side of the Atlantic generally saw the Yishuv as a solution to their inherently problematic existence in Europe. American Zionists, however, championed the need for a Jewish state abroad while continuing their commitment to maintaining Jewish communities in the United States. While American Zionism was infused with imagery of the Yishuv and absorbed with its internal politics, the movement remained based in the diaspora both physically and culturally. The American Zionist mission of garnering recognition and support for the new Jewish homeland among both Jewish and non-Jewish Americans required creating a special discourse, in which American and Zionist values were presented as compatible, even mutually enhancing. Beginning with Louis Brandeis's rhetoric linking Zionism with American patriotism in the 1910s, this notion continued to be elaborated during the interwar years, culminating in Abba Hillel Silver's exhortations of "the common ground between Zionism and liberalism, Judaism and America."[5]

The development of American Zionist culture coincided with the rapid rise of a new national consumer culture, the result of both a booming postwar economy and the flourishing of new mass media during the 1920s — newspaper rotogravure sections, commercial radio broadcasting, "talking" motion pictures — all driven by a burgeoning advertising industry. In his 1929 history of advertising, Frank Presbrey writes that the industry "had its greatest development" during "the ten years which include American participation in the World War and after effects of the war." Campaigns for Liberty Bonds and the Red Cross during the war years employed advertising techniques for the purposes of propaganda and fundraising in unprecedented ways — and with financially impressive results: "Advertising did not win the war, but it did its bit so effectively that when the war was over advertising and its manifold mediums had the recognition of all governments as a prime essential in any large undertaking in which the active support of all the people must be obtained for success."[6]

Eager for mass support of their cause among the nation's Jews and non-Jews alike, American Zionist organizations relied heavily on the "manifold mediums" of public relations to promote their cause to fellow citizens during the interwar years. Indeed, it is an irony of Zionism that it could not have garnered the international support essential for fulfilling its agenda without the existence of an international, cosmopolitan, public space—the antithesis of the close, autonomous, agrarian society envisioned for Jewish settlers in Palestine. This new public space was, like the traditional Jewish diaspora, a virtual locus; as Stuart Ewen has observed, it was "less and less a particular place, but had become an increasingly boundless phenomenon," sustained in the minds of many disparate individuals by modern mass media.[7]

Being an American Zionist thus entailed not simply an ideological or financial commitment, but also the public demonstration of this commitment. In 1935, for example, the Zionist Organization of America issued a *Guide Book for Observance of Palestine Day* (held on January 20), which contained over 100 pages of "material for addresses, radio talks, newspaper articles, editorials and general information." While the event itself was intended to have wide appeal, publicizing it was described as the special responsibility of the Zionist: "Remember that Palestine Day should be observed by ALL Jews—and that Zionists should merely take the initiative in stimulating its observance. Palestine Day should be observed by Jews and Christians. See that this is done."[8] The aesthetic protocols and ideological sensibilities of the modern American marketplace of ideas and material goods shaped American Jewry's presentation of Zionism; similarly, this new idiom of public culture informed the role that American Jews might play as the backers and shapers of a Jewish state in Palestine.

From its inception in late-nineteenth-century Europe, the Zionist movement has striven to span the disparity between its visions of an autonomous Jewish polity and its dependency on political and financial support from the diaspora. This is epitomized by the institution of the shekel in 1897, which symbolically links political activism focused on the Yishuv with philanthropy from Jewish communities based elsewhere. In the United States, the configuration of this relationship entailed distinctively American idioms. Here, the "selling" of Zionism frequently involved an appeal to the values of the American marketplace; like theatrical impresarios seeking financial backers for their productions, American Zionists vaunted the worthiness of their cause as they promoted the financial wisdom of supporting the Yishuv.

Thus, while much of Zionist political ideology in the Yishuv and in Europe championed a collective life as prescribed by socialist principles, American Jews were often presented with the image of the Jewish state-in-the-making as a sound investment. A 1925 promotional brochure for the American-Palestine Bank of Tel Aviv, for instance, invited American Jews to "help build Palestine at a profit to yourself" by becoming shareholders. Advertisements in American Zionist periodicals, notably *The New Palestine,* repeatedly exhorted Jewish readers to buy land in Palestine. "Every Jew should own land in Erez Israel," began one such appeal from the American Zion Commonwealth in 1923. But while the mandate of owning property in Palestine was construed as an act of Jewish patriotism, it was not equated with settlement. Prospective buyers might "settle yourself or a relative or a pioneer." In any case, one would "own an inheritance in the land of your forefathers," thereby satisfying both financial and patriotic aspirations.[9]

Remarkably, America often served as the model in Zionist promotions, providing Jews in the United States with a self-reflexive vision of the Yishuv. An advertisement for the colony of Balfouria promoted the new settlement to American investors as both attractive to the visiting tourist—assumed to be the mode in which the American Jew would most likely encounter the site—and inspired by modern urban planning in California. (Similar comparisons were made to entice American travelers to vacation in Palestine. One tourist agency promoted a salubrious holiday in Tel Aviv as a trip to "the Palestinian 'Atlantic City.'")[10]

The appeal to invest in land, settlements, and other institutions in the Yishuv followed the precedent of advertisements for produce raised by Jewish farmers in Palestine, which had appeared in American Jewish publications since the turn of the century. Indeed, an appeal to loyalty to the Zionist cause could prove instrumental in staking one's claim in the competitive market of Jewish holiday products. In 1907 the Carmel Wine Company warned readers of the *Jewish Daily Forward* to beware of competitors selling "all kinds of garbage under the name of Carmel." Such imposters not only cheated the consumer, they also offended "thousands of the best children of our people, on whom the colonization and development of Palestine depends."[11]

By the 1920s, purchasing wine, oranges, almonds, honey, olive oil, and the like from Jewish farms, vineyards, and orchards was championed as an act of Zionist patriotism. Advertisers frequently linked the ideological with the sensory; through these purchases one could not only support Jewish-owned and -run industries in Palestine, but could also savor the taste—or, in the case of Lubliner Palestine cigarettes, the aroma—of the Land of Zion. An advertisement for "Palestine Almonds for Pesach" in *The New Palestine* asked readers: "Have you ever thought how good the famous sweet Palestine almonds must be on Yom Tov only to be told that America is not a market for Palestine products? You must have hoped more than once that Palestine colonists would turn to America so that American Jews could taste the fruits of the Land of Israel. . . . This Yom Tov, you will not only taste the best fruit of its kind, but you will also be helping us create in America the market for our products which is so necessary for our welfare."[12]

Advertisements suggested that supporting Jewish settlements in Palestine was compatible (or at least not incompatible) with other Jewish agendas. The Mizrach Wine Company touted the purchase of their wares as the simultaneous fulfillment of traditional devotion and the support of the Yishuv: "Use Palestine Wine for Sacramental Purposes and Help Support the Jewish Colonists in Palestine." The Herzl Paint Company offered American Jews the opportunity to support the Zionist cause while simultaneously patronizing—and validating—Jewish entrepreneurship in the diaspora. A 1927 advertisement for the company in the *Jewish Daily Forward* features paint cans whose labels bear the portrait of the famous Zionist leader, framed by a six-pointed star, accompanied by the following copy: "For the first time in the history of the paint trade—a Jewish firm, the Herzl Paint Company of Brooklyn, a company under the management of experienced professionals with a great deal of capital, with the latest contrivances of science and technology. This firm has striven to show the world that the

Jewish spirit can also work wonders in the field of house paint. . . . We contribute a certain percentage of all purchases of our merchandise to the Jewish National Fund."[13]

Even with regard to regional produce, the United States served American Zionists as a material standard by which Palestine's performance ought to be measured. A 1920 advertisement in the *Jewish Daily Forward* for the American Fruit Growers of Palestine, based in New York City, exhorted investors to help provide funds to make Palestine "the California of the Orient." The advertisement called on American Jews to help colonists in Palestine realize their long-awaited dream and send them machinery, which would help bring their fruit production up to the level then maintained in California. The results would bring both profit and pride to the colonists. "Every Jew can lend a hand in helping to build the future of the fruit industry in our own land, and thereby also realize large profits from his investment."[14]

Elsewhere, America's heartland served as the implicit standard for envisioning the transformation of arid Palestine into a land of agricultural bounty. Jewish National Fund and United Jewish Appeal promotional pamphlets of the period typically featured illustrations of young pioneers gazing out over vistas of gently rolling fields, dotted with clusters of buildings or livestock—scenes that were clearly inspired more by an "American rural landscape" than by any Palestinian scene. Publicity photographs in the files of the United Palestine Appeal depicted *halutzim* restoring "the ancient fertility of the soil . . . with the aid of American agricultural machinery."[15]

The American standard was even extended to the healthy production of Jews born in Palestine: A 1937 Hadassah fundraising bag thanks American children for donating money to "help the children of Israel become as healthy and happy as the children of America." Had a child been born in Palestine before 1921, when the American-based women's Zionist organization established its modern infant welfare centers there, "his birth would have been attended by old women bearing magic charms which, they claimed, drove the Evil Spirit away. Dogs' teeth, birds' beaks and metal hands would have been pinned on the newborn's clothes. If the infant were a girl, mascara would have been put on her eyes and rouge on her lips." However, Hadassah boasts in a 1937 promotional report on child welfare in

Palestine that thanks to the organization's efforts, "the rate of fatality at delivery among Jewish mothers . . . has been reduced to 1.9 out of 1,000 cases—one of the lowest such records in the world"—surpassing even the death rate among mothers at childbirth in the United States.[16]

At the same time that American Zionists promoted the nascent Jewish state in Palestine in terms that conformed to bourgeois American material standards, they envisioned cultural as well as financial returns on their investment in the Yishuv. Although some American Jews would reap their spiritual reward through travels to Palestine or, in a few cases, by becoming halutzim, this was experienced most extensively and powerfully at home and in performative terms.

Many American Zionist leaders believed that "the Zionist revival in Eretz Yisrael promised to radiate spiritual and cultural sustenance . . . for American Jews."[17] Performance proved essential to the realization of Zionism as a cultural force in the diaspora. Indeed, American Zionist leaders often recognized—and not always begrudgingly—that the physical, emotional, and aesthetic aspects of performance enabled forms of communion with the spirit of Zionism unmatched by intellectual or polemical engagement.

The performance culture of American Zionism proved to be not only extensive and diverse in scope, but also of strategic importance to the movement's success in the United States. These performances bridged the gap between political rhetoric at home and pioneer struggles abroad. Whether as audiences or participants, American Jews could find in Zionist performances affective and visceral experiences simulating the achievements of remote settlers. Remarkably, this semblance of involvement in the Yishuv, this virtual realization of *halutsiut* (pioneering), became the basis of a diaspora Jewish culture that celebrated Zionist achievements while remaining at a distance from them. For many American Jews, creating, attending, and financing these performances became a cultural end in itself.

The ties between performance and fundraising in American Zionist culture are extensive and complex. Most directly, American Zionists have relied on a wide array of performative events to promote support for their cause and to situate Zionist activism in American Jewish communal life. Since the 1920s, much fund- and consciousness-raising centered around the importing of so-called Palestinian performances—Jewish folk dance troupes, soccer teams, or propaganda films featuring athletic halutzim making the desert bloom — much like wine, almonds, oranges, and other exotic produce from the Yishuv. During the interwar years both American and European producers made a series of films in Palestine for use as propaganda and to solicit support. As Hillel Tryster observes in his study of Zionist filmmaking in the pre-state era, the medium quickly proved an unrivaled vehicle for fundraising. By 1923, film accounted for the largest share of the JNF's propaganda budget. Zionist fundraising films were distributed throughout Europe and North America, with careful instructions as to when and how to appeal for and collect funds during the presentation. In some films, donating to the Zionist cause becomes a dramatic, even magical, cinematic moment, with stop-action animation sequences depicting the currencies of the world propelling themselves into a JNF *pushke* (charity collection box).[18]

In addition to importing Palestinian performances, American Zionists proved adept at creating their own. During the interwar years, activities such as benefit concerts, charity balls, protest rallies, lectures, and music and dance recitals became regular features of the public life of American Zionism. Often these were hybrid occasions, combining Jewish rituals with American-style political speeches and celebrity appearances, as well as featuring musical performances from an array of traditional, Zionist, popular, and classical repertoires. A case in point is the third seder, a secular communal ritual modeled on the traditional domestic Passover ceremonial meal. First practiced in the United States by secular Yiddishists in the early 1930s, the ritual was quickly adopted by American Zionist groups. The 1939 Annual Third Seder Festival held by the Zionist Organization of America in Atlantic City, New Jersey, featured the Philadelphia Hadassah Choir and the Hebrew theater troupe Habimah performing dramatic and musical pieces based on the Bible and Jewish folklore as well as works by modern Hebrew poet Hayyim Nahman Bialik and French composer Maurice Ravel. Like many similar programs, the seder concluded with the singing of both America's national anthem and the Zionist anthem "Hatikvah," a performative gesture that endowed the Yishuv with the status of a sovereign state.

Music, drama, and dance figured prominently in providing Americans with an aesthetic simulation of Zionist pioneering. Performances by folksingers, instrumentalists, and dancers from the Yishuv demonstrated a new

"Palestinian" aesthetic being created by Zionists. Their repertoire was quickly adopted by local Zionist youth groups, Jewish schools, and summer camps to provide physically and emotionally engaging activities that would appeal to young Americans and inspire in them a connection to the Yishuv. With its extensive focus on children, the performative culture of American Zionism frequently linked edification with recreation. As I. Sheldon Posen writes about the role of singing at Jewish summer camps, these activities "offered children self-made entertainment," were "a superb collective activity," and could be called upon by leaders "to help them achieve their . . . philosophical . . . and social goals."[19] Similarly, staging Bible plays or simulating kibbutz life at a camp encouraged young American Jews to imagine — and feel — themselves part of the Israelite past or the Zionist future. Activities such as learning to play baseball in Hebrew construed Zionism as a performative culture that could be realized in the diaspora and integrated into the most American of idioms.

Musical performances also enabled Zionists to present the Yishuv to a larger public of listeners as a nation-in-the-making with both a proud history and a promising future. Beginning with its title, *Song and Soil* — a recording of "Palestinian folk songs" performed by the United Synagogue Chorus in the 1940s — equates the physical Yishuv with its performative manifestation. In his foreword to this recording American Jewish composer Leonard Bernstein proclaims, "The Jews of Palestine are producing a culture all their own, rooted in its own soil, proud of itself, strongly and unashamedly Eastern. . . . Its folk art speaks out for all the world to perceive."[20]

Promoters often conceptualized these performance arts as dynamic links between Israel's ancient present and its utopian future. In the foreword to their 1941 instructional volume *Palestine Dances!* Corinne Chochem and Muriel Roth trace the origins of "the dance of new Palestine" by modeling its history on the Zionist master narrative, proceeding from origins in an idealized, ancient pastoral setting to a liberating return to this site from the restrictions of the urban diaspora. The *hora,* readers are informed, is rooted in dancing that celebrated the harvest as part of "primitive ritual," which employed "leaps, high jumps and the upward movement of the arms to symbolize the growth of the grain." Encountered by Sephardic Jews in the Balkans (whence its name, derived from Serbo-Croatian), the hora became "a dance of joy" performed at weddings and holidays, but it also "took on a more enclosed—an indoor—character and consequently became more restrained." The *bulgar* followed a similar path among Ashkenazim, as "the same agricultural dance . . . underwent a restraining influence in the crowded ghetto milieu" (although it "became more expressively emotional," responsive to the "fervor of the Hassidim"). Early halutzim from Eastern Europe "revived the old Sephardic Horah" in Palestine, where it takes on "an even more authentic color," as it is "once again danced under the open sky, bringing it still closer to its original agricultural source." Now, Chochem and Roth write, "the Horah subtly fuses the healthy energy of the youthful builders with the mystic ecstacy and abandon of their Hassidic forbears. . . . After long hours of hard labor in the fields and factories, a people engaged in the upbuilding of a new land find new enthusiasm, new strength and new hope with which to face the difficult years ahead when they dance the Horah, their dance of affirmation. . . . To see Palestine dance," the authors claim, is nothing less than to witness "a people reborn."[21]

From modest amateur theatricals to lavish professionally mounted spectacles, public performances were often instrumental in raising money for building up and defending the Yishuv. Some, such as the June Night Frolic for Palestine Land Redemption, held in Yankee Stadium in summer 1935, followed the format of vaudeville. The event featured a wealth of popular entertainers, Jewish and non-Jewish—among the twenty-nine acts were appearances by Milton Berle, Paul Draper, Ed Sullivan, Major Bowes, Molly Picon, Sophie Tucker, and Baby Rose Marie—as well as numbers by a Zionist chorus, an opera ensemble, and the Radio City Ballet. Other fundraising performances were more aesthetically original and ambitious in their mission—none more so than the epic pageants created under the leadership of Zionist activist (and, for much of the 1930s and 1940s, theatrical producer) Meyer Weisgal.

In his memoir Weisgal characterizes pageantry as the antithesis of American Zionism's traditional predilection for speechifying; he describes his initial embrace of "music, drama, spectacle" as a "reawakening" of a movement "strewn with dry bones and a thousand speeches." Inspired by a production of *Aïda* at the Chicago Opera House, Weisgal borrowed its sets ("How far is Egypt from Palestine?") to produce his first pageant on the occasion of

Chanukkah, in 1932. At Weisgal's insistence, "the highlight of the evening was to be: *no speeches!*" The event proved successful as a feat of showmanship, a fundraiser, and a generator of publicity for the Zionist movement. These goals were intertwined from the production's inception: Weisgal's ensemble included "hundreds of Jewish schoolchildren, knowing that every kid who took part would fill ten seats with parents and relatives." The Chanukkah production was shortly followed by *The Romance of a People,* a large-scale enactment of "four thousand years of Jewish history." Staged in conjunction with the 1933 Chicago World's Fair, it also proved an artistic, fundraising, and public relations success, traveling on for an extended run in a New York City armory.[22]

Weisgal's involvement with performance grew from an interest in theater as an instrument of fundraising for the Yishuv to performance as an act of American Zionist cultural expression in its own right. The contract Weisgal drew up with stage director Max Reinhardt, composer Kurt Weill, and playwright Franz Werfel to create *The Eternal Road* (which eventually opened at the Manhattan Opera House in 1937) was nothing less than a mandate to create "a musical biblical morality play to express the spiritual origin, the earliest mythical history and the eternal destiny of the Jewish people." As he explained to Reinhardt, Weisgal envisioned the production as a cultural expression equivalent to the mission of the Yishuv: "This spectacle must be our answer to Hitler."[23]

Other performances were the end result, rather than the instrument, of American Zionist fundraising efforts. Historian Arthur A. Goren recalls a "battle of paid advertisements" in American newspapers and magazines waged during the immediate post–World War II years between a group of Revisionist Zionists and members of the Labor Zionist youth movement Habonim. With funds raised by their appeals in the press for support, Habonim decided in fall 1947 to produce a record album, entitled *Haganah: Songs of the Jewish Underground*. The recording featured performances "in English translation followed by the Hebrew original, thus making them accessible to the American public." As Goren notes, the order of the songs performed on the recording "traced the saga of 'the return to the land' "—first, "*Hora* in a Foreign Land"; second, a song describing an *aliyah-bet* (illegal) ship's approach to the coast of Palestine; third, a song about life on a kibbutz; and fourth, the "Palmach" hymn of the elite unit of the Haganah — in effect, enabling the American listener to make vicarious aliyah.[24]

Volunteering and fundraising were similarly imbued with performative significance that simulated the arduous defense and construction of the Yishuv. Volunteers for the Keren Hayesod campaign were "called to the colors" to "take [their] place in the peaceful army of Palestine" and devote three full days — not just "leisure time in the evening" — to canvassing contributions from neighbors and colleagues. "If you are serious about the rebuilding of Palestine, if you really mean business, you will meet the test," an appeal in *The New Palestine* challenged readers in the early 1920s. A 1938 appeal for funds to build the Hadassah Medical Center on Mt. Scopus transforms donations into symbolic bricks and the donor into a "builder in Palestine."[25]

Halutzim provided American Zionists with compelling role models of the "new" Jewish man and woman — proud, athletic, activist, visionary, and committed to modern, collectivist ideals. Their images in propaganda photographs and films became icons that young American Zionists emulated in training camps and at public performances. Thus, at the New York premiere of the 1935 Keren Kayemet fundraising film *Land of Promise,* which featured heroic images of halutzim at work in the fields, a group of American would-be pioneers were brought in "from their training farm in New Jersey for the event. Dressed in white shirts with pitchforks and rakes on their shoulders," they posed in the movie theater lobby for publicity photographers covering the event.[26]

Yet Palestine's halutzim were exemplars for American Jews to admire and support, rather than to imitate. While Zionist propaganda typically depicted young female pioneers in Palestine at work on farms and in factories, Hadassah exhorted American Zionist women in 1934 to "serve Palestine with the labor of your hands" by forming sewing circles. These groups produced clothing for halutzim and also provided American Jewish women with opportunities to socialize, recruit, and promote the Zionist cause. One "tested method of promoting sewing circle activities" had members "asking their young daughters to accompany them to the sewing group. The girls thus learn how to knit and at the same time hear about Hadassah's work."[27]

Perhaps the most popular and symbolically powerful act of support for the Yishuv from abroad was donating money to plant trees in Palestine, fulfilling the vision of early Zionist leaders to "reforest" the Land of Israel. These contributions — sometimes tangible in the form of special fundraising cards, in which the donor purchased leaf-shaped stamps that foliated an illustration of a tree, or in which coins were inserted in slots to simulate leaves — rendered donors as virtual foresters in what Simon Schama has described as "the nursery of the [Jewish] nation."[28]

American Zionism's impresario culture was not only distinct from pioneering in the Yishuv but also differed significantly from other forms of American Jewish culture, including other activities centered around fundraising. As the shekel poster cited earlier indicated, money was being raised both to build the Yishuv and to aid European Jewry. Eastern Europe was, of course, the other major focus of interwar Jewish philanthropy. Some organizations, notably the Joint Distribution Committee, supported both causes simultaneously.

Most of the fundraising for Eastern Europe was localized, focusing on an individual community or even family. *Landsmanshaftn* (hometown associations) generated the lion's share of funds and goods donated to Eastern European Jews. These mutual aid organizations were concerned largely with the welfare of particular *shtetlekh* (towns) or other localities, with which American members had direct blood ties.[29] For the most part, however, there were no such family bonds linking American Jews to the Yishuv. There the agenda was national in scope, more ideological than sentimental.

Moreover, while fundraising for the Yishuv was directed forward in time, parallel efforts for the *alte heym* (old home, as this term suggests) generally looked backward. Eastern Europe was seen as being literally old, a vestigial Jewish world. The rhetoric and imagery of appeals for support focused primarily on caring for an aging, enfeebled culture. During World War I and after, political cartoons calling for American assistance for beleaguered Jewish Eastern Europe repeatedly represented the Old World community with the figure of an elderly, pious Jewish male, usually bent over or prostrate, often in tatters, sometimes with arms outstretched in supplication. The Soviet utopia of Biro-Bidjan, celebrated in Yiddish primers for the International Workers Order (IWO) schools in the 1930s, or the Jewish Labor Bund's 1935 documentary film *Mir kumen on,* which raised money for the

Medem Sanitorium near Warsaw, were radical exceptions. As a rule, American Jews did not publicly envision a future for Jewish Eastern Europe, especially after the rise of Nazism and Stalinism.[30]

Palestine, however, as represented in American Zionist productions from world's fair pavilions and protest rallies to sporting events and folkdance recitals, was all about the future. It would be a future in which most American Jews would take part not as actors on the stage of the Jewish state, but rather as producers—providing not only support, but also inspiration, authority, and appreciation.

NOTES

This chapter grew out of research conducted at the Center for Judaic Studies by the author, together with Beth Wenger, during the 1996–1997 fellowship year for the 1998 exhibition "'Holy Land': American Encounters with the Land of Israel in the Century before Statehood," displayed at the National Museum of American Jewish History, Philadelphia, and the Kamin Gallery, University of Pennsylvania Library. A shorter version of this essay was presented by the author at the 29th Annual Conference of the Association for Jewish Studies, Boston, on December 22, 1997, as part of a joint presentation with Dr. Wenger.

1. Michael Berkowitz, *Zionist Culture and West European Jewry before the First World War* (Cambridge, 1993), p. 119.

2. Rachel Arbel, ed., *Blue and White in Color: Visual Images of Zionism 1897–1947* (Tel Aviv, 1997), p. 42.

3. Milton Goldin, *The Music Merchants* (New York, 1969), p. 22.

4. Melvin I. Urofsky, *American Zionism from Herzl to the Holocaust* (1975, reprint; Lincoln, Nebraska, 1995), pp. 312–13.

5. See Louis Brandeis, "Zionism and Patriotism," (New York, 1915); Hasia R. Diner, "Zion and America: The Formative Visions of Abba Hillel Silver," *Journal of Israeli History* 17:1 (Spring 1996), p. 48.

6. Frank Presbrey, *The History and Development of Advertising* (1929, reprint; New York, 1968), pp. 565–66.

7. Stuart Ewen, *PR!: A Social History of Spin* (New York, 1996), p. 68. Ewen's discussion of public space here is indebted to the pioneering work of sociologist

Gabriel de Tarde, whose early writings on the workings of public opinion were inspired, in part, by the Dreyfus trials, which similarly spurred Herzl's involvement in political Zionism.

8. *Guide Book for Observance of Palestine Day* (New York, 1935), p. I.

9. Brochure, "A Message to American Jewry," The American-Palestine Bank, Ltd., Tel Aviv, 1925; Cyrus Adler Papers, Box 18, Folder 4, Center for Judaic Studies, University of Pennsylvania; advertisement for the American Zion Commonwealth, *The New Palestine,* Jan. 5, 1923, p. 16.

10. "Settle in Balfouria," *The New Palestine,* Mar. 2, 1923, p. 156; advertisement for Palestine & Oriental Shipping Service Co., *The New Palestine,* Apr. 20, 1923, p. 294.

11. Advertisement for Carmel Wine Company, *Jewish Daily Forward,* Mar. 7, 1907, p. 6 (in Yiddish; my translation).

12. Advertisement for Lubliner Palestine Cigarettes, *The New Palestine,* Mar. 27, 1925, inside front cover; advertisement for Palestine Almonds, *The New Palestine,* Mar. 17, 1922, p. 176.

13. Advertisement for Mizrach Wine Company, *The New Palestine,* Mar. 17, 1922, p. 176; advertisement for Herzl Paint Company, *Jewish Daily Forward,* Jan. 10, 1927, p. 10.

14. Advertisement for American Fruit Growers of Palestine, *Jewish Daily Forward,* Oct. 12, 1920, p. 2 (in Yiddish; my translation).

15. Arbel, *Blue and White in Color,* p. 78. See also the cover of "Rebuilding the Land of Israel," a 1926–1927 United Palestine Appeal pamphlet, reproduced in Jeffrey Shandler and Beth S. Wenger, eds., *Encounters with the "Holy Land": Place, Past and Future in American Jewish Culture* (Philadelphia, 1997), p. 49; "Harvest Time in the Holy Land" [photograph], United Palestine Appeal, ca. 1940s; RG 120 (Israel, General), Folder 85, YIVO Institute for Jewish Research Archives.

16. Fundraising bag, "Dear American Children," (1937); RG 17, Box 1, Folder "Child Welfare Fund," Hadassah Archives. The notion of the Western middle-class setting an economic standard for Jewish life in Palestine has its antecedents in non-Zionist fundraising for the region's religious Jewish community, which was largely impoverished and depended on charitable support from the diaspora. A turn-of-the-century set of fundraising stamps for the Matzoh Fund of the Central Committee Knesseth Israel of Jerusalem, for example, juxtaposes a scene of a pious middle-class American (or perhaps European) family around the seder table with the image of Palestine's Jewish community receiving packages of Passover food from the charity. See Shandler and Wenger, *Encounters with the "Holy Land,"* p. 33,

illustration, "Hadassah Child Welfare in Palestine" [brochure, 1937]; RG 17, Box 1, Hadassah Archives.

17. Arthur A. Goren, "Spiritual Zionists and Jewish Sovereignty," in Robert M. Seltzer and Norman J. Cohen, eds., *The Americanization of the Jews* (New York, 1995), p. 169.

18. Hillel Tryster, *Israel before Israel: Silent Cinema in the Holy Land* (Jerusalem, 1995), chap. 4, passim.

19. I. Sheldon Posen, "*Lomir Zingen, Hava Nashira:* An Introduction to Jewish Summer Camp Song," in Jenna Weissman Joselit with Karen S. Mittelman, eds., *A Worthy Use of Summer: Jewish Summer Camping in America* (Philadelphia, 1993), p. 30.

20. *Song and Soil/Shir Ha-moledet* [record album], sung by United Synagogue Chorus (New York, ca. 1940s). Sound Archives, YIVO Institute for Jewish Research.

21. Corinne Chochem and Muriel Roth, *Palestine Dances! Folk Dances of Palestine* (New York, 1941), pp. 5–8, passim.

22. Meyer Weisgal, . . . *So Far: An Autobiography* (New York, 1971), pp. 106–15, passim. On Weisgal's pageants, see also Atay Citron, "Pageantry and Theater in the Service of Jewish Nationalism in the United States, 1933–1946," Ph.D. diss., New York University, 1989.

23. Weisgal, . . . *So Far,* p. 117.

24. Arthur A. Goren, "Celebrating Zion in America," in Shandler and Wenger, eds., *Encounters with the "Holy Land,"* pp. 54–55, passim.

25. Advertisement for Keren Hayesod campaign, *The New Palestine,* Mar. 23, 1923, p. 23; "Pile Brick on Brick NOW" [raffle ticket, 1937]; RG 17, Box 2, Hadassah Archives.

26. Goren, "Celebrating Zion in America," p. 51.

27. "A Stitch in Time" [pamphlet], 1934; RG 17, Box 3, Hadassah Archives.

28. Simon Schama, *Landscape and Memory* (New York, 1995), pp. 5–6. In recent years the symbolic investment that diaspora Jews have made in "reforesting" Israel has been challenged by environmentalists, who question its impact on the region's native ecology. The time-honored practice has even become the subject of American Jewish humor. The front of a card published recently by American Greetings reads, "In honor of your birthday, a tree has been planted in Israel in your name"; inside, the card reads, "Your day to water it is Thursday!" (birthday card, L'Chayim To Life! series, American Greetings, Cleveland Ohio, n.d.; purchased 1997).

29. See Daniel Soyer, *Jewish Immigrant Associations and American Identity in New York, 1880–1939* (Cambridge, MA, 1997).

30. See Jack Kugelmass and Jeffrey Shandler, *Going Home: How American Jews Invented the Old World* [exhibition catalog] (New York, 1989), p. 16. See, e.g., J. Foshko, "Helft!" [cartoon], *Der tog,* Aug. 16, 1915, p. 4; Lola, "A briv fun Amerike" [cartoon], *Der groyser kundes,* Jan. 26, 1917, p. 1; Zagat, "Ratevet!" [cartoon], *Jewish Daily Forward,* May 15, 1919, p. 3. On children, see e.g., "Kinder in Sovetn-farband" (p. 134), "A sovetn Amerike" (p. 135), "A briv fun Biro-Bidzshan" (p. 139), "Der ershter may in Moskve" (p. 157), in D. Tarant and B. Fridman, *Kinder: onfanger lernbukh farn ershtn yor* (New York, 1933); on *Mir kumen on,* see J. Hoberman, *Bridge of Light: Yiddish Film Between Two Worlds* (New York, 1991), pp. 226–31.

THREE

Moroccan Jews and the Shaping of Israel's Sacred Geography

YORAM BILU

In the late 1970s Kenneth Brown, an anthropologist who had been working in Morocco among Jews and Muslims, made a photographed tour of Israel. In the publication that followed, designated "A Journey through the Labyrinth," he sought to present and ponder the many faces of Israeli society he met on his way. Joining the pilgrimage to the popular shrine of Rabbi Shimon Bar-Yohai in Meron on Lag Ba'Omer (the thirty-second day after Passover), he made the following observations:

> The area around the shrine was filled with people who had camped there during the night. Most of them had set up tents and tables and chairs. They were eating, drinking, playing music, dancing, sleeping, or wandering around observing one another and the goods for sale that have been set up by hawkers. The crowd was decidedly Oriental [of Middle Eastern and North-African background] and so was the atmosphere—the sounds of music and voices (a mixture of Hebrew and

> Arabic as pronounced by Oriental Jews) and the smells of food. *The scene bore a striking resemblance to the pilgrimage fairs celebrated in Morocco by Muslims and Jews alike* [emphasis added].
>
> As we approached the building of the shrine that housed the tombs of Bar Yohai and his son, the composition of the crowd changed. Inside the courtyard most of the men were dressed in the typical clothing of Orthodox Eastern European Jews—long black coats and black or fur hats. And they were dancing to and singing Hasidic melodies, all the while carrying the small male children on their shoulders.[1]

Brown's conclusion seems to be informed by the correspondence model of pilgrimage. "The pilgrimage fair at Meron brought together Oriental and European Jews but it did not integrate them. The separation existed here as it did in most sectors of life in Israel. The inequalities and imbalances should be noted: the Ultra-orthodox European Jews, a minority but nonetheless at the center, dominated the ritual aspect of the pilgrimage. The Oriental Jews, although a majority, remained on the periphery."[2]

Brown's symbolic reading of the pilgrimage, although suggestive, appears overstated. The ultra-Orthodox Hasidim flocking to Rabbi Shimon's tomb can hardly be taken as representing the hegemonic Ashkenazi mainstream in Israel. And the dispersal of celebrants of Eastern (Mizrahi) extraction in Safed's outlying mountain slopes seems to reflect a traditional pattern of camping and picnicking in the open air rather than the oppressive domination of Ashkenazi "ritual specialists." In this respect, it is illuminating to read the lamenting response of an Orthodox Ashkenazi writer to the changing face of the *hillulah* (death anniversary celebration). Comparing contemporary pilgrimages to the one he had first attended in 1935, he bemoans the Oriental takeover. "Where are the dancers of that time? the joy, the exuberance, the ecstasy? An undefined monster has emerged in their place . . . an *Oriental fantasia,* like the *ziara* of Nebi Rubin or the fantasia of Nebi Musa in the 1920s" [emphasis added].[3]

Indeed, the changes that the festival in Meron has been undergoing, in terms of ethnic composition and patterns of celebration, have been noted in other pilgrimage sites as well. These changes are strongly associated with the astonishing proliferation of the cult of the saint in present-day Israel. As a multifaceted and widespread phenomenon, this hagiolatric revival clearly exceeds narrow ethnic boundaries, but the imprint of Maghrebi hagiolatric traditions has been evident in many of its manifestations. In this chapter I would like to situate the Jewish Moroccan contribution to current cultic manifestations in the proper historical and sociocultural context, to present its major manifestations, and to explore some of its possible meanings for present-day Israeli society.

The folk-veneration of saints played a major role in the lives of the Jews in nineteenth-century Morocco and constituted a basic component of their ethnic identity. In form, style, and prevalence this cultural phenomenon clearly bears the hallmarks of indigenous saint worship, perhaps the most significant feature of Moroccan Islam. At the same time, however, it was also reinforced by the deep-seated conception of the *tsaddiq* (saint) in classical Jewish sources. In various Jewish groups outside North Africa, pious rabbis were accorded saintly attributes and their tombs became centers of popular pilgrimages. In the case of Eastern European Hasidism the ideology of *tsaddiqim* (pl.) crystallized into a religious movement that spawned many dynasties of venerated rabbis, each with its own organizational infrastructure and institutions. In the Maghreb, institutionalization of this scope did not take place. Yet the unique fusion of Jewish and Muslim influences created a viable and pervasive folk-religious system.[4]

Most of the Jewish Moroccan saints were charismatic rabbis, distinguished by their erudition and piety. These rabbis were believed to possess a special spiritual force, which did not fade away after their death. This force, akin to the Moroccan Muslim *Baraka*, could be utilized for the benefit of the saints' adherents.[5] In contrast with their Muslim and Hasidic counterparts, most of the Jewish Moroccan tsaddiqim were identified as such only after their death. Therefore their miraculous feats were usually associated with their tombs. At the same time, however, the strong sense of inherited blessedness inherent in the Jewish notion of *zechut avot* (literally, the virtue of the ancestors) allowed for the emergence of *some* dynasties of tsaddiqim, the most well-known of which were the Abu-Hatseras, the Pintos, and the Ben-Baruchs.

Virtually every Jewish community, including the tiniest and most peripheral, had one or more patron saints. While the popularity of most of these saints was quite circumscribed, some of them acquired reputations and followings which transcended regional boundaries. Sainted figures like Rabbi Ya'aqov Abu-Hatsera, Rabbi David u-Moshe, Rabbi Amram Ben-Diwan, and Rabbi David Ben-Baruch were venerated in many areas of the country. Some of the saints were well-known historical figures, while many others seemed to be legendary characters, recognized as blessed with holiness only after manifesting as posthumous apparitions, most typically in dreams.[6]

Generally, the presence of the saints was a given in the social reality of Moroccan Jews, a central idiom for articulating a wide range of experiences. The main event in the veneration of each saint was the collective pilgrimage to his tomb on the anniversary of his death and the hillulah there. In the case of the more renowned saints, many thousands of pilgrims from various regions would gather around the tombs for several days, during which they feasted on slaughtered cattle, drank *mahia* (arak), danced and chanted, prayed, and lit candles. All these activities, combining marked spirituality and high ecstasy with mundane concerns, were conducted in honor of the tsaddiq.

In addition to collective pilgrimages, visits to saints' sanctuaries were made on an individual basis in times of plight. As intermediaries between God Almighty and the believers, the problems which saints were considered capable of solving included the whole range of human concerns. The presence of the saint was also strongly felt in daily routine, as people would cry out his name and dream about him whenever facing a problem. At home, candles were lit and *se'udot* (festive meals) were organized in his honor; and male newborns were conferred his name. In many cases the relationship with the saint has amounted to a symbiotic association spanning the entire life course of the devotee.

Rather than a frozen set of cultural vestiges, Jewish Maghrebi hagiolatry was a dynamic system, accommodating to shifting circumstances, in which new saints and shrines successively emerged, sank, and resurfaced. Intriguingly, the 1930s and 1940s, decades of rapid modernization, were also the golden period of saint worship among Moroccan Jewry. In fact, until the establishment of the French Protectorate the tenor of Jewish Moroccan hagiolatry was personal and local. Prior to that period, the general lack of economic resources and the unsafe travel conditions in the rural hinterland of *bled es-siba* (country without government control), where most of the saints' tombs were concentrated, made it highly improbable for the reputation and followings of a given tsaddiq to transcend local boundaries. Following pacification, communication and locomotion between the Jewish communities became relatively easy, and the improved economic and political conditions facilitated organizational efforts designed to maintain and publicize many shrines on the communal level. In addition, rapid changes brought by modernization, manifested in massive processes of urbanization, industrialization, migration, and secularization, shattered the social fabric of the traditional Jewish family and community. Under the resultant conditions of disorientation and anomie, the salience and appeal of the traditional dispensers of solace and protection grew.

The mass immigration of Moroccan Jews to Israel during the 1950s and 1960s confronted the newcomers with a major challenge of maintaining cultural traditions rejected by the Israeli mainstream. Saint worship appeared particularly vulnerable in the new country, because it was linked to specific places now remote and inaccessible. Immigration to Israel meant, among other things, a painful dissociation from the tsaddiqim, and this loss exacerbated "the predicament of homecoming."[7]

Clearly, the attractiveness of the saints' shrines, as centrifugal sacred sites located in the Diaspora, could not compete with the centripetal messianic fervor generated by the establishment of the State of Israel. But the religious ascendancy of Zion vis-à-vis the peripheral shrines in the Maghreb did not mean that the saints were forgotten. Their followers could not easily forgo the support of the tsaddiqim as a cultural resource in the face of enormous difficulties after immigration. Yet the pressures exerted on the newcomers to shed their ethnocultural heritage and embrace the reigning ideology of secular-collectivist Zionism, together with the disengagement from the Maghrebi sites, contributed to the general diminution and decentralization of the *hillulot* (pl.). They had been reduced to domestic affairs, modestly celebrated at home or in the neighborhood synagogue.[8]

Once the immediate difficulties of absorption were mitigated, however, Moroccan Jews responded to the separation from the saints by embracing various substitutes for the tombs that had been left behind. Apparently, the newcomers had to become more rooted in the local scene and more confident in their Israeli identity in order to proudly assert their hagiolatric heritage. This dialectical pattern, incompatible with a naive melting pot ideology, has fueled the resurgence of ethnic sentiments in many immigrant-absorbing countries. Given the central role of saint worship in the life-space of many Moroccan Jews before *aliya,* it is no wonder that this tradition in particular emerged as an emblem of ethnic pride. As an "act of concentrated religious fervor, highly dramatic and fused with emotions," yet one which is quite undemanding in terms of the minutiae of religious observance, participation in hillulot was tailor-made for many Israelis of North African background, who remained believers at heart despite a growing distancing from strict ritual practice.[9]

THE REVIVAL OF MAGHREBI SAINT WORSHIP IN ISRAEL

In what follows I discuss six avenues through which Moroccan Jews have expressed their devotion to the tsaddiqim in the new country. These avenues may be viewed as accommodations in response to the disengagement from the tsaddiqim of the Maghreb.

1. *"Appropriating" old-time native pilgrimage sites.* Most accessible among the compensatory alternatives were the tombs of local, Eretz Israeli tsaddiqim, mainly from the biblical and the talmudic eras. The "Moroccanization" of these old-time pilgrimage traditions has been particularly noted in the popular, all-Israeli hillulot of Rabbi Shimon Bar-Yohai ("Rashby") in Meron near Safed and of Rabbi Meir Ba'al HaNess in Tiberias. For the mystically oriented Jewish communities in Morocco, the fact that Rabbi Shimon was the alleged author of the sacred *Zohar* (the *Book of Splendor*), the canonical text of kabbalah mysticism, granted him a particularly elevated stance among the tsaddiqim. Rabbi Shimon's hillulah in Israel brings together up to 200,000 celebrants—about 4 percent of the state's entire Jewish population. North African Jews and their descendants form the majority of the pilgrims in Meron and Tiberias, and they imbue the pilgrimage with a distinctive Maghrebi style.[10]

2. *"Annexing" local, community-based pilgrimage sites.* Maghrebi Jews living in development towns throughout the country have adopted burial sites of native tsaddiqim in their vicinity. Although most of the pilgrimages thus created have not exceeded local or regional boundaries, the resultant pattern of devotion appears closer than the "national hillulot" to the traditional Maghrebi pattern of a community with its own patron saint. The creation of the hillulah of Honi HaMe'agel (the circle-maker), a legendary talmudic sage, in the northern town of Hatsor Haglilit, is perhaps the most well-known case among the regional hillulot. An old-time tradition identified an ancient burial cave some fifteen miles east of Safed as the tomb of Honi, but the site was frequented only sporadically, in times of drought (the termination of which was considered Honi's specialty).

   Honi's finest hour came about after the development town of Hatsor Haglilit had been founded near the cave. His popularity mounted after the wars of 1967 and 1973, during which the town, situated not far from the border with Syria, did not suffer the slightest damage, ostensibly owing to the tsaddiq's miraculous intercession. Consequently, Honi's hillulah was scheduled to fall on Israel's Day of Independence. The celebration in Hatsor is a medium-size pilgrimage attracting several thousand celebrants from the town and its environs.

   The same Maghrebi pattern of a community with its own patron saint could be seen evolving in other new towns, like Yavneh, Carmiel, and Beit-Shemesh. In Yavneh, for example, a local cult emerged around the tomb of Rabban Gamliel, located in a Muslim shrine in the center of the town. The hillulah was designated for the eighteenth day of Sivan, the death anniversary of a venerated scion of the Abu-Hatsera family, Rabbi Israel, buried in Colombe-Bashar, Algeria, simply because the son-in-law of the late tsaddiq was the head of the local municipality. In some places, a reappropriation of sites connected with the forebears of the tribes of Israel (Jacob's sons) but associated for years with Muslim saint worship has been taking place. Examples are the sanctuaries of Dan (near the town of Beit-Shemesh), Benjamin (near Kefar Saba), and recently Reuben (near Ashdod and Yavneh).

3. *Creating new contemporary saints.* Given the dynamic nature of saint

veneration in Morocco, it is not surprising that in Israel, too, new cult centers have been established around the tombs of contemporary rabbis. The most impressive example is that of Rabbi Israel Abu-Hatsera, nicknamed Baba Sali, a descendant of the most revered Jewish family in southern Morocco. Since his death in 1984, Baba Sali's tomb in the southern development town of Netivot has become a popular pilgrimage center, second only to Rabbi Shimon's sanctuary. On regular days, the site is probably the most "active" holy location in Israel after the Wailing Wall.[11] The growing popularity of the shrine at Netivot has resulted from the meteoric rise of Baba Sali to the status of a national tsaddiq, the saint of Israel of the 1980s and 1990s.

In contrast to other hillulot, the festival in Netivot is the object of intense "promotion campaigns," complete with media coverage, official invitations, special bus lines, organized markets, and an elaborate "holy industry" in which the saint's portrait adorns a wide variety of artifacts, from prayer books and bottles of arak to key chains and holograms. Moreover, the hillula also draws organized political interest groups and personages such as the prime minister and cabinet ministers, party leaders, and local officials, as well as representatives of the chief rabbinate. The conscious planning evident in the effective system for "selling" the saint that Baba Baruch, Baba Sali's controversial son and successor, had set in motion is an example of the extent to which charisma can be manufactured or synthesized.[12]

Baba Baruch's entrepreneurial endeavor is impressively inscribed in the land of Netivot. The tsaddiq's tomb was enclosed in a spacious whitewashed sanctuary and an opulently decorated synagogue was erected next to it. This impressive edifice, visible from a distance, is now part of a larger, walled enclosure that includes a parking lot, a picnic area, vendors booths, and other facilities. In addition, the father's (now Baruch's) residence was enlarged and the foundations for Kiriat Baba Sali, a big religious campus, were laid. Today the campus includes several buildings housing the headquarters of Baba Baruch's organization, a *yeshiva* (religious academy), a *Talmud Torah* (religious school), and a kindergarten. These were built in a distinctively Moorish style, contrasting dramatically with the plebeian neighborhood surrounding them. In 1996 the sanctuary was officially declared a holy site by the ministry of religious affairs. Two years later the Jewish National Fund began to transform the empty space between Kiriat Baba Sali and the shrine into Baba Sali's Park, in the shape of a huge *hamsah* (hand-shaped amulet).[13]

Another contemporary case concerns Rabbi Hayyim Houri, a Tunisian rabbi who died in 1957 in the southern town of Beer-Sheva. The limited accessibility of the tomb, inconveniently located in the midst of a densely populated municipal cemetery, does not stop crowds from transforming the cemetery into a scene of joy and ecstasy during the hillula. At the same time, it points to the spontaneous, unplanned nature of Houri's emergence as a sainted figure, "the saint of Beer-Sheva."[14]

4. *Transferring Jewish Moroccan Saints to Israel through Dreams*. Although the "Moroccanization" of local hillulot and the creation of new saints have contributed to the preservation of hagiolatric practices under changing circumstances, their function should be seen as *compensatory* rather than *restorative*. To cope with the painful loss of the Maghrebi saints, a more direct and daring accommodation has been necessary, namely, the "symbolic translocation" of saints from Morocco to Israel.[15] Here we deal with the spontaneous initiative by people who had been inspired by a series of visitational dreams in which they had been urged by a Maghrebi tsaddiq to erect a site for him in their home. The initiators, whom I have designated "saint impresarios," were middle-aged men and women who were typically among the rank and file.

The most well-known Jewish Moroccan tsaddiq to be transferred to Israel via dreams is Rabbi David u-Moshe, with sites in Safed, Ashkelon, and Ofakim. The "House of Rabbi David u-Moshe" in Shikun Cana'an, Safed, erected immediately after the 1973 war, became a sweeping success, with thousands of devotees flocking to the domestic shrine (originally the bedroom of the impresario and his wife) on the hillula day (the first day of Heshvan). The founder, an afforestation worker (now retired), has become an inspiring model for several other impresarios. Shrines of other translocated Maghrebi saints were erected in Beit Shean (Rabbi Avraham Aouriwar), Kiriat Gat (Rabbi Machluf Ben Yosef Abuhatsera), Ramle (Slat L'ktar, a Tunisian female saint), and recently Or-Akiva (Rabbi David Ben Baruch) and Beer-Sheva (Rabbi Ya'aqov Wazana).

5. *Situating local sainted figures in new shrines through dreams*. A variant of the previous pattern is a dream-based shrine referring to a local rather than imported tradition. According to a legendary tradition mentioned in the Babylonian Talmud (Eruvin 19a), the entrance to the Garden of Eden in its terrestrial form is located in the town of Beit Shean in the Jordan Valley. In 1979 a Beit-She'ani inhabitant announced that he had discovered this entrance in the backyard of his house. Elijah the Prophet, the gatekeeper of the Garden of Eden, and the protagonist of the dreams that precipitated the discovery, is the patron saint of the site. Other dream-based shrines, reviving or inventing local traditions, have been added in recent years to Israel's sacred geography, from Yeruham in the Negev (where a domestic shrine for Rabbi Shimon Bar-Yohai was established by a female impresario) to a *moshav* in the upper Galilee (where the tomb of Isaiah the Prophet was recently discovered).
6. *Reinterring the remains of Jewish Moroccan saints in Israel*. Another, more palpable restorative method has been to exhume the remains of well-known saints buried in Morocco—until recently a clandestine affair—and reinter them in Israel. A recent case, well-covered by the media, was that of Rabbi Hayyim Pinto from Ashdod. Rabbi Pinto, the chief rabbi of Kiriat Mallachi, entombed there the remains of four holy ancestors of his which he had managed to smuggle from Morocco in a suitcase. An impressive shrine covers the quadripartite tomb, which draws a fairly large following. In recent years, the remains of other cherished rabbis from Morocco have been reinterred in Israel by their descendants.

Following the peace treaty with Egypt, Moroccan-born Israelis have been allowed to visit their country of origin. As a result, the shrines there have become accessible once more. Indeed, judging from their itineraries, many of the tours from Israel to Morocco are pilgrimages no less than touristic ventures.[16] But the number of visitors is still too small to render the Israeli alternatives redundant. In addition, the notion of a patron saint bespeaks an intimacy and easy availability associated with a strong sense of localism which remote shrines cannot provide.

NETIVOT AS THE BENARES OF ISRAEL: THE "SANCTIFICATION" OF DEVELOPMENT TOWNS

In seeking to situate the renaissance of Maghrebi hagiolatry in the wider context of contemporary Israeli society, the fact that most of the urban arenas for this revival were "development towns" (*ayarot piuah*) appears highly significant. The peak of the population dispersion policy initiated by the Israeli government in the early 1950s coincided with the first massive waves of aliya from the Maghreb. Consequently, many Moroccan Jews found themselves relegated to these hastily built, "planted" communities on the periphery of Israel, where they were assigned pioneering roles veteran Israelis were unwilling to assume. They constituted the largest ethnic group placed in development towns, and their partaking of the Zionist dream was marred by the many ills of these disadvantaged communities. These ills included limited occupational opportunities resulting from an under-developed infrastructure and reliance on one type of industry based on manual, low-paying jobs, an almost total dependence on government services, a poor education system, and a high rate of population turnover in which the more resourceful, upwardly mobile inhabitants left the towns while the poor and the less able tended to stay.[17]

Because of these chronic problems, development towns were depicted derogatorily as "residual communities" or "sinks" for the less resourceful immigrants.[18] In contrast to this stigmatic image, the optimistic goal-directedness and grand vision of early statist Zionism is reflected in the appellations of such development towns as Netivot ("Pathways"), Ofakim ("Horizons"), and Shderot ("Boulevards").

Many of the socioeconomic and political ills that characterized these towns in the 1950s and 1960s still haunt them in the 1990s. At the same time, however, the inhabitants who did stay in the towns, despite their social and economic difficulties, have slowly developed a genuine attachment to the localities. The growth of these "natural" sentiments of belongingness and rootedness in one's own community finds expression in and is further enhanced by the association with saints in these towns. This presence grants metahistorical depth to places that were without a recognized and validated past, thus making them a more integral part of Israel. The tsaddiq endows the town with an aura of sanctity, and the residents' sense of attachment is placed within a larger meaning-giving system, based on the idioms encoded in their Maghrebi traditions. In the case of Netivot, the most impressive case in this process, this peripheral, backward town became the sacred abode, in life and death, of a mystical luminary, a spiritual ally of Rabbi Shimon and Abraham the Patriarch, who had staked his tent in nearby Gerar. This acquired transcendence, based on ideological tenets sharply at odds with those underlying the pre-state Zionist settlements of *kibbutzim* and *moshavim,* has provoked a comparison of Netivot with the Hindu pilgrimage city, Benares, India. The designation of Netivot as "the Benares of Israel" reflects the mixture of condescension, mild disdain, and paternalistic concern with which development towns were viewed by mainstream Israelis[19] But for many denizens, the saints represent a congenial and welcome urban transformation. Evaluating the changes in the town following the death and rapid sanctification of Baba Sali, one local said with a modicum of pride: "A town that was 'outside' of Israel's map, is now not only 'on' the map, thanks to Baba Sali it is also 'above' it."

In this context, it is significant that the same event—a firm decision to change a place of residence by moving to a less peripheral town or neighborhood—precipitated the dream apparitions of most of the "saint impresarios" who had erected domestic shrines to Jewish Moroccan tsaddiqim. The recurrent pattern may have reflected the ambivalence the protagonists felt toward their communities as well as the resolution of that ambivalence. The ongoing presence of the saint who came to stay has inextricably bound the initiators to their newfound homes; the initial plan to "desert" the town was countervailed by a solemn vow to stay forever in the old houses now turned into shrines.

This process whereby sacred cities are being added to the country's landscape is strongly associated with the changing context of ethnic consciousness in Israel. The folk-veneration of saints (along with the preservation or revival of other practices associated with Sephardi or Mizrahi Jews, like the ethnic festivals of the Mimuna, Saharane, and the like) have provided many Maghrebi Jews with a set of cultural means to deal with their situation. By discovering and establishing sacred sites associated with the saints, they express their integration into Israeli society. In this sense, the hillulot in various sites resemble "ethnic renewal ceremonies."[20] They reflect the growing confidence of an emigré group in being part of the contemporary Israeli scene while, at the same time, indicating a strong sense of ethnic distinctiveness.

A leading Israeli social scientist has designated the process whereby core cultural identities from the Moroccan past have been revived and transplanted in the new country a "symbolic diasporization" of Israel.[21] Note, however, that as a result of the importation of Maghrebi tsaddiqim to Israel and their integration within the contemporary scene, these identities have been reconstituted in a new context and made reflective of the problems of a living reality quite remote from those of traditional Morocco. Hence the hagiolatric revival by which many Jewish Moroccan saints have been incorporated into Israel's sacred geography may be viewed as reflecting genuine attachment to the local scene and a process of "Israelization." Admittedly, the sociocultural matrix which constitutes the rise of the saints bespeaks of a new vision of peoplehood and society unforeseen by the founding figures of Israel.

NOTES

1. Kenneth Brown and Jean Mohr, "Journey Through the Labyrinth," *Studies in Visual Communication,* 8 (1982), 2–81, quotation on p. 43.

2. John Eade and Michael J. Sallnow, Introduction to J. Eade and M. J. Sallnow, eds., *Contesting the Sacred: The Anthropology of Christian Pilgrimage* (New York, 1991), pp. 1–29, quotation on p. 44.

3. Yoseph Haglili, *Sefer Meron* (Meron, 1987), p. 93 (in Hebrew).

4. Vincent Crapanzano, *The Hamadsha: A Study in Moroccan Ethnopsychiatry* (Berkeley, 1973); Dale Eickelman, *Moroccan Islam: Tradition and Society in Pilgrimage Center* (Austin, 1976); Clifford Geertz, *Islam Observed: Religious Development in Morocco and Indonesia* (Chicago, 1968); Ernest Gellner, *Saints of the Atlas* (Chicago, 1969); Harvey E. Goldberg, "The Mellahs of Southern Morocco:

A Report of a Survey," *Maghreb Review* 8 (1983), 61–69; Norman A. Stillman, "Saddiq and Marabout in Morocco," in Issachar Ben-Ami, ed., *The Sephardi and Oriental Jewish Heritage Studies* (Jerusalem, 1982), pp. 485–500.

5. Paul Rabinow, *Symbolic Domination: Cultural Forms and Historical Change in Morocco* (Berkeley, 1975); Edward Westermarck, *Ritual and Belief in Morocco* (London, 1926).

6. Issachar Ben-Ami, *Saint Veneration Among the Jews in Morocco* (Jerusalem, 1984); Goldberg, "The Mellahs of Southern Morocco"; Yoram Bilu, "Jewish Moroccan 'Saint Impresarios,' in Israel: A Stage-Developmental Perspective," *Psychoanalytic Study of Society* 14 (1990), 247–69.

7. Shlomo Deshen and Moshe Shokeid, *The Predicament of Homecoming* (Ithaca, NY, 1974).

8. Erik Cohen, "Ethnicity and Legitimation in Contemporary Israel," *Jerusalem Quarterly* 28 (1983), 111–24; Norman A. Stillman, *Sephardi Religious Responses to Modernity* (Luxembourg, 1995); Alex Weingrod, *Studies in Israeli Ethnicity: After the Ingathering* (New York, 1985); Weingrod, *The Saint of Beersheba* (Albany, 1990).

9. J. W. Bennett, ed., *The New Ethnicity: Perspectives from Ethnology* (St. Paul, MN, 1975); S. N. Eisenstadt, "Some Reflections on the Study of Ethnicity," in Ernest Krausz, ed., *Migration, Ethnicity and Community*, Vol. 1 (New Brunswick, NJ, 1980), pp. 1–4; Shlomo Deshen, "Political Ethnicity and Cultural Ethnicity in Israel During the 1960s," in Abner Cohen, ed., *Urban Ethnicity*, ASA *Monograph* 12 (London, 1974), pp. 281–309.

10. Yoram Bilu and Henry Abramovitch, "In Search of the Saddiq: Visitational Dreams among Moroccan Jews in Israel," *Psychiatry* 48 (1985), 83–92.

11. Yoram Bilu and Eyal Ben-Ari, "The Making of Modern Saints: Manufactured Charisma and the Abu-Hatseiras of Israel," *American Ethnologist* 19 (1992), 29–44.

12. Ronald Glassman, "Legitimacy and Manufactured Charisma," *Social Research* 42 (1975), 615–36; Richard Ling, "The Production of Synthetic Charisma," *Journal of Political and Military Sociology* 15 (1987), 157–70.

13. Alex Weingrod, "Changing Israeli Landscapes: Buildings and the Uses of the Past," *Cultural Anthropology* 6 (1993), 370–87.

14. Weingrod, *The Saint of Beersheba*.

15. Yoram Bilu, "Jewish Moroccan 'Saint Impresarios' in Israel"; Bilu, "Personal Motivation and Social Meaning in the Revival of Hagiolatric Traditions among Moroccan Jews in Israel," in Zvi Sobel and Benjamin Beit-Hallahmi, eds., *Tradi-*

tion, Innovation, Conflict: Jewishness and Judaism in Contemporary Israel (Albany, 1991), pp. 47–69.

16. André Levi, "To Morocco and Back: Tourism and Pilgrimage among Moroccan-Born Israelis," in Eyal Ben-Ari and Yoram Bilu, eds., *Grasping Land: Space and Place in Contemporary Israeli Discourse and Experience* (Albany, 1997), pp. 25–46.

17. Michael Inbar and Chaim Adler, *Ethnic Integration in Israel* (New Brunswick, NJ, 1977); Myron, J. Aronoff, *Israeli Visions and Divisions: Cultural Change and Political Conflict* (New Brunswick, NJ, 1973); Judah Matras, "Israel's New Frontier: The Urban Periphery," in M. Curtis and M. S. Chertoff, eds., *Israel: Social Structure and Change* (New Brunswick, NJ, 1973), pp. 3–14; Moshe Semyonov, "Effects of Community on Status Attainment," *Sociological Quarterly* 22 (1981), 359–72.

18. Erik Cohen, "Development Towns: The Dynamics of 'Planted' Urban Communities in Israel," in S. N. Eisenstadt, ed., *Integration and Development in Israel* (Jerusalem, 1970), pp. 587–617; Seymour Spilerman and Jack Habib, "Developmental Towns in Israel: The Role of Community in Creating Ethnic Disparities in Labor Force Characteristics," *American Journal of Sociology* 81 (1976), 781–812.

19. Harvey E. Goldberg, *Greentown's Youth: Disadvantaged Youth in a Development Town in Israel* (Assen, 1984), p. 7.

20. Weingrod, *The Saint of Beersheba*.

21. Erik Cohen, "Ethnicity and Legitimation in Contemporary Israel."

FOUR

Identity, Ritual, and Pilgrimage: The Meetings of the Israeli Exploration Society

MICHAEL FEIGE

During the 1950s and 1960s, the annual meetings of the Israeli Exploration Society[1] (henceforth, IES) drew audiences of thousands to hear academic lectures on the archaeology, geography, and history of the land of Israel. Presidents, prime-ministers, and army generals attended regularly, not only as honorary guests but also as active participants. Most meetings took place on the social and geographical periphery, places such as Beit Shean, Eilat, Ashkelon, Acre, and Safed, which were not easily accessible using the transportation means of the time. Israeli author and journalist Amos Elon, writing for an American public, tried to convey the uniqueness of the phenomenon in the following way: "Imagine about 150,000 people attending a similar seminar in the United States."[2] Had he added a scholarly lecture by the U.S. president and the event taking place in Wyoming or Alaska, his comparison would have been even more appropriate.

In what follows I will try to explain the popularity of the meetings, as well as their subsequent decline. In order to do so, I shall place the events in two contexts. The first is the role of biblical archaeology in the formation of Israeli identity during the early state years. This academic field was conceived as being able to supply tangible proof to the truth claims of the Zionist narrative, and to support an integrative national ethos for a society of immigrants. The second context is the creation of new Jewish peripheries in the form of economically backward development towns, and the state's problem of their socio-cultural integration. I shall contend that the annual meetings of the IES served as a Zionist ritual and pilgrimage, attributing national value to space through its connection to a meaningful narrative. While the annual meetings served as an important mechanism for creating, sharing, and distributing knowledge, their formal structure served national and social goals. The conference/pilgrimage form was constructed in order to enhance the sacred legitimacy of the state, strengthen the temporal integration of its historical narrative, further the symbolic appropriation of its territories, and construct the unity of its Jewish population. I claim that, concomitantly, the IES meetings served the seemingly opposite function of symbolizing and strengthening power relations within Israeli society. The productive and reproductive functions of the meetings can serve to explain their initial success. It can also explain their subsequent decline, starting in the mid-1960s and leading to today, when the meetings hold limited weight within the academic milieu and have hardly any general social significance.

THE IES AND ITS MEETINGS

The IES meetings shared many characteristics with other Zionist rituals of early state years, among them Independence Day and Remembrance Day for the Fallen Soldiers. They occurred annually in regular intervals, involved the political leadership, and centered upon cherished national values, especially the sacred connection of the present to the past and of the people to the land. There were, however, important differences, such as their academic content and shifting locations. Not least among the differences was the fact that they were not state rituals but were rather initiated, organized, and carried out by a voluntary association within the civil society. Through the means of these conferences, the nation- and state-building project was being helped enthusiastically by an important section of the intellectual elite, represented by the IES.[3]

The "Israeli Exploration Society" was founded as the "Jewish Palestine Exploration Society" in 1914. From its initiation, the society had a defined role of contributing to the national effort. The first general manager, Nahum Slutz, addressed its members in the institution's first publication: "The creation of a Hebrew institute for the study of the land of Israel is needed not only from a cultural-Hebraic perspective, but also for national-political reasons. Coming to build our national home and to make it the center for Israel culture, we can not stand idle against the industrious and purposeful competition of other nations and their sages in researching the land of our fathers." The main contribution of the IES to the Yishuv (pre-state Jewish community in Palestine) — and later Israeli — social and cultural activities, was in sponsoring research and publications and holding conferences where research could be presented to professional and lay audiences alike. During the pre-state years, paying membership included many of the major political and intellectual figures of the era, and membership abroad, especially among the American and British Jewish communities, was also impressive. The society had around 1,500 paying members during the 1950s. From 1944 onward the leading figure of the organization was general manager Yosef Aviram, while the top Israeli archaeologists (including Binyamin Mazar and Yigael Yadin) served as presidents. A tribute to the place of the organization in Zionist and Israeli history was given in 1989, with the award of the prestigious "Israel Prize" for contribution to state and society.[4]

The first IES meeting was held in Jerusalem under the name "the week of the Hebrew past," in Tabernacles (Sukkot) 1943. Since then it became a tradition to hold the meetings at that holiday; it was convenient for schoolteachers because of the vacation. It was also symbolically meaningful because of the holiday's ancient tradition of pilgrimage. On the following year the event took place in Tel Aviv and then Haifa and Tiberias, and in 1949 in besieged Jerusalem. After the establishment of the state, the meetings became a fixture on the Israeli national calendar. During the 1950s and early 1960s they were scheduled respectively for the following places: Tel Aviv,

Acre, Beit-Yerah (Kinneret valley), Beer-Sheva, Ashkelon, Kiriat Tiveon (Israel valley), Jerusalem, Haifa, Safed, Jaffa–Tel Aviv, Jerusalem, Beit-Shean, Eilat, Naharia-Acre, and Masada. The Jerusalem meeting of 1956 turned out to be the most dramatic: during a visit to the Ramat Rahel excavations, shots were fired from across the Jordanian border, killing four participants and injuring many more. The late 1950s meetings saw the development of the conflict between Israel's two top archaeologists, Yigael Yadin and Yohanan Aharoni, the consequences of which accompanied Israeli archaeology for many years to come.[5]

The three-day meetings had a structure much like other academic conferences. Each opened with a gala evening event, featuring speeches of dignitaries. During the first decade of the state the speakers included government ministers, often the prime minister himself, a representative of the Jewish Agency, the mayor of the city or town where the event took place and a representative of the Israel Defense Forces (IDF) — at times even the chief of staff. The "patron saint" of the IES and its meetings was Yitzhak Ben-Tzvi, the second president. He attended almost every meeting and frequently presented a paper based on his own ethnographic studies. Indeed, the meetings were a public event, and audiences reached the thousands. Newspaper reports reflect the celebratory nature of the events: "The large hall of the new 'Keren' theater was packed with scientists, representatives of the national and local institutions, lovers of the study of the land from all around the state, many guests and residents of Beer Sheva, on which the conference lent a festive atmosphere. . . . The president and his wife were greeted by a police unit that presented its arms, and the great audience standing outside greeted them with cheers." The following report came from another meeting: "They came from all over the land, Ministers and Knesset members, archaeologists and historians, physicians and lawyers, engineers, teachers and guides, members of rural settlements and lovers of antiquity." Teachers and kibbutz members are repeatedly mentioned.[6]

The meetings had a distinct local flavor, as was reflected by the names given to many of them: "The Land of the Negev" (Beer-Sheva), "The land of the Philistines" (Ashkelon), "All the land of Naphtali" (Tiberias). Each year the same experts were required to prepare a lecture that was centered on, or was relevant to, the host town or region. An important part of the meetings was the field trips to local historical sites, and especially to archaeological excavations in progress. The meetings addressed the historical time span of various regions in its totality—from prehistoric humanity through the ancient world, Muslim periods until the history of the past few years, and even plans and programs for future development. Various scientific bodies of knowledge, such as botany, climatology, and geography, were presented. However, biblical archaeology enjoyed a privileged status. The organizers and leaders of the conferences were archaeologists and historians of early antiquity. Of the first fifteen meetings of the state era, two were dedicated to general—as opposed to regional—discussions, and they concentrated on an overview of the archaeological research in Israel.

NATIONALISM AND ARCHAEOLOGY

From a cross-national comparative perspective, archaeology has had an important role in nation- and state-building. Anthony Smith has noted that nationalism needs physical tangibility and stations in time, that are supplied by archaeological excavations. Benedict Anderson referred to the importance of the ancient site as a symbol of ancient greatness for the national aspirations of colonized people. Many Middle Eastern and Mediterranean states have used archaeology at crucial stages of their nation-building process. For the Yishuv and later Israel, archaeology held great symbolic importance, and was described in terms of a substitute for religion and a national hobby. Archaeological excavation fulfilled an important role in the forging of Israeli identity, through the promise of verifying the nationalist claims of ancient Israeli greatness, and the establishment of so-called instant roots for an immigrant society. Popular enthusiasm over the findings of the Dead Sea Scrolls, Masada, and the Bar Kochva letters attests to the place of the practice in Israeli civil religion. Yaakov Shavit observed: "In Israel . . . archaeology never meant only sites, ruins or the various material findings. It meant 'greater archaeology': an archaeology that renders new pictures of the past, a new concept and new narrative of history." The mass participation at the IES meetings serves as a further proof, possibly the most important, of the national role of archaeology.[7]

Constructing identity was not done by the presentation of the findings in themselves. Archaeological artifacts are mute in the sense that they hold no inherent meaning and are open to contradictory interpretations. The stone statue, piece of clay pot, or human remains have to be placed in a historical context in order to become meaningful to professional archaeologists, historians, and laypeople alike. That is especially true regarding the field of biblical archaeology, where very few written texts were found, and even those have been subjected to numerous conflicting interpretations. The meetings had a mediating role of communicating the scientific findings to the wider public, placing them in a national context and thereby transforming them into identity-forming historical roots.[8]

The nationalization of archaeology was done through the context and structure of the meetings themselves. The fact that archaeological findings were presented within the framework of a national celebration, preceded by speeches of nation-building leaders, gave the scientific results ideological meaning. Regardless of actual results, archaeology was proclaimed as lending scientific proof to the truth claims of the Zionist historical narrative. The keynote speakers were most explicit about the role allotted to the science. Prime Minister David Ben-Gurion said in 1950: "The Jewish archaeology will find its rightful place in the wisdom of Israel. All her victories make our past present and realize our historical continuity on the land." Prime Minister Levi Eshkol observed in 1963: "You reveal our roots in the past and we plant new roots on the same soil." As late as 1970, Minister of Education and Culture Yigael Alon claimed that archaeological excavations render undeniable proof that "all our myths are true, and the land hid all the needed evidence for the real and spiritual connections between the people and the land."[9]

The integration of past and present was most conspicuous in the role played by top army officers in these events. The complex interconnections of the army and archaeology has been noted by researchers. Through active participation in the events, the military establishment has affirmed its central place as an integral part of society and as heir to the great warriors of the past. At the 6th meeting (1950) Yigael Yadin, still chief of staff, presented a paper on the strategic geography of the Galilee. Yadin compared the three times the people of Israel used force in order to gain independence on their land—namely the ancient occupation by Joshua, the Maccabean revolt, and the war of Israeli independence, which he himself had directed two years earlier. Five years later, Chief of Staff Moshe Dayan greeted the participants coming to the eleventh meeting: "The IDF soldiers, patrolling the land, know that they are walking in the land of Pleshet, walking the path of the hero soldiers of days gone by."[10]

The meetings were meant to encompass the entire temporal spectrum of human life on the land of Israel, from prehistory to planning the future regional development. Thus, for example, the tenth meeting in Beer-Sheva started with biblical archaeology, moved on to geography and climatology, and ended with a day of lectures dedicated to the new Israeli settlements of the Negev. The sixteenth gathering, at Beit Shean, started with findings regarding prehistoric humanity, and ended with a lecture by an army major on the area's defense, a discussion on the process of the Gilboa mountains' forestation, and a talk by Yosef Weitz of the Keren Kayemet describing the Jewish settlement in the Beit Shean valley. Each of the regions discussed received a similar treatment. It was placed firmly within a historical narrative, leading from ancient times to the present. The current settlement effort —in each region and in the Land of Israel in general—was presented as a culmination and logical outcome of history. By creating a continuous history that incorporates the present, the structure of the meetings legitimized and normalized the Jewish settlement project. Furthermore, the meetings evoked scientific truth claims, thereby endowing the settlement project with an aura of scientific credence and neutrality. Part of their role was to construct the Israeli "imagined community" in the sense described by Benedict Anderson: a collectivity which recognizes a shared past, and moves simultaneously into a shared future.[11]

THE DEVELOPMENT TOWNS AS FRONTIER AND PERIPHERY

The fact that many of the meetings took place in development towns was important, for it complemented the message of temporal integration with a message of spatial and social integration. This should be understood against the backdrop of the mass immigration of the 1950s and the emerging problems of creating solidarity amid apparent cultural, economical, and ecological inequalities. Admittedly, there were other practical reasons for choosing sites at the periphery. The meetings took place in connection with major excavation work going on, and proximity to the digging site was helpful for the field trips, which were an integral part of the meetings. However, that cannot explain why the development towns were chosen over the nearby kibbutzim and moshavim, many of which had the facilities to hold mass gatherings. Holding the meetings in development towns was meant to stress their symbolic importance in the nation-building ethos.

During the early state years, as it is today, the socio-economic situation in the development towns was much worse than that of the older Jewish settlements. The immigrants arriving there came mostly from Islamic societies, and those from European origins soon left. The result was the gradual creation of a self-perpetuating segregated ethno-class. Furthermore, the newcomers were alienated from their newly allotted places. Having neither residential options nor the needed resources to move at will, they experienced residence in a development town as no more than a meaningless and arbitrary coincidence. The more successful residents often left, draining the towns of the forces that could bring about change, and aggravating the despair of those left behind.[12]

The socio-economic and regional gap, accompanied by the disappointment and frustration of the newcomers, was an embarrassing refutation to the national leadership claim that all Jews are welcome in the Jewish state. The melting pot ideology was challenged by the fact that the lingering disparities between segments of society were tightly correlated with their respective land of origin. A partial solution, presented by the political elite, was to construct the experience of the immigrants in a way that would render meaning to their hardship and obscure the ethnic divide. The new immigrants were hailed as the new pioneers, joining, or even substituting, the former holders of the title. As Moshe Dayan said in 1963, "Degania, Ein Harod and Nahalal are no longer symbols for essential settlement centers, nor do they answer our problems of national existence. Nowadays the enhancement of these issues is typified by the (development towns of) Beer Sheva, Ashdod and Dimona."[13]

The IES meetings contributed to this cognitive construction. By holding the annual events in development towns, it addressed the issue of symbolically incorporating the Jewish peripheries into the established social and cultural order. Moshe Dayan, IDF chief of staff, explained how disseminating knowledge of the land's history can integrate new immigrants. In his 1955 address he noted that soldiers who are new immigrants live on a land whose history they do not know. Once they receive knowledge "they stop being the Moroccans that were recruited from the transit camp by the military police, and become soldiers of the nation, writing the Jewish history with their own bodies."[14]

Eilat, located at the remotest southern point of Israeli territory, hosted the meeting in 1962. The event can serve as one example of the interaction that evolved between the Israeli center and its most forsaken peripheries. Eilat at that time, before the arrival of mass tourism, was a poor development town, suffering from its proximity to the Egyptian and Jordanian borders. High rates of outward migration indicated its residents' frustration. Yosef Aviram, the IES general manager, explained that the site was chosen because Eilat was "terra incognita" for most Israelis, and the society had decided to bring knowledge of the region to a wide audience. Knowledge, however, was also brought to the residents of Eilat. Aviram added: "We decided to conduct the 18th meeting of the Society in Eilat in order to give its population a cultural-spiritual boost in the context of the crisis it was undergoing lately."[15]

Other speakers specified the nature of the boost. In his opening address, Yadin stressed the importance of Eilat to national security. He presented the map of Israel as analogous to an ancient weapon: "Eilat is the point of the spear of the state of Israel, and if the point will be blunt the entire spear will be blunt." David Ben-Gurion evoked pioneering imagery: "You were the first who dared to come to this desolate and empty place. The next generations will marvel at your courage." Apart from information regarding their contemporary role in the Zionist saga, Eilat's residents received lectures telling them of the history of their locality. This knowledge helped build pride and identity among the population. Unmentioned was the fact that most residents of Eilat were "reluctant pioneers" (to use Alex Weingrod's term regarding the new immigrants in the moshavim) living in that location, where they had been settled by the government through no wish of their own.[16]

In honor of the meetings, Eilat was decorated and full of lights as if in celebration of a national holiday. In fact, the visit of so many dignitaries was a rare celebration in the development town's unwritten history. The daily newspaper, *Davar*, reported condescendingly that "Eilat receives the visitors with the warmth characteristic of its residents." The mayor of Eilat used the opportunity to demand resources from the national leadership, in accordance with its own claims regarding pioneering, and especially the blossoming of the desert. The residents of Eilat were given a usable past and a promise of a glorious future. They were given the opportunity to honor the national leadership and convey feelings of trust and solidarity. For three days Eilat was positioned at the core of the national narrative, its story was told affectionately by experts, and its population was hailed as the carriers of Zionist values. Yigael Yadin said in his concluding remarks: "We shall leave as ambassadors of Eilat and the Negev, and that will be the benefit of this meeting." In other words, Israel's foremost archaeologist had declared that the national and social goals of the conference were more important than the academic and professional ones.[17]

One of the functions of the IES meetings was, therefore, to assist in constructing a tangible cognitive structure that would lend meaning to the socio-economic disparities among regions and ethnic groups. The meetings placed the gap into a socially accepted and even prestigious context. The new immigrants were portrayed as pioneers or as civilian-soldiers guarding the borders. As such, their plight was seen either as temporary—a greatly admired step taken before by other immigrant groups—or as part of the heroic struggle for national security.

Furthermore, the IES meetings served to cast the development towns as meaningful "places." In Zionist settlement-building, places achieved identity through their connection to the general national narrative using "key scenarios."[18] Archaeology was used at times in order to create local meanings. The words of Eliezer Sukenik, Yadin's father, convey this identity formation. In regard to the discovery of the Beit Alfa ancient synagogue, he commented: "There was a feeling that this piece of ground, for which people had suffered so much, wasn't just any plot of land but a piece of earth where their forefathers have lived fifteen hundred to two thousand years ago. Their work in the present was cast in a different light. Their history was revealed to them and they saw it with their own eyes."[19]

In the case of the development towns, however, the residents of the places did not tie their forced settlement to Zionist key scenarios. For the new immigrants, leaving their homes and coming to a new land, space—not being connected to an apprehensible narrative—became meaningless, or at least did not hold the acceptable Zionist connotations. Because they had been arbitrarily brought to alien territories and "stuck" in those non-places, their attachment was weak and superficial. By bringing historical knowledge, the IES meetings transformed meaningless spaces into meaningful places, thereby supplying the building blocks for the construction of local identities. Israel's Jews were told that, wherever their residence may be, they could be proud not only of their collective national identity but also of their local one. The IES meetings, then, can be interpreted as an attempt to create and impose instant local patriotism and nativeness on a population of newcomers, and to connect their identity to a valued place.[20]

THE IES MEETINGS AS PILGRIMAGE

The meetings, secular by virtue of their subject, share many characteristics of religious pilgrimages, as anthropologist Victor Turner depicted in his celebrated article "The Center Out There: Pilgrim's Goal." A pilgrimage is a journey leaving the political and social center of life in order to visit a symbolic and religious center located on the geographical periphery. In the case of religious pilgrimage, the sacred place is located where a heirophany, an appearance of the holy, has occurred. In most religions, this place is fixed and unchangeable. In the case that I am describing, the "pilgrim's goal" was decided by the IES politically and bureaucratically, according to social and national considerations.[21]

More similarities can be found in anthropologist Clifford Geertz's historical analysis. In his essay "Centers, Kings and Charisma," he wrote: "When kings journey around the countryside, making appearances, attending fetes, conferring honors, exchanging gifts, or defying rivals, they mark it, like some wolf or tiger spreading his scent through his territory, as being physically part of them." One of Geertz's examples is the travels of Queen Elisabeth through the English countryside. Her journeys were meant to symbolically establish the rule of the Crown over the entire land, and to enable her subjects to show submission, loyalty, and respect.[22] A similar mechanism was at work in the IES meetings: representatives of statehood and national power paid courteous visits to the peripheries, thus stating that they were not forsaken, and that they were all part of a sacred collectivity. The pilgrimage of the center to the periphery also established that throughout the land the state reigns supreme, not only as a bureaucratic organization but also as a moral idea. The monarchical role was played largely by David Ben-Gurion, Moshe Sharet, Yitzhak Ben-Tzvi, Moshe Dayan, and other Israeli political leaders, but it was also performed by academic scholars researching the past.

The pilgrimage framework not only transformed space to place but also gave the place an aura of symbolic centrality. However, the fact that the allotted center changed annually is important for the understanding of the construction of "Israel" as a place through these meetings. The shifting sites meant that the sacred center could be—in principle—located anywhere in the land of Israel. No one place was then symbolically "higher" than any other, and all share a sacred history.[23] Establishing pilgrimage to shifting symbolic centers was an attempt at homogenizing the national space through consecrating it in its entirety. Each region of the country was symbolically incorporated into the national body at the same level of importance as any other. All regions of Israel were considered to have histories relevant enough to evoke national interest. Therefore the periphery was not considered as such, but rather as a possible center.

On the face of it, the meetings were an equalizing vehicle for Israeli society. However, integrating space and population did not mean equalizing the social status of the people living on the periphery with that of the people living at the socio-economic center. Although the meetings were presented as encompassing the entire population, they were in fact celebrations of the mainly Ashkenazi elite strata. The meetings dramatized and visualized the difference between the highly educated and relatively affluent elite, and the educationally and economically deprived population residing in the development towns, and thus re-created the center-periphery continuum each time anew. By the very fact that the elite stratum held its conferences among the people of the periphery, it accentuated its advantage, even regarding knowledge of the very place where the new immigrants lived. The pilgrimage to elective sites meant that the elite was composed of translocal, cosmopolitan Israelis, while the periphery population was constructed as metaphorically bounded to its place, as local or even native.

The "dialogue" between the center and the periphery of development towns was one-sided, because the periphery was silent regarding the definition of its own identity. Information and knowledge, resulting from excavations in the periphery areas, were channeled one way as the politicians and scientists ascribed identity to the periphery through the act of pilgrimage. If a dialogue actually existed, it was rather between the central and the local elites, namely the members of the kibbutzim surrounding the development town. The kibbutzim took an active part in organizing the events, and frequently hosted some sessions (though not the grand opening). Their population revealed much interest not only in the very existence of the event but also in the content of the lectures. Some of their members were autodidactic relic collectors, and in some kibbutzim archaeological museums were built. Unlike the new immigrants, they shared the elite's cultural and ideological universe and participated actively in their settlement's identity formation according to the acceptable Zionist key scenarios.[24]

Because the subjects discussed in the meetings were connected to the land and not to the histories of the populations currently residing on it, the pre–Israeli Diaspora history of the new immigrants was defined by the conferences. The meetings forwarded a local Jewish-Israeli identity, a Hebraic or even Canaanite one, with roots in the ancient past of the region. The immense popularity of the IES meetings had, therefore, much to do with the "negation of the exile" ideology, and reflected the new state's lines of inclusion and exclusion.

The meetings drew a line around Israeli Jewish citizens, including new immigrants, and excluded Israeli Arab citizens. Owing to the military rule imposed upon them, they could not have participated even if they wanted to, but the meetings excluded them in more profound ways. Their story was indeed told—the Arab and Muslim history of the land had a prominent part in the conferences from their beginnings, as did the Byzantine and Crusader history. Their exclusion was in the fact that the pilgrimage never elected their towns and villages as a site and therefore as a potential symbolic center for Israeli society. They were depicted as part of the past, not of the present or future.

THE DECLINE OF THE MEETINGS

Gradually, the IES meetings lost their social impact. The event that had symbolized the change most of all was the twenty-first meeting, in 1964: the chosen location for that year was Greece. Even though the leadership of the IES was reluctant to admit it, professional curiosity and academic opportunity were clearly taking precedence over the national function of the event. The following year the meetings were held in connection with, and in the shadow of, the opening of the Israel Museum in Jerusalem. In 1966 the event again moved abroad, this time to Turkey. An attempt at reversing the trend followed the Six-Day War. In 1967 the event was scheduled in Jerusalem and was dedicated to the reunited city. In the following years the meetings concentrated on different parts of the newly occupied territories, in a renewed attempt to gain wide social relevance. The days in which the IES meetings had been important national celebrations were, however, already over.

The IES meetings continue to exist today, but only as a professional gathering, holding the interest of experts and some knowledgeable laypeople. Inside the academic community they have to compete against other professional archaeological conferences and historical meetings, organized by universities and research institutes. In 1961 Israeli geographers founded their professional society, and later other academic research centers and professional associations entered the field. Yet the decline has more profound historical origins. New generations of Israeli-born did not feel the same need for identity-forming mechanisms as had their immigrant parents, and the public interest in archaeology dwindled accordingly. Those now searching for roots tend to turn to religion.

Deep socio-cultural changes, especially the crystallization of social divisions, changed the place of archaeology vis-à-vis different social groups. Modern science, not to mention biblical archaeology, is no longer an integrative force in Israeli society. Recurrent bitter conflicts between archaeologists and the ultra-Orthodox over grave excavations attest to this fact. However, archaeology has not fared well with the secular Zionists either, who have been reluctant to take a firm stand in the conflicts against the ultra-Orthodox. Archaeology is apparently losing the battle for the right to ascertain Jewish and Israeli authenticity, even within the populations of the past who had used it as a way of recovering roots.[25]

One of the reasons for the archaeologists' "fall from grace" is their professionalism. While some critics claim that the nationalization of archaeology and the cultural hegemony of Zionism have been reflected in the academic writings, others tend to agree with Amos Elon's claim that: "[The Israeli archaeologists] may have been prejudiced in their choice of study but not, in most cases, in their analysis of the results." They did not hesitate to bring forth, in public meetings and professional writings, findings and interpretations that did not conform with the basic tenets of the Zionist narrative. Yaakov Shavit notes that while "greater archaeology" was used to enhance nationalism, "lesser archaeology," namely the academic product of professional archaeologists, held potentially subversive messages and eventually neutralized its own nationalist usefulness. Incremental evidence enabled a prominent Israeli archaeologist to write, for example: "The biblical description is the absolute opposite of the description of the history of Israel as is accepted today by all scholars."[26]

The radicalism of this statement should not be overstated. Most mainstream Israeli archaeologists will agree to the following statement as well: "Take the Bible out of the archaeology of the second and first millennia BCE and you have deprived it of its soul." Yet research has brought about a new, sometimes revolutionary understanding of the biblical era. Ironically, the IES itself, dedicated as it is to archaeological professionalism, participated in publishing works that portrayed new visions of ancient Israel.[27]

Yet the professionalization of Israeli archaeology was only part of the reason for the decline of the meetings as national rituals. The idea of pilgrimage to development towns lost credence also because of the socio-cultural changes at these locations. Alienation of the Mizrahim in the peripheral towns became much more evident, and the pretense of their being pioneers became clear. Moreover, new cultural formations appeared in development towns, partly as a protest against the attempt to impose western concepts from above. Saint worship became a local way of acquiring high symbolic value in Israeli society, and an alternative channel for becoming a center for pilgrimage. The development towns formed their new identity as sites of mass ethno-religious celebrations by transplanting and transforming traditions from their pre-immigration history and culture. These roots were not excavated from the land, were not prescribed patronizingly by the political center, and have little to do with western scientific rationality. Unlike the secular pilgrims to the IES meetings, the pilgrims to development towns today are Mizrahim of lower socio-economic status.[28]

Further research revealed the complex process of local identity formation. The Baba-Sali shrine built in the southern development town of Netivot is an implant of Moroccan architecture into the landscape. As anthropologist Alex Weingrod has claimed, this can be seen as a protest against the identity imposition of the early state years. In a recent, growing phenomenon, Jews of North African origin have been traveling to their places of birth. This can be understood as pilgrimage to an elective symbolic center, and as an expression of estrangement from Israeli identity. However, anthropologist André Levi, who has done research on these travels, has found that the encounter with Morocco has actually made the commitment to Israeli identity even stronger. The accumulating research shows that immigrants have constructed their own version of Israeli identity, using the resources of their pre-immigration traditions, and that they have a conflictual and rebellious relationship with the identity that the Israeli center has tried to impose upon them.[29]

An intriguing difference is the one between the two types of academics to appear in the secular academic meetings of the early state years and religious celebrations (*hillulot*) of today. In the IES meetings the linchpins have been the archaeologists, whose allotted role has been to construct integration through revealing the ancient roots, the "sameness," common to all Jews. They have been replaced by anthropologists, coming not to participate in the strict sense of the word but rather to "do participant observation." The difference is important because of the traditional role of anthropologist to interpret the "other." By choosing the development towns as objects of research, Israeli anthropologists have stated the claim that residents of these places have traits inherently different from the upper-middle-class Ashkenazi Israeli elite, that these traits are stable fixtures of the socio-cultural reality of the places, and that they merit interpretation. Eyal Ben-Ari and Yoram Bilu stressed the point to its extreme in one of their articles, written for a Hebrew reading public. They systematically collected and analyzed manifestations of mainstream Israelis' fears and misconceptions of the Baba-Sali and the Netivot celebrations before offering an anthropological interpretation of the event. They sought to show explicitly the cognitive distance between the emergent culture of the development towns and the culture of the Ashkenazi elite in Israel.[30]

The choice of development towns as objects of anthropological study reflects their transformation from a Zionist frontier to an Israeli periphery. In today's deeply divided post-ideological Israel, the idea of a secular pilgrimage to development towns is unthinkable. The science of archaeology and the task of building national or local identities have thus parted ways.[31]

NOTES

1. Direct translation from Hebrew would be: "The Society for the Study of the Land of Israel and Its Antiquities."

2. Amos Elon, "Politics and Archaeology," *New York Times Review of Books* 41 (15), 1994, p. 16.

3. See Maoz Azariahu, *State Cults: Celebrating Independence and Commemorating the Fallen in Israel* (Sede Boker, 1995) (in Hebrew); Eliezer Don-Yehiya, "Festivals and Political Culture: Independence Day Celebrations," *The Jerusalem Quarterly* 44 (1988), 61–84.

4. The Jewish Palestine Exploration Society's history has not been researched. See Yosef Aviram, *Biblical Archaeology Today: Proceedings of the International Congress on Biblical Archaeology,* Jerusalem, April 1984 (Jerusalem, 1985), pp. xv–xvi; "Lecture on the Acts of the Hebrew Society for the Research of the Land of Israel and Its Antiquities" appeared in the first collection of articles published by the society, 1941 (in Hebrew).

5. On the conflict and its interpretation see Neil Asher Silberman, *A Prophet from Amongst You: The Life of Yigael Yadin, Soldier, Scholar and Mythmaker of Modern Israel* (New York, 1994); Shulamit Geva, "Israeli Biblical Archaeology at Its Beginning," *Zemanim* 42 (1992), 92–102 (in Hebrew). The main thrust of the argument was on the nature of the Hebraic occupation of the Land of Canaan.

Yadin favored a theory of military occupation, while Aharony tried to show a process of gradual infiltration.

6. *Davar* Sept. 27, 1953 (in Hebrew); *Davar* Oct. 14, 1962 (in Hebrew).

7. Anthony D. Smith, *The Ethnic Origins of Nations* (New York, 1988), p. 188; Benedict Anderson, *Imagined Communities,* 2nd edition (London, 1992); Neil Asher Silberman, *Between Past and Present: Archaeology, Ideology and Nationalism in the Modern Middle East* (New York, 1989); Amazia Baraam, *Culture, History and Ideology in the Formation of Ba'thist Iraq* (New York, 1991); Charles S. Liebman and Eliezer Don-Yehiya, *Civil Religion in Israel* (Berkeley, 1983), pp. 110–12; Yaakov Shavit, "Truth Shall Spring out of the Earth: The Development of Jewish Popular Interest in Archaeology in Eretz Israel," *Cathedra* 44 (1987), 27–54 (in Hebrew); Aharon Kampinski, "The Impact of Archaeology on Israeli Society and Culture," *Ariel* (1994), 100–101, pp. 179–190 (in Hebrew); Amos Elon, *The Israelis* (New York, 1971), pp. 365–78; Elon, "Politics and Archaeology"; Geva, "Israeli Biblical Archaeology"; Silberman, *A Prophet from Amongst You;* Yael Zerubavel, *Recovered Roots: Memory and the Making of Israeli National Tradition* (Chicago, 1995); Nahman Ben-Yehuda, *The Masada Myth: Collective Memory and Mythmaking in Israel* (Madison, WI, 1995); Yaakov Shavit, "Archaeology, Political Culture and Culture in Israel," in Neal A. Silberman and David Small, eds., *The Archaeology of Israel* (supplement of the *Journal for the Study of the Old Testament,* 1997), p. 51.

8. This point is stressed in every textbook referring to biblical archaeology. See Roni Reich, *Introduction to Archaeology* (Tel Aviv, 1995) (in Hebrew).

9. *Yedion Haaguda,* 1950, p. 125 (in Hebrew); *Davar* Oct. 11, 1963 (in Hebrew); *Davar* Oct. 18, 1970 (in Hebrew).

10. See Zerubavel, *Recovered Roots,* pp. 57–60, and Silberman, *A Prophet from Amongst You; Yedion HaHevra* (1955), p. 62.

11. Anderson, *Imagined Communities.*

12. The literature on development towns is extensive. See Elisha Efrat, *The New Towns of Israel* (Munich, 1989); S. Ilan Troen, "New Departures in Zionist Planning during the Great Wave of Immigration: The Development Towns in the First Decade of Independence," in Dalia Ofer, ed., *Israel in the Great Wave of Immigration* (Jerusalem, 1996), pp. 261–84 (in Hebrew); Oren Yiftahel and A Meir, eds., *Ethnic Frontiers and Peripheries: Landscape and Inequality in Israel* (Boulder, CO, 1997); Esther Schely-Newman, "The Nocturnal Voyage: Encounters Between Immigrants and Their New Homes," in Dalia Ofer, ed., *Israel in the Great Wave of Immigration* (Jerusalem, 1996), pp. 285–98 (in Hebrew).

13. In Aharon Kellerman, *To Become a Free Nation in Our Land: Transition of Zionist Objectives and Their Geographical Implementation* (Haifa, 1987), p. 49 (in Hebrew).

14. *HaBoker* Oct. 3, 1955 (in Hebrew).

15. *Davar* Oct. 12, 1962 (in Hebrew).

16. *Davar* Oct. 15, 1962 (in Hebrew); *Davar* Oct. 15, 1962 (in Hebrew); Alex Weingrod, *Reluctant Pioneers: Village Development in Israel* (Ithaca, NY, 1966).

17. *Davar* Oct. 12, 1962 (in Hebrew); *Davar* Oct. 18, 1962 (in Hebrew).

18. Tamar Katriel and Aliza Shenhar, "Tower and Stockade: Dialogic Narration in Israeli Settlement Ethos," *Quarterly Journal of Speech* 76:4 (1991), 359–80. Eyal Ben-Ari and Yoram Bilu, Introduction to *Grasping Land: Space and Place in Contemporary Israeli Discourse and Experience* (Albany, NY, 1997).

19. Quotation from Elon, "Politics and Archaeology," p. 14.

20. There were other connections between Israeli archaeology and development towns at the period. Before Yadin's Masada excavations and the extensive use of volunteers, the development towns supplied the work force for the excavations. To a large extent, this is the situation today as well. Yadin's album-book on Hazor reflects the expectations that the workers be interested in digging at sites of the common biblical past. Furthermore, immigrants are photographed with ancient findings, alluding to the conceptions of Mizrahim "authenticity."

21. Victor Turner, "The Center Out There: Pilgrim's Goal," *History of Religions* 12 (1978), 191–230. Mircea Eliade, *The Sacred and the Profane* (New York, 1961).

22. Clifford Geertz, *Local Knowledge* (New York, 1983), p. 125.

23. An exception is Jerusalem. Approximately every fifth meeting took place in Jerusalem, and the keynote speakers stressed its sacredness and unique importance. The meetings, therefore, had also a role in establishing the centrality of Jerusalem.

24. This is reflected in the kibbutz museums. See Tamar Katriel, "Remaking Place: Cultural Production in Israeli Pioneer Settlement Museums," in *Grasping Land: Space and Place in Contemporary Israeli Discourse and Experience* (Albany, NY, 1997), pp. 147–76.

25. For one of these struggles, see Myron J. Aronoff, "Establishing Authority: The Memorialization of Jabotinski and the Burial of the Bar Kochva Bones in Israel under the Likud," in M. J. Aronoff, ed., *The Frailty of Authority* (New Brunswick, NJ, 1986), pp. 105–30.

26. See Geva, "Israeli Biblical Archaeology." More radical is: Keith W. Whitelam, *The Invention of Ancient Israel* (London, 1996); Elon, "Politics and Archaeology,"

p. 15; Shavit, "Archaeology, Political Culture"; Nadav Na'aman, "Historiography, Collective Memory and Historical Consciousness of the People of Israel at the End of the First Temple Period," *Zion* 60 (1995), p. 450 (in Hebrew).

27. Amnon Ben-Tor, *Introduction to the Archaeology of the Land of Israel at the Times of the Bible* (Tel Aviv, 1990), p. 43 (in Hebrew); Nadav Na'aman and Israel Finkelstein, eds., *From Nomadism to Monarchy* (Jerusalem, 1990) (in Hebrew).

28. Some of the extensive research on development town local saints and *hillulot:* Eyal Ben-Ari and Yoram Bilu, "Saint's Sanctuaries and in Israeli Development Towns: On the Mechanism of Urban Transformation," *Urban Anthropology* 16:2 (1987), 243–71; Alex Weingrod, *The Saint of Beersheva* (New York, 1990).

29. Alex Weingrod, "Changing Israeli Landscapes: Buildings and the Uses of the Past," *Cultural Anthropology* 8:3 (1993), 370–87; André Levi, "To Morocco and Back: Tourism and Pilgrimage among Moroccan Born Israelis," in *Grasping Land: Space and Place in Contemporary Israeli Discourse and Experience* (Albany, NY, 1997), pp. 25–46.

30. Yoram Bilu and Eyal Ben-Ari, "Netivoth's Western Wall," *Politika* (1990), 56–59 (in Hebrew).

31. Shlomo Hasson, "From Frontier to Periphery," in *Eretz Israel* (1991), 85–94.

FIVE

Mirror, Mirror on the Wall: Clothing, Identity, and the Modern Jewish Experience

JENNA WEISSMAN JOSELIT

"A great deal of happiness may be had from a study of dress and its requisites," observed fashion doyenne Mary Brooks Picken in her 1918 bible of sartorial propriety, *The Secrets of Distinctive Dress*. "As we study, observe and apply, our inner selves will awaken to the artistic side of dress, and once awakened will develop to such an extent as to give us understanding and appreciation."[1] In what follows, I take my cue from Picken, hoping to awaken and stimulate interest in sartorial matters on the part of Jewish historians who have been impervious to its charms and inattentive to its relevance. For a host of reasons, dress has not figured prominently on their mental maps. In some quarters, the study of clothing—indeed, the material world as a whole—has been dismissed out of hand as trivial and mindless: an instance of *veibishe zakhn* (the frivolous preoccupations of women) at its worst. In others, it is seen as a distraction from and as a sideshow to more central and representative Jewish concerns: politics, economics, Torah.

And yet, over the past century, and on both sides of the Atlantic, few issues have consistently aroused as much public interest and sustained as much controversy within the modern Jewish community as the sartorial practices—and lapses—of its members. From editorials in Sunday school newsletters suggesting that young Jewish girls "tone down their taste in dress and avoid all flaunting colors" and pronouncements from the pulpit about the evils of the rouge-pot ("the daughters of nice people don't use make-up," categorically declared Rabbi Stephen S. Wise) to an abiding fascination with "hatlessness," much was made of the way Jews dressed.[2]

In fact, long before Roland Barthes devised his "fashion system" with its complex algorithms of style, the Jews of America and England had come up with their own, equally elaborate, set of sartorial norms and aesthetic standards. In both countries, where the "Jewish question" tended to be played out in the dock of public opinion rather than the legislature, Jews repeatedly drew on this "Jewish fashion system" to measure their collective transformation from "outcasts and wanderers" into refined gentlefolk, the "products of civilization."[3] Appearance, as modern-day Jews came to know well, was no private matter, subject only to personal fancy and the idiosyncrasies of style and taste, but a public construct, bound up with the social order.

It's to the public face of clothing that this chapter attends. Drawing from a large wardrobe of issues, it selects two case studies as representative of the relationship between the clothing worn by Jews in the modern era and the aesthetics of daily life. The first case study, set at the turn of the twentieth century, fastens on excess and extravagance; the second, set in the 1960s and early 1970s, is about ease. What joins them together, like a hook-and-eye, is the way they give shape to historical notions about the limits and possibilities of acculturation in the modern era.

OSTENTATION AND JEWS

During America's Gilded Age, Jewish women were generally believed to possess an "innate" affinity for "conspicuous and flashing jewelry," an affinity that allegedly stretched as far back as the Bible. "Hebrew women," gamely explained one of their number, Countess Annie de Montague, "are often reproached [for] their inordinate love for precious gems. This is a heritage from their forefathers, a natural tendency for the brilliant and the beautiful." More to the point, there is nothing the least bit unseemly about either the "heritage" or the "tendency." The "dark, Oriental beauty of Hebrew women," declared Montague, is "enhanced by the wearing of flashing jewelry and their love for special ornaments has been fostered by centuries of customs and environments."[4]

By the turn of the century, an increasing number of latter-day "Hebrew women" began not only to dispute such claims but to reject them out of hand. Vowing to become "more like [shrinking] violets and less like sunflowers," they instituted a strikingly modern form of sumptuary legislation that sought to do away with "flashing jewelry" and other outward forms of excess. In a radical departure from centuries of tradition in which matters of dress and of external appearance were regulated by the rabbis and enforced by the community, or *kehillah,* American Jewish women, acting independently of both institutions, relied instead on the gentle art of persuasion and on a female network of support. Through feature articles and editorials in such publications as the *American Jewess,* a monthly widely reputed to be "the first American magazine to appeal particularly to Hebrew women," and by word of mouth, middle-class American Jewish women urged one another to cultivate modesty and to practice restraint. There's no need for us to become Quakers, they conceded, but we must "cease to become conspicuous for flashy dressing."[5] This attempt at social control, no less potent for being tacit, voluntary, and gendered, not only reflected the limits of rabbinic authority in late-nineteenth-century America but also located an alternative source of authority in lay women.

They made their voices heard at least twice a year: in the spring, shortly before the start of Confirmation celebrations, and on the cusp of summer, when thoughts turned to vacation, two occasions often marred by extravagance and excess. In the first instance, what ought to have been the sacred simplicity of Confirmation was tarnished by overelaborate attire and way too much jewelry. "The admission of girls to Confirmation is a quiet step towards the religious equality of the sexes," declared the monthly magazine. "Women should, therefore, take especial care to observe this day with true religious fervor. . . . Confirmation is no social event. Costly ornaments and jewels should never be displayed." Summoning up the sine qua non of good breeding—tastefulness—the paper concluded: It is, after all, "in wretched taste to have a dress parade on a religious platform."[6]

Meanwhile, the prospect of summering by the sea or in the mountains inspired even fiercer rhetoric. Jewish women who take to the mountains or the sea come July and August should realize just how accountable they are, the *American Jewess* dutifully advised its readers, direly warning of the perils of excess: "The Jewess represents a race, the Christian an individual. Hence it does not suffice for the Jewess to be as refined as her Christian sister; she must out-distance her in every desirable social quality." Lest their readers fail to understand what was at stake, the *American Jewess* spelled it out for them by drawing a scenario featuring the fictional Mesdames Brown and Abrahams. "If Mrs. Brown chooses to bedeck her ample, Merdle-like bosom with glittering gewgaws," to "talk and laugh boisterously and occupy three chairs on the piazza," it is just Mrs. Brown that is held up to opprobrium. "Be she Baptist, Methodist, Presbyterian or Catholic, it is only the little, insignificant unit—Brown—that is branded as a vulgar, undesirable upstart." With the Jews, however, it's a different matter entirely, cautioned the magazine. The collective good name of the Jews stands or falls on the behavior of each individual member. "Let Mrs. Abrahams indulge in the same offenses against the canons of good breeding—and Jewish womanhood, en masse, must atone for her sins. With one fell sweep, all Jewesses are forthwith pronounced loud, common, obtrusive."[7]

Admittedly, this situation is not as it ought to be, quickly conceded the *American Jewess*. In the best of all possible worlds, Jews would not be held accountable for the lapses of some members. In the meantime, Jewish women should do their best "to face [this situation] philosophically and to act accordingly," a course of action that consisted of following in the footsteps of social arbiters such as Walter Houghton, author of *American Etiquette and Rules of Politeness,* and a resolute champion of restraint, the hallmark of the American bourgeoisie. "Elegant dressing," he declared aphoristically, "is not to be found in expense; money without judgement may load, but never can adorn. A lady may be covered with jewels and yet not show the slightest good taste."[8]

The *American Jewess* sounded a similar note. Be sure "strenuously" to eschew all forms of ostentatious display and to cultivate "unobtrusive modesty," it told its middle-class readers. Above all, "avoid decking out your children, the little tots, like miniature fashion plates. There is nothing which more inevitably shocks and repels the truly refined than to see children put to such base uses."[9] Against a steady drumbeat of "dos and don'ts," Americans learned to practice what Houghton and the *American Jewess* preached: a bourgeois sartorial code that held that "foreigners" were given to excess and ostentation whereas the "truly refined" American was not.

A few years later, subsequent developments within the American Jewish community strongly suggest that many American Jewish women had taken such advice to heart; at the very least, the *American Jewess* seemed quite pleased by the way things had turned out. Happily, the magazine reported sightings of modestly clad women at fancy dress balls and charity fairs and of ringless women promenading on the piazza. Cause, no doubt, for equal amounts of approbation and relief, such sightings also gave rise to one of the most fascinating and revealing editorials in American Jewish history: an 1899 editorial entitled "Jewels No Longer Synonymous with Jewess." The piece, fusing sociology with moral fervor, began by praising the American Jewish woman for coming to her senses, for recognizing the "fact that the rich tints of her coloring and the brilliancy of her eyes do not need to be accentuated by glittering tinsels." Having internalized American notions of attractiveness, the American Jewish woman "at last realizes that golden ornaments are not becoming to her style of beauty. A flash of rare gems will ever be a desirable addition to her brilliant appearance, but the massive and conspicuous jewelry which she used to wear in abundance, made her look vulgar and showy and gave her the reputation of courting extravagance."[10]

But that "reputation" is increasingly a thing of the past, the *American Jewess* eagerly pointed out, noting how Jewish women had come to jettison their old ways and to embrace a new, American aesthetic. "Heaven be praised, that jewels are no longer synonymous with Jewess," it crowed, inadvertently furthering the association between Jewishness and jewelry. "All hail this new American beauty, who, satisfied with her natural, God-given endowments, discards flashing ornamentation and to a certain extent boycotts jewelry." All hail, indeed. Only when the modern Jewess "conquered" her "innate desire to display jewels," it seemed, did she stand poised to blend in with the rest of America.[11] The socially acceptable Jewess, emerging from the chrysalis of restraint, was no longer the Oriental beauty of yesteryear, festooned with glittery baubles; the socially acceptable and truly modern Jewess was reborn instead as a natural, American beauty who went without.

The perception of the Jew as the Orientalized outsider was just as pronounced in early-twentieth-century England as it was in turn-of-the-century America. Henry James, viewing John Singer Sargent's portrait of Mrs. Carl Meyer and her two well-dressed children arrayed on a settee, thought the likeness a good one. The children's faces, he wrote, are "Jewish to a quaint orientalism, faces to peep out of the lattice of the curtains of closed seraglio or palanquin." Sargent, like his good friend James, also applied the "language of excess" to his portraits of the Wertheimer family, members-in-full of the Anglo-Jewish haute bourgeoisie.[12] Whether painting the Wertheimer women in exuberant evening attire, in rich velvets and luminescent silks or swathed in pearls, a turban, and a filmy costume, the leading portraitist of his day saw his subjects as extravagantly exotic.

Before long, British Jews came to see themselves as Sargent and others saw them: as creatures of excess. In summer 1907, the equanimity of the London Jewish community was put to the test as its newspaper of record, the *London Jewish Chronicle,* carried a number of increasingly heated exchanges among its readers on the relation of Jews to excess and ostentation, a subject reportedly so disturbing that it sent "a shudder through the frame of all fellow-Jews with the least suspicion of refinement." In the Old World, as in the New, belief in its ubiquity was not only widespread, it was taken for granted, prompting quite a few contemporaries to speak of "Jewish ostentation" as if it were either an innate, biological trait or a religious obligation. You couldn't walk down the street, go marketing, or enjoy a holiday by the sea without encountering "hordes of Jewesses," clad in "gaudy and hideous costumes . . . [and] enormous and gruesome hats," related one "disgusted Jew," his stomach in an uproar at the sight of such tastelessness. "For downright vulgarity, it's hard to beat the Jewess."[13]

Jewish women, though, were by no means the sole target of Anglo-Jewry's ire. Men, especially young Jewish males of the "parvenu type," were also taken to task for their boorish manners, loud voices, and slavish devotion to fashion and frippery. "Who doesn't know the type who will only wear the very latest style in clothes, the latest-shaped hat, the latest tie, the latest cane — the creature that wears the gaudiest of colored waistcoats, who walks with his elbows stuck out, ostentatiously puffing a fat cigar, occupying as much of the pavement as he can and speaking as loudly as possible. . . . What type of human being . . . is more objectionable than the Jewish parvenu? He is the embodiment of ostentation, obtrusiveness and vulgarity. Why?"[14]

Why, indeed? But then, the British Jews voicing their collective distaste at the sartorial mores of their coreligionists were less inclined toward soul-searching as they were toward registering their disapproval and making high-minded, if vague, statements about the pressing need to correct the situation. "It behooves those Jews whose finer feelings are not yet blunted to take a stand against this cankerous enormity," they ringingly declared, insisting "we must have a vigorous, persistent and systematic onslaught on the whole gamut of its manifestations."[15]

What such high-minded declarations meant in practice turned out to be something else again. Nearly everyone involved (or so it seemed) had a different notion of what constituted "systematic onslaught." Some believed it behooved the clergy to issue "mild rebukes" from time to time about the importance of restraint. Others felt that statements of a "homiletical strain" carried no weight whatsoever. Instead, the leaders of boys and girls clubs were urged to use their "refining influence" to modify the behavior of those under their supervision. Still others counseled patience, insisting that the issue would ultimately correct itself: with the passage of time and sustained exposure to the British way of life, the "vulgar and ostentatious *will become* the most fastidious and refined."[16]

And they were right. Only a few years later, journalist Gabriel Costa could write approvingly of those "metamorphosed Cinderellas," the "girls of the London ghetto." According to Costa, "There was a time when nothing but the gaudiest colors, the most aggressive feather would please her ladyship. Her sole desire was to be seen. She *was* seen, from afar." But then, he continues, "there came a desire for quieter garments. The oriental desire for garish color in cloth and plumage made way for greater chromatic sobriety; and there seems no sign of a reversion to the old and conspicuous array."[17] In England, as in America, a muted palette was a badge of integration.

What are we to make of these two expressions of public, communal concern with overdressing and its consequences? It's tempting, to be sure, to cast these episodes in classical terms, to see them simply as another in a long series of jittery responses to the potential threat of anti-Semitism, as reflections of anxiety about drawing unwarranted attention to one's Jewish self and, by extension, to the community at large lest "race prejudice" arise. But that is only part of the story. Even as the *American Jewess* and her British cousin, the "disgusted Jew," fretted over their coreligionists' appetite for flashy jewelry and gaudy waistcoats, what worried them had little to do with anti-Semitism or, for that matter, with the elements of style. What worried them was the viability of modernization itself. Reading clothing, like tea leaves, for signs that Emancipation had actually taken hold, inside as well as out, Anglo-American Jews of the late nineteenth and early twentieth centuries were extremely sensitive to anything—from "glittering appendages" to shiny patent leather shoes—that suggested the Jews were destined to remain outside the pale of western civilization, a nation of pariahs and parvenus forever "under the spell of Eastern fancies."[18]

Little wonder, then, that American Jews and their British cousins of the late nineteenth and early twentieth centuries were given to closely scrutinizing—and criticizing—one another's attire: like citizenship papers, it furnished proof of their collective determination to conform. A deliberate cultural strategy designed to highlight the Jews' assimilability, dressing like a proper lady or gent proved central to the Jewish project of westernization or what, in some circles, went by the grimly determined yet apt name of deorientalization. Nothing, it seemed, more vividly bespoke the Jewish community's commitment to modernity than its willingness to "sacrifice at the shrine of frivolity" and its insistence that ostentation was not an "inherent trait of character but an imposition of circumstance," susceptible to change.[19]

OUR SABBATH BEST

Like the fin-de-siècle, the 1960s and 1970s were marked by a heightened attentiveness to clothing except that, this time around, clothing no longer supported the social order; instead, it seemed to defy, even undermine it. Rejecting restraint and refinement in favor of freedom and "authenticity," growing numbers of Americans, members-at-large of the counterculture, increasingly substituted casual wear for gray flannel suits and chunky beads for dainty pearls. Charles Reich, one of the movement's most impassioned chroniclers, explains in his influential book *The Greening of America* that these mass-produced, machine-made, and inexpensive "new clothes express profoundly democratic values." He asserts they do so by denying the "importance of hierarchy, status, authority, [and] position." More to the point, they are a vivid and powerful "declaration of sensuality, not sensuality-for-display as in Madison Avenue style, but sensuality as a part of the natural in man."[20]

Many American Jews, much to the consternation of their leaders, embraced this new sensuality just as readily as their suburban neighbors. With gleeful abandon (or so it seemed), they took to wearing casual attire even when attending synagogue. Where once married female worshipers had come to shul "wearing expensive and knowing hats" and smartly tailored dresses, they now thought nothing at all of wearing "unisex" pants suits or, for that matter, of unceremoniously perching a yarmulke atop their uncoiffed heads. But then, as several eyewitnesses were quick to point out, "propriety of dress in the synagogue is not altogether a woman's subject; men too are involved." Benjamin Kreitman, the rabbi of Brooklyn's Congregation Shaare Torah, a Conservative synagogue, recalled looking out at a sea of congregants one Sabbath morning and "Behold, the bar mitzvah, his family and his friends were attired as if the synagogue was the first link on the golf course."[21]

Dressed in sports jackets or blazers and slacks, more and more male shulgoers turned their backs on the Prince Albert frock coats, or *prinz yankels,* fancied by an earlier generation of would-be natty dressers. That generation's love—and faith—in clothing has been beautifully captured (and at times, even gently mocked) by S. N. Behrman in his short story "Mr. Wolfson's Stained-Glass Window." Mr. Wolfson epitomized the *gvir,* or local bigshot. Proud president of his local shul, Wolfson delighted in wearing a silk top hat, a Prince Albert frock coat, and striped trousers on Shabbos morning, as did many of his fellow officers. "The fabulous circumstance," writes Behrman knowingly, "was that Mr. Wolfson owned these garments outright."[22]

By the 1960s, as men's striped trousers and women's saucy hats went the way of spitoons, snuffboxes, and Mr. Wolfson, a number of rabbis sought one another's counsel. A steady stream of *shaylahs* (ritual questions) on the vagaries of fashion now made its way onto the agendas and the files of American Jewry's denominational law committees, attesting to clothing's stranglehold on the contemporary religious imagination. Some clergymen wanted to know whether "lady's pants suits" were verboten in the sanctuary. They were dutifully informed that inasmuch as "the pants suit is no longer an exceptional garment worn by some bold woman to attract attention, but by now has become established as a normal type of women's garment," it was to be tolerated, grudgingly. Where the pants suit was deemed an acceptable form of temple-wear, the mini-skirt, another popular sartorial convention of the 1960s, was not. The mini-skirt was labeled "provocative," and American Judaism's legal arbiters recommended that it be barred from the precincts of the sanctuary.[23]

Meanwhile, as the practice of wearing hats to synagogue (and church) tumbled from grace, a few rabbis were moved to inquire about requiring married women to cover their heads while in the sanctuary. Was this mandatory or customary, they wondered, to which the Conservative movement's Committee on Jewish Law and Standards supplied the following answer: There is no "halakhic requirement that a woman must wear a head covering specifically in shuel." But, it hastened to add, if the wearing of hats or head coverings is an "accepted custom in the community, the rabbi should consider preserving the custom."[24]

Still other rabbis, like Benjamin Kreitman, went a step further by publicly taking a stand in favor of distinctive shul attire, even if it happened to be downright unfashionable. Together with his wife Joyce, a former clothing designer, the Brooklyn rabbi published a detailed essay in the pages of the *United Synagogue Review* on "fashions for the synagogue." The latter "cannot shut itself away from the changing times and from the passing parade, which includes the fashions of the day," the Kreitmans acknowledged. Still, the synagogue must be ever mindful of the past and of tradition and in all things, including "apparel," seek "the delicate balance of the old and the new." Once upon a time, the Brooklyn couple went on to explain, the sight of a woman's exposed arms was considered improper; today, however, when different, looser, notions of modesty prevail, "it would be senseless for the synagogue to insist that modesty requires the woman to cover her arms."[25]

The same could not be said, however, of women dressed in pants suits and yarmulkes, attire the Kreitmans utterly disdained. "Our voices will go unheeded outside the synagogue, but certainly *in* the synagogue . . . unisex styles must be banned. We should recommend that at no time should women be admitted to synagogue services . . . wearing pants suits or slacks. . . . Such clothes are a 'declaration of sensuality,'" they insisted, pointedly referring to Reich's remarks in *The Greening of America,* "and they clash, we insist, with the synagogue's 'declaration of spirituality.'" Yarmulkes atop female heads also clashed with the imperatives of proper synagogue attire at Congregation Shaare Torah. "In their eagerness to impose their own standards of modesty, some rabbis require women to don yarmulkes if they come to the synagogue without hats," the Kreitmans related with considerable finesse. "This is most unfortunate. A lace chapel cap should be made available for women entering the sanctuary. The yarmulke should be used by the men."[26]

In their insistence on the yarmulke as a male form of attire, the Kreitmans were not arguing against equality as much as they were standing firm in defense of propriety. From where they sat, women in yarmulkes looked wrong, unseemly, even sloppy. Much the same could be said of brightly colored trousers, sports jackets, and other latter-day manifestations of casual male attire; they, too, looked wrong. "We need not and cannot return to the synagogue etiquette of yesteryear with its silk hat, morning coat and striped trousers," the Kreitmans explained, noting how that ensemble "imprisoned the worshiper in a meaningless and stiff formalism. Would that the rabbi today could gain release from his formal rabbinic robe . . . and exchange it for something less formal and more appropriate! But certainly the 'casual' has no place in the synagogue."[27]

Many American Jews, however, strongly disagreed and instead of anathematizing the "casual," actively sought it out. Readers of *The Jewish Catalog,* one of American Jewry's best-selling publications and the manual, or *shulkhn arukh,* of the Jewish counterculture, placed a premium on comfort and ease. Rejecting the dressy, bourgeois aesthetic of their parents and grandparents as un-natural, inauthentic, and un-Jewish, they preferred to dress "in the manner of a Shabbat service at Camp Ramah or a USY *kinus*" (United Synagogue Youth convention), in oversized, tie-dyed *tallitot* (prayer shawls), simple white shirts, and loose-fitting cotton skirts. The more homespun and homemade an article of clothing, the more authentically Jewish it was perceived to be. "The orientation [of *The Jewish Catalog*] is to move away from the prefabricated, spoon-fed, nearsighted Judaism into the stream of possibilities for personal responsibility and physical participation," stated the text, offering detailed instructions, replete with childlike drawings, on how to tie ritual fringes, or *tzizit,* an act described in the parlance of the times as "ritual macrame," crochet "beautiful and original kippot," and make a "poncho-shawl" tallit suitable for both men and women. In fact, *The Jewish Catalog* gently encouraged women to wear a prayer shawl. "Women are not obligated to wear a tallit, nor are they prohibited from wearing one," it explained. "The importance and need for a prayer robe in which to wrap and immerse yourself during tefillah (prayer) is certainly equal for both men and women."[28]

The sight of young men and women enveloped by handmade tallitot undoubtedly inspired a number of rabbis to take stock of and question some of their own sartorial conventions, like the wearing of flowing, floor-length black pulpit robes. "The appropriateness of pulpit robes," explained Solomon Freehof, dean of American Reform rabbis, in response to a question regarding its acceptability, "depends upon the motivation which led to their adoption. If it could be demonstrated that they were adopted simply for the purpose of making our service appear more like the Christian service, then, the wearing of robes would indeed be repugnant to the spirit of Jewish law." But if, said Freehof reassuringly, their purpose was "to add dignity to the service . . . such garments are fully within the scope of Jewish law and are praiseworthy."[29]

For some, the robe represented the modern rabbinate. A symbol of office, like a "shingle hanging outside the door of a professional," the black floor-length gown, said one of its champions, "is tantamount to a sign that conveys the following to the congregation: Do you know whom I am? I am your rabbi. Some rabbis need that." For others, it added color and ceremony to the service, satisfying the people's need for what one rabbi called "the theurgy they crave."[30]

Still others felt the severely styled costume distanced the rabbi from his congregation, rendering him stiff and aloof. "Nothing turns off the younger generation," allowed Los Angeles rabbi Hillel Silverman, "[more] than the spectacle of the rabbi on the pulpit at Sabbath services in untraditional, Protestant-type, black robes. Our children are seeking authenticity and for them, robes are a symbol of the aura of the sanctimonious establishment." Eager to win them over, Silverman, for one, chose to "disrobe." "It was not a simple matter for me personally to dispense with the robe," he admitted. "However, after many months of experimentation in just tallit and yarmulke, I feel very much more at ease—natural and comfortable."[31]

Silverman's East Coast colleague, Rabbi Edward Sandrow, also modified his appearance, exchanging his black robe for a large tallit and his cantorial-like mitre for a "real kippah," but for a different reason: the teachers and rabbis after whom he styled himself did not wear such garb. Sandrow elected to wear just a yarmulke and tallit, he explained, "because this was always part of the normative symbolism of synagogue Judaism." While the long-time Cedarhurst rabbi had no qualms about changing his costume, his congregants saw things differently, wondering whether their rabbi had taken leave of his senses as well as his robe. They "wanted to know what had happened to me," Sandrow later recalled. "They thought that a spirit of radicalism (!) had over taken me—that it was not Jewish, that it was not 'dignified,' etc., etc." Eventually, after weeks of rancor and "intense debate, during which we even dragged in the 'freedom of the pulpit' principle," Sandrow recollected, his congregants grew accustomed to the sight of their robe-less rabbi and even welcomed the change as a sign that their rabbi was truly "with it."[32]

In Sandrow's suburban congregation, as in hundreds of synagogues across the nation, the counterculture cast a long shadow. While some American Jews dug in their heels and resisted, many others freely appropriated its rhythms, sensibilities, and fashions, eager to demonstrate that late-twentieth-century Judaism could be "with it," too. Like the jewel-less Jewess of the fin-de-siècle and her somberly suited male cousin of the early 1900s, their descendants—the bell-bottomed, tie-dyed, casually attired American Jews of the 1960s and 1970s—proclaimed their affinity with modernity by dressing the part.

When, in 1899 or 1907 or 1973, Anglo-American Jews looked in the mirror, what did they see? Overdressed and "showy exhibitions of gems and golden trinkets?" Models of restraint, studies in "chromatic sobriety?" Exemplars of psychedelic chic? I suspect that what they saw, if only they looked hard enough, was the desire to fit in. The shape of that desire, like the latest styles, varied from generation to generation, but in each and every instance, the Jews answered to a higher authority than Dame Fashion. After all, when they looked in the mirror, what stared back was the unforgiving face of community.

NOTES

1. Mary Brooks Picken, *The Secrets of Distinctive Dress* (Scranton, PA, 1918), p. iii.

2. "What Our Girls Can Do," *The Sabbath School Companion of K. K. Beth Elohim,* Vol. 1, No. 1 (Charleston, SC, January 1895), p. 7; Arthur Strawn, "Stephen S. Wise—Prophet A La Mode," *Reflex* 2:1 (January 1928), p. 59; "Letter to the Editor from E. Carmel," *London Jewish Chronicle,* August 8, 1919, p. 13. Writes Carmel: "The hatless Hebrew, like the mad hatter, invariably turns up."

3. Roland Barthes, *The Fashion System* (New York, 1983); Kathleen Manning, "Jewish Ostentation," *London Jewish Chronicle,* Aug. 23, 1907, p. 9; "Missionaries Needed," *American Jewess* 9:4 (May 1899), p. 46.

4. "Go on Conquering," *American Jewess* 10:3 (January 1899), p. 45; Countess Annie de Montague, "Love of Jewels Justified," *American Jewess* 5:6 (September 1897), p. 264.

5. "What Our Girls Can Do," *Sabbath School Companion.*

6. "Abuses of Confirmation," *American Jewess* 1:2 (May 1895), p. 91. See also, "A Plea for Simplicity by a Non-Jewess," *American Jewess* 2:8 (May 1896), pp. 411–13; Julia Richman, "Ada's Confirmation Presents," *Helpful Thoughts* 1:3 (April 1896), pp. 20–21.

7. "The Jewess at Summer Resorts," *American Jewess* 11:3 (June 1895), p. 139.

See also, Jenna Weissman Joselit, "Jewelry: The Natural Gift," in Ulysses Grant Dietz, ed., *The Gold and the Glitter: Fashioning America's Jewelry* (Newark, NJ, 1997), pp. 19–33.

8. Walter Houghton, *American Etiquette and Rules of Politeness,* 7th edition (New York, 1883), p. 257.

9. "The Jewess at Summer Resorts," pp. 139–40.

10. "Jewels No Longer Synonymous with Jewess," *American Jewess* 8:3 (January 1899), pp. 44–45.

11. "Jewels No Longer Synonymous with Jewess," p. 45; "Go on Conquering," p. 45. See also Rosa Sonnenschein, "The American Jewess," *American Jewess* 6:5 (February 1898), pp. 205–9. The modern American Jewess, Sonnenschein declared, loves her country dearly enough to "sacrifice her gold and her jewels as readily as the ancient Jewess did for her religion."

12. Henry James, *The Painter's Eye: Notes and Essays on the Pictorial Arts* (Madison, WI: 1989), p. 257, quoted in Kathleen Adler, "John Singer Sargent's Portraits of the Wertheimer Family," in Norman Kleeblatt, ed., *John Singer Sargent: Portraits of the Wertheimer Family* (New York, 1999), pp. 25, 31.

13. "A 'Disgusted Jew' Writes on Jewish Ostentation," *London Jewish Chronicle,* Aug. 16, 1907, p. 9; Kathleen Manning, "Jewish Ostentation," *London Jewish Chronicle,* Aug. 23, 1907, p. 9; Anrasius, "Jewish Ostentation," *London Jewish Chronicle,* Aug. 9, 1907, p. 10.

14. " 'A Disgusted Jew,' " *London Jewish Chronicle.*

15. Anrasius, "Jewish Ostentation," *London Jewish Chronicle,* pp. 9–10.

16. "Jewish Ostentation," *London Jewish Chronicle,* Aug. 30, 1907, p. 11; Manning, "Jewish Ostentation," p. 9.

17. Gabriel Costa, "The Girls of the London Ghetto," *American Hebrew*, Feb. 6, 1914, p. 419.

18. Anrasius, "Jewish Ostentation," p. 9; Emil G. Hirsch, "The Modern Jewess," *American Jewess* 1:1 (April 1895), p. 1. See, too, Hannah Arendt's classic essay, "The Jew as Pariah: A Hidden Tradition," *Jewish Social Studies* 6:2 (April 1944), pp. 99–122.

19. Hirsch, "The Modern Jewess," p. 11; quoted in Marion Golde, "The Modern Ghetto Girl: Does She Lack Refinement? Discussed by Mrs. Asch, Mme. Nazimova and Mr. Foshko," *American Weekly Jewish News* 1:3 (Mar. 29, 1918), p. 11. I thank Riv-Ellen Prell for sharing this reference with me.

20. Charles Reich, *The Greening of America* (New York, 1970), pp. 236, 238.

21. Leah Morton, *I Am a Woman—And a Jew* (New York, 1926), p. 238. See

also, Milton Himmelfarb, "Going to Shuel," *Commentary,* April 1966, pp. 66–70; Benjamin and Joyce Kreitman, "Fashions for the Synagogue," *United Synagogue Review* 25:1 (Spring 1972), pp. 15, 31.

22. Sarah Schack, "O'Leary's Shul—And Others," *Menorah Journal* 16:5 (May 1929), p. 464; S. N. Behrman, "Mr. Wolfson's Stained-Glass Window," *The Worcester Account* (New York, 1954), p. 198.

23. "Lady's Pants Suits," Solomon B. Freehof, *Contemporary Reform Responsa* (Cincinnati, 1974), pp. 123–26.

24. "Minutes of the Steering Committee Meeting of the Rabbinical Assembly Committee on Jewish Law and Standards," July 6, 1978, p. 2. See also, Rabbi Norman Shapiro to the Committee on Jewish Law and Standards, Dec. 31, 1957, and "Minutes of the Committee on Jewish Law and Standards," November–December 1957, Archives of the Rabbinical Assembly. I thank Rabbi Joel Meyer, executive director of the Rabbinical Assembly, for graciously allowing me to consult these records.

25. Kreitman, "Fashions for the Synagogue," pp. 14, 15.

26. Kreitman, "Fashions for the Synagogue," p. 15.

27. Kreitman, "Fashions for the Synagogue," p. 31.

28. Edward Sandrow, "Robes and Sermons," *United Synagogue Review* 26:1 (Spring 1973), p. 11; Richard Siegel, Michael Strassfeld and Sharon Strassfeld, eds., *The Jewish Catalog: A Do-It-Yourself Kit* (Philadelphia, 1973), pp. 9, 49, 50, 51, 57.

29. Solomon B. Freehof, "Pulpit Robes," *Reform Jewish Practice and Its Rabbinic Background,* Vol. 2 (Cincinnati, 1963), p. 53.

30. Sandrow, "Robes and Sermons," pp. 10, 11.

31. Hillel Silverman, "New Directions for the Synagogue and the Rabbinate," *United Synagogue Review* 25:3 (Fall 1972), p. 8.

32. Sandrow, "Robes and Sermons," p. 11.

SIX

Sculpting an American Jewish Hero: The Monuments, Myths, and Legends of Haym Salomon

BETH S. WENGER

Myth-making and the creation of heroes are a part of every society. The legends of George Washington, Betsy Ross, and Abraham Lincoln have become staples of American culture. Their tales of heroism have been firmly implanted within popular narratives of American history and their images preserved in monuments and memorials.[1] Likewise, modern Jews have created their own icons, from Moses Mendelssohn to Theodor Herzl to Rebecca Gratz. Generations after their deaths, their images are continually reproduced and their legacies invoked by Jews seeking communal honor and legitimation for their own causes. American Jews have created a pantheon of heroes and heroines and molded their legends to fit the unique circumstances of Jewish life in the United States. The first and perhaps most enduring heroic figure of American Jewry was Haym Salomon. Salomon's patriotic service during the American Revolution inspired scores of tributes and memorials and triggered some of the most contentious battles about the myth-making and public commemoration of an American Jewish hero.

This chapter focuses on the many attempts to memorialize Haym Salomon, conducted by several Jewish groups, in various cities, over the course of more than a century. The campaigns to build monuments honoring Salomon and the controversies that surrounded them are episodes that reveal the contested process of shaping public memory in the American Jewish community. The debates about whether Salomon deserved to be memorialized, how he should be honored, what kind of monument would be appropriate, and where such a memorial should be located recurred in different generations and reflected the political and social issues that preoccupied the Jewish community at the time. The various movements to memorialize Haym Salomon were ultimately not about Salomon himself, but rather about the ways that his mythic legend intersected with Jewish communal politics and revealed competing visions of American Jewish identity.

HISTORY AND LEGEND

The legend of Haym Salomon evolved despite—and perhaps partly because of—the sketchy evidence surrounding his life and activities in colonial America. There is no documented likeness of Salomon (a fact that made his physical appearance vary widely in commemorative representations). The murkiness of some parts of his life combined with the documented evidence about his service to the Revolutionary cause provided the perfect balance of fact and fiction to fuel the myth of Haym Salomon as patriotic hero. Salomon was born in 1740 in Lissa (Leszno), Poland. He probably came to the United States in 1772, at the time of the first partition of Poland. Many of the details of his early career in New York are unknown. During the time that New York was occupied by the British, Salomon probably served as a commissary agent supplying the Hessian troops. He was reputed to have been arrested and imprisoned by the British, to have spied for the Americans, and helped prisoners to escape. However, there is little evidence that any of these activities actually occurred.

After fleeing New York for Philadelphia in 1778, Salomon began the second phase of his career, where he earned his mythic status as the "Financier of the Revolution." Salomon was well-known as a financial broker within the Philadelphia community, advertising his services in local newspapers,

Figure 1. Portrait of Haym Salomon. There is no record of Haym Salomon's likeness. This portrait represents the artist's imaginative conception of the revolutionary patriot. The portrait hangs today in Brooklyn's Haym Salomon Home for Nursing and Rehabilitation. Source: Artist unknown. © Haym Salomon Home for Nursing and Rehabilitation, Brooklyn, New York. Courtesy American Jewish Historical Society, Waltham, Mass., and New York, NY.

and buying and selling bills of exchange. When the Revolution broke out, Superintendent of Finance Robert Morris asked Salomon to secure funds for the Revolutionary cause. In his diary, Morris indicates his high esteem for Salomon's talent as a broker and explicitly details Salomon's financial contributions to the Revolution. As a broker, Salomon offered a valuable service to the Revolution by raising funds and negotiating bills of exchange with several foreign governments. Many colonial Jews were involved in international trading and finance and several worked on behalf of the Revolution, but Salomon's financial prowess earned him a place of distinction in the colonial community.[2]

As the legend of Haym Salomon evolved, the story of his patriotic contributions came to include the claims that he singlehandedly financed the Revolution at his own personal expense, that his loyalty to the cause left his family completely impoverished, and that the government never repaid its financial debt to him. These highly distorted assertions resurfaced in many of the attempts to memorialize Salomon. Haym Salomon was indeed a patriot and a broker who provided important financial services to the Revolution, often at no interest charge. Salomon distinguished himself within the new American nation and also championed the cause of religious equality. He was not only a successful businessman, but also an active member of and key contributor to Philadelphia's Mikveh Israel synagogue. Salomon's economic advice and trading skills were highly valued by Revolutionary leaders, but he did not provide personal funds for the war, as was widely asserted. He died in 1785 while only in his mid-forties and did leave his family in debt, largely because he had accumulated government notes of credit that had depreciated after the war. Such insolvency was, in fact, quite common in the years following the Revolution. There is no denying Salomon's key role in securing financial support for the American cause, but his vaunted title as Financier of the Revolution was much exaggerated.[3]

FROM FAMILY PETITIONS TO COMMUNAL ICON

The heirs of Haym Salomon first promoted him as an unappreciated American hero. Seeking payment from the government, Haym M. Salomon, the son of Haym Salomon, asserted his right to claim the alleged debt owed his father. In 1846, at the age of sixty-one, Salomon's son brought his first petition for monetary compensation before Congress. In a series of petitions submitted periodically through the Civil War years, he insisted that the government repay the principal debt to his father plus interest, which he estimated at sums ranging from three hundred to six hundred fifty thousand dollars. Several congressional committees reviewed Salomon's petitions and some bills advanced to the floor of the Senate, but all were ultimately rejected by Congress.[4]

Thirty years later, a new generation of Salomon heirs renewed the quest to gain recognition for Haym Salomon's contributions. In 1893, Salomon's descendants altered their goals, petitioning not for monetary compensation but for a medal to commemorate Salomon's service to the Revolution. As historian Samuel Rezneck has observed, this effort to honor Salomon took place during the years that such organizations as the Sons and Daughters of the Revolution were being founded. In a climate of heightened interest in historical commemoration and honor societies, the campaign to recognize Salomon was a conscious effort to place Jews at the center of an emerging public memory of the American Revolution. The House Committee on the Library did recommend that the Salomon medal be issued, but this venture, like previous efforts, was defeated in Congress.[5] Although the attempts by Salomon's heirs were unsuccessful, they marked the beginning of a process of public debate about Haym Salomon. In fact, many of the unsubstantiated claims put forth before Congress in the nineteenth century were repeated and accepted as fact in the twentieth-century campaigns to memorialize Haym Salomon.

By the turn of the twentieth century, the dialogue surrounding Haym Salomon's legacy shifted from petitions for compensation by his heirs to a public debate within the Jewish community. The American Jewish community of the early 1900s had become better organized than in previous years, and its leaders were building an array of institutions and associations. The legend of Haym Salomon often took center stage as American Jews worked to establish Jewish institutions and construct an American communal self-definition. For Jews positioning themselves within American culture, Haym Salomon provided an ideal symbol of Jewish patriotism.

In 1910, the *American Hebrew,* a widely read Jewish newspaper, reported an effort by an organization calling itself the Haym Salomon National Monument Committee to erect a statue honoring Salomon in Washington, D.C. The movement received significant support, even from President Taft, who spoke before a Washington congregation "to second the motion that a memorial be raised to the Jew who stood by Robert Morris and financed the American Revolution." Although this effort quickly faded, the statements issued by proponents of the plan revealed how thoroughly the inflated legend of Haym Salomon had penetrated public consciousness.

Only one year later, the *American Hebrew* reported a new proposal, supposedly initiated by the Federation of Jewish Organizations, a lobby group that represented a small contingent within the Eastern European immigrant community. In 1911, the newspaper carried an article announcing that the federation had endorsed a campaign to collect on the financial claims of Salomon's heirs and use the funds to build a Haym Salomon National University in Washington, D.C. According to the report, the university would be designed as a nonsectarian humanistic college. This plan immediately generated controversy. Leaders of the federation denounced the project and denied that they had ever endorsed such a proposal. Louis Marshall, the prominent leader of the American Jewish Committee, who had been listed in the newspaper as a supporter of the movement, vehemently condemned the plan and sharply denied his own involvement in the affair. "It seems to me utterly ridiculous and absurd," Marshall wrote to the general secretary of the federation, expressing his hope that those individuals who had supported the plan "may be dissuaded from making themselves, and the Jewish people generally, ridiculous, by undertaking such a movement." Even Reverend Madison Peters, who was a self-proclaimed advocate of the monument project and author of a book-length tract about Jewish patriotism, denounced the national university project as "foolish," urging Marshall to oppose it. The debate over Salomon's right to a memorial persisted both inside and outside the Jewish community. At the height of the controversy in 1911, historian Worthington C. Ford wrote a column in *The Nation,* denouncing the historical record of Salomon's service and challenging his right to be commemorated as a hero.[6]

Neither a monument nor a university honoring Salomon was ever realized. After a flurry of discussion in 1911, the campaign to memorialize

Haym Salomon disappeared briefly from public debate. But the stage had been set: Salomon's legend had been promoted and popularized as well as challenged and condemned. In years to come, his legacy would become an increasingly contentious source of conflict within the Jewish community.

IMMIGRANT HERO

Following several years of inactivity, a new Haym Salomon campaign began in 1925 in New York City. This movement both made more progress and generated more controversy than any previous attempts to memorialize Salomon. The Federation of Polish Hebrews (later renamed the Federation of Polish Jews in the mid-1920s) initiated the new campaign to build a monument to Haym Salomon. In this movement, Salomon was no longer the "New York Jew" or the "Philadelphia Jew" but rather the "Polish Jew" whose heroism symbolized the loyalty and long-standing patriotism of Polish Jews in America. The efforts of the Polish association must be seen in the context of the many cultural and political challenges facing American Jewry in the early twentieth century. By the 1920s, the steady stream of Eastern European immigrants had dramatically altered the shape of the American Jewish community. Immigrant Jews had begun to challenge the existing structure of Jewish institutions, to create their own associations, and to assert the primacy of their brand of ethnic Jewish culture in the United States. When the Federation of Polish Hebrews chose to honor Haym Salomon in a monument, its members were also waging a broader campaign for communal respect as well as fighting against the climate of immigration restriction in America. Against the backdrop of the approaching sesquicentennial of the American Revolution, the battle for control within the Jewish community, and the political struggle to liberalize immigration quotas, the organized Polish community publicly claimed Haym Salomon as its American Jewish hero.

In 1925, Zigmunt Tygel, secretary and chief spokesperson for the Federation of Polish Hebrews, wrote an informational brochure entitled, "Haym Salomon . . . The Polish Jew Who Helped America Win the War for Independence." The brochure recounted Salomon's life story in the most exaggerated terms, including a completely fictional account of George

Washington sending an urgent message to Salomon in a moment of crisis on the eve of Yom Kippur in synagogue. According to Tygel, Salomon gladly interrupted his worship to come to the aid of the Revolutionary cause. This particular story, which became a standard vignette included in subsequent retellings of the legend of Haym Salomon, blended Salomon's religious devotion with his patriotic service. The federation celebrated Salomon as a Jew, a patriot, and an immigrant, calling him "the first Jewish immigrant from Poland." The organization announced a $100,000 fundraising campaign to build a monument that would publicly acknowledge Salomon's contributions. Imagining the project in the grandest terms, Tygel urged his fellow Jews to "pay the debt [to Salomon] by erecting one of the most beautiful and imposing monuments, the first memorial in the history of American Jewry to be built to perpetuate and honor the memory of a fighter, revolutionary, and backer of America's great struggle for independence and liberty, of one who at the same time was one of the noblest Jews that ever lived."[7]

The Federation of Polish Hebrews created the Haym Salomon Monument Committee and commissioned a model for its proposed monument. From five models submitted by prospective sculptors, the federation chose a design by sculptor Aaron Goodelman that it deemed worthy of representing Salomon's image and contributions. Goodelman's statue of bronze and granite portrayed a standing Haym Salomon draped in a Revolutionary era cape. Scenes of the Revolutionary period were etched in the sides of the pedestal, and on the four corners of the base were reliefs symbolizing the themes of patriotism, liberty, immigration, and peace. In 1925, the New York Municipal Art Commission reviewed the proposal submitted by the committee and considered building the statue near Madison Square Park, at 23rd Street. The commissioners, however, were not convinced "that Haym Salomon was entitled to the distinction of such a monument," given the shaky historical evidence concerning him. In its report, the commission quoted the opinion of historian Worthington C. Ford, who insisted that there was "no reason for connecting Haym Salomon's name with the nation's history." Ford maintained that "only as an estimable merchant has he any claims to recognition." The commissioners expressed serious doubt about the design of the monument itself and about whether Salomon

Figure 2. The stationery (circa 1931) letterhead created by the Haym Salomon Monument Committee for its campaign contained a depiction of the proposed monument along with an endorsement of the cause by a leading Harvard University professor. Courtesy Jacob Rader Marcus Center of the American Jewish Archives, Cincinnati, Ohio.

deserved to be memorialized alongside Admiral Farragut and William H. Seward, whose monuments already stood in the square. After some debate, the commission voted to deny the petition for "so elaborate a design and so important a location for a monument to a private citizen."[8]

Despite being turned away, the Federation of Polish Jews persisted in its campaign. The federation commissioned a new model and proposed a different New York site. The new Salomon monument was to be built at Broadway and 66th Street, at Lincoln Square, a site the federation considered "one of the choicest points in the metropolis for such a memorial." Federation leaders boasted that with the creation of the monument, "Haym Salomon will be looking down Broadway and, played upon by the constant Southern light, will always present a clear, unshadowed figure."[9] The new sculptor, Anton Schaaf (whom the federation described as "not a Jew himself" but someone who had "caught the vision of the great American Jewish patriot") had designed several other public monuments, including the Benjamin Franklin statue displayed at the sesquicentennial exposition in Philadelphia.[10] Schaaf created a model of granite and bronze, depicting Salomon

Figure 3. This 1925 model for a Haym Salomon monument, designed by sculptor Aaron J. Goodelman, was rejected by the New York City Art Commission. Courtesy Art Commission of the City of New York.

in Revolutionary garb, holding his hat close to body and looking decidedly like a patriotic hero. In 1928, three years after denying the first proposal, the New York Art Commission recommended preliminary approval for this new monument, provided that the size of the monument and pedestal be reduced from the original plan and that the historical claims about Salomon depicted on the statue be substantiated and approved by a reputable scholar. After receiving the commission's report, the federation chose to include only Haym Salomon's name and the dates of his life on the pedestal of the monument. On the half-circle that surrounded the statue, the sculptor etched several bronze reliefs designed to "represent in allegory and symbol the dominant motifs in the life of Haym Salomon and his services to the country." Clearly, the Federation of Polish Jews hoped to avoid any opposition by toning down any specific historical claims about Haym Salomon, his contributions to the Revolution, or the alleged unpaid debt owed him.

But opposition followed the Haym Salomon monument project from its inception. During the years that the Federation of Polish Jews campaigned for a Salomon memorial, many prominent Jews expressed vehement objection to the project. The chief opponents of the monument were members of the more established German Jewish community who believed that Haym Salomon's contributions to the Revolution had been much exaggerated and were fearful of a public campaign that might ultimately expose the Jewish community and its chosen hero to severe criticism. Max Kohler, secretary of the American Jewish Historical Society, led the campaign to thwart the monument, garnering the support of Louis Marshall, Nathan Straus, George Kohut, Stephen Wise, and other leaders of the Jewish community. Zigmunt Tygel and members of the federation met several times with their opponents, trying to make the case for a Haym Salomon memorial and to forge some cooperative alliance. At these meetings, Louis Marshall and his colleagues called for further historical research about Haym Salomon and also suggested alternative memorial efforts that might list the names of several Jewish revolutionary patriots instead of a sole focus on Haym Salomon. But the Federation of Polish Jews refused to abandon the Salomon plan. The organization's members did not want simply a monument to Jewish patriots; they wanted a monument that celebrated Polish Jewish heritage.

Figure 4. The Federation of Polish Jews received preliminary approval from the Art Commission for a Haym Salomon monument based on this 1928 model. The monument, designed by sculptor Anton Schaaf, was to be built at Lincoln Square in New York. Courtesy Jacob Rader Marcus Center of the American Jewish Archives, Cincinnati, Ohio.

At stake in the debate over the monument was not only the memory of Haym Salomon, but a power struggle between different sectors of the Jewish community. At one of the initial meetings concerning the monument, Benjamin Winter of the Polish Jewish Federation explained that the idea for a memorial "had arisen out of a desire of the Polish American Jews *as opposed to other Jewish groups in America* to establish a memorial to serve as an inspiration to them and their descendants by way of the example of the patriotic services of Polish American Jews to our Government." He added, "It is hoped that this memorial and the services which it will commemorate, will help off-set the inferior position which the Polish Jews are said to hold in the questionable hazy Jewish scale." By the late 1920s, it became clear that the Federation of Polish Jews would not be pressured into abandoning its plan. To bolster its case, the federation commissioned Charles Edward Russell, a Pulitzer Prize–winning author, to write a biography of Haym Salomon. Russell's book, published in 1930, recounted Salomon's life in the most reverential, heroic, and often fictional terms, eliciting harsh condemnation from scholars and from opponents of the monument. In a letter to Stephen Wise, Nathan Straus called Russell "a publicist of a facile gift of expression."[11]

The Jewish communal leaders who opposed the Haym Salomon memorial worried about the specter of creating a public monument to a Jew who was, in the words of Louis Marshall, "only a money-lender" and whose patriotic contributions might be questioned by historians. Max Kohler, perhaps the most ardent opponent of the monument, insisted that the Salomon memorial was being built "on the pedestal of forgery, fabrication and concealment." At the urging of Kohler, the American Jewish Historical Society initiated its own historical study of Haym Salomon, known as the Oppenheim Report (after the project's chief researcher, Samuel Oppenheim), that investigated Salomon's life and activity, refuting in detail the claims of the Federation of Polish Jews and attacking the assertions put forth in Charles Russell's book. Monument opponents hoped that the report would discourage the federation from pursuing the project, but federation leaders refused to be dissuaded. Concluding that the internal lobbying effort to "restrain this Polish crowd" would not succeed, Max Kohler published an open letter to New York Congressman Emanuel Celler in 1931. In what was actually a lengthy article, Kohler's "open letter" presented a point by point refutation of the federation's claims about Salomon and harshly criticized the monument effort. By the time Kohler issued a public condemnation of the monument, almost every prominent Jewish leader of the era had participated in the debate at some level. Even historian Salo Baron, contacted by Stephen Wise for his opinion on the matter, confessed that although he had not thoroughly researched the issue, he "instinctively . . . suspected the facts to be at least exaggerated."[12]

In 1931, the communal debate over the Haym Salomon monument reached its most fevered pitch, as the Federation of Polish Jews proceeded with its campaign and several Jewish leaders publicly denounced it. The federation responded to Max Kohler's open letter with a virulent response in the Jewish press, accusing Kohler of adopting a tone worthy of the Ku Klux Klan and of insulting "his own brethren of the Polish Jewry." Members of the Polish Federation considered Kohler's letter an act of betrayal and an affront to their community. In a private letter, Benjamin Winter, who had assumed the chairmanship of the Haym Salomon Monument Committee, angrily wondered what had motivated Kohler to "go before the Art Commission and denounce an effort which was approved by many authoritative bodies, by the Commission itself, and urge it to reverse itself in the matter of the monument, because of the flimsy discoveries that at any rate do not diminish by one iota the value of the man Salomon and his great contributions to the American Revolution." The debate over the monument was filled with rhetoric about historical accuracy, but at the heart of the controversy was a fierce struggle over ethnic pride and power within the Jewish community. As they condemned their opponents, members of the Federation of Polish Jews firmly insisted that "The monument to Haym Salomon will be erected. The figure of the Polish immigrant Jew will rise in granite to testify as a symbol of Jewry's participation and aid in the trying days when America was born."[13]

The monument campaign ultimately disintegrated in the mid-1930s, apparently defeated by a lack of funds rather than by any ideological or political victory. In the early years of the Great Depression, the Federation of Polish Jews appealed to its members to contribute to the project "despite the present economic conditions," urging them to "remember that Haym

Salomon gave all that he had to his country at a time when the country was in the grip of an economic stringency."[14] The difficulties of the Great Depression, combined with the heightened movement to collect money for European Jewish relief (an abiding concern of the federation through the years), seemed to have depleted the resources of monument supporters. As the monument controversy receded, so too did the heated public conflict within the Jewish community.

The debate over the Haym Salomon memorial had fundamentally centered on Salomon's symbolic meaning within two American Jewish cultures and their differing beliefs about public expressions of Jewish identity. Salomon as a mythic figure occupied center stage in the monument controversy. In one of the most telling moments of the debate, Louis Marshall, a strong opponent of the monument, argued against building the statue and even against conducting any further research on the matter, "declaring it preferable and more beneficial to future generations to retain the myth." In a confidential letter to members of the Jewish press, Marshall called upon Jewish reporters to "let this agitation die." "Otherwise," he explained, "another fiasco will confront us — a beautiful myth like that of William Tell will melt away, 'a great patriot' will be found in the scrap-heap and the Jews subjected to deserved criticism." To some extent, both sides of the monument controversy were interested in preserving Salomon's symbolic role. Even the most ardent opponents of the project were willing to claim Haym Salomon as a symbol of Jewish patriotism. Although this particular monument campaign did not succeed, the mythic Haym Salomon survived the controversy and endured as legend.[15]

THE "BUILT" MONUMENTS

No monument to Haym Salomon was ever built in New York or Philadelphia, the cities in which Salomon had lived and worked. But in Chicago and Los Angeles, two cities far removed from the East Coast, campaigns to memorialize Haym Salomon met with greater success and less rancor.

The first monument to depict Haym Salomon was built in Chicago, amid a scenario far different from the contentious struggle that had occurred in New York. Barnett Hodes, a lawyer and Chicago politician of Polish

Jewish heritage, had initiated the "Great Triumvirate of Patriots" monument project in the mid-1930s. George Washington, Robert Morris, and Haym Salomon constituted the "Great Triumvirate" depicted in the Chicago monument. Unlike previous efforts to memorialize Haym Salomon, this campaign was not defined as a Jewish project, but rather as part of a broader effort to commemorate the Revolution and its heroes. The Patriotic Foundation of Chicago, led by Barnett Hodes, set out to pay tribute to Salomon in the context of honoring other Revolutionary patriots. The choice of these three figures reflected the organizers' intent to emphasize that civilians as well as soldiers contributed to the Revolution and to underscore that "people of all creeds and origins participated from the beginning in the upbuilding of the nation." According to Chicago's Patriotic Foundation, "Salomon, a civilian and a Polish Jewish immigrant, symbolizes both concepts when standing with Washington and Morris." The foundation initiated a successful five-year fundraising campaign to raise the money needed to erect the statue. The project began in 1936, against the backdrop of an emerging Nazi threat. From the outset, the monument was a celebration of American democracy and tolerance, not a memorial that focused exclusively on Salomon.[16]

The Chicago Patriotic Foundation commissioned sculptor Lorado Taft to design the Great Triumvirate of Patriots monument, which stands in the city's Heald Square. Taft constructed a large and imposing piece, depicting Washington at the center, with Morris and Salomon on either side. The three men stand together, hand-in-hand, on a seven-foot, six-inch pedestal. On one side of the monument's base, beneath the towering figures of the three Revolutionary heroes, Taft etched George Washington's famous proclamation that "The government of the United States gives to bigotry no sanction, to persecution no assistance." On the other side of the base, he depicted the Goddess of Liberty holding her torch with arms extended above the people of the United States, who were purposefully drawn to represent the multiracial, multi-ethnic composition of the American population.

This monument honors Haym Salomon, but it is more pointedly a statement about American democracy in the face of intolerance at home and abroad in the 1930s and 1940s. The monument's supporters, which included President Franklin Roosevelt and many other leading politicians,

ROBERT MORRIS · GEORGE WASHINGTON · HAYM SALOMON
THE GOVERNMENT OF THE UNITED STATES
WHICH GIVES TO BIGOTRY NO SANCTION · TO PERSECUTION
NO ASSISTANCE · REQUIRES ONLY THAT THEY WHO LIVE UNDER
ITS PROTECTION SHOULD DEMEAN THEMSELVES AS GOOD CITIZENS
IN GIVING IT ON ALL OCCASIONS THEIR EFFECTUAL SUPPORT
PRESIDENT GEORGE WASHINGTON 1790

Figure 5: The Great Triumvirate of Patriots Monument, designed by sculptor Lorado Taft, stands at Wacker Drive in Chicago. The monument depicts Robert Morris and Haym Salomon standing at either side of the figure of George Washington. Courtesy, Jacob Rader Marcus Center of the American Jewish Archives, Cincinnati, Ohio.

considered the project an ideal public tribute at a time when racial and ethnic tensions were running high in the United States and when Europe was gripped by Nazism and World War II. The Chicago Patriotic Foundation scheduled the dedication of the monument for December 15, 1941, which President Roosevelt had proclaimed "Bill of Rights Day," a celebration of the one hundred and fiftieth anniversary of the adoption of the Bill of Rights. As it happened, the Pearl Harbor attack occurred only a week before the dedication ceremony. "Thus, when unveiled to reveal the larger-than-life figures of Washington and his co-patriots," one chronicler of the event observed, "the monument stood with more immediate meaning than had been envisioned."[17]

Haym Salomon was carefully positioned in the narratives that surrounded the Chicago monument. Aware of the controversy that swirled around the New York monument effort, Barnett Hodes and the Chicago Patriotic Foundation explicitly avoided any exaggerated claims about Salomon, acknowledging only that he was "a patriot during the Revolution, a man who served the cause of independence." For the purposes of the Chicago campaign, Haym Salomon represented a civilian who contributed to the Revolution and an example of the participation of people of many creeds in the fight for American independence. Despite the concerted effort to present a balanced account of Salomon's contributions, however, many of the fictional stories that had become part of the Haym Salomon legend remained. In a 1936 brochure promoting the Great Triumvirate of Patriots monument, a slightly altered account of the often repeated Yom Kippur tale appeared. In this account, Robert Morris sends an urgent message to Haym Salomon in the middle of Yom Kippur services, telling him that immediate funds must be raised for the Revolution. (In many previous renditions of this tale, it is George Washington who issues the urgent request.) The brochure reports that one of his fellow worshipers questions, "'Aren't you forgetting what occasion this is?'" But Salomon solemnly replies, "'It is for the cause.'" In the Chicago monument project, just as in previous campaigns to memorialize Salomon, the mythic legend endured and reinforced popular historical understanding of Haym Salomon as an American Jewish patriot and hero.[18]

Less than a year after the Chicago monument dedication, the Polish

Figure 6. On January 7, 1944, residents of Los Angeles gathered to watch the unveiling of this statue of Haym Salomon, sculpted by Robert Paine. Courtesy Herald Examiner Collection, Los Angeles Public Library.

American Jewish Federation in Los Angeles (an organization similar to the Federation of Polish Jews) began a campaign to erect a monument to Haym Salomon in California. Unlike the plan sponsored by New York's Polish Jewish community, the Los Angeles project precipitated no heated Jewish communal conflict. Perhaps because the schisms among ethnic factions within the Jewish community were less pronounced by the 1940s and never as sharp in California as they had been in New York, the attempt to memorialize Haym Salomon in Los Angeles met with little resistance. In the mid-1940s, with the United States embroiled in World War II, the effort to honor Salomon took shape as an expression of American patriotism. In 1942, sculptor Robert Paine, a descendant of the revolutionary pamphleteer Thomas Paine, petitioned the Los Angeles Parks Commission to approve a site for his Haym Salomon monument. Paine insisted that the monument would "greatly stimulate the bond-selling" campaign in the city and suggested that it be placed at the site where war bonds were being sold. He constructed a statue of "heroic size" that depicted Salomon in a seated posture, closely resembling the image of Abraham Lincoln sitting solemnly at the Lincoln Memorial in Washington, D.C. In 1944, the Haym Salomon monument was dedicated at a large public ceremony in Hollenbeck Park. However, unlike the Chicago monument, which remains a fixture in the city's Heald Square, the Salomon statue in Los Angeles has shifted locations and custodianships several times since 1944; it stands today outside one of the city's community centers.[19]

Both the Los Angeles and Chicago monument projects took shape within the climate of World War II. In that context, both promoted Haym Salomon as an American hero, a model of the patriotic devotion of immigrants and an example of American tolerance and diversity. The memory of Salomon was thus shaped not only within the Jewish community, but also through public campaigns to promote American ideals. A complex interplay of Jewish communal efforts and broader attempts to create symbols of national pride set in motion the various commemorations. The mythic Salomon that emerged was multidimensional—a product of many different communal campaigns and an amalgam of the commemorative ventures, sometimes conflicting agendas, and imparted legends that had created him.

AMERICAN JEWISH HERO

By the 1940s, a popular portrait of Haym Salomon as patriotic hero had been established and widely embraced. The disputes over historical claims still existed, but they took place among a small group of scholars and community leaders. "Repaying the debt" to Haym Salomon ceased to be a source of political or communal contention and became instead a symbolic campaign waged in Jewish textbooks and children's stories. Tales of Salomon's heroism and sacrifice on behalf of his country became part of the shared heritage of American Jewry. Beginning in the 1930s and continuing to the present day, a steady stream of popular writings and representations of Haym Salomon have perpetuated the legend—without the controversy.

Haym Salomon became a favorite topic in popular historical fiction and children's books, where he was often depicted as a fighter in the Revolution. The opening illustration that accompanied Charles Spencer Hart's 1936 reverential treatment, *General Washington's Son of Israel,* portrayed Salomon being dragged away by British soldiers.[20] Representations of Salomon often constructed him not only as a broker and financier, but also as a soldier in the Revolution. Salomon was a gendered hero. Despite the fact that his contributions were primarily economic, Haym Salomon served as a model of heroic masculinity for the American Jewish community. His legend placed Jewish men squarely within the narrative of bravery and resistance so prevalent in popular interpretations of the Revolution. (Similar icons, such as Rebecca Gratz, provided analogous models of ideal American Jewish womanhood.) In both Jewish and American lore, Salomon secured a position as a courageous American patriot. When Warner Brothers made a film about his life, actor Claude Rains was chosen to play the lead.[21]

The proliferation of popular books about Haym Salomon helped to sustain the many legends. The Yom Kippur story appeared in virtually every account, as did several other tales about Salomon's heroism, sacrifice, and dual devotion to American democracy and Jewish tradition. In 1941, the well-known author and communist Howard Fast (Fast wrote many children's books and works of historical fiction) published a volume entitled *Haym Salomon: Son of Liberty*.[22] This book, like many others, offers a series of fictionalized accounts of Salomon's life, including an often repeated scene in which friends and family mourn his death at his gravesite. In fact, Salomon's grave is unmarked, and the exact site where he is buried is unknown. Salomon's grave lies somewhere in Philadelphia's Mikveh Israel cemetery, but the family could not afford a headstone at the time of his death. Years later, the city placed a plaque at the cemetery to commemorate the fact that Haym Salomon had been buried there.

As the Haym Salomon legend persisted throughout the twentieth century, the historical errors about him merged seamlessly into popular narratives about his life and service to his country. But the mythic Salomon should not be interpreted merely as a compilation of factual inaccuracies. Haym Salomon as patriot and hero was a fabricated but valuable part of American Jewish heritage. As David Lowenthal has observed, "Heritage everywhere not only tolerates but thrives on historical error. Falsified legacies are integral to group identity and uniqueness."[23] The legend of Haym Salomon positioned Jews at the center of the story about America's founding. As a heroic figure, Haym Salomon inspired ethnic pride and put forth an ideal vision of Jewish patriotism. In the post–World War II years, popular histories, children's stories, and Sunday school plays not only kept the legend of Haym Salomon alive in public consciousness, but also imbued it with particular meanings that emphasized American ethnic diversity and Jewish devotion to America.

Like any successful legend, Haym Salomon became so integral to popular narratives that his name could be invoked playfully as well as seriously. By 1974, the Great Triumvirate of Patriots monument in Chicago was so much a part of the city's landscape that it was used in a local advertising campaign. An advertisement for office space in Heald Square displayed a picture of the monument and put words in the mouths of each of the three Revolutionary figures. The campaign depicted George Washington saying, "Word is this building is filling up fast!" Robert Morris comments, "With some blue chip tenants, too," and the caption emerging from Haym Salomon's lips proclaims, "There goes the neighborhood!"[24] With a hint of ethnic humor, this advertisement demonstrates that Salomon had become so thoroughly accepted as a public figure that he could be utilized with a touch of levity in a sales pitch.

Within the Jewish community, Haym Salomon's legacy has usually been invoked more seriously, his legend employed as a means to assert Jewish belonging in America and devotion to democratic principles. As the United States approached the Bicentennial, the Jewish community accelerated efforts to honor Haym Salomon within the national celebration. In 1975, after a successful campaign to gain public recognition for Salomon's contributions to the Revolution, the United States Postal Service (USPS) issued a postage stamp honoring Salomon. As part of a series that paid tribute to "Contributors to the Cause," the stamp identified Salomon as a "Financial Hero." Despite this rather ambiguous category of heroism, the USPS praised Salomon as a "businessman and broker." Repeating some of the exaggerated claims about him, the USPS described Salomon as "responsible for raising most of the money needed to finance the American Revolution and later to

Figure 7. As part of the Bicentennial celebration, the United States Postal Service issued this 1975 commemorative stamp honoring Haym Salomon as a "Financial Hero." Courtesy United States Postal Service.

save the new nation from collapse." The years leading up to the Bicentennial also witnessed a flurry of other commemorative efforts within the Jewish community. In 1972, the Jewish-American Hall of Fame commissioned a Haym Salomon medal, designed to honor the "neglected patriot" who had been denied a medal in 1893. Three years later, the Jewish Publication Society marked the upcoming Bicentennial by publishing a new popular account of Salomon's life. The cover of Shirley Milgrim's *Haym Salomon: Liberty's Son* (1975) depicts Salomon dressed in Revolutionary clothing and carrying a Torah, making a graphic point about Salomon's dual role as a Jewish and American hero.[25]

Commemorations of Haym Salomon continue to the present day. In 1997, shortly before Memorial Day, a group of Jewish War Veterans in Philadelphia marched with Mayor Ed Rendell in a public ceremony to lay a wreath at the plaque for Haym Salomon at Mikveh Israel cemetery. Just a

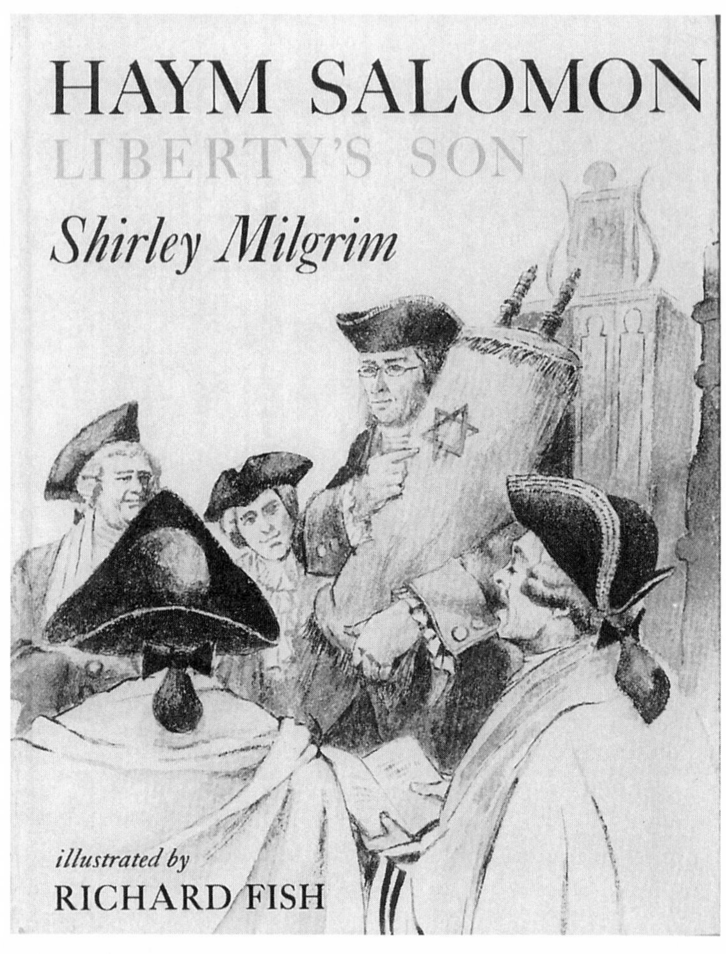

Figure 8. The image of Haym Salomon displayed on the cover of this popular account depicts Salomon as both a devoted Jew and a patriot. Shirley Milgrim, *Haym Salomon: Liberty's Son* (1975). Courtesy Jewish Publication Society of America.

Figure 9. In 1997, residents of Philadelphia dedicated an official state marker honoring Haym Salomon with a celebration that included a parade by the First Continental Regiment and a firing of muskets. Photographer: Beth S. Wenger.

few months later, the State of Pennsylvania approved an official state historical marker to honor Haym Salomon as "Financier of the Revolution." The marker was placed outside Philadelphia's Mikveh Israel synagogue. The elaborate dedication ceremony included a parade and gun salute by the First Continental Regiment, dressed in the uniforms of the Continental army and carrying muskets. The state marker, which contains some distorted historical claims about Salomon, came to fruition as a result of a successful lobbying campaign from the Philadelphia Jewish community as well as through official sanction by the Pennsylvania Historical and Museum Commission. Once again, the legend of Haym Salomon was reinforced and perpetuated through multiple channels—through the efforts of the Jewish community, which wanted to honor one of its own, and through government agencies seeking to create symbols of national pride.[26]

In the past fifty years, the mythic quality of Haym Salomon has grown even stronger. He is invoked more frequently and with less controversy as an American Jewish hero. The emergence of Salomon as a symbol of Jewish patriotism has probably been aided by the sketchy historical evidence about him. Because many of his early activities are undocumented and there is no record of his likeness, he can be represented in many different ways and is particularly malleable as a heroic figure. To be sure, the legend of Salomon has evolved through a combination of fact and fiction. But separating fact from fiction in the legend of Haym Salomon is, in the final analysis, a less compelling project than recognizing the meaning of myth itself as a formative element in what has become a shared piece of American Jewish heritage.

The efforts to memorialize Haym Salomon provide a lens on certain formative moments in the construction of public Jewish identity. At the height of the controversy over building a monument to Salomon, different sectors of the Jewish community laid claim to "owning" the memory of Salomon as a way of asserting their competing self-definitions as American Jews. The efforts to fix an image of Haym Salomon in legend and lore, and in bronze and granite, were part of a contested process to create a symbolic American Jewish hero. That process, although less contested, continues to the present day.

NOTES

1. Studies of American public commemorations and memory include John Bodnar, *Remaking America: Public Memory, Commemoration, and Patriotism in the Twentieth Century* (Princeton, 1992); Michael Kammen, *Mystic Chords of Memory: The Transformation of Tradition in American Culture* (New York, 1991).

2. My brief summary of Haym Salomon's life and contributions to the Revolution are based largely on the following histories: Jacob Rader Marcus, *United States Jewry, 1776–1985 Vol. I* (Detroit, 1989), pp. 66–77; Samuel Rezneck, *Unrecognized Patriots: The Jews in the American Revolution* (Westport, CT, 1975); Edwin Wolf and Maxwell Whiteman, *The History of the Jews of Philadelphia from Colonial Times to the Age of Jackson* (Philadelphia, 1957), pp. 98–113.

3. Rezneck, *Unrecognized Patriots,* pp. 81–97; Marcus, *United States Jewry,* pp. 66–77.

4. Rezneck, *Unrecognized Patriots,* pp. 215–16; Marcus, *United States Jewry,* pp. 73–75.

5. Rezneck, *Unrecognized Patriots,* pp. 215–17; Kammen, *Mystic Chords of Memory,* pp. 218–20.

6. *American Hebrew* (July 29, 1910), p. 313; *American Hebrew* (May 19, 1911), p. 66; Arthur A. Goren, *New York Jews and the Quest for Community: The Kehillah*

Experiment, 1908–1922 (New York, 1970), pp. 22–23, 40; *American Hebrew*, May 30, 1911; June 9, 1911, p. 171; June 16, 1911, p. 217; Aug. 11, 1911, p. 418; letter from Louis Marshall to Nissim Behar, May 31, 1911, Louis Marshall Papers, Box 1580, Folder "May 1911," American Jewish Archives, Cincinnati, Ohio (hereafter, AJA); letter from Madison Peters to Louis Marshall, May 30, 1911, Louis Marshall Papers, Box 111, Folder "P," AJA; Madison C. Peters, *The Jews Who Stood By Washington* (New York, 1915). The chapter on Salomon, entitled, "Haym Salomon as the Real Financier of the Revolution," was delivered as a lecture in 1911; *The Nation* 102 (1911), 647; Rezneck, *Unrecognized Patriots*, pp. 230–31.

7. Zigmunt Tygel, "Haym Salomon: His Life and Work, The Polish Jew Who Helped America Win the War of Independence" (New York, 1925), pp. 4, 6, 8. (The organization later changed its name to the Federation of Polish Jews.)

8. Ibid., p. 7; Report of Art Commission, Sept. 15, 1925, Salomon Memorial Application, Series 1344-A, Municipal Art Commission, New York; Report of Art Commission, June 9, 1925, Salomon Memorial Application, Series 1344-A, Municipal Art Commission, New York.

9. Pamphlet, "Haym Salomon Monument," ca. 1931, p. 15, contained in Louis Marshall Papers, Box 85, File 2, AJA.

10. "Haym Salomon Monument," pp. 14–15; Report of Art Commission, July 20, 1928, Salomon Memorial Application, Series 1344-A, Municipal Art Commission, New York.

11. Minutes of Conference Called for Further Discussion of the Haym Salomon Memorial Project, Apr. 12, 1927, p. 2, Box 139, Folder "S," Louis Marshall Papers, AJA [emphasis added]; see also Conference for the Discussion of the Haym Salomon Memorial, Feb. 26, 1926, Box 137, Folder "S," Louis Marshall Papers, AJA; Charles Edward Russell, *Haym Salomon and the Revolution* (New York, 1930); Nathan Straus to Stephen Wise, Dec. 23, 1930, Stephen Wise Papers, Collection P-134, Box 39, American Jewish Historical Society, Waltham, MA.

12. Minutes of Conference Called for Further Discussion of the Haym Salomon Memorial Project, Apr. 12, 1927, p. 2, Box 139, Folder "S," Louis Marshall Papers, AJA; Max Kohler to William Finishriber, Nov. 21, 1930, Small Collections 1068, AJA; Max Kohler to Emanuel Celler, Feb. 7, 1931, Small Collections 1068, AJA; Max Kohler, *Haym Salomon, The Patriot Broker of the Revolution: His Real Achievements and Their Exaggeration, An Open Letter to Congressman Celler* (1931); Salo Baron to Stephen Wise, Oct. 31, 1929, Small Collections 1068, AJA.

13. *Jewish Daily Bulletin*, Mar. 25, 1931, pp. 1, 4; Benjamin Winter to James Marshall, Mar. 27, 1931, Marshall Papers, Box 85, File 2, AJA. An interesting

subplot to the monument debate was a controversy over Louis Marshall's position on the issue. Marshall had died in 1929, in the middle of the monument campaign. Although he had opposed the effort, the Federation of Polish Jews listed him as a supporter. In 1931, James Marshall, the son of Louis Marshall, insisted that the federation refrain from using his father's name in its campaign. In a letter to Zigmunt Tygel, James Marshall admonished, "[Y]ou should not have used my father's name as a supporter" for that effort or tried to capitalize on his memory in the interest of a movement of which he did not approve. James Marshall to Zigmunt Tygel, Feb. 9, 1931, Louis Marshall Papers, Box 141, Folder "S," AJA; see also *Jewish Daily Forward,* May 12, 1929, Section 2, p. 1.

14. "Haym Salomon Monument," p. 23.

15. Minutes of Conference Called for Further Discussion of the Haym Salomon Memorial Project, Apr. 12, 1927, p. 2, Box 139, Folder "S," Louis Marshall Papers, AJA; confidential letter sent by Louis Marshall to various Jewish newspapers, July 23, 1927, Louis Marshall Papers, Box 141, Folder "S," AJA.

16. Harry Barnard, *This Great Triumvirate of Patriots* (Chicago, 1971), p. 76; Pamphlet, Patriotic Foundation of Chicago, "1936 Repays 1776: A Debt of Honor," (1936), Small Collections, Box A76, 701, Hebrew Union College Library, Cincinnati, Ohio.

17. Ibid., pp. 78–101; Rezneck, *Unrecognized Patriots,* pp. 233–34; Barnard, *This Great Triumvirate of Patriots,* p. 94.

18. Barnard, *This Great Triumvirate of Patriots,* p. 76; Patriotic Foundation of Chicago, "1936 Repays 1776," p. 8.

19. Rezneck, *Unrecognized Patriots,* p. 234; Deborah Dash Moore, *To the Golden Cities: Pursuing the American Jewish Dream in Miami and Los Angeles* (New York, 1994), p. 62; Correspondence between Robert Paine and Board of Parks Commissioners, July 1942, Southern California Jewish Historical Society; Bernard Postal and Lionel Koppman, eds., *A Jewish Tourist's Guide to the U.S.* (Philadelphia, 1954), p. 42; Letter from Ruth Isaacs, executive director, Southern California Jewish Historical Society, to the author, Feb. 3, 1997.

20. Charles Spencer Hart, *General Washington's Son of Israel and Other Forgotten Heroes of History* (Philadelphia, 1936).

21. Dianne Ashton, *Rebecca Gratz: Women's Judaism in Antebellum America* (Detroit, 1997), pp. 239–56. At a 1939 fundraiser for the Chicago monument, the crowd of supporters watched a Warner Brothers film entitled, "Sons of Liberty." Barnard, *This Great Triumvirate of Patriots,* pp. 91–92; Warner Brothers apparently produced another film about Salomon in the 1940s, entitled "My Country First." Rezneck, *Unrecognized Patriots,* pp. 276–77, n. 19.

22. Howard Fast, *Haym Salomon: Son of Liberty* (New York, 1941); Priscilla Murolo, "Life in the Fast Lane: Howard Fast and the Historical Novel," in Susan Porter Benson, Stephen Brier, and Roy Rosenzweig, eds., *Presenting the Past: Essays on History and the Public* (Philadelphia, 1986), pp. 53–64.

23. David Lowenthal, "Fabricating Heritage," *History and Memory: Studies in Representations of the Past* 10:1 (Spring 1998), p. 11.

24. *Chicago Daily News,* Jan. 28, 1974.

25. Caption printed on back of 1975 United States postage stamp honoring Haym Salomon. Leonard W. Stark, "Haym Salomon: After 75 Years, a Patriot Earns a Medal," *The Jewish Veteran* (December 1972), p. 26; Shirley Milgrim, *Haym Salomon: Liberty's Son* (Philadelphia, 1975).

26. *Philadelphia Jewish Exponent,* May 22, 1997; Program, "The Dedication of an Official State Historical Marker in honor of Haym Salomon, Jewish patriot," Sept. 7, 1997.

PART II

Contested Identities

SEVEN

Imagining Europe: The Popular Arts of American Jewish Ethnography

BARBARA KIRSHENBLATT-GIMBLETT

"Practically everyone has seen the prize-winning musical about the lovable people in that little village in Old Russia called Anetevka [sic]. Well, as far as we're concerned, 'Fiddler' made a GOOF!" *Mad* magazine's irreverent parody of the Broadway show (1964) and film (1971) "takes this famous musical about the problems of people who had *nothing,* and updates it with a version about the problems of people who have *everything*—mainly America's Upper Middle Class."[1] This 1973 spoof ends with the people of Anatevka arising from the depths of an American Jewish unconscious to haunt the nightmares of their dysfunctional descendants. Don't blame us for your problems, they say. *Fiddler on the Roof,* as theater, cinema, and comic, is a prime example of how the popular arts of American Jewish ethnography have been used to imagine Europe.

Before the Holocaust, anthropologist Franz Boas tried to protect Jews from ethnography, because he saw cultural difference as a liability in the fight against anthropological theories of race. During the same period, progressive social worker Boris D. Bogen used the popular arts of ethnography to celebrate Jewish cultural diversity in the service of a more humane approach to Americanization. For Bogen, the Jewish diaspora offered a model for American cultural diversity.

After the Holocaust, the relationship between professional and popular uses of ethnography shifted. Boas's worst fears had been realized. Race science had been the handmaiden to genocide. Denying Jewish cultural specificity and avoiding ethnography had not worked in the way Boas had hoped. What role might ethnography now play in the wake of the destruction of European Jewish communities? For the first time, American anthropologists, several of them students of Boas, made Eastern European Jewish culture the subject of sustained research.[2] The success of their ethnography, *Life Is with People* (1952), derives in no small measure from the literary works it took as models—Maurice Samuel's *The World of Sholom Aleichem*, Bella Chagall's *Burning Lights*, and Abraham Joshua Heschel's *The Earth Is the Lord's*. All of them are examples of the popular arts of ethnography. These are the kinds of texts that the creators of *Fiddler on the Roof* consulted when they adapted Sholom Aleichem's *Tevye the Dairyman*, a collection of short stories, for stage and screen.[3]

Fiddler on the Roof was intended to address a mainstream audience by imagining an Old World that was not "too Jewish" and by presenting its dissolution as symptomatic of the challenges facing "tradition" in modern life.[4] Though it does not make any direct reference to the Holocaust, *Fiddler on the Roof* uses the popular arts of ethnography to perform a distant, vanished world into life, while figuring its dissolution in ways that resonate with tragic events in recent memory. The mass exodus of the Jews from the fictional Anatevka cannot but evoke the fate of European Jewry during World War II. In *Fiddler on the Roof* two kinds of Holocaust memory converge. The first attempts to recover a destroyed world. This is the mode that dominates *Fiddler on the Roof*. The second documents the destruction and commemorates those who perished. This mode is suggested but not fully realized in *Fiddler on the Roof*'s theme of dissolution.

Not long after *Fiddler on the Roof* debuted on Broadway in 1964, a proliferation of Holocaust museums and memorials would ensure that the genocide and its victims would be remembered unflinchingly. In recent years, the fear that the world will know more about how Jews died than about how they lived in the past has given to the recovery of an obliterated world a new role in the commemoration of its tragic destruction. At the Museum of Jewish Heritage: A Living Memorial to the Holocaust, which opened in Manhattan in 1997, the first floor is devoted to Jewish life before the Holocaust and the third floor to life after the Holocaust. They serve to contextualize the central exhibit—the Holocaust itself.

ERASING THE SUBJECT

Franz Boaz, a German Jewish immigrant himself, settled in New York in 1887. His work offers something of a limit case for thinking about the popular arts of ethnography because Boas, a founder of American anthropology, saw the key to Jewish survival in cultural disappearance. Opposed to theories of racial formalism and immutability, Boas not only insisted that culture was independent of race—nothing cultural was biologically inherited—but also celebrated the capacity of immigrants to shed their European culture. By showing that immigrants could and did adapt to American culture, he hoped to counteract hostility to immigrants and efforts to restrict immigration.

Anti-immigration sentiment, which culminated in the quotas of 1921 and 1924 and was fueled in the 1930s by the rise of fascism, made race—and the question of Jews as a race—a very charged topic. During this period, anthropology was for all intents and purposes an applied science and provided support for restrictive immigration policies, eugenics, and social welfare programs. In his efforts to protect Jews from the liability of difference, Boas went beyond proving that they were not a race. He also argued that they were without a distinctive culture. Given the stakes, Jews could not afford to be different, ethnographically speaking. It was thus virtually impossible, or at the very least too dangerous, for American anthropologists before World War II to imagine Jews as an ethnographic subject. Instead, they rallied virtually the same arguments they had used to demonstrate that Jews did not constitute a race in order to prove that they were also without a distinctive and/or distinguishable culture. If Jews did not exist—either in racial or in cultural terms—then perhaps they might cease to be a target of anti-Semitism. They could certainly be spared from ethnography or, at least, from the kind of ethnography that would fix cultural differences and attribute those differences to racial inheritance.

Whereas the loss of culture had prompted eleventh-hour salvage ethnography among Native Americans, it was the fear that immigrants would not give up their distinctive ways that prompted anthropological research to document their ability to disappear. Accordingly, Boas framed all considerations of cultural change among immigrants exclusively in terms of *loss*—not retention or acquisition—of culture. His sole concern was with the disappearance of distinguishing characteristics, not with the process by which natal culture persisted or "American culture" was acquired, and certainly not with the impact of immigrant cultures on the American scene.

For Boas, cultural death was the most powerful evidence of the plasticity of human behavior. It also reflected his personal philosophy as expressed in "An Anthropologist's Credo," which appeared in *The Nation* in August 1938, and his way of answering American nativists and Nazi racists. In a rare moment of personal accounting, toward the end of his life, Boas stated that his "parents had broken through the shackles of dogma. My father had retained an emotional affection for the ceremonial of his parental home without allowing it to influence his intellectual freedom. Thus I was spared the struggle against religious dogma that besets the lives of so many young people." The outcome was his conviction that the "individual must be valued according to his own worth and not to the worth of a class to which others assign him." Moreover, "It must be the object of education to make the individual as free as may be of automatic adhesion to the group in which he is born or into which he is brought by social pressure."[5]

There is a painful paradox in Boas's thinking. In his scholarly work on North American Indians, he affirmed the relativistic values of anthropology that accord equal worth to all cultures. But in his anthropology of European immigrants and in his personal credo, Boas expressed his belief in the need and capacity for distinctive cultures to disappear and for everyone to accept universal and absolute ethical values. Utopia meant freedom from the "shackles of tradition." It meant the disappearance of competing claims to cultural superiority, while recognizing that "the solidarity of the group is presumably founded on fundamental traits of mankind and will always remain with us." The historical context in which Boas wrote had put anthropology's sacred principle of cultural relativism to the ultimate test and Boas took a stand: "The study of human cultures should not lead to a relativistic attitude toward ethical standards."[6]

Clearly, the battle in Boas's time was to be free of involuntary categorizations, to be free *not* to identify or be identified with a particular group. Boas almost always defined identification in negative terms as the fate of outsiders who are consigned to despised groups by the in-group. These are the terms in which Boas spoke of modern group life. Boas exemplified what Roland Barthes has called constitutive negativity.[7] Following an agenda set by the opposition, Boas tried to erase the subject, not only in anthropometric but also in cultural terms. But to erase the subject, he had first to constitute it. Only then could he eliminate the necessity for ethnography by demonstrating and celebrating the disappearance of its subject.

By 1920, as anti-immigration measures were gaining ground, Boas looked beyond physical anthropology for cultural evidence to support his argument that Jews were not a race. He saw in the gap between generations an opportunity to document cultural assimilation and support his case for the mutability of immigrants in the United States. Noting that "the break between the younger generation and the older generation" is "one of the most serious problems," Boas urged Leah Rachel Yoffie, a high school teacher in St. Louis, to record "what the people bring over in the way of folk-lore and folk-customs and how much it is lost in the younger generation." Boas did not have in mind salvage ethnography but rather hoped to provide evidence of "the process of assimilation of the Jewish community in this country." Yoffie, explaining that she was "gradually gathering all the Jewish folk-lore in St. Louis," declined the invitation, adding that: "The break between the two generations is no greater nor more serious [?] to-day than it always has been among Jews. . . . I am sorry I can't get up my enthusiasm on the wide breach between the two generations, but it is because I have not seen it. I believe that is a sentimental postulate based by a few emotional social-workers in New York on a few picturesque cases, and not founded on figures and facts."[8]

Characteristically, Boas affirmed that he was "not wedded to any particular theory" and encouraged Yoffie to gather the material to support her observation, which she did.[9] This overture was a rare exception to

Boas's strict avoidance of immigrant culture as a subject for study. He encouraged his own students to study "acculturation," but only among Native Americans, not among immigrants. By the 1920s, Boas had lost the fight against restrictive immigration. By the 1930s, he saw clearly what was happening in Europe. He was prepared to use any means he could in his fight against racial theories, even ethnography—the ethnography of cultural disappearance.

EXPOSITION OF THE JEWS OF MANY LANDS

Yoffie's comment about social workers might well have applied to Boris D. Bogen, himself a Russian Jewish immigrant. In contrast with Reform Jews, who, in Bogen's view, worried that to suggest any kind of national distinction was un-American, Bogen saw Jewish culture as a resource. He used the popular arts of ethnography to redirect the entire project of Americanization.[10]

Social workers who fostered appreciation of immigrant cultures during the first decades of the twentieth century hoped that if immigrants were valued they would be treated more fairly and would respond more warmly to Americanization efforts. Liberal intellectuals such as Horace Kallen, who coined the term *cultural pluralism,* and Randolph Bourne, who proposed a "trans-national America," condemned the position that immigrants should be stripped of their "ancestral endowment." They proposed instead that cultural differences be respected as part of "American civilization." In the paper that he read at the Thirty-First Annual YIVO Conference in 1957, Kallen contrasted emancipation in Europe, which "was particularly intolerant of the Jewish culture complex," with emancipation in the United States, which "came to be interpreted as an opportunity to enhance and enrich Jewish cultural heritage with new content and new values." These views informed social work among immigrants, nowhere more clearly than in the many homelands exhibitions, festivals, and pageants during the first half of the twentieth century.[11]

Inspired by the national pavilions and foreign villages so prominent at international expositions, Bogen mounted "Exposition of the Jews of Many

Lands," a Jewish world's fair in miniature, at the Jewish Settlement House in Cincinnati in 1913. As early as 1909, the Settlement House board was seeking ways to shake the "growing indifference to the good and wholesome old." When lectures by renowned speakers and amateur theatricals on Jewish subjects did not work, a comprehensive plan was proposed, at the beginning of 1912, "to modify the entire work of the Settlemtnt [sic] with the view of making Jewish culture the central idea of all activities." This work culminated in the Exposition of the Jews of Many Lands.[12]

The exposition answered the question "Should this culture and art be preserved, or should it give way as speedily as possible to Americanism?" This question animated the pages of the journal *Jewish Charities* during this period: "The value of the foreign culture that the immigrant brings to this country has been extolled by Miss Jane Addams; but she is partial to the immigrant, and has a keen sense for the artistic and picturesque in him, whether of custom or craft, and a fine regret for their neglect and rapid obliteration in America." Bogen argued that to think of cultural preservation as an impediment to Americanism was to forget that "besides the advisability of making the parents more modern and putting them, so to say, in a shape lovable to the children, it is also important that the children should be able to realize the strong and positive sides of their parents, not only as much as they have succeeded in modifying themselves in the process of Americanization; but, aside from it, the child should be able to appreciate the merits of their parents as they are." By focusing on the Jew rather than on Judaism, by making "Jewish culture the central idea of all activities," and by avoiding a "policy of inflexible Americanization," Bogen hoped to close the gap between immigrant generations and reduce the divisiveness among Jewish groups.[13]

For Jewish leaders in Cincinnati, the first step in the adjustment of immigrants to America was their adjustment to one another. In his introductory words to the program booklet, George Zepin pegged the exposition's success to its showing "that men may be different in dress but alike in soul-complexion, different in manners but alike in fine heart-throbs. At any rate, it will be our endeavor to show that difference does not mean inferiority. And, if this contributes to make us feel more keenly the brotherhood of

Israel, it has done enough." Jews were unified, in Bogen's view, by a common legacy of persecution, a sense of responsibility to co-religionists, and "a high standard of moral integrity of the home."[14]

The theme of persecution unsettled any easy celebration of the Old World, understood as the countries from which Jews had emigrated. How, for example, could they sing the national anthem of a country that had persecuted them? "A chorus of boys and girls, clad in the garb of all the nations in which Jews are citizens, sing native songs. Saturday night the chorus sang the Russian hymn 'God Save the Czar,' and men and women who had fled to America from Russian persecution hissed. 'Why should the Czar be saved?' they asked. 'Did he spare us?' So the song was eliminated from the program."[15]

Instead, "The Russian department presented a recital of continuous suffering and oppression. The orthodox rabbi, the soldier, the political prisoner, the revolutionist, the different types of women, represented by immigrants from Russia, reenacted actual episodes of Jewish life in the Dark Russia, with a background of scenery representing the interior of a Russian *izba*-soldiers' guard booth and appropriate music and national dances." This was not the shtetl of *Life Is with People* or the Anatevka of *Fiddler on the Roof*. Similarly, many of the domestic objects loaned by the immigrants for display commemorated historical events. For example, Miss Numa Kochman, "whose parents were killed in the Kishineff massacre," loaned "a prayer shawl, the weaver of which was also killed in the massacre."[16]

The Jewish home became the prime site of Jewish cultural revival and intergenerational rapprochement. The great danger in the United States, in Bogen's view, was "a totally unprecedented breakdown of the Jewish home." He attributed the worst effects of Americanization not only to external factors—bad influences from the environment—but also to internal ones, most importantly the weakness of the Jewish family to withstand those influences. Americanization had driven a wedge between parents and their children that expressed itself in "estrangement from the old tradition of religious ceremonial life." This estrangement, for Bogen, involved Jewish culture more than Judaism. To stem the tide, Bogen advocated "a strenuous effort . . . in different directions to revive the interest toward Jewish ideals; to return to Jewish culture; to develop an interest toward Jewish history, and to strengthen the weakening ties of the Jews of all the world." He pointed to the Exposition of the Jews of Many Lands as an example of this "educational crusade."[17]

What did the popular arts of ethnography look like on the eve of World War I? From January 18 to 26, 1913, the entire building of the Jewish Settlement House in Cincinnati was "utilized for booths, each one representing the settlement of Jews in another land, and each presided over by men and women in the picturesque costume of that land." Twenty-seven countries were represented, "beginning with the United States and ending with Abyssinia." The event brought together 400 volunteers, 51 local Jewish organizations, and 12 national, philanthropic, and educational organizations representing a wide spectrum of the Jewish community, including labor unions, Zionist associations, fraternal organizations, synagogues, schools, and social clubs. This event was to coincide with the convention of the Union of American Hebrew Congregations.[18]

Two modes of cultural competence converged at the Exposition of the Jews of Many Lands—the vernacular and the elevated. The vernacular mode, as manifested in the humble forms of everyday life associated with Jewish homes, expressed the heterogeneity of Jewish culture. The Jewish home of the Old World lent itself to the popular arts of ethnography, and domestic objects figured prominently in the displays. Everyone was asked to help: "You can assist by loaning curios, costumes, treasures, etc." Over 500 objects, most of them brought by immigrants from the Old Country, were exhibited. The abundance of embroidery and lace made by women was taken as an indication of "the innate love for the beautiful."[19]

The elevated mode, which operated in the media of fine art, was used to present general Jewish themes in a universalizing idiom. Performances included orchestral and choral arrangements of national songs, pageants on the theme of Israel Zangwill's "Melting Pot," tableaus, or "living pictures," on such themes as the "Maidens of Many Lands" (including Egyptian, Babylonian, Persian, Grecian, Spanish, Russian, Jewish, and American "maidens"), and Samuel Hirszenberg's painting *Galut* (exile).

While each of the twenty-seven Jewish groups was distinct and even incommensurate with the others, several methods integrated them into a larger whole. The statistical surveys, displayed in the form of charts, made it possible to compare groups. Modular displays, by designating a booth for each country, provided a consistent template for displaying comparable differences. Every group was represented, accepted as part of the Jews and portrayed as distinctive. Choral and dance ensembles performed an eclectic repertoire that represented all the participating groups within unifying choral or choreographic styles and arrangements.

Cincinnati's Exposition of the Jews of Many Lands was a tour de force of the popular arts of ethnography. It integrated a diverse immigrant community, while affirming its heterogeneous cultures, by involving the participants in the display and performance of their doubly diasporic "heritage." They had been displaced, first from an ancient homeland and later from an Old World. Immigration had assembled the diaspora in America. By reviving interest in Jewish culture, this event was supposed to help close the gap between generations, divert youth from the worst influences of tenement life, and integrate Jews into American society. Jewish heterogeneity both challenged Jewish solidarity and, as the exposition would demonstrate, modeled American cultural diversity.

LIFE IS WITH PEOPLE: THE CULTURE OF THE SHTETL

During the first half of the twentieth century, Boas had felt compelled to protect Jews from anthropology. After World War II, his students felt a moral obligation to use ethnography to save a vanished culture from oblivion. *Life Is with People,* which appeared in 1952, represents the first time that American anthropologists made Eastern European Jewish culture the subject of a sustained ethnography. Like the Exposition of the Jews of Many Lands, *Life Is with People* was an example of autoethnography by and for the Jews depicted therein. Jewish immigrants in New York City were the informants for this study of Eastern European Jewish culture at a distance. The authors of the book intended it to be read by those it was about and hoped that readers would recognize their culture in its pages. The recognition factor was due in no small measure to textual devices that have come to be associated with popular uses of ethnography. Like its models, this book tried to evoke a total world. However flawed as a professional ethnography, *Life Is with People* has been immensely successful among the wide audience for which it was written. The book has sold almost 132,000 copies during almost fifty years in print.[20]

By the time American anthropologists were finally ready to study Eastern European Jews, they were too late to study them in situ. They had no choice but to study them at a distance, much as they had studied the "broken" culture of Native Americans "at a distance." Operating in the mode of salvage ethnography, anthropologists interviewed immigrants about a way of life in Europe that no longer existed. In this way, those who studied Jewish culture from afar came to use the popular arts of ethnography in the service of one of two major modes of Holocaust memory—re-creating a *world* that had been destroyed. That mode reached its apogee with the Broadway musical *Fiddler on the Roof* in 1964.

In my Introduction to the 1995 edition of *Life Is with People*, I trace the history of the book, how it constructed the shtetl, and how it came to identify all of Eastern European Jewish culture with the shtetl. Consistent with its literary models, *Life Is with People* produced a composite portrait of a virtual town, not an empirical description of an actual one. The goal was to delineate the general patterns of Eastern European Jewish culture, rather than inventory its customs, in order to illuminate how cultural practices shape personality. After a brief historical prologue, the book opens with the Sabbath, before proceeding to social organization and stratification, the life cycle, and sacred texts and religious rules. There follow chapters on women's lives, the lowest social strata, and Hasidism, as well as charity and community services, social life and conflict resolution, and work. The final chapters deal with marriage, family life, children, growing up, the kosher home, and holidays. By the end of the book, the shtetl has become a protagonist in its own right. The final chapter, "How the Shtetl Sees the World" opens with this statement: "The shtetl views the universe as a planned whole, designed and governed by the Almighty." The conclusion continues, in this fashion, to speak of the shtetl in anthropomorphic terms, so fully animated had it become for the authors.[21]

Life Is with People, which developed out of the Research in Contemporary Cultures project at Columbia University, is a classic example of Cold War anthropology. Funded by the Office of Naval Research in 1946, this project was designed by Ruth Benedict and Margaret Mead to delineate the national character of the countries of strategic interest to the United States and provide a basis for forging a postwar peace. China and the Soviet Union were central to the project, and Jews were not part of the original plan. When it became apparent that many of the informants for the Eastern European countries were Jews and that many of the researchers were also Jews, the Jewish research group was formed. Their book, *Life Is with People,* was to become the most enduring publication to arise from the larger project.

Although Benedict and Mead had persuaded the Office of Naval Research to fund the research, Mead turned to the American Jewish Committee (AJC) for money to write the book. In making her case to the AJC, Mead clearly positioned the projected volume within the context of the popular arts of ethnography. She argued that this book would help mobilize "positive attitudes towards the traditional East European Jewish culture, which is part of the cultural legacy of contemporary American culture" and thereby serve "indirectly to refute or to illuminate current stereotypes about the Jew." This pitch met with a sympathetic response from the AJC's Department of Scientific Research, which had originated from conferences on anti-Semitism held during World War II. A book like *Life Is with People* not only was good "counterpropaganda," but also would strengthen Jewish self-identification at a time of low morale—or so it was hoped.[22]

When *Life Is with People* appeared in 1952, the American Jewish Committee issued a press release stating that "For millions of Americans, this book will open the door to a new understanding of their heritage. Such understanding is indispensable to that sense of identity which makes for a wholesome, integrated life in the present," echoing almost verbatim the words that had persuaded the AJC to fund the project in the first place.

Anthropology has always been, to some degree, an applied science, and *Life Is with People* shows the discipline applying itself to the situation of American Jews in the immediate post-war period. Margaret Mead was determined that the book would be written in an accessible style. And the book was, indeed, accessible, in large measure because of the models it followed, including the classics of Yiddish literature (for the most part in translation) and films on Jewish subjects. While content analysis of a wide range of material was a methodological requirement of the culture-in-a-distance approach, only *Life Is with People* modeled itself on the form and style of popular literary works. Moreover, the people interviewed had also read the Yiddish classics and seen the films.

Life Is with People was modeled on three texts, all of them published in the 1940s and examples of the popular arts of ethnography in their own right: Maurice Samuel's *The World of Sholom Aleichem;* Bella Chagall's *Burning Lights;* and Abraham Joshua Heschel's *The Earth Is the Lord's: The Inner World of the Jew in Eastern Europe*. These works stand in a recursive relationship to one another in terms of theme, form, and sensibility. Sholom Aleichem's literary constructions become the basis for writing the *World of Sholom Aleichem,* a mediation that informs subsequent ethnographic inscriptions (*Life Is with People*) and embodiments (*Fiddler on the Roof*). Such examples of the popular arts of ethnography demand attention not only to their content and form, but also to their structures of feeling. In the moment of their appearance and in their reception thereafter lies a history of changing sensibility.

THE WORLD OF SHOLOM ALEICHEM

Appearing in 1943, *The World of Sholom Aleichem* carried a solicitation for war bonds on its back leaf and the marks of wartime publication in its "full compliance with all government regulations for the conservation of paper, metal, and other essential materials."[23] Searching for metaphors to describe his book, Samuel called it a "pilgrimage" to the lost world of our "grandfathers and grandmothers." It was an "act of piety." It was a sin, the sin of "necromancy, or calling up the dead, which was the sin of Saul. For that world is no more." Samuel's self-appointed task was nothing less than resurrection of the dead. He intended to "recapture the warm, breathing original creation" using that "mirror of Russian Jewry," Sholom Aleichem. *The World of Sholom Aleichem* is an early example of the popular arts of ethnography put to the service of the mode of Holocaust memory that recovers a lost world. A striking feature of this book, written and published in the midst of World War II, is its attribution of the "obliteration" of the "strange world" of Sholom Aleichem to a half century of cataclysmic events, including "two gigantic wars and a major revolution." This characterization suggests that the enormity of the genocide of World War II, its difference from other dramatic events of the century, had not yet registered.[24]

The "world" of Sholom Aleichem, as Samuel explains, is not only the world in which Sholom Aleichem lived (he is "himself its focus and miniature"), but also "the world which appears in his books." With this formulation, Samuel attributes to Sholom Aleichem "complete self-identification with a people" and the "fusing [of] external and internal material in a natural whole."[25]

The operative term is *world,* what philosopher Alfred Schutz calls "a province of meaning." *World* also suggests the immediacy of being there, which accounts for the strategic realism of the account. If we are to believe Samuel, "We could write a *Middletown* of the Russian-Jewish Pale basing ourselves solely on the novels and stories and sketches of Sholom Aleichem, and it would be as reliable a scientific document as a 'factual' study; more so, indeed, for we should get, in addition to the material of a straightforward social inquiry, the intangible spirit which informs the material and gives it its living significance." This idea was repeated by a reviewer of *Life Is with People* about ten years later: "With all due respect to Ruth Benedict, Margaret Mead, and the authors of *Life Is with People,* it can be safely asserted that the greatest 'anthropologist' of the *shtetl* was the Yiddish novelist and writer Mendele Mocher Seforim."[26]

As literary scholars disabuse naive readers of the illusion that literature is ethnography, anthropologists are insisting that ethnography is literature.[27] This does not make Sholom Aleichem an anthropologist or the authors of *Life Is with People* novelists. But it does make *The World of Sholom Aleichem* the missing term in the equation. In *The World of Sholom Aleichem,* Samuel fashioned a hybrid genre that mediates between literature and ethnography, between retelling the Tevye stories and providing an ethnographic gloss on them.

Whereas Samuel referred his observations about Eastern European Jewish culture to Kasrielevky, a fictional Jewish town, Mark Zborowski and Elizabeth Herzog referred their observations to an unnamed, prototypical, equally "virtual" Jewish town—the shtetl. In the absence of an actual Jewish community in Eastern Europe, the anthropologists posited an imagined one and always kept it in mind. The Jewish "world" called forth in Yiddish literature provided a vivid model for visualizing the virtual shtetl of *Life Is with People* and for integrating otherwise disparate information from more than a hundred informants from many different locations.

The World of Sholom Aleichem and *Life Is with People,* like *The Earth Is the Lord's* and, for that matter, *Burning Lights,* offered a spiritualized account of Jewish culture. This approach arises in part from an elegiac mission that finds consolation in the indestructibility of a spiritual legacy. The notion that Jewish culture is inherently spiritual, rather than material, becomes a matter of necessity.[28] It sacralizes the loss. The popular arts of ethnography become a mode of worship.

BURNING LIGHTS

Written in 1939, *Burning Lights* appeared in Yiddish as *Brenendike likht* in 1945, the year after Bella Chagall died. The English translation was published in 1946.[29] Both versions included drawings by Marc Chagall, her husband. By stressing cultural intactness and writing in the present tense, Bella Chagall's memoir takes on an ethnographic quality, however soft the focus of this "portrait of the warm world of Russian Jewry," as the book is described on its cover.[30] *Burning Lights* contains no dates, place names, or family surnames. It is *not* organized chronologically from Chagall's birth in 1895 into a well-to-do Hasidic family, through her graduation from the Vitebsk Gymnasium for girls, where she studied Russian, to her entrance into the University of Moscow in 1912, "where she writes her thesis on 'the liberation of the Russian peasants' and Dostoievski."[31] These facts appear in the publisher's prefatory note, not in her account.

Although memoir and autobiography have long served as genres of Jewish autoethnography, Bella Chagall breaks with convention by writing about childhood alone. More typically, as in the memoirs of Yekheskl Kotik and Pauline Wengeroff, childhood is not only the site of a world lost or rejected (and minutely described) but also the prelude to a transformative experience and a coming of age. In *Burning Lights,* the chapters roughly follow the holidays of the Jewish calendar year as seen through the innocent eyes of a little girl who never grows up. As one reviewer commented, "We find very little personal experience in *Burning Lights*. The ego of the author is dissolved in the general atmosphere of a life conducted according to fixed Jewish customs. . . . The same thing, more or less, has been done during the last eighty years by almost every Yiddish and Hebrew writer."[32]

The book's opening chapter, "Heritage," establishes the elegiac tone of the memoir. Like *The World of Sholom Aleichem, Burning Lights* seeks to bring the dead to life. Bella Chagall's childhood years return with such force that "they could be breathing into my mouth." Fearing that her memories would die with her, she sets out to "draw out a fragment of a bygone life from fleshless memories." Her description of that task, "I am unfolding my piece of heritage," anticipates the opening song of *Fiddler on the Roof,* "Tradition."[33]

Like *Burning Lights, Life Is with People* is lyrical, elegiac, and idealized. *Life Is with People* offers a romantic and generalized portrait based on the themes of piety, poverty, and insularity. Even Mead was caught up in this spirit when she wrote of *Life Is with People,* "This book, this record of a whole way of life, has been written from the inside, where the mother's tears of mingled joy and sorrow glistened through her fingers as she lit the Sabbath candles."[34] That very image was to appear on the cover of *Burning Lights*. The title is an allusion to the Sabbath and to all the other holidays when candles are lit. Both books launch their evocations of a lost Jewish world with an account of Sabbath bliss, an icon of Old World Jewish joy.

THE EARTH IS THE LORD'S: THE INNER WORLD OF THE JEWS OF EASTERN EUROPE

The Earth Is the Lord's, by Abraham Joshua Heschel, valorized the inner life of Ashkenazic Jewry and offered its enduring value as the basis for Jewish spiritual continuity in the face of physical annihilation. It did so by allegorizing a barely material Jewish world in order to redirect ethnography to the project of Jewish spiritual survival. Heschel seemed to suggest that by not entrusting to the material world that which they most cherished, the Jews of Eastern Europe had created a spiritual legacy beyond the reach of those who annihilated them. In a mode that was at once autoethnographic and anti-ethnographic, Heschel enacted in his own text the very qualities that he attributed to his subjects.

Heschel first delivered the essay that became *The Earth Is the Lord*'s in Yiddish at the Nineteenth Annual Conference of the YIVO Institute for Jewish Research in 1945. As Deborah Dash Moore has reported, "When he finished speaking, the audience of several thousands was moved to tears, and a spontaneous Kaddish [mourner's prayer for the dead] was uttered by many who were committed secularists and nonbelievers."[35] Attesting to the indestructibility of spirit in the face of physical annihilation, Heschel presented a transcendent account of the "inner world" of Eastern European Jewry. Here, as in *The World of Sholom Aleichem,* the operative term is *world,* not *shtetl*. Indeed, the English text makes no reference to "shtetl" whatsoever. It refers instead to an era or period, to a people, or to "little Jewish communities in Eastern Europe" and "a typical Jewish township."[36]

Without ever using the term *ethnography,* the 1949 preface to *The Earth of the Lord's* invokes this modality and transmutes it. Heschel takes as his subject "a whole people," rather than exceptional individuals. After all, a whole people had been annihilated, and it was their way of life as an achievement in its own right that Heschel set out to define and praise. To have done otherwise would have been to suggest that some lives were worth more than others, that some deaths were more tragic than others, that the outstanding contributions of exceptional individuals, or of an entire people, had made their annihilation more terrible. It was therefore not his "intention to dwell upon the various achievements of that period, such as the contributions to science and literature, to art and theology, the rise of the *Wissenschaft des Judentums,* the revival of the Hebrew language, the modern Hebrew and Yiddish literatures, the development of the Yiddish language, Zionism, Jewish socialism, the establishment of new centers, the rebuilding of Israel, the various attempts to modernize Jewish life and to adapt it to changing conditions." Rather than judge this era by "progress in general civilization," Heschel took as his measure "how much spiritual substance there is in its everyday existence." Not only was the spiritual all that remained, but, in what might be seen as a homeopathic gesture, Heschel suggested that Jewish life had always been defined in spiritual terms. By valorizing the "spiritual integrity" of everyday life, he celebrated a capacity that had been denied Jews by their murderers.[37]

Finding the defining pattern of Eastern European Jewish culture in its inwardness, Heschel could be said to have taken as his ethnographic subject "the Jewish soul" and to have created a text that effects a kind of transmigration of soul from a world lost to one yet to be gained. Anticipating the objection that his account is idealized, Heschel stated, "There is a price to be paid by the Jew. He has to be exalted in order to be normal. In order to be a man, he has to be more than a man. To be a people, the Jews have to be more than a people."[38] After all, they had been murdered for being less than human and less than a people.

Ethnography, however attenuated, offered Heschel a model for finding the exceptional in the ordinary. Accordingly, he made *culture* rather than *Culture* his focus and drew on two approaches in the American anthropology of his time, salvage ethnography and patterns of a culture. But he transmuted them both. Like the salvage ethnographies of Native Americans that Boas and his students had produced, *The Earth Is the Lord's* was written into the face of its disappearing subject, but with this critical difference. Anthropology as a field had been complicit with the institutions and policies that decimated Native American communities and destabilized their cultures. For that reason, it could be said that the discipline of anthropology had helped to produce the necessity for its own salvage practices. In the case of *The Earth Is the Lord's*—and for that matter *Life Is with People,* which was modeled on it—salvage ethnography was deployed by and on behalf of those who had suffered incalculable losses at the hands of others. These works were not only salvage ethnographies (and salvage ethnographies of a special kind); they were also autoethnographies. Autoethnography, as figured in Heschel's work, is history's alter ego. In the *longue durée* of eight hundred years, "the Ashkenazic period," an era defined by the Catastrophe (*khurbn*), which closed it against its will, Heschel found his ethnographic present. In this "golden period in Jewish history, in the history of the Jewish soul," Hasidism, with its valorization of simple piety over erudition and notion of divine sparks in the commonplace, provided Heschel with the inner mandate for a theologically infused ethnography.[39]

Salvage ethnography, by its very nature, required piecing together fragmentary information to form a larger cultural whole that no longer existed. How was the larger whole to be constituted? Not by making a complete inventory of the outer world, the observable practices and artifacts, of Jewish culture. Consistent with the trend in American anthropology during the 1940s, Heschel "had to inquire into the life-feeling and life-style of the people." Ruth Benedict, whose *Patterns of Culture* (1934) became one of the best-selling works in the history of American anthropology, offered a model compatible with Heschel's project. He aimed to describe the "pattern of life of a people" and to delineate "the character of a people as reflected in its way of living throughout generations." These goals were virtually identical with those of the configurationist anthropology of Ruth Benedict and Margaret Mead, which sought to identify the patterns of a culture and the relation between culture and personality or national character. Heschel's text applied these concepts to Eastern European Jewish culture even before *Life Is with People* was conceived.[40]

The anti-ethnographic character of *The Earth Is the Lord's* arises from its refusal to objectify its subjects, to treat them as specimens. By focusing on cultural patterns and inner life, *The Earth Is the Lord's* studiously avoided the objectifying tendencies of salvage ethnography, which tended to inter, even as it inscribed, its disappearing subject. Heschel sidestepped the museological effects of clinical descriptions of the "outer world" of his subjects. As he would later state, "Eastern Europe is not a collection of antiques to be relegated to a museum. It must become part and parcel of the mode of life of Jews born in America."[41] To avoid delegating a lost world to the museum, Heschel offered an account that was more inspirational than informational.

Instead of re-creating with clinical detachment the tangible world of those who had perished, Heschel gave sensuous presence to the inner life of Eastern European Jewry. Taking his lead from his subject, about whom he states that "Audacious doctrines were disguised as allegories," Heschel allegorized from the concreteness of "ethnographic" detail, which he understood as "habits and customs," "attitudes," "values," and "style"—in other words, the "unique and enduring features" of Ashkenazic Jewry. Thus, although Eastern European Jews "had no affinity with things," Heschel made objects metaphors for intangible and inexpressible features of an unseen though fully experienced inner world. He anthropomorphized icons of the world of Ashkenazic Jewry in the service of portraiture. The physiognomy of the Jew in Eastern Europe "was not like a passage in an open book—a static picture of uniform lines with a definite proportion of text and margin—but like a book whose pages are constantly turning." Similarly, "The little Jewish communities in Eastern Europe were like sacred texts opened before the eyes of God so close were their houses of worship to Mount Sinai."[42]

In this and other ways, Heschel enacted in his own text qualities he attributed to his subjects. "Everywhere they found cryptic meaning." So, too, does Heschel. "The purpose [of their piety] was to ennoble the common, to endow worldly things with hieratic beauty." Such is Heschel's purpose as well. His allegorization of a barely material Jewish world redirected ethnography to the project of Jewish survival after the Catastrophe.[43]

When Heschel spoke in 1945, his words resounded in the void of the Catastrophe to a YIVO audience that was in a state of shock and grief. Although the Catastrophe had infused Heschel's 1945 account of the Eastern European era, he had not addressed the genocide directly in what was a text of consolation for an inconsolable community. *The Earth Is the Lord's* sought to fan the spiritual flame of Eastern Europe that it might survive in the lives of American Jewry. The physical destruction was barely mentioned, so raw was the sense of loss, as the spontaneous Kaddish uttered by the YIVO audience attests.

Twelve years later, in 1957, Heschel again addressed a YIVO audience, this time to admonish American Jewry for their complacency. Not only was the younger generation ignorant of the world that had been destroyed, but also "there are in America now young Jews who maintain that extermination of six million Jews is a myth." By 1957, some members of the American Jewish community had become self-satisfied, and Heschel reproached them: "Dark are our days and we do not even kindle the Sabbath lights. Six million Jews passed away in smoke. Blood is not silent, but our conscience is as unresponsive as the wall. We have become intoxicated and giddy with the vanities of the world." He exhorted his audience "to prevent a second extinction of Eastern Europe. The body of the six-million community, the body of an entire generation was destroyed by the barbarian. Shall we permit a second extinction of the spirit of Eastern Europe, the spirit of all the generations?" For the present generation, "the name of Las Vegas is more meaningful than

Vilna." As a result of their shame, ignorance, and complacency, "The heritage of Eastern Europe is being dissipated nowadays." "YIVO's Task Now," the title of the published summary of his remarks, was "To serve as a memory, to remember, to remind, and to study the world that we have lost." Stressing the importance of "the study and elucidation of the heritage of East European Jews" for Jewish survival, Heschel placed heritage, which is at the heart of the popular arts of ethnography, at the fore.[44]

When Heschel's *The Earth Is the Lord's* appeared in English as a book in 1950, it was illustrated with Ilya Schor's hieratic wood engravings. Schor's engravings were inspired by Eastern European Jewish folk art, including tombstone carvings, papercuts, manuscript illumination, ritual silver, and synagogue embroidery. Photography is absent from this book as well as from the other texts discussed here. There was no scarcity of photographic images. Rather, a particular kind of artistic mediation was necessary to spiritualize these otherwise documentary projects, and that mediation operated both textually and visually, even in photograph albums such as Roman Vishniac's *Polish Jews: A Pictorial Record*.

Vishniac's photographs had been exhibited by YIVO in January 1944 and again in January 1945, to coincide with the YIVO conference at which Heschel delivered his legendary elegy. If anything, these photographs needed a textual intervention to mitigate what Vishniac himself described as "real life unposed." That intervention took two forms in *Polish Jews,* an album of thirty-one photographs, most of them portraits, which Schocken published in 1947 and again, as a paperback, in 1965. First, part of Heschel's 1945 YIVO address served as the introduction to this album, which took as its theme "the religious absorption of Jewish life in Poland." Selected from more than two thousand photographs made by Vishniac in 1938, "These pictures are largely concerned with what was the major aspect of East-European Jewish life: its intense religious quality." Second, the captions are cryptic: Fish Seller, Exegesis, Chant, Heder, Storekeeper with Nothing to Sell, Grandfather and Granddaughter, Courtyard, Old Man. Thanks to such captions, which include the general locations where the images were taken (Cracow, Warsaw, Carpathian Ruthenia, Munkacevo, Poland, and Russo Poland), persons, places, and scenes tend toward the typical, rather than the particular. Together, Heschel's introduction and the cryptic captions intensify the tension between the ethnographic character of the album as cultural portraiture and its anti-ethnographic avoidance of detail.[45]

Just before and after the opening of *Fiddler on the Roof,* Schocken brought out the first paperback editions of *Burning Lights* (1962), *Life Is with People* (1962), and *The World of Sholom Aleichem* (1965). The covers of these books were illustrated not with photographs but with the line drawings of Marc Chagall and Ben Shahn. Shahn, who had illustrated Arnold Perl's 1953 play, *The World of Sholom Aleichem,* designed the cover for the paperback edition of Samuel's *The World of Sholom Aleichem*.[46] The central image is a sketch of a fiddler. Shahn's fiddler stands on his own two feet, with his back to the reader, not perched precariously on a shtetl rooftop. Marc Chagall's drawing of a mother and daughter blessing Sabbath candles appeared on the cover of *Burning Lights*.[47] His drawing "A House in Vitebsk" appears on the cover of *Life Is with People*.[48] The title of *Fiddler on the Roof* was inspired by a Marc Chagall painting, not by the Sholom Aleichem stories, and Chagall's paintings were also the visual inspiration for Boris Aronson's stage designs. They were supposed "to capture the flavor and special essence of Chagall and at the same time to serve the spatial needs of [director] Jerry Robbins."[49] The tension between the suggestiveness of drawings and the literalness of photography finds its parallel in the stage and film versions of *Fiddler on the Roof*.

FIDDLER ON THE ROOF

Mad magazine's "Fiddler Made a Goof" may well resonate more fully with Heschel's 1957 exhortation than does *Fiddler on the Roof*. Writer Frank Jacobs and artist Mort Drucker, in inimitable *Mad* style, tell the story of a dysfunctional (Jewish) family in the suburbs. The scenario is a group therapy session. Dad, who looks like Zero Mostel, complains to the psychiatrist, who looks like Freud, about his materialistic wife and three disaffected daughters: Sheila is a hippy and sex fiend; Nancy is a junkie; Joy is a political radical turned lesbian. The session ends with Dad, on the psychiatrist's couch, narrating a nightmare: "It's — it's THEM! It's our ancestors from the Old Country!" Images of the characters in *Fiddler on the Roof* flood the dreamscape. They loom over scenes of industrial pollution, labor unrest, Yippie protests, and police brutality. They point their accusing fingers at

Mom and Dad, who cringe in their bed, the covers pulled up, terror on their faces. Singing to the tune of "Miracle of Miracles," the ancestors make their final indictment of Tevye, Golde, Motel, Yente, and "all the other people from Anetevka [sic]" with the following words: "God may make a fuss / And . . . some . . . how . . . blame . . . you . . . on . . . us!" The Old World talks back! In a preemptive strike, dead ancestors distance themselves from their living descendants. If *Fiddler on the Roof* universalized a Jewish story about the dissolution of Old World tradition, "Fiddler Made a Goof!" does the same for New World materialism and links the two situations by making the characters in *Mad* the descendants of the characters in *Fiddler*.[50]

Both *Fiddler on the Roof* and "Fiddler Made a Goof!" address the generation gap, which they locate not only within their narratives of family strife, but also within the lives of their respective audiences. They do this from opposing generational vantage points. The musical speaks for an older generation in an elegiac mode. It exhorts the next generation to take responsibility for "tradition." The comic speaks for a younger generation in an irreverent mode, blaming arriviste parents for the disaffection of their countercultural offspring. It does this through the venerable mode of ethnographic burlesque, which repudiates what it describes in order to repulse, rather than attract, its readers.[51]

Such examples of the popular arts of ethnography demand attention not only to their content and form, but also to what Raymond Williams calls a "structure of feeling." Williams distinguishes feeling ("meanings and values as they are actively lived and felt") from ideology ("formally held and systematic beliefs"), noting that they are of course interrelated in practice: "Methodologically, then, a 'structure of feeling' is a cultural hypothesis, actually derived from attempts to understand such elements [affective elements of consciousness and relationships] and their connection in a generation or period, and needing always to be returned, interactively, to such evidence."[52] These invocations of the Old World are an archive of changing structures of feeling and their generational character, nowhere more apparent than in the various versions of *Fiddler*.

The Broadway musical debuted on September 22, 1964, and broke a record with three thousand performances in its eight-year run. *Fiddler on the Roof* was released as a motion picture in 1971, the year a history of the production was published.[53] The play, musical score, sound recordings, and video release of the film remain in print. So powerful was *Fiddler*'s presence at the time of the Broadway musical that the dust jacket for Sholom Aleichem's *Tevye's Daughters* carried the statement, directly under the title, "The stories on which the great musical FIDDLER ON THE ROOF is based."[54] While its Broadway record has since been broken, *Fiddler*'s afterlife in amateur productions may be even more impressive, if less celebrated, than its Broadway and cinematic success.

From the outset, its creators sought ways to avoid *Fiddler* being "just an ethnic show with limited appeal." Indeed, they hesitated to approach a producer because "If we had gone to a producer and said, 'Hey, we've got an idea for a musical about a bunch of old Jews and they have terrible trouble and there's a pogrom,' he'd have thrown us out of his office, even though we were all fairly well known writers in the field." They also had difficulty raising money because "Everybody thought it was far too special, too ethnic and parochial for any kind of open audience." Richard Altman, who was the researcher for the production and wrote a history of it, explained to each company as it was about to go into rehearsal that "This is not just a show about Jews living in Russia in 1905, although it is that, on the surface. At its heart, it's about the enduring strength of the human spirit—and man's ability to grow, to change, to overcome adversity." While the performance itself aimed to bring out the universal meaning of a Jewish story and transcend Tevye as "an ethnic symbol," the producers also wanted the audience to meet the production halfway by subordinating their own "cultural identification" and "private prejudices."[55]

Two months before rehearsals were to start, director Jerome Robbins gave the following instructions to Joseph Stein, who wrote the book: "Dramatize the story of Tevye as that of a man in the state of transition. This is the story we are telling; without it our show is just a touching narrative Jewish *Cavalcade*. . . . The audience must be strongly directed to Tevye's ambivalences and struggle to keep his traditions while being assailed by outside forces that are projected in terms of his daughters and their suitors." Robbins quickly realized that "if it's a show about tradition and its dissolution, then the audience should be told what that tradition is." To do so succinctly, Robbins suggested that they "create a song that would be tapestry against which the whole show would play." Slowly and with great difficulty, Jerry Bock, who composed the music, and Sheldon Harnick, who wrote the lyrics, created "Tradition." Bock worried that this song would just compound the show's problems: "I was terrified that the whole show was too long and that it was going to be too serious and too Jewish and a disaster." Contrary to his fears, "'Tradition' became the key to *Fiddler*'s meaning" and to every scene and character. It is in the staging of tradition that we can see the popular arts of ethnography at work and differences in the approaches of the stage and screen versions of *Fiddler*.[56]

Fiddler on the Roof's success as a theatrical work derives in no small measure from its suggestiveness. As the opening song attests, it is Tradition, not traditions, that is the focus of the production. Even when Tevye refers to traditions, they are so generic that anyone could fill in the blank with his or her own customs: "Here in Anatevka we have traditions for everything—how to eat, how to sleep, how to wear clothes." Who doesn't? Even when "the little prayer shawl" is mentioned, as evidence of "our constant devotion to God," it turns out to be arbitrary and determining: "You may ask, how did this tradition start?" Tevye answers his own question, "I don't know! But it is a tradition. Because of our traditions, everyone knows who he is and what God expects him to do." A kosher home, the Holy Book, the rabbi, and the Sabbath are about as specific as Tradition gets. As a result, a Jewish audience could fill the blanks with all that it already knew about the imagined Jewish world of Anatevka, while other audiences would not be prevented by too much Jewish detail from making their own connections. A key to such differential response was a coded Jewishness, which was decipherable only by those who could hear it in the accent, idiom, and style of the performance itself.[57]

The challenge for the team was to etherealize (rather than spiritualize) the Jewishness of Anatevka. They produced "Jewish lite"—the flavor, style, and feel of a vaguely Jewish world—by suppressing markers thought to be too overtly Jewish, even though the team demanded detailed research as a foundation for their work. As official researcher for the production, Altman was asked to find "as much information as could be found on Jewish life and lore at the turn of the century, specifically the way people live in the *shtetls* of Eastern Europe, the work they did, their professions." To that end, he "scoured the secondhand bookstores on lower Fourth Avenue. I also visited the library of the Yivo Institute on upper Fifth Avenue to bring Jerry books and illustrations that would provide him with a visual flavor of the times. This research gave him the basis for attempting to communicate with Boris [Aronson] something of the scenic values he wanted."[58]

How they got from detail to flavor can be seen in their handling of language, which Stein saw as part of the "too Jewish" problem. He was "very careful not to have any Yiddish words or phrases in the script—and there are only one or two Yiddish words in any of the songs. But through the quality of the talk, the construction of sentences, there is a kind of ethnic rhythm without any Yiddishisms." Harnick explained the decision not to use Yiddish words as follows: "I remember seeing so many nightclub comics, including Lenny Bruce, get cheap laughs by throwing in Jewish phrases. So we were careful." Harnick understood the special affective associations that Yiddish had acquired as it became obsolescent for a generation that remembered a time when the language was vital vernacular. He also agreed with Robbins that "even one noticeable accent would destroy the illusion that the characters were all speaking their native tongue."[59]

To prepare for the Broadway production, members of the team drew on their childhood memories, "fieldwork" in Hasidic communities in New York, and library research. Bock wrote the music from what he described as "a conglomerate spiritual feeling" and "instinctive knowledge" based on his childhood memories of Jewish music. Stein also drew on his childhood memories. He had grown up in a Yiddish-speaking family in the Bronx. Robbins and Altman attended Hasidic weddings in New York, including one at "the baroque Ansonia Hotel on Manhattan's upper West Side," because Hasidim "adhered strictly to a kind of tradition, in form and spirit, that Jerry hoped to re-create in *Fiddler*'s wedding sequence." Every time they went to a Hasidic wedding, Altman reported, "we felt as though we had hurtled back through time and been plunked into another world." They observed the costume, the modesty of women, the arranged marriages, and the customs associated with the wedding ceremony—smashing the wine glass, crying out "*Mazl tov,*" and the merrymaking. As Altman explains, "Jerry absorbed all these details and selected from them, without forsaking their validity." Specifically: "One evening, during the entertainment that followed the wedding ceremony, a Jewish comedian did a funny dance while balancing an empty wine bottle on his head. Jerry said nothing about it at the time, but I remembered the rapt smile on his face and his almost hypnotic absorption. The impression obviously remained strong with him, for to climax the exuberant wedding celebration in Act One, he added the relatively brief but intensely exciting "Bottle Dance," during which four male villagers did a spectacular dance with wine bottles balanced precariously on their heads."[60]

The team also looked to the Yiddish theater. "If I Were a Rich Man" was "inspired by a performance the composers had seen at a Hebrew Actors Union benefit held at a theatre on Second Avenue." It reminded them of a "boy-boy-boy" syllabic song they had heard at a Simchas Torah celebration in Williamsburg.[61] In these ways, the team identified religious orthodoxy with tradition and staged tradition as heritage through a theatrical mediation of the ethnographic.

Producers and reviewers alike felt that the slickness of a Broadway production was fundamentally at odds with the simplicity—and ugliness—of Tevye's world. The first task was to make the performers look less like singers and dancers and more like villagers—and specifically, like Anatevkans, which were a species unto themselves. As the production concept coalesced, the virtual village of Anatevka became more "real." Robbins had each actor "write an essay describing the character he played. . . . to heighten their self-awareness and the pride they were to feel at being Anatevkans." For at least one reviewer, they did not entirely succeed: "*Fiddler on the Roof* takes place in Anatevka, a village in Russia, and I think it might be an altogether charming musical if only the people of Anatevka did not pause every now and then to give their regards to Broadway, with remembrances to Herald Square."[62]

While priding themselves on there being "nothing glamorous about *Fiddler on the Roof*," which the team praised as "the opposite of conventional showmanship," they depended on theatrical mediation to aestheticize what Hal Prince, for one, saw as an otherwise alien genre and ugly people—"there is a certain beauty in ugliness when enlightened artists deal with it."[63] Reviewing the musical in the *New York Times*, Brooks Atkinson noted that this "major artistic achievement" makes the "shabby clothes" and "unlovely" environment look "extraordinarily beautiful." This is not Heschel, who looked to inner life for beauty. In *Fiddler,* the surface is Jewish, however attenuated, and the "heart" is the human spirit.

According to Altman, "Inevitably, the screen *Fiddler* became more ethnic than the play," in large part because of how the producers understood the nature of the film medium at the time. Film provided a preternaturally realistic surface, in contrast with the suggestiveness of theater. It was not simply a matter of filming the musical. As Altman explains, "What Jerry Robbins was able to *suggest* on the stage had to be *shown* on the screen. Jerry could be selective, but Norman [Jewison] had to fill the screen with realistic detail. The camera's very literalness was Norman's greatest obstacle in trying to retain those delicate and special qualities that had brought *Fiddler* so beautifully to life on the stage." The Anatevka of the stage could be more suggestive because, "In the theatre it is easier to accept a stylized, unreal atmosphere." Not so in a film that is set in "the real world, with real scenery and real sounds." Because "most films are more realistic than ever," filmmaker Jewison believed that it was "very difficult to use music and poetry and to suspend audiences' disbelief, as *The Wizard of Oz* once did so perfectly." In other words, "We can't have the villagers all lined up, coming down the road, singing 'Tradition.'" If the stage production's suggestive and stylized approach produced a generically ethnographic effect, the film version aimed to make realism evocative by creating "the feeling of a place untouched by time or the twentieth century."[64]

Fiddler on the Roof was shot in Yugoslavia, within thirty miles of Zagreb in the village of Lekenik, which was "built entirely of wood and has a Chagall-like quality in its random design." This set was a veritable ethnographic village, not only by virtue of its intactness but also because of the standards of ethnographic accuracy that guided the construction of the film set. So complete was Lekenik that for it to become Anatevka, "All that had to be built there was Tevye's house, barn and cheese hut, and these were deliberately constructed with tools and material that dated from the turn of the century, so that on film there would be no way to tell the old from the new, the real from the artificial." The part of the story that takes place in Russia was shot in the village of Martinska Ves, which was chosen for its "totally Slavic" architecture. A marketplace and synagogue were constructed in Mala Gorica, and "The clutter of shops and stalls that was fashioned there was so convincingly realistic that one day, at the peak of shooting, a local peasant tried to buy a horse." Preferring "hardy peasant faces evocative of Eastern Europe rather than Central Casting," Jewison used few American actors and depended on local people for extras. Their horses, carts, chickens, and ducks were rented for the film.[65]

Jewison wanted to retain the original conception of *Fiddler,* while using his "Panavision camera to enter the daily lives of Jews in the village, to see the rich, broad expanse of European farmland—how hard the people worked there, how close they were to the earth and to their faith." The Jewishness of this world was as fuzzy as the dream sequence, which was shot through a silk stocking in order to produce warm earth tones and a "feeling of Chagall."[66] The ethnographic effect was concentrated on the surface of the film, as the camera captured "everyday" life, none of it particularly Jewish, in sharp and concrete detail.

Fiddler on the Roof spoke to a suburbanized Jewish public removed from old immigrant neighborhoods and reassured by the existence of a Jewish homeland in Israel, not Europe. *Fiddler* ends by charting all the exits from Tevye's disintegrating world. That world had already been foreclosed by such representations of it. Those representations evince a kind of sincerity that would later seem sentimental, nostalgic, or even kitsch. They stand in sharp contrast to the more recent protocols of Holocaust memory, which are predicated on confrontation, the impossibility of representation, and the centrality of evidence, witnessing, and mourning.

In the course of a century, American Jews have been protected from an ethnography that would racialize them and saved by an ethnography that would make children proud of their parents and inspire American Jewry to continue the spiritual legacy of Eastern Europe. They have been consoled by elegiac invocations of a vanished world and admonished by Abraham Joshua Heschel and *Mad* magazine alike for succumbing to the materialism of American middle-class life in the course of their postwar suburbanization. Through books, expositions, performances, images, and films, American Jews would find in the popular arts of ethnography a way to remember a world that was destroyed. Until they could face the genocide itself more directly, invocations of a lost world would serve as their primary mode of Holocaust memory. More eulogy than document, the popular arts of ethnography of the postwar period exhibit not only an autoethnographic, but also an anti-ethnographic character. Such aesthetically mediated self-portraiture was intended to inspire, more than to inform, for its goal was cultural survival rather than museological preservation.[67]

Fiddler on the Roof brought this mode of Holocaust memory to its apogee during the period when the televised Eichmann trial forced American Jewry to confront the genocide more directly than ever before.[68] In the years that followed, documenting the genocide and remembering its victims would take precedence over the recovery of a lost world. Nonetheless, that world would continue to be the elusive object of modern forms of heritage tourism, pilgrimages to hometowns, and documentary projects to recover through interviews, photography, and film the remaining traces of Jewish life in Eastern Europe.[69]

In recent years, American Jews have also been exporting Europe back to itself, as the success of klezmer music and young American klezmer musicians in Europe attest. With such developments, American Jews are not the only ones producing and performing an imagined Europe. Klezmer music is following a precedent set by *Fiddler on the Roof,* which continues to be performed in Europe and the United States by Jews and non-Jews alike. An instance of the popular arts of ethnography in its own right, klezmer music sounds the sensibility of a new generation as it takes on the challenge of imagining Europe.[70]

NOTES

I thank Jeffrey Shandler for his generosity and expertise. I am grateful to Zachary Baker, formerly the head librarian at the YIVO Institute for Jewish Research and currently at the Stanford University Library, Barbara Gilbert and Grace Grossman of the Skirball Museum, Jenna Weissman Joselit, Kevin Profitt of the American Jewish Archives, and Jennifer Turvey of Schocken Books for answering my queries and bringing material to my attention. This chapter was revised at the Swedish Collegium for Advanced Study in the Social Sciences, Uppsala. My deep appreciation to SCASSS for supporting my spring 1999 residency.

1. Mort Drucker and Frank Jacobs, "Antenna on the Roof," *Mad,* 1:156 (January 1973), 4. This comic strip appeared in the "Fiddler Made a Goof Department" of the magazine.

2. Many of Boas's students were Jews, but they had chosen to study the Winnebago (Paul Radin), Ojibwa (Ruth Landes), and Pueblo Indians (Ruth Bunzel), the Dahomeyans (Melville and Frances Herskovits), and African-Americans (Hortense Powdermaker).

3. *Life Is with People: The Jewish Little-Town of Eastern Europe* (New York, 1952) was retitled *Life Is with People: The Culture of the Shtetl* (New York, 1962) for the paperback edition. The 1995 edition included my new introduction. Maurice Samuel, *The World of Sholom Aleichem* (New York, 1943); Bella Chagall, *Burning Lights,* Norbert Guterman, trans. (New York, 1946); Abraham Joshua Heschel, *The Earth Is the Lord's: The Inner World of the Jew in Eastern Europe* (New York, 1950). On the relationship of *Fiddler on the Roof* to the history of the Sholom Aleichem texts, see Ken Frieden, "A Century in the Life of Sholom Aleichem's *Tevye,*" The B. G. Rudolph Lectures in Judaic Studies, New Series, Lecture One, 1993–1994 (Syracuse, 1997) and Seth L. Wolitz, "The Americanization of Tevye or Boarding the Jewish *Mayflower,*" *American Quarterly* 40 (1988), 514–36.

4. Richard Altman, and Mervyn Kaufman, *The Making of a Musical: Fiddler on the Roof* (New York, 1971), p. 14.

5. Franz Boas, "An Anthropologist's Credo," *The Nation* 147:6 (August 1938), 201–2.

6. Boas, "An Anthropologist's Credo," pp. 202–3.

7. Roland Barthes, "The Third Meaning: Research Notes on Some Eisenstein Stills," *Image, Music, Text,* Stephen Heath, trans. (New York, 1977), 64.

8. Letter from Franz Boas to Leah Rachel Yoffie, Mar. 4, 1920, and Yoffie to Boas, Mar. 29, 1920, in *The Professional Correspondence of Franz Boas,* microfilm edition (Wilmington, DE, 1972).

9. Boas to Yoffie, Mar. 31, 1920. Between 1916 and 1949, Yoffie published five collections of folklore from St. Louis in the *Journal of American Folklore,* which Boas edited from 1908 to 1924. Her first two articles, "Present-Day Survivals of Ancient Jewish Customs," *Journal of American Folklore* 29:113 (1916), 412–17, and "Yiddish Proverbs, Sayings, Etc., in St. Louis, Missouri," *Journal of American Folklore* 33:128 (1920), 134–65, must have caught his attention.

10. Boris D. Bogen, *Born a Jew* (New York, 1930), p. 74.

11. Horace Kallen, "Democracy Versus the Melting Pot," *The Nation*, Feb. 18

and 25, 1915, 190–94, 217–20; Randolph Bourne, "Transnational America," *Atlantic Monthly* 118 (July 1916), 86–97. A summary of Kallen's paper, "The Antithesis of Emancipation," appeared in a report of the conference in *News of the YIVO* 64 (March 1957), 1. On homelands exhibitions see, for example, Ilana Abramovitch, *America's Making Exposition and Festival (New York, 1921): Immigrant Gifts on the Altar of America,* Ph.D. dissertation (New York University, 1996); Allan H. Eaton, *Immigrant Gifts to American Life: Some Experiments in Appreciation of the Contributions of Our Foreign-Born Citizens to American Culture* (New York, 1932); and David Glassberg, *American Historical Pageantry: The Uses of Tradition in the Early Twentieth Century* (Chapel Hill, NC, 1991).

12. Boris D. Bogen, "History of the Exhibit," in *Jews of Many Lands: Exposition Arranged by the Jewish Settlement, January 18 to 26, 1913, Cincinnati, Ohio* (Cincinnati, 1913), p. 6.

13. Editor, "The Month in Brief," *Jewish Charities,* 3:10 (May 1913), 2; Boris D. Bogen, "Jews of Many Lands," *Jewish Charities,* 3:10 (May 1913), 5; Bogen, "History of the Exhibit," p. 6; Bogen, *Born a Jew,* p. 57.

14. George Zepin, "Introductory Words," in *Jews of Many Lands,* p. 3. Bogen repeats these words verbatim in "Jews of Many Lands," p. 10, and in Boris D. Bogen, *Jewish Philanthropy: An Exposition of Principles and Methods of Jewish Social Service in the United States* (New York, 1917), p. 257, which raises the question of whether he or Zepin is their author. Bogen, "Jews of Many Lands," p. 3.

15. "Show Jews' Progress in Exposition," *The Post,* Jan. 20, 1913, p. 1.

16. Bogen, "Jews of Many Lands," *Jewish Charities,* p. 7. "Show Jews' Progress in Exposition." See Steven J. Zipperstein, "Shtetls Here and There," in *Imagining Russian Jewry: Memory, History, Identity* (Seattle, 1999), pp. 16–39. Zipperstein suggests a shift in orientation toward the Old World from predominantly negative in the case of first-generation immigrants to more positive on the part of later generations. The popular arts of ethnography show how immigrants during the first half of the century negotiated conflicting feelings about the places from which they had come.

17. Bogen, "Jews of Many Lands," pp. 3–5.

18. Bogen, *Born a Jew,* p. 79; Bogen, "Jews of Many Lands," p. 6. The numbers vary. In *Jewish Philanthropy,* p. 253, and "Jews of Many Lands," p. 5, Bogen indicates fifty-one organizations. In *Jews of Many Lands,* p. 6, he indicates forty-five organizations. Perhaps additional organizations joined the venture after the program had gone to press. It was the first of the three sources to appear. For a discussion of this event in the context of Jewish participation in world's fairs, see

Barbara Kirshenblatt-Gimblett, "Exhibiting Jews," in *Destination Culture: Tourism, Museums, and Heritage* (Berkeley, 1998), pp. 111–17.

19. "First Notice," Hebrew Union College Broadside Collection, SC 13:1, 3:7, 1904:1 + ? [sic]. Whereas in 1913, Bogen borrowed artifacts from immigrants, in January 1944, YIVO would solicit material from the American Jewish public for a permanent Museum of the Old Homes (*Muzey fun di alte heymen*). Bogen, "Jews of Many Lands," p. 6.

20. The title of this book in 1952 was *Life Is With People: The Jewish Little-Town of Eastern Europe* (New York, 1952). The authors are Mark Zborowski and Elizabeth Herzog. The subtitle was changed to *The Culture of the Shtetl* in 1962, when Schocken published the paperback edition. As of May 1999, the hardcover had sold 12,000 copies and the paperback 119,956 copies. Schocken allowed the book to go out of print in 1998, for the first time in its history. The original publisher, International Universities Press, plans to publish its own paperback edition in 2000.

21. Zborowski and Herzog, *Life Is with People* (1995), p. 409.

22. "Suggested Project on Jewish Culture," submitted by Margaret Mead, Mar. 3, 1949. RG 347, American Jewish Committee Records, Gen-10, 73, Box 211, File: Mass Media, Books, "Life Is with People," Archives of the YIVO Institute for Jewish Research. For the historical context in which the texts considered here were written, see Arthur A. Goren, "The 'Golden Decade' for American Jews: 1945–1955," in Peter Y. Medding, ed., *A New Jewry? America Since the Second World War,* Studies in Contemporary Jewry, 8 (1992), 3–20.

23. This statement appears on the verso page of the B'nai B'rith Hillel Foundations edition, which appeared in May 1943. The foreword by Abram Leon Sachar that appeared in the first edition was dropped from the later paperback edition. It largely repeated what Samuel himself had written in the first chapter of the book.

24. Samuel, *World of Sholom Aleichem,* pp. 3, 5; Sachar, Foreword to *World of Sholom Aleichem,* n.p. Sachar is echoing Samuel's characterization, p. 3.

25. Samuel, *World of Sholom Aleichem,* p. 6.

26. See Alfred Schutz, *The Phenomenology of the Social World,* George Walsh and Frederick Lehnert, trans. (Evanston, IL, 1972). Samuel, *World of Sholom Aleichem,* pp. 3, 6–7. *Middletown,* by Robert S. Lynd and Helen Merrell Lynd (New York, 1929), was an early experiment in studying "an American community as an anthropologist does a primitive tribe," as Clark Wissler characterized this book in his foreword to it. Moshe Dector, "The 'Old Country' Way of Life: The Rediscovery of the Shtetl," *Commentary* 13:6 (1952), 604. For a critique of this

view, see Dan Miron, *Der imazsh fun shtetl: dray literarishe shtudyes* (The Shtetl Image: Three Literary Studies) (Tel Aviv, 1981).

27. See, for example, James Clifford and George Marcus, eds., *Writing Culture: The Poetics and Politics of Ethnography* (Berkeley, 1986).

28. Samuel, *World of Sholom Aleichem,* p. 5.

29. *Brenendike likht* (New York, 1945). Two English translations have appeared: *Burning Lights,* Norman Guterman, trans. (New York, 1946), and *First Encounter,* Barbara Bray, trans. (New York, 1983), which includes additional material. The book has also been translated into French, German, and Hebrew.

30. This phrase appears on the front cover of the first Schocken paperback edition (1962), seventh printing (1974).

31. Chagall, *Burning Lights* (1962), p. 7.

32. Yekheskel Kotik, *Mayne zikhroynes* (Berlin, 1922), 2 vols.; Pauline Wengeroff, *Memoiren einer Grossmutter: Bilder aus der Kulturgeschichte der Juden Russlands im 19. Jahrhundert* (Berlin, 1908–1910); J. Ayalti, "By Sabbath Candlelight," *Commentary* 2 (July–December 1946), 598.

33. Chagall, *Burning Lights* (1962), pp. 9–10.

34. Margaret Mead, Foreword to *Life Is with People,* p. 21. A drawing of a mother blessing the Sabbath candles, one of thirty-six drawings Marc Chagall prepared for Bella Chagall's memoir, made its way to the cover of the paperback edition of *Burning Lights*. The paperback cover of *Life Is with People* also bears an evocation of *Burning Lights*—Marc Chagall's illustration "House in Vitebsk." Bella was born in the Byelorussian city of Vitebsk, and Marc in Liozno, a small town nearby. Like *Burning Lights, Life Is with People* begins, after a short prologue, with a chapter on the Sabbath. During this period, Heschel also published an essay on the Sabbath, both as a separate book, *The Sabbath, Its Meaning for Modern Man* (New York, 1951), illustrated by Ilya Schor, and as an expanded edition of *The Earth Is the Lord's and The Sabbath* (Cleveland, 1963).

35. Deborah Dash Moore, Preface to *East European Jews in Two Worlds: Studies from the* YIVO Annual, ed. Deborah Dash Moore (Evanston, IL, 1990), viii. Moore reprints Heschel's "The Eastern European Era in Jewish History." The talk was published as an essay in Yiddish in *Yivo bleter* 25:2 (1945), in English translation in the *YIVO Annual of Jewish Social Science* 1 (1946), and in an expanded version as *The Earth Is the Lord's: The Inner World of the Jews in Eastern Europe* (New York, 1950), copyrighted in 1949, with illustrations by Ilya Schor. Various forms of this essay/book were also translated from Yiddish or English into other languages. The complicated publication history of this essay is detailed by Jeffrey Shandler, "Heschel and Yiddish: A Struggle with Signification," *Journal of Jewish*

Thought and Philosophy 2 (1993), 245–99. See also Edward K. Kaplan and Samuel H. Dresner, *Abraham Joshua Heschel: Prophetic Witness* (New Haven, CT, 1998), and Edward K. Kaplan, *Holiness in Words: Abraham Joshua Heschel's Poetics of Piety* (West Fulton, NY, 1996)

36. Heschel, *The Earth Is the Lord's,* pp. 42, 92.

37. Heschel, *The Earth Is the Lord's,* pp. 8–9.

38. Heschel, *The Earth Is the Lord's,* pp. 10, 64.

39. Heschel, *The Earth Is the Lord's,* pp. 8, 10.

40. Ruth Benedict, *Patterns of Culture* (New York, 1934); Heschel, *The Earth Is the Lord's,* 7–8.

41. Heschel, "YIVO's Task Now," *News of the YIVO,* 64 (March 1957), 2.

42. Heschel, *The Earth Is the Lord's,* pp. 59, 7–10, 15, 92–93.

43. Heschel, *The Earth Is the Lord's,* pp. 57, 20.

44. Heschel chaired the opening session of the Thirty-First Annual Conference of YIVO. His remarks were summarized as "YIVO's Task Now," *News of the YIVO* 64 (March 1957), 2–3. In Israel, Yom Hashoah became the official day of commemoration in 1951.

45. Back cover of fourth printing, in 1973, of the first Schocken paperback edition of Roman Vishniac, *Polish Jews: A Pictorial Record* (New York, 1965). The book first appeared in 1947. The colophon indicates that "The introductory essay by Dr. Abraham J. Heschel is part of an address delivered at the Nineteenth Conference of the Yiddish Scientific Institute of New York, by whose permission the present version is printed."

46. Arnold Perl's *The World of Sholom Aleichem* (New York, 1953) consists of dramatizations of three Yiddish stories by Sholom Aleichem and I. L. Peretz. The play was released as a motion picture in 1959 and as a sound recording around the same time.

47. This image appears on the seventh printing (1974) of the first Schocken paperback edition (1962) of *Burning Lights*.

48. This image appears on the fifth printing (1967) of the first Schocken paperback edition (1962) of *Life Is with People*. The changing cover art of these books deserves further study.

49. Altman, *Making of a Musical,* pp. 40, 46–47. Aronson, who was born in Russia, had worked in the Yiddish theater before 1935, the year he designed his first Broadway show.

50. Drucker and Jacobs, "Antenna on the Roof," p. 10. It is no accident that this parody appears in the January issue, which takes up Christmas themes in the aftermath of the holiday. When Dad, lying on the psychiatrist's couch, sings "Millions

just like us / Throughout ev'ry state!" to the tune of "Matchmaker, Matchmaker!" he is speaking directly to the "modern Christmas Spirit" (p. 5). Who is the "us"? The American descendants of the people of Anatevka. The back cover of this post-Christmas January issue of *Mad* features a wreath of dollar bills. "The Mad Christmas Hate Book" in this same issue includes a cartoon whose caption reads "DON'T YOU HATE . . . when your class is preparing religious Christmas displays and rehearsing the Christmas Pageant . . . and you're Jewish" (p. 37).

51. See Barbara Kirshenblatt-Gimblett, "Problems in the Early History of Jewish Folkloristics," *Proceedings of the Tenth World Congress of Jewish Studies,* Aug. 16–24, 1989, Division D, Vol. 2, *Art, Folklore, and Music,* David Assaf, ed. (Jerusalem, 1990), 21–32.

52. Raymond Williams, "Structures of Feeling," *Marxism and Literature* (New York, 1977), pp. 132–33. I explore this idea in relation to klezmer music in "Sounds of Sensibility," *Judaism,* issue 185, 47:1 (1998), 49–78.

53. Altman's *Making of a Musical* is a history of the creation of *Fiddler on the Roof.* Altman kept a detailed journal of his observations, just as he had done for *Tenderloin,* another Broadway show. A Ford Foundation grant supported the documentation of *Tenderloin*'s development. See Altman, *Making of a Musical,* p. 26.

54. Sholom Aleichem, *Tevye's Daughters,* Frances Butwin, trans. (New York, n.d.). This edition is copyrighted 1949. While no publication date is indicated, it was probably published around the same time as the deluxe edition, with illustrations by Ben Shahn, in 1965, which was also published by Crown.

55. Altman, *Making of a Musical,* pp. vii, 9, 21–22, 150.

56. Altman, *Making of a Musical,* pp. 31–32, 43.

57. Henry Bial, in "The Men Who Would Be Tevye: Zero Mostel and Topol in *Fiddler on the Roof*" (unpublished essay, 1997), compares the interpretation of Tevye in the stage and film versions of *Fiddler* to show how the coding of Jewishness in the performance itself structures the way different audiences will respond to it. This work points to the need for an analysis of the production that goes beyond its literary sources, script, and score.

58. Altman, *Making of a Musical,* pp. 89–90, 108.

59. Altman, *Making of a Musical,* pp. 39, 118, 140. Nonetheless, Zero broke the rules and "let loose with a stream of Yiddish, under his breath" (p. 118). On the special affective associations acquired by obsolescent languages, among them Yiddish, see Uriel Weinreich, *Languages in Contact: Findings and Problems* (The Hague, 1968), 95.

60. Altman, *Making of a Musical,* pp. 35–36, 64–65, 67–68.

61. Altman, *Making of a Musical,* 100.

62. Altman, *Making of a Musical,* pp. 90–91, 106.

63. Altman, *Making of a Musical,* 111.

64. Altman, *Making of a Musical,* pp. 184, 194–96, 204.

65. Altman, *Making of a Musical,* pp. 199, 196.

66. Altman, *Making of a Musical,* pp. 203–4.

67. Beth Hatefutsoth (Museum of the Diaspora), which was conceptualized in the 1960s and opened in Tel Aviv in the 1970s, had the aura of a Holocaust memorial (and contained within itself such a memorial) from the outset. The diaspora is figured here, in the Israeli context, not only in a museum but as museological. Moreover, this museum made a radical departure from conventional practice by deciding not to collect or exhibit original objects. The diaspora could be exhibited in facsimile. Such an approach would have been unthinkable at the Book of the Shrine, where facsimiles supplement fragments of the original Dead Sea Scrolls but do not supplant them.

68. *Fiddler on the Roof* has gone on to have a life of its own beyond anything envisioned by its creators. Not only is it often performed by amateurs, Jews and non-Jews alike, but also it has become a kind of proof text for church sermons. Ray C. Steadman of Peninsula Bible Church in Palo Alto, California, compares Tevye's struggle with the violation of tradition to the Gospel of Mark and the conflict between the ministry of Jesus and the traditionalism of the Pharisees. This text appeared in the series "The Servant Who Rules" (Scripture: Mark 6:53–7:30, Message: No: 12, Catalog No: 3312, Jan. 26, 1975), *http://www.pbc.org/dp/stedman/mark/3312.html,* last modified June 6, 1997.

69. See for, example, Theo Richmond, *Konin: A Quest* (London, 1995). See also, Jack Kugelmass, "The Rites of the Tribe: The Meaning of Poland for American Jewish Tourists," in *Going Home,* ed. Jack Kugelmass, YIVO *Annual* 21 (1993), 395–453. Though beyond the scope of this essay, the proliferation of memorial books (*yizker-bikher*) during the postwar period should be noted. They are an important example of the popular arts of ethnography and, in particular, of a vernacular autoethnography. See Jack Kugelmass and Jonathan Boyarin, eds., *From a Ruined Garden: The Memorial Books of Polish Jewry* (New York, 1983). The appearance of this volume and such books as Lucjan Dobroszycki and Barbara Kirshenblatt-Gimblett, *Image Before My Eyes: A Photographic History of Jewish Life in Poland* (New York, 1977), is a reaction to the diffuse and sentimentalized ways in which Europe had been imagined by *Life Is with People* and *Fiddler on the Roof,* among others.

70. See *Judaism* issue 185, 47:1 (1998), which is devoted to klezmer music.

EIGHT

The Shoah as Israel's Political Trope

GULIE NE'EMAN ARAD

Locating a place for the Shoah in Israel's national narrative proved complicated and controversial from the beginning.[1] However, only in recent years has the placement and displacement, centrality and marginality, and use and misuse of the Shoah been subjected to critical analysis. Of course there is nothing particularly surprising that a time span of fifty years would yield changes in the ways in which a past event is remembered and understood. Organic lapses in memory, modified self-understanding, new research findings, and the creation of expectations as a result of social and political transformations can alter not only our relationship to a particular past but also our general perspective about a people's position within history. However, for Jews the Shoah has not been perceived as just another event within history. It has been regarded as a cataclysmic watershed, the ultimate rationale for restoration through the founding of a Jewish state.[2]

While a time perspective is essential to analyze changes in perception, especially with regard to a formative event, the shift in direction can readily be discerned. Yet, because periods of transition, however alluring for historians, are extremely difficult to decipher, great caution must be exercised to avoid the inclination to emphasize the elements of "change" and attenuate the forces of the "continuum." Indeed, it is not my intention here to claim or infer that the Shoah as a national-ideological trope has become peripheral to Israel's collective consciousness, that its rhetoric is no longer deployed, or that the trauma has lost its hold on the popular imagination. Rather, it is my contention that a cross section of Israeli citizenry contests the perception of the Shoah as a vital organ in Israel's body politic and as a salient component of its collective self-understanding.

Far from spontaneous, the evolution of collective memory is mostly orchestrated from above. We remember and/or forget largely because we are driven by those who have the power and interest to have us remember a certain past in a particular way. The resulting hegemonic narrative reflects a unity between the elite and the ideas that legitimate its rule. Thus official remembrance reflects political designs that are subjected to pressures as a result of changed political circumstances. At critical junctures contesting memories are likely to emerge and challenge the previously hegemonic version of the past.[3]

Within these parameters this chapter sets out to examine the application of the Shoah as a political trope in Israeli society. It proposes to show how this past has been both recruited and discharged to confirm and deny various rights and responsibilities of the state and how initial indifference to the Shoah evolved into an obsession. The chapter further proposes to examine the manifestations and results of such a fixation and its potential impact on the kind of society Israel will become.

In 1947 Abba Kovner, poet and legendary leader of the Vilna ghetto's underground and one of the leading architects of Israel's remembrance of the Shoah, said: "To remember everything is madness, but to forget is a betrayal."[4] In the immediate postwar period most Jews the world over agreed that keeping this trauma alive is dangerous. Only a minority regarded forgetting as treachery. In Palestine as well, neither Zionists nor recently arrived survivors saw much sense in keeping the quintessential negative Jewish experience alive.

In a community that aspired above all to gain independence, the memory of the millions who went to their death like "sheep to the slaughter" was largely disclaimed as an ideological liability. There was no space in the public sphere to house the existential-personal ordeals of the victims, whose experiences were at best kept at a distance if not entirely removed from everyday life. For their part, the surviving remnants eager to start a new life were not proud of their recent past. In their hope to gain acceptance, these emotionally fragile people agreed to plow the past under and treat it as a "foreign country." Indeed, disremembering was considered as the only "healthy" option. As the writer Aharon Appelfeld, himself a survivor, recalls: "The first years in Israel were years of repression, denial, and the construction of a personality without a trace of what you went through and who you were. . . . The inner world was as if it did not exist. It shrunk and sunk into deep sleep. . . . Whoever survived and came here brought with him much silence. It was tacitly accepted not to speak about certain matters and not to touch certain wounds."[5]

Yet the legendary heroism of the ghetto fighters was recruited to serve as a role model for young Palestinian Jews to emulate while sacrificing their lives in the struggle for an independent Jewish state. It is true that heroes of the uprisings were identified as zealous Zionists, but they were not entirely free of the negative stigma associated with being diaspora Jews. Hence, it was somewhat ironic that during the 1948 War of Independence the military chief appropriated their exilic experience to mobilize his own troops. On the occasion of the fifth anniversary of the Warsaw ghetto uprising he issued an order of the day which read in part: "the victory in the Ghetto is the victory of the Jewish people—to die honorably, weapons in hands—and not be led like sheep to slaughter. Let those Ghetto fighters be example to us in our present struggle."[6]

In line with the Zionist's activist self-image, the emerging new state carefully embraced only the "heroic" version of the Shoah. The heroic epics of the ideologically accredited few were recovered and integrated into the redemptive narrative of the new state. The powerlessness and vulnerability of the Jewish victims, on the other hand, served as a heuristic device to prove the "negation of the Diaspora" and confirm the validity of the Zionist prognosis that Israel is the only solution to the so-called Jewish problem. As such the archetypal negative consequence of dispersion, as defined by the Zionist doctrine, unified the ingathering of the Jews in an independent Israel.[7]

The selective use of the Shoah by the state reflected the ideology of *mamlakhtiut* (statism) — denoting the principle that state interests receive priority. With regard to the Shoah this intention became clearly visible in the early 1950s during the Knesset's deliberations on the Holocaust and Heroism Remembrance Law. According to the state's agenda two objectives were to be achieved by including this past in the national pantheon: it would preclude the emergence of memory adverse to the state's interest, and crown the State of Israel as the supreme sovereign of the Jewish people, dead and alive.[8]

Minister of Education and Culture Ben-Zion Dinur articulated these aims most succinctly when during the Knesset's discussions on the establishment of Yad Vashem he insisted that the state-sponsored remembrance authority ought to "combine all the existing (memorial) institutions in Israel, to guide them and unite them." Dinur's concern that contesting memories emanating from both the extreme right and left would gain legitimization became evident when he argued against the phenomenon of multiple institutions, decentralization, and separation. To avoid it, he stressed the necessity of including all commemoration efforts under one central body supervised by the state. Such hegemony was justified because the state was pronounced the supreme sovereign of the Jewish people and "the only heir" to the victims of the Shoah.[9] How to commemorate the Shoah did not arouse much interest among the Israeli public. As some Knesset members complained prior to the hearing on the Law of Holocaust and Heroism Remembrance — Yad Vashem, when none of the ministers were present, the Knesset did not find "one single hour" in all of five years to discuss the Shoah.[10]

The difficulties in working through a trauma of such unprecedented proportions and the fear that it might become an obstacle in creating a "normal" national identity had encouraged a closely controlled search for closure. If the commemoration of the event was entrusted to the legislative branch, reckoning with its historical actors was consigned to the judiciary. Indeed, just as the war allies and the enemy (Germany) had turned to the judicial system for a clean bill of health for their respective societies, so, too, did Israel. Staffed by seemingly apolitical professionals who are bound by laws of procedure, the judiciary has been perceived as the most functional and efficient system by which to settle moral-historical issues. But in Israel, unlike everywhere else, it was the victims, not the perpetrators, who were to have their day in court.

The reception extended to the survivors was tinted with the hue of the national ethos. Hence, for the most part they were objectified and framed within a "guilt discourse." Such an environment helped create a dichotomous portrayal of the survivors. They were depicted as either "ordinary" or "heroic," dishonorable or sacred, guilty or innocent. The attitude of Israeli society toward the survivors was to a large extent shaped by the implementation of the Law for the Punishment of Nazis and Their Collaborators.[11]

When the law was introduced to the Knesset in 1950, the prime aim was not to bring to trial Nazi criminals. As Justice Minister Pinkhas Rosen explained, "It may be presumed that Nazi criminals who have been convicted of those crimes discussed by this law will not dare to come to Israel." Rather this judicial procedure was designed to deal primarily with "crimes committed by the Nazis' subordinates," since Israel "unfortunately, cannot be sure that such persons are not found within our ranks." The purported suspects were the Jewish victims who served in the Jewish police, the *Judenrat,* or as *Kapos* in the Nazi death camps and allegedly mistreated other Jews.

The call for such legislation presumably came from below. Complaints and charges that survivors brought against other survivors could not be settled within the framework of the existing laws. The Knesset was quick to meet the demand for suitable legislation. Although it was intended "to punish the guilty and exonerate the innocent," in the righteous climate of the 1950s guilty and innocent were not pure legal categories, they were heavily invested with ideology. As Rosen made clear, the law also aimed to purge the Zionist camp of what was considered dishonorable Jewish conduct. Especially for the victims of Nazi persecutions it was not a simple matter to include in a single category both "a Jewish Kapo, even if he has beaten other prisoners and a Nazi, both of whom had been in Auschwitz." However, to differentiate between Jewish and non-Jewish blood was totally unacceptable in legal terms. After some fierce debate a compromise was reached: the same criminal responsibility would apply to the persecuted and the persecutor, but in sentencing for the same crime a distinction between the two would be made.[12]

The subcommittee deliberations on the Law for the Punishment of Nazis and Their Collaborators reveal how legal principles and political interests were intermixed. The main and fiercest speaker, Michael Bar-Yehudah of Mapam, focused on the moral aspects of collaboration when he argued "against freeing such a person [a collaborator] since he did what he did out of cowardice." Moreover, he insisted "that every member of the Judenrat who was not actually forced to join was a criminal, and that [in doing what he did] he helped the Nazis, by playing on that basic bestiality, inherent in every man—of saving his own life." But Bar-Yehudah, who closely identified with the Jewish resistance movement, suggested an amendment to the law to absolve of criminal responsibility those who had committed such acts under the order of the resistance.[13]

Contrary to popular collective memory, Israeli society of the 1950s first confronted the Shoah by focusing on the "disreputable" behavior of the victims and not by attending to the crimes of perpetrators. Around forty cases of Jewish functionaries in Nazi-occupied Europe were tried under the Law for the Punishment of Nazis and Their Collaborators. None attracted much public interest or media coverage, except one. This was the "Kasztner trial."[14]

The affair began as a libel suit brought against one Malkiel Gruenwald, who had charged in a defamatory pamphlet that Rudolph Israel Kasztner had collaborated with the Nazis in Hungary and sacrificed the local Jewish community to gain safety for his relatives and friends. As an active member of the Ha-Mizrahi (a religious wing of the Zionist movement), Gruenwald was not politically innocent, since Kasztner, who headed the Zionist Rescue Committee in Budapest, was closely identified with the ruling MAPAI Party. He joined the party when he came to Israel after the war and shortly after his arrival was appointed spokesman for the Ministry of Trade and Industry, not least because of his MAPAI connections. At this point Gruenwald made his accusations public. His intentions were not at all hidden. He had hoped that by recovering Kasztner's past during the war he would embarrass MAPAI, force Kasztner to resign from his new job, and mobilize public opinion to establish a committee of inquiry that would investigate the fate of Hungary's Jews. His achievements, so it seems, far exceeded his expectations. MAPAI, sensing correctly a potential political scandal, moved to preempt it. None other than the attorney general urged Kasztner to sue Gruenwald for libel or be forced to resign from his government job. Kasztner complied and sued. The affair turned into a protracted four-year case: the trial in 1954, in which the plaintiff became the defendant; Kasztner's guilty verdict in spring 1955; his assassination in 1957; and in 1958 the Supreme Court ruling which overturned the lower court's decision. The impact of the trial has not faded to this day.[15]

Seeking the source for the murderous consciousness that ended in Kasztner's assassination, author Moshe Shamir located it in the Israelis' sense of entitlement "to judge the survivors of the Shoah and to divide them into heroes and traitors." Although this is an extreme formulation, it appears to hold much truth. Such attitudes, it seems, exemplified the closely linked insecurity and callousness that prevailed in Israeli society during the critical period of nation building. Empathy for the victims was considered almost anathema for the 1948 generation that chose to embrace a heroic self-image, not least in order to ensure an absolute separation between the cowardly "them" and the courageous "us."[16]

There was hardly any space for the past of the "cowardly" victims in the social domain. But in the political sphere their misery was put to use. Tinkering with their memories and fine-tuning their reality, the Zionists depicted the victims' plight as a negation of core Zionist values and experiences. The memory of the Shoah was meant to serve as an ideological vaccine for Israel's body politic.

Moreover, under the reductionist code of the "six million," the Shoah was used as leverage for persuading the nations of the world of their unrecoverable moral debt to the Jewish people. Before long this ideologically unacceptable past was appropriated for realizing the nation's political and economic agendas. The moral debt was soon settled by a unique financial agreement that Germany bizarrely named "*Wiedergutmachung*." For David Ben-Gurion, negotiating with Germany was a national responsibility that transcended any moral considerations. Having "Zionized" a postmortem of all the victims, he reasoned that "had the six million not been murdered, they would have served as the chief instrument of rebuilding the state and we would have gained five or six million Jews for the State of Israel." Hence, he reasoned that building up the country was "the only memorial fitting to commemorate the exterminated European Jewry," and if the realization of this goal meant ties with Germany, "we'll do it."[17]

The Reparations Agreement between the German Federal Republic and the State of Israel was signed in September 1952, much before Israeli society was willing or able to work through the human dimensions of the Shoah and its universal implications. The fervent debates on the financial settlement and Israel's future relationship with Germany during the early 1950s reflected the political and ideological dissension between the left and the right. For the Herut Party under Menachem Begin's leadership, hating the Germans and boycotting Germany was a value-laden normative stand in its struggle against MAPAI's rule and in preserving the lessons and memory of the Shoah. "Approved" survivors, such as the ghetto fighters, shared these sentiments. It was one thing for the survivors to wish to suppress their private pain, but on a collective level negotiating with Germany was for them proof that the Jew "has no national memory or dignity to speak of." Jews, they lamented, "can be bought for next to nothing." Among the surviving victims it was strongly felt that the state had a moral obligation not to bargain over their past.[18]

In comparison with Herut, MAPAI's historical orientation was more ambivalent. While basing the need for a Jewish state on the Catastrophe, it wished at the same time to eliminate the Diaspora experience from Jewish consciousness. Reflecting on the heated reparations debate, Ben-Gurion castigated those who "cling stubbornly to the emotions of the past. They cannot perceive the transformations that take place . . . and recognize new relationships and new needs." While he did not deny that there were differences between nations, he based his views not only on memories of "the situation of their Jewish communities, but also on account of the national needs of the State of Israel." Ben-Gurion was not nostalgic for any aspect of the exilic past: "I ran away from the national dignity of the ghetto when I was nineteen," he said, "and you won't bring me back there."[19]

Nowhere were these stands of Ben-Gurion more clearly manifested than in his attitude toward the Eichmann trial. This meticulously staged production was intended as the ultimate historical proof that Zionism, as embodied in the Jewish State, was the only solution to the problems of the Jews. The trial would affirm Israel's strength and sovereignty, and crown the Jewish State as the sole legitimate representative of the Jewish people and as the exclusive heir of their victims. As Gideon Hausner, Israel's attorney general, who also served as the chief prosecutor, revealed, the trial aimed to establish "the correct historical perspective." In trying to meet this non-juristic objective witnesses were repeatedly subjected to the senseless rhetorical question: "Why didn't you resist?" In the Zionist courtroom in Jerusalem there could be only one acceptable answer: the Jews were powerless because they lacked political independence. Indeed, only after the Jews established a strong state of their own were they able to effect "Operation Final Solution to the Eichmann Problem," as the insensitive headline of one evening newspaper chose to report his execution.[20]

Opening in Jerusalem in April 1961, the trial was designed to reflect Israel's official attitude toward the Shoah, and Hausner prepared his opening speech with that aim in mind. He sent Ben-Gurion the draft for review and comments, a rather unusual step if the trial had been strictly a legal procedure. Ben-Gurion attended only to the first part of the text, for as he later noted, the other sections seemed to have had no "special political significance." Indeed, as evidenced by the three corrections that Ben-Gurion requested, he was less concerned with the history than with the political impact that such a trial would have on Israel's relations with West Germany. "Every time reference is made to the crimes of 'the German,'" he suggested, "it should, in my opinion, say 'Nazi Germany.'" He further advised forgoing the argument that Nazism was inevitable, claiming that it would provide a "pseudo-scientific excuse" for the Nazi regime that would weaken the case of the prosecution. He also feared that such a deterministic argument would open a debate, "not necessary for our purpose," on the German character and whether there could ever be "a different Germany." Hausner deleted this paragraph. The third change that the prime minister recommended was to underscore Hitler's guilt, perhaps thereby releasing Germany from the "collective guilt" charge. In his opinion "Adolf Hitler should be given precedence over Adolf Eichmann, even though Eichmann is the defendant." Hence, he instructed Hausner "to mention first the main and central factor, Hitler, and only then Eichmann."[21]

Notwithstanding the efforts to appropriate the Shoah for ideological ends, the testimonies of the carefully chosen witnesses seem to have produced a most "undesirable" result. The life stories of the "cowardly" victims who had managed to survive, their daily encounters with isolation, terror, starvation, and death, touched the minds and souls of the "heroic Israelis." Indeed, following the trial armed resistance was no longer perceived the only act of bravery; the mere tenacity to survive another day under Nazi rule came to be appreciated as an act of great fortitude. This is not to say that stereotypes quickly dissipated: the "shame" of having "merely" survived lingered on among survivors. Yet, particularly among Israel's younger generation, the tragic accounts of the survivors, while reinforcing the conviction that a strong Israel was needed, also generated much anxiety which translated into increased sympathy for the victims of the Shoah. Hence, whereas the Eichmann trial was designed as a national undertaking that aimed at earning the right to collective closure of the Shoah, it seems to have produced the opposite effect. For the next twenty-five years Israel became deeply preoccupied if not obsessed with this past.[22]

The images of the Shoah, which Israeli society so zealously wished to eradicate from its future and for which it found so little use during the 1950s and early 1960s, were never as widely deployed as during the three-week "waiting period" before the Six-Day War. During these weeks recovered memories of the Jews' passive and powerless experience during the Shoah were summoned to legitimize the demands for "war now" and a "strong man" to lead the nation to victory. Suggestions that were made to try to settle the crisis by diplomatic means were compared to Munich. Nasser was the new Hitler, and Israel was not about to become another Czechoslovakia. At issue, as one columnist wrote in *Haaretz,* was "the existence or nonexistence of the Jewish people. We must crush the scheme of the new Hitler at the outset, when it is still possible to demolish them and survive. It is irresponsible folly not to believe what Nasser has been writing and saying for the last twelve years." The message of many news articles was "Never consider such rhetoric as merely that."[23]

"Conventional" dangers, so it seems, were deemed inadequate to enlist Israelis to mobilize in response to the crisis. There was hardly any talk about the dangers that Israel might be conquered and destroyed, or its inhabitants killed by the Arab armies. Rather, the Arabs were transformed into Nazis who were ready to "exterminate Israel." As proof, one newspaper compiled a list where it compared threats made by Hitler and by Nasser. One such equivalence was drawn between Nasser's threat in 1967 that "If Israel wants war—fine: Israel will be destroyed!" and Hitler's warning in 1939 that "If the Jews drag the world into war, world Jewry will be destroyed."[24]

Psychologically, most Israelis accepted the threat of annihilation in 1967 as real. Almost overnight they adopted a vicarious victims' mentality, not least the fighters who won the war. Reflecting shortly after the war, one young soldier recalled that he and the troops in his company "believed we would be exterminated if we lost the war. We got this idea—or inherited it—from the concentration camps. It's a concrete idea for anyone who had grown up in Israel, even if he personally didn't experience Hitler's persecution. Genocide—it's a real possibility. . . . That's the lesson of the gas chambers."[25]

Although in six days the threat of "extermination" was dispelled as not real, the angst generated became a permanent fixture in Israel's politics. One source for this irrational—however authentic—fear can be traced back to an indigenous ideological paradox that permeates Israel's attitude toward the Shoah. If on the one hand the Jewish state was viewed as the only way to eliminate the anxiety of exilic existence as epitomized by the Shoah, on the other hand Israel continuously invoked the catastrophe ideologically and psychologically. The destruction of European Jewry has mobilized such diverse interests as the legitimation of Israel's establishment, the need to go to war, the necessity to occupy territories and people, and the justification of caution in embarking on the road to peace.[26] Reality complicated matters even more; because Israel could not offer physical security, it lost much of its edge over life in the Diaspora.

In order to be effective, the destruction of European Jewry could not be turned into history; it had to be kept alive. Indeed, especially since the Six-Day War, meeting future challenges was linked to the collective understanding of the lesson of the Shoah. In total negation of one of Zionism's major doctrines such a calamity was adopted as a permanent possibility. The notion that "It could happen again" and that Israel must be strong enough at all times to strike back and win, or else, constituted a major shift in its self-understanding. This mind-set is closely linked to the "never again" doctrine, which Israel chose to communicate as the prime lesson of the Shoah. Framed as a historical-moral obligation, "never again" explained why Israel could not return to its pre-war 1967 borders, which former Prime Minister Yitzhak Shamir dubbed the "Auschwitz border"; why it must expand its military capabilities; why it could trust only itself.[27]

As some feared, the national drama of the Eichmann trial encouraged popular hubris among Israelis. It fostered "a victim mentality, a sense of self-righteousness and excessive nationalism" which helped weaken the already shaky universal basis of Israel's political culture. This mood was expressed in a commemoration address delivered in 1969 by one of the heroes of the 1948 war, the then deputy prime minister and minister of education Yigal Allon. "We have decided not to be apologetic about our existence," Allon said. Now, after the victory in the 1967 war, he argued, the Jewish people could determine their own destiny and nobody would be entitled to teach them about morality. Israel, he concluded, was free to decide what is needed for its security and how to reach a settlement with its Arab neighbors.[28]

While on the one hand victory in the field was quickly translated into imprudent political arrogance, on the other hand Israel was also criticized for its new role as an occupation force. The feeling of increasing isolation and the subjection to a number of terrorist attacks such as airplane hijackings and the massacre of the Israeli athletes during the Olympic Games — in Munich, no less — fostered a growing empathy for the plight of Jews under Nazi domination. The confidence of many Israelis that their country was the only true safe haven for Jews was shaken. Yet, the fact that this sense of insecurity was linked to the unresolved Arab-Israeli conflict went unacknowledged. For the most part the Palestinian problem continued to be disregarded or at best was reified by both the government and the shapers of public opinion, while the Jewish problem was concretized with images of the powerless past. Indeed, during the period following the Six-Day War the Shoah acquired status as a national asset. It was used as a permanent reminder to the nations of the world of their unpaid and overdue moral debt, and to justify any and all of Israel's actions and policies regardless of their moral or political fairness.

Following the Yom Kippur War in 1973 such attitudes became much more deeply entrenched. To work through its difficult problems—among them, the threat of war, sanctions, boycotts, and condemnation by the international community—Israel repeatedly rehearsed the Nazi past, anti-Semitism, and the world's abandonment of the Jews. This appeared particularly in the debates about the future of the occupied territories. No longer confined to the past, the Shoah became part of Israel's present and future. As Golda Meir said on Holocaust Remembrance Day in 1976, "The Shoah, which was aimed at the individual Jew, became a collective Shoah directed against the state of Israel." On the same occasion another speaker asked the world to "atone for its moral apathy" during the Shoah and feel obliged "to stand constantly at Israel's side by rendering political, military and economic aid." Some years later none other than Shimon Peres declared the Shoah to be a "national lesson." Central to this lesson was the belief that "the whole world is against us." And as such, as Peres insisted, "We must not rely on others. . . . Our fate depends on the Jews."[29]

However, in order for the Shoah to be admissible as a Zionist national lesson, its "dishonorable" repute had to be tempered. This could be achieved by sanctifying the previously disreputable victims as *kedoshim* (martyrs) and consecrating all the survivors as *giborim* (heroes). Indeed, they were embraced in their transfigured status as role models for meeting Israel's future challenges. "If you wish to know the source from which the Israeli army draws its power and strength," the Israeli defense forces chief of staff, General Mordechai Gur, told an audience in Yad Vashem in 1976, "go to the holy martyrs of the Holocaust and the heroes of the revolt."[30] Following the trauma of the 1973 war, the Shoah's badge of timidity was exchanged for a badge of courage. In its revised version, the Catastrophe increasingly gained acceptance.

The Yom Kippur War was won in the battlefield, but Israeli society is still struggling with its ramifications. Following this earthquake an inward journey could not be avoided, because little of what was had remained the same. The war had destroyed the myth of Israel's invulnerability, and as a result the military lost its position as a quasi-sacred institution. Terrorist activities compromised the sense of national and personal security. The 1975 United Nations resolution (passed on the anniversary of Kristallnacht), which defined Zionism as "a form of racism and racial discrimination," was a bruise not easily healed. Since the 1973 war the notion of patriotism as an unqualified readiness to die in war was redefined to mean a willingness to take a risk for peace, and following the 1982 war in Lebanon the belief that Israel engages only in just wars was seriously questioned. Concurrently many of Israel's most time-honored assumptions have begun to be challenged by generations for which neither the Shoah nor the birth of the state constituted "living memories."[31] Feeling liberated from some of the burdensome "isms," the younger generation have questioned whether a Jewish state is the only solution to the "Jewish problem," the Jews' victimized past is a sound dictum for Israel's future definition, and Israel rightfully deserves moral discount when her conduct is considered because of the Shoah.

This self-probing process articulated a growing political and social rift that had been dividing Israeli society since the Six-Day War. It found ultimate expression in the right-wing nationalist Likud victory in 1977, which ended the secular Labor Ashkenazi hegemony.[32] The new prime minister, Menachem Begin, who for many years had been the invincible pariah of Israeli politics, pledged to bring about unity of "*Am yisrael*" (the people of Israel). He tried to make his promise good by restructuring Israeli identity around the lessons of the Shoah. However, for the new members of the political elite—the Mizrachim (Jews who had come from Arab countries) and the Orthodox—the centrality of this event in its Eurocentric Zionist interpretation was largely responsible for making them feel like outsiders in Israeli society. Rather understandably these groups desired a national narrative that would express their own heritage and view of history. Indeed, the ethnic and cultural diversity that gained recognition following the 1977 election results could no longer be contained and subsumed under the previous Zionist model. As a result, alternative narratives contested the meanings of Israel's central pillars of identity—Zionism, Judaism, and the Shoah. The Shoah, especially, has become a major weapon in current battles that engage Israeli society, and the war with Lebanon has brought the politicization of the event to new heights.[33]

Informing his cabinet of the upcoming invasion of Lebanon, Begin presented the options in genocidal terms. Everything was done to prevent war, he told his ministers, "but such is our fate in Israel . . . to fight selflessly. Believe me, the alternative is Treblinka, and we have decided that there will be no more Treblinkas." For Begin, sending Israeli soldiers to destroy Arafat's headquarters in Beirut was, as he wrote to President Reagan, as if he were dispatching them to destroy Hitler's bunker in Berlin. And when the international community began to voice criticism of Israel's war operations, Begin resorted to Israel's standard explanation. "No one," he told the Knesset, "anywhere in the world, can preach morality to our people."[34]

But this was neither 1967 nor 1973. A new generation no longer accepted that the Jews' tragic past rendered Israel's present behavior beyond reproach. For the first time wide segments in Israeli society denounced the appropriation of the Shoah to justify war. "Hitler is already dead, Mr. Prime Minister," author Amos Oz wrote in response to Begin's "rationale" for bombing Beirut. The nonconsensual war in Lebanon and some fifteen years as occupiers among the Palestinian people persuaded many that Israel could not be a "light unto the nations," that indeed it might be casting a dark shadow on its own future. Israelis evinced a growing readiness "to replace the power-oriented message" of the Shoah "with a more humanistic one." There also appeared an apparent disparaging attitude toward symbols and expressions of national heroism based on military strength alone.[35]

Beyond the immediate historical contingencies, Begin's extreme instrumentalization of the Shoah as a political trope for goading a nationalistic and victim-like mentality seems to have stimulated his political adversaries to challenge the significance of the Shoah as a central element in the forging of Israel's national identity. A growing perception of an obsessive need to keep the raw wound open, to "reproduce" the tragedy emotionally and politically and utilize it for political ends, has generated a reaction which, as Amos Elon has put it, calls "to cure the wound instead of only administering to it."[36]

One way to heal the wound was suggested by the well-known public intellectual Boaz Evron. In a 1980 article entitled "The Holocaust: A Danger to the Nation," Evron presented a moral-ideological critique on the "uniqueness of the Shoah" paradigm and its effect on the future of Israel.

"Since the world is always presented as hating and persecuting us," he wrote, "we see ourselves free of the need for any moral considerations in our attitude toward the world." He further warned that adhering to a self-definition of the "chosen people" who "dwell alone" may, when backed by sufficient power, promote among some Jews a mentality that non-Jews were subhuman and, for all intents and purposes, emulate the racist ideas of the Nazis.[37] Young Israelis who grew up believing they were members of the tribe of Goliath were receptive to such criticisms. With the costly fiasco in Lebanon it became all the more difficult for them to understand why the state that was established in order to efface the Jews' abnormal exilic existence kept clinging to the Shoah as the epitome of aberration, as a focus of its national life.

Without much time to reflect upon the moral crisis engendered by the war in Lebanon, the next generation was called to perform yet another controversial task of subduing the Palestinian Intifada. Watching daily on television how the historical victims were being transformed into victimizers and how their society's moral fabric was unraveling before their eyes shocked a public that had been taught to believe their righteousness was unimpeachable. One of the most powerful responses came from none other than a Holocaust survivor. Four months into the Intifada, Yehuda Elkana published a call for "The Need to Forget." A philosophy professor who was ten years old when he was taken to Auschwitz, Elkana argued that what happened in Germany can happen anywhere, "with any people, including my own." His plea occurred in the wake of a noticeable rise in press reports of "excesses" committed by Israeli soldiers against Palestinians. According to him such brutalities were motivated by a "profound existential 'Angst' fed by a particular interpretation of the lessons of the Shoah, and the readiness to believe that the whole world is against us, and we are its eternal victims." He urged Israelis to "displace the Shoah from being a central axis of our national experience." Basing the understanding of human existence on the Shoah was in his view "disastrous."[38]

Elkana was not "overlooking the historical importance of collective memory," but he questioned the wisdom of a nation that "determines its attitude to the present and shapes its future by emphasizing the lessons of the past." The late Prime Minister Yitzhak Rabin recognized that "holocaustal"-based anxieties could have political ramifications, especially with regard to the peace process. In a policy statement made in the Knesset on future peace talks with Syria, Rabin delivered a preemptive strike against the opposition. Israel, he made clear, "will not return to the days of 'there is no one to talk to,' we will not return to the days of 'we are waiting for a phone call,' we will not return to the days of 'the world is against us.' . . . We will not return to those days. We are going forward."[39]

Shulamit Aloni, then the minister of communication, science and the arts, had sounded an alert that Israel's perception of reality was distorted by the traumas of the past. On the occasion of the Israel Prize ceremony on Independence Day 1996, she declared, "The world has changed; our place among the nations of the world is secure and stable. The struggle for physical survival is over. Only people with anachronistic mind-sets are still scaring us with fears of the past, referring to an insane terrorist act as an existential threat, and are still seizing the sensations of victimization and persecution, preaching for isolation and worshipping divine-egoism and power."[40]

Aloni's plea to abandon the "holocaustal" mind-set has not gained many converts. Many Israelis cannot accept the idea that they must see themselves as a normal nation rather than as the moral inheritors of the Shoah and thus forgo the political self-righteousness they arrogated to Israel. This is especially the case among the nationalist zealots who are fighting their last round for a "greater Israel." But the appropriation of the Shoah is not limited to the specific political agendas of the Right. At a time when Zionism, socialism, and Jewish consciousness have been losing their efficacy as agents of cohesion in Israeli society, the Shoah has been discovered as a useful past to scare the younger generation back to their Jewish roots. Annually, thousands of high school students (in recent years close to 12,000) are taken on a pilgrimage to Europe's death camps. Interestingly, the kibbutz movement first deployed the Shoah as a weapon in its depleted ideological arsenal. Educators were pleased with the results, because the youths, on the eve of starting their military service, returned with such Zionist insights as "In Poland I understood the importance of the State of Israel," "Now I am certain I will never leave Israel." Since 1988 the Labor government's Ministry of Education and Culture has taken charge of organizing these identity-boosting trips. Rather ironically, the Zionist state is sending its sons and daughters to reinforce their Jewish identity to the same memorial locations that had been rejected by the founders of modern Israel. The nationalistic mind-sets that these programs aroused received much criticism even within the Ministry of Education. There have been some attempts to revise and expand the educational objectives of these tours to depict Poland not only as the largest graveyard of the Jewish people, but also as the home of a rich Jewish culture. Yet, for most the Shoah serves to evoke a sense of national commitment and buttress a Zionist Israeli identity.[41]

To that end a new tradition was established in 1992, when Ehud Barak, then chief of staff of the Israeli Defense Forces, was the first to head a delegation of soldiers and officers to Auschwitz. The visit was staged as a redemptive play. There was the national flag, the national anthem, and the traditional Kaddish prayer. At the opening to the crematorium, after saluting the ashes of the dead, Barak delivered the Zionist redemptive oratory. "We the soldiers of the IDF [read: of Zionism]," he opened, "arrived here fifty years later, perhaps fifty years too late." He continued: "My brothers, sons of the Jewish people, forty-seven years ago the fire in these crematoriums were put out, and three years later a Jewish state was born. A straight line extends from these death fields to the revival of Israel in its historical homeland. . . . For the State of Israel the IDF is the symbol of our promise and vow that what happened here will never happen again. Zahal's might is the only real life guarantee to the pledge: Auschwitz Never Again!"[42]

On the eve of the Shoah Day of Remembrance in 1998, the general staff held a special meeting in Yad Vashem. Afterward, the chief of staff Amnon Shahak said: "We need from time to time to fill up the batteries. We all came out of here a little bit stronger." A few days later IDF cadets led "The March of the Living" between Auschwitz and Birkenau. At the end of the march Prime Minister Netanyahu said: "Look at these wonderful soldiers of the IDF. They represent the Jewish peoples' army. This is the lesson of the Shoah: the existence and revival of the Jewish people depend on a Jewish army and Jewish sovereignty, and are strengthened by Jewish belief." General (Ret.) Yossi Ben-Hanan, who had accompanied the prime minister, stated that if he had a say he would very much want to see every Israeli student visit those sites. He further suggested that from time to time "the swearing in ceremony of the IDF's elite units should take place in Majdanek or Birkenau." Such an act in the place where Jewish existence had been most in jeopardy, he explained, would express the sincerity of Israelis' commitment to defend the Jewish people.[43]

The Shoah Day of Remembrance has turned into a media event reminding one of the close connection that can exist between kitsch and death. For some time, every prime minister has made a photo opportunity pilgrimage to Auschwitz. There, before the world media, Israel's leaders perform the annual ritual of vowing to remain strong, and promise that what happened there will not happen in Israel. This, they declare, is indeed a supreme responsibility of all political leaders everywhere. Regarding the Jews, the responsibility is double-edged: Jews should never again become victims but they should also never become victimizers. This is not a simple promise to fulfill, especially for a state that has only recently acquired political independence and great military might and still lives amid unresolved conflict with its neighbors. Indeed, those who are concerned with the humanistic lessons of genocide should be wary of Jewish nationalism based on the Shoah. Such a collective self-definition could transform into Jewish fascism, which is as dangerous as anti-Semitism and just as destructive of the memory of the Shoah and its victims.

The Shoah can be viewed as peripheral to the internal war raging within Israeli society. But whether Israel will become a civil democratic society of all its citizens or remain an ethnic Jewish state will depend in great measure on how it works through this dark chapter in human history. Indeed, a closer look reveals that because of the Shoah's primacy in the state's ideology and culture, it has been a significant weapon in this conflict. Hence, whether the humanistic or the militaristic lessons of the Shoah have a greater impact on Israel will be decisive in affecting its future. Because this internal conflict is far from being resolved, all sides are doing their best to improve their position. The results extend from the reinvention of history to the segmentation of memory.

One example is what is taking place in the Orthodox camp. If the Zionist version was construed as a countermemory to traditional Jewish memory, the Orthodox and traditional elements in Israeli society are currently fighting to create a religious version of Holocaust remembrance. In 1995 the chief rabbi of Israel, Rabbi Israel Lau, initiated a strictly religious observance to commemorate the fifty years since the end of World War II. In arguing for a ceremony separate from Holocaust Remembrance Day, he claimed that religious youth lack awareness of the Holocaust because it does not relate to secular rituals of remembrance. Around the same time ultra-Orthodox circles threatened to boycott Yad Vashem if photographs of naked female victims, on display since the museum opened, were not removed. In a telling interview, the deputy mayor of Jerusalem, Chaim Miller, who had headed the campaign, said: "Until now I was afraid to raise the issue, but now I feel with my two feet on the ground in the State of Israel, and I want to improve our position here." Miller's position was clear: "We are conducting a war," he said, and if the demands were not met, he warned, the ultra-Orthodox would open "competing organizations" to commemorate the Shoah in an "orthodox spirit." Concurrently the ultra-Orthodox are busy reinventing the history of both Zionism and the Holocaust.[44] Imagining themselves to have been the ancestors of secular Zionist settlers in Palestine and arguing falsely that the majority of European Jews prior to the Holocaust had been Orthodox are preliminary steps in the cultural-political war the Orthodox are waging against a modern democratic Israel.[45]

Among the Mizrachim there were also alternative expressions of commemoration of the Shoah, at least some of which appear to be dissenting gestures against Israel's Eurocentric orientation and its Ashkenazi cultural hegemony. One such example was the decision of a high school principal in a predominantly Mizrachi neighborhood to de-nationalize and de-Ashkenize Holocaust Remembrance Day. This was intended as a lesson to respect others and otherness. In this particular version the Armenian, gypsy, African American, Native American, and homosexual holocausts were remembered alongside the Jewish Holocaust. The cultural program was also de-canonized by choosing only texts written by Mizrachim. Genocide was remembered as a universal phenomenon rather than as a particular European-Jewish catastrophe.[46]

The notion that "We Are One" is perhaps a useful slogan for the United Jewish Appeal or other fundraising organizations. But as a characterization of modern Jewry, whether in Israel or elsewhere, it is little more than a fancy fabrication of reality. Not only among the nations of the world but within

Israel as well, the memory of the Shoah is being integrated by associating it with particular historical and cultural meanings. Hence, the expanding global awareness of the Holocaust is derived from and linked to the universalization of the Shoah. As such, more than one authentic and exclusive memory of the event will be formed, not least because remembrance traditions cannot exist without change, including changing modes of reception. What ought to concern us is how change is introduced or accepted. To accommodate the inevitability of change and its limitation, it seems futile to opt for an "authentic" version or "correct" interpretation. The aim should be for "rights of inclusion," thereby making manifest that which does not belong.

Yet another issue calls for contemplation: the crucial difference between obsession with victimization and preoccupation with survival. Victimization concerns murder and death, domination, and helplessness. Survival describes coping, going on. The Holocaust ought to survive; it ought not to become a victim of memory. Perhaps, the deluge of commemoration rituals in which our contemporary sensibilities have been immersed confirms the absence of memories. If that is indeed the lamentable modern human condition, we are all the more obliged to efface the rhetorical, political, and religious misuses to which this catastrophe has been put; to guard that what we remember is the victims' truth in as innocent a manner as their tragic fate was.

NOTES

1. See Yechiam Weitz, "Political Dimensions of Holocaust Memory in Israel During the 1950s," *Israel Affairs* 1:3 (Spring 1995), 129–45, and *idem*, "Shaping the Memory of the Holocaust in Israeli Society of the 1950s," in *Major Changes Within the Jewish People in the Wake of the Holocaust*, Proceedings of the Ninth Yad Vashem International Historical Conference (Jerusalem, 1996).

2. On the theory and history of expectations see Reinhart Koselleck, *Futures Past: On the Semantics of Historical Time*, Keith Tribe, trans. (Cambridge, MA, 1985).

3. See Iwona Irwin-Zarecka, *Frames of Remembrance: The Dynamics of Collective Memory* (New Brunswick, NJ, 1994). On the representation of collective

memory, see the very engaging essay by Alon Confino, "Collective Memory and Cultural History: Problems of Method" (AHR Forum), *American Historical Review* 102 (December 1997), 1386–1403.

4. Abba Kovner speaking at a meeting dedicated to the establishment of Yad Vashem during the first Congress for Jewish Studies, July 13–14, 1947. Cited in Dalia Ofer, "Israel," in David S. Wyman, ed., *The World Reacts to the Holocaust* (Baltimore, 1996), p. 857.

5. Mark Dworzecki, "The Surviving Remnant in Israel," *Gesher* 1 (1956), 115–83; Aharon Appelfeld, "Fifty Years after the Great War," *Yediot Aharonot,* Apr. 20, 1995, 28–29 (in Hebrew).

6. Cited by Hanna Yablonka, "The Formation of Holocaust Consciousness in the State of Israel: The Early Days," in Efraim Sicher, ed., *Breaking Crystal: Writing and Memory after Auschwitz* (Urbana, 1998), p. 122.

7. For two opposing interpretations on this issue, see Eliezer Don-Yehiya, "Memory and Political Culture: Israeli Society and the Holocaust," *Studies in Contemporary Jewry* 9 (1993), 139–62, and Moshe Zuckermann, "The Curse of Forgetting: Israel and the Holocaust," *Telos: A Quarterly Journal of Critical Thought* 78 (Winter 1988–89), 43–54.

8. Don-Yehiya, "Memory and Political Culture," p. 144. See, for example, MK Beba Idelson (MAPAI) in *Divrei Ha-Knesset* (Proceedings of the Knesset, May 18, 1953), 25:1336–37 (in Hebrew).

9. Proceedings of the Knesset, May 12, 1953, 25:1310–14.

10. Don-Yehiya, "Memory and Political Culture," p. 148.

11. On the initial reception accorded to the survivors see, Hanna Yablonka, *Akhim Zarim* (Jerusalem, 1994) (in Hebrew). On this law see the two path-breaking articles by Yechiam Weitz, "The Law against the Nazis and Nazi Collaborators and the Relationship of Israeli Society in the 1950s to the Shoah and Its Survivors," *Katedra* 82 (December 1996), 153–64, and Hanna Yablonka, "The Law against the Nazis and Nazi Collaborators: An Additional Perspective to the Issue of Israelis, Survivors and the Shoah," *Katedra,* in *idem,* 135–52 (in Hebrew).

12. Proceedings of the Knesset, Mar. 27, 1950, 4:1148.

13. For the discussion of the Knesset subcommittee on the proposed law, see Proceedings of the Knesset, Aug. 1, 1950, 6:2393–95, and Yablonka, "The Formation of Holocaust Consciousness," pp. 124–29, quotations on pp. 125–26.

14. For the Kasztner affair I draw on Yechiam Weitz, *The Man Who Was Murdered Twice* (Jerusalem, 1995). See also Penina Lahav, *Judgment in Jerusalem: Chief Justice Simon Agranat and the Zionist Century* (Berkeley, 1997), pp. 121–44.

15. Yechiam Weitz, "The Holocaust on Trial: The Impact of the Kasztner and Eichmann Trials on Israeli Society," *Israel Studies* 1:2 (December 1996), 13.

16. Moshe Shamir, "A People that Does Not Know," *Al Hamishmar,* Mar. 22, 1957, quoted in ibid., 7. For the more widely known critique, see Natan Alterman, *Al Shtei Ha-Derachim* [Between Two Roads], ed. Dan Laor (Tel Aviv, 1989) (in Hebrew). For the exceptions see Haim Guri, "On Books and What Is in Between Them," *Alpayim* 14 (1997), 9–30 (in Hebrew).

17. Ben-Gurion in a speech before the Journalists' Association, Nov. 29, 1951, cited in Neima Barzel, "Dignity, Hatred and Memory? Reparation from Germany: the Debate in the 1950s," *Yad Vashem Studies* 24 (1994): 266–67.

18. On Begin's stand in the reparation debate see Tom Segev, *The Seventh Million: The Israelis and the Holocaust,* Haim Watzman, trans. (New York, 1993), pp. 189–252. Cited in Barzel, "Dignity, Hatred and Memory," p. 260.

19. David Ben-Gurion, "Israel's Security and Her International Position," in *Israel Government Year Book,* 1959/1960 (Jerusalem, 1960), pp. 72–73, 77. Ben-Gurion is quoted in Barzel, "Dignity, Hatred and Memory," p. 267.

20. See Michael Keren, "Ben-Gurion's Theory of Sovereignty: The Trial of Adolf Eichmann," in Ronald Zweig, ed., *David Ben-Gurion: Politics and Leadership in Israel* (London, 1991), pp. 40–42. Gideon Hausner, *Ha-Shoah bi-Re'i ha-Mishpat* [The Holocaust on Trial] (Tel Aviv, 1988), pp. 8–9; *Yediot Aharonot,* June 1, 1962, cited in Lahav, *Judgment in Jerusalem,* p. 161.

21. Hausner to Ben-Gurion, Mar. 24, 1961; Ben-Gurion to Hausner, Mar. 28, 1961, cited in Segev, *The Seventh Million,* pp. 346–47.

22. On how witnesses were chosen see Rachel Auerbach, "Edim Veeduiot Bamishpat," *Yediot Yad Vashem* 28 (1961), 35–41. See Dalia Ofer, "Israel," in David S. Wyman, ed., *The World Reacts to the Holocaust* (Baltimore, 1996), p. 878.

23. This observation on the "waiting period" is based on the press, Knesset proceedings, and other published material. On the Six-Day War, see Moshe A. Gilboa, *Shesh Shanim Shisha Yamim* [Six Years Six Days] (Tel Aviv, 1969) (in Hebrew). Eliezer Livneh, "The Danger of Hitler," *Haaretz,* May 31, 1967, p. 2. See "Between Hitler and Nasser," *Haaretz,* June 5, 1967; Letters to the Editor, *Haaretz,* May 30, 31, June 5, 1967, p. 4; *Davar,* May 28, June 4, 1967, p. 3 (in Hebrew).

24. Segev, *The Seventh Million,* pp. 389–91.

25. Henry Near, ed., *The Seventh Day: Soldiers' Talk about the Six-Day War* (Tel Aviv, 1970), p. 160 ff.

26. For a similar analysis see Zuckermann, "The Curse of Forgetting."

27. *Yediot Aharonot,* May 18, 1993.

28. On the evolving particularistic mentality and Justice Simon Agranat, see Lahav, *Judgment in Jerusalem,* pp. 149–61 (quotation on p. 161). *Haaretz,* Apr. 15, 1969, p. 2.

29. *Maariv,* Apr. 27, 1976; *Haaretz,* Apr. 27, 1976; Apr. 14, 1988.

30. Quoted in James Young, "When a Day Remembers: A Performative History of Yom ha-Shoah," *History & Memory* 2 (Winter 1990), 68.

31. On the concept of "deep memory," see Lawrence L. Langer, *Holocaust Testimonies: The Ruins of Memory* (New Haven, CT, 1991), esp. chap. 1; and Saul Friedlander, "Trauma, Transference and 'Working through' in Writing the History of the Shoah," in *History & Memory* 4:1 (1992), 40–41.

32. The Likud, a center-right alignment, was formed in 1973. Begin's Herut party was the Likud's largest faction.

33. On the place of the Shoah in the nationalist discourse see, Hanna Torok Yablonka, "The Commander of the Yizkor Order: Begin, Herut and the Holocaust," in Selwyn Troen and Noah Lucas, eds., *Israel: The First Decade of Independence* (Albany, 1995), pp. 211–31. On the politicization of the Shoah by Prime Minister Begin see Segev, *The Seventh Million,* pp. 396–401.

34. Arieh Naor, *Government at War: How the Israeli Government Functioned during the Lebanon War, 1982* (Tel Aviv, 1986), pp. 47–48; Arieh Zimuki, "Begin to Reagan: I Feel Like I have Sent the Army into Berlin to Destroy Hitler in His Bunker," *Yediot Aharonot,* Aug. 3, 1982, p. 1 (in Hebrew). Begin cited in Segev, *The Seventh Million,* p. 399.

35. Amos Oz, "Hitler Is Already Dead, Mr. Prime Minister," *Yediot Aharonot,* June 21, 1982, p. 6 (in Hebrew); Eliezer Don-Yehiya, "Memory and Political Culture: Israeli Society and the Holocaust," *Studies in Contemporary Jewry* 9 (1993), 159.

36. See Amos Elon, "Israel and the End of Zionism," *The New York Review of Books,* vol. 43, no. 20, Dec. 19, 1996, p. 24; see also *Politika* 8 (June–July 1986), which was devoted entirely to the Shoah, and especially Adi Ofir, "On the Renewal of the Name," 2–7 (in Hebrew).

37. Boaz Evron, "The Holocaust: A Danger to the Nations," *Iton* 77:21 (May–June 1980), 12 ff.

38. Yehuda Elkana, "The Need to Forget," *Haaretz,* Mar. 2, 1988, p. 13. All quotations in this paragraph are from this article.

39. Prime Minister Rabin, policy statement to the Knesset, Oct. 3, 1994, Israel Information Service.

40. The speech of Minister Shulamit Aloni, Apr. 24, 1996, on the occasion of the Israel Prize ceremony, published by Israel Information Service.

41. On the trips to Poland see, Nili Keren, "Student Trips to Poland—A Memory Forming Journey," in Yoel Rappel, ed., *Memory and Awareness of the Holocaust in Israel* (Tel Aviv, 1998), pp. 93–100; Tom Segev, "Katav Zar," *Haaretz,* Nov. 2, 1990, B5; idem, *Haaretz,* Nov. 9, 1990; Shevach Weiss, "The War on Memory," *Al Hamishmar,* Oct. 1, 1992, p. 10. All these items are in Hebrew.

42. Full text of the speech appears in *Maariv,* Apr. 8, 1992.

43. Both quotations are cited by Avner Ben-Amos, "A Dangerous Attachment," *Haaretz,* May 3, 1998, p. B2; *Haaretz,* Apr. 24, 1998, p. A4 (in Hebrew).

44. See David Assaf, "The Assassins of Memory," *Haaretz,* Feb. 17, 1995, B7; Rami Rosen, "Thank God There Are New Historians," *Musaf Haaretz* Dec. 6, 1996, 42–4.

45. Ilan Sachar, "Rabbi Lau Initiates a Separate Religious-Orthodox Memorial," *Haaretz,* Mar. 29, 1995. Nachum Barnea, "Miller's Hand and Name," *Yediot Aharonot,* Feb. 10, 1995. See also news reports in *Haaretz,* Feb. 3 and 9, 1995, and Apr. 12, 1995 (in Hebrew).

46. See *Haier* Apr. 21, 1995, pp. 16–18.

NINE

"I Am Other": The Holocaust Survivor's Point of View in Yehudit Hendel's Short Story "They Are Others"

NURITH GERTZ

A central dichotomy in Israeli culture between Diaspora Jew and Hebrew Israeli aims to eliminate Israeli culture's hybridity and consolidate a homogeneous Hebrew identity. Zionism fashioned the Hebrew-Israeli identity by negating everything that threatened this homogeneity, especially the Jewish Diaspora. This dichotomy of Diaspora Jews and Israeli Hebrews is most saliently expressed in works dealing with Holocaust survivors. In these texts, the Holocaust survivor embodies Diaspora culture and history, and his identity, cultural world, and fate contrast with Hebrew culture, the history of *Eretz Israel* (the land of Israel), and the Zionist program.

Many stories, novels, and films written and produced in the 1940s and 1950s put Israel's recently arrived Holocaust survivors through an educational process in which they exchanged their Diaspora Jewish identity for a Hebrew-Israeli one, emerging at the end as pronouncedly pure Israelis.[1] These stories do address most of their "sympathy" to Holocaust survivors but "nullify" them as independent, separate, differentiated characters with their own past, identity, and experiences.

Even in most works that attempt to dismantle this simple linear process of transformation, their heterogeneity is eventually blurred. Ultimately all the survivors' biographies merge by analogy into one account: that of the transformation that turns Diaspora Jews into Israelis. This is the Zionist narrative that all protagonists who carry "Diaspora Jewish traits" experience, each in his or her own way and time, each ascending a hierarchical ladder on which strength emanates from the top, the Israeli top. This intent, which informed much of the fiction produced in those decades, changed direction in subsequent literature and cinema, produced mainly in the 1980s and thereafter, and in literature written by Holocaust survivors themselves. These works dispense with the dominant narrative that leads Diaspora Jews to their Hebrew-Israeli identity. As a result, details and events that are meaningful in the films and novels of the 1950s become meaningless, arbitrary, and incomprehensible. In contrast, the later works organize previously ignored biographical details of survivors into a narrative that elevates them to a position of centrality.[2]

In this sense, Yehudit Hendel's short story "They Are Others" (1949–1950) differs from most contemporaneous works of the 1950s. Its main protagonist, a Holocaust survivor, meets a woman with whom he forms an intimate relationship on the ship on his way to Israel and from whom he is separated on shore, where he is sent to the Israeli army to fight in the War of Independence. The story neither retells the popular Zionist narrative nor shatters and dismantles it. The Jewish survivor is not an outsider who must adopt an Israeli identity. Neither is the survivor's identity depicted as the one and only authentic identity. Hendel tells both accounts: that of the Zionist Hebrew society that attempts to refashion the survivor in its own image, and that of the survivor who cannot integrate into this society and assimilate the identity dictated to him. Hendel adopts the Zionist narrative of her time and describes it understandingly, but she examines it through the eyes of the disintegrated outsider. From this point of view, the narrative seems insensitive and cruel. The author actually pinpoints the phase at which two equivalent narratives, two histories, and two national identities confront each other: that of the "Hebrew" society, which subjects the Diaspora to total repudiation, and that of the survivor, who has come from that same Diaspora. Thus the perspective of Yehudit Hendel, quite innovative for her time, is located between the narrative of the 1950s and that of the 1980s. She was the first to describe the Hebrew culture of the 1950s as a hybrid.[3]

The two counterpositioned narratives create a state of ambivalence which dictates the poetics of Hendel's story. It fluctuates between masculine and feminine male heroes, between action and contemplation, passivity and activity, causal progress in time and static spatial descriptions. This poetics employs central and fringe models in the writing of its own time, models of writing that the contemporary culture considered masculine, and those adopted by women writers and, therefore, considered feminine. It also anticipates future models.

Yury Lotman describes ambivalent texts that fuse historical, ideological, and cultural models of different eras, culled from different locations in the cultural system.[4] Lucien Goldmann asserts a correlation between textual ambivalence and the situation of groups of intellectuals positioned between social classes and, for this reason, between different ideologies. According to Goldmann, only intellectual groups in such a situation can perceive the ideological contradictions of their time.[5] Homi Bhabha describes the national narration as an ambivalent one—a narrative in which the other is shaped as an object of attraction and fantasies on the one hand and an object for control and investigation on the other.[6]

Yehudit Hendel's writing may bridge these three definitions of ambivalence. She belonged to the cultural elite of the War of Independence generation, but men determined the literary and cultural norms of that generation. This situation, beyond her own talents and inclinations, allowed her to contemplate her surroundings from the outside (the fringe) *and* the inside (the center) and, for this reason, to adopt the ideological and poetic models of both. Thus she expressed social awareness from the point of view of the excluded outsider, to use Bhabha's term,[7] and revealed the fissures in the homogeneous voice of the mainstream hegemony, to which she simultaneously gave voice.

My claim in this chapter is that Yehudit Hendel, because she wrote from the perspective of a woman "torn" between two cultures, was able to break the mold of the hegemonic Zionist narrative and to present other narratives—those of the fringe of her time and those that would come to dominate Israeli culture only years later.

MULTIPLE POINTS OF VIEW

In literature and other texts written in the 1950s, the vantage point is that of the Israeli-born. In texts written since the 1970s, the vantage point is that of the Holocaust survivors. In Yehudit Hendel's story, both points of view dominate, thus expressing the author's ambivalence. The woman narrator of the story articulates this ambivalence by simultaneously taking the side of the coterie of War of Independence fighters and of Sheftel, the Holocaust survivor, who is not part of the group. "The fellows were again awash in smoke and conversation." In this intimate tone, that of the insider, she describes Sheftel's encounter with the group of sabras at the café. However, she immediately changes this insider's tone by adopting the point of view of the outsider, to whom the group members are strangers: "And the young guy with the checkered scarf, who considered himself the chief orator here, answered in a thick, rude voice" (p. 62). Although the point of view is that of Sheftel, the outsider who does not know the people in the group, the narrator reports conversational details in Hebrew, which Sheftel, of course, cannot understand. Thus, the point of view has become again that of the narrator. This point of view, however, is also ambivalent because the narrator reports only those fragments of conversation that may interest Sheftel: a discussion of the *Gahal* (overseas recruited fighters), most of whom were Holocaust survivors. Thus the story slides between two points of view, two angles—that of the sabras and that of Sheftel—and, practically speaking, adopts both.

The ambivalence of the story is based throughout on the confrontation between these two points of view. In the novels and films of the time, the Israeli tends to adopt the admiring look of the outsider, the survivor, and uses it to consolidate his sense of confidence and supremacy and present himself as an admired hero. After the survivor himself becomes a Hebrew-Israeli and adopts his hosts' point of view, he can confirm the Israeli identity by emulating and identifying with it.

Yehudit Hendel sculpts the survivor's admiring regard of the Israeli but exposes its meaning and changes its purpose. On the one hand, the survivor does confirm the Israeli's sense of supremacy. Sheftel and his friend regard the old-time Israelis, the sabras, as everything that Zionism has taught them to admire — active people, healthy in mind and body, courageous and vital, rooted in the country and its soil — and try to resemble them. In so doing, however, they take on the sabra point of view and, by means of it, repudiate their own identity, which, however, refuses to disappear and clashes with the Israeli identity throughout the story.[8]

The two points of view create a never-ending conflict between the two narratives — the Israeli Zionist narrative and that of the Holocaust survivor raised in the Diaspora — and constantly test and re-test each narrative in the light of the other. The reader, identifying with Sheftel's point of view, may judge those who send him to the army without allowing him to part with his girlfriend, the man who attempts to take his rucksack (the receptacle of all his belongings and memories), those who send him into combat without training, and those who consider him and his comrades "a bunch of misfits." However, Sheftel's point of view also admires them, justifies them, and judges Sheftel himself according to their point of view. He pictures himself moving about with a filthy rucksack, he blames his commander's death on his own stupidity, and he perceives himself and his comrades as a bunch of misfits. The account itself does not take an equivocal stance in this struggle between points of view, as the facts attest. The clerks make fun of Sheftel's rucksack but do not deprive him of it. The commander does not explain the combat orders to Sheftel but forfeits his life by returning to the battlefield to look for him after the retreat. The comrades in the café pay no attention to him most of the time but do try on several occasions to befriend him. Thus the point of view of the other, the stranger, leaves the Zionist narrative in place but purges it of its totality, as Bhabha says, by forcing us to contemplate it from an additional perspective, that of one who tries to adopt it but cannot.

Ambivalence also guides the way the story is read. As the plot progresses, contemporary Israel-born readers must abandon their point of view and adopt that of a Holocaust survivor. From this vantage point, they are urged to contemplate those who represent them in the story — the sabras, the soldiers, the group at the café — and to criticize them.

Tension between the two points of view surfaces in the very title of the story, "They Are Others." For contemporary Israeli readers, the "others" are of course the survivors. Only after they adopt the survivors' point of view can they perceive themselves and their representatives in the story as others —others in the eyes of immigrants and, in fact, strangers to their own identity. This is because the identity of the Diaspora Jew is a part of their own identity that they are trying to repress and banish from memory. This point is confirmed when Sheftel uses the term to describe the Israeli-born as others: "They are different," he tells his new friend Leizer, "They are simple and natural" (p. 37).

The blend of perspectives creates a mixture of categories and identities. Sheftel is a man described and observed through the eyes of a female author. He observes himself from the contemptuous point of view of Israelis, and thus repudiates his own identity. Concurrently, however, his look makes the Israeli himself a stranger to his identity, past, and origins. The vantage point of each participant in this story undermines his / her own ethnic identity and that of all the others, and thus the very definition of national ethnic identity changes and becomes, instead of a demarcated, homogeneous, and permanent "place," a crossroads with many possibilities.[9]

FLUIDITY OF IDENTITY

To shatter the Zionist canon of her time, Hendel attacks the integration that this canon creates between gender and nationality—between Zionism and masculinity and between Diaspora Judaism and femininity.

In many novels and films of the 1940s and 1950s, Jewish identity is converted by the plot into Hebrew identity in a simple process of substitution, one collection of traits succumbing to another. Immigrants to Israel are typified by a pool of "negative" Jewish traits, some of which were assessed as analogous to nonmasculine traits.[10] Cowardly and passive, these immigrants refuse to work and fight. Aloof to the place and landscape, they can neither circulate in this landscape nor contemplate it—two actions that symbolize, more than anything else at that time, masculine control of the country. Instead of clinging to the land and the new Hebrew collective, they adhere to memories of home and family—the space of the women. Ultimately, they shed these traits and replace them with those considered Israeli and masculine. The others, who are left out, remind us at all times that the Zionist conversion process cannot be complete. In addition, the failure of those left out underscores the success of those who have made their way in, who have stopped being Jewish and have become Hebrew and Israeli.

Yehudit Hendel reveals the mechanics of this process and shows how fluid identity is when it hinges on constant definition of who is "in" and who is "out," and how limited are definitions of identity when built on rigid dichotomies of Jew and Israeli, female and male.

The hero of Hendel's story, Sheftel, cannot experience a process similar to the one that occurs in the other texts, simple or complex, because from the very outset he carries both kinds of traits: Diaspora-Jewish and Hebrew-Israeli, feminine and masculine. His transformation in the course of the plot is not from a Diaspora Jew into an Israeli but from a carrier of a hybrid collection of traits into a person without them, who nevertheless tries to adhere to his heterogeneous identity: Jewish and Israeli, feminine and masculine. In this sense, Sheftel also differs from survivors in the works of the 1980s and 1990s, who discover the supremacy of their world and values relative to those of native Israelis.

On the ship, en route to Israel, Sheftel reconstructs the masculine roles he had played before the war—as husband and father—by taking care of and protecting the young woman he met on his journey, Paula. Although Sheftel's role aboard the ship is masculine, it depends on traits often described as characteristic of the "femininity" of the Diaspora Jew, the exile, the survivor. He exhibits tenderness and sensitivity; his range of memories embraces the core family.[11] He contemplates reality at length but takes little action in it. His look is not the penetrating masculine gaze with which the Israeli protagonists dominate their landscape and control others, but rather a humane, subjective look that yearns to communicate, a look that carries a heavy load of memories and feelings, the look of women in Hendel's other works.[12]

The connection between Sheftel's gendered and national identity is already articulated aboard the vessel. True, he converses with his friend Paula in Yiddish, but his speech is reported in correct Hebrew that underscores Paula's halting, fractured rhetoric. The possibility of controlling his fate and of integrating into the Israeli nation, as we learn during the story, hinges on his ability to become fluent in Hebrew, regarded as one of the main characteristics of the new Hebrew identity. He possesses this fluency aboard the ship (where his Yiddish language is "translated" by the work into a fluent Hebrew) and, as we shall see later, he is deprived of it when he comes ashore.[13]

On the ship, Sheftel speaks the right and wrong language at the same time. His pride in his achievement is ambivalent, accompanied by a sense of insult and defilement that, like his other traits and feelings, is reflected in the surroundings and the landscape. The filthy sailors, the miserable, lost man with the suitcase, the porter carrying a sack, the polluted water at the port, the oily rust in the water, and the "befouled deck" all reflect his feelings about himself—his filthy, redolent rucksack, his greasy hair, and so on.

Thus, when he interacts with Paula on the ship's deck, Sheftel is a person with "double" gendered and national identity that also contains clashing traits. Sheftel feels he controls his life, but he has also lost everything in the war, despises his identity, and expects to rebuild himself in Israel.

This ambivalence also typifies the other characters in the story and Sheftel's relations with them. Paula has tender feelings for Sheftel but probably exploits them for her own purposes. Leizer behaves like a tough, crude sabra, but also like a "Diaspora" Jew, a survivor, a recent immigrant. Each protagonist's contradictory traits shatter the story's simple Israelis-and-survivors dichotomy and fracture the facile conversion of Diaspora Jewish identity into Israeli selfhood.

When he reaches the country, Sheftel parts with Paula and is sent to an army camp. From then on, he is defined by the uniform and rifle given to him. He must display his masculine traits in other ways, neither by means of women nor through personal, human, or family relations but in combat, as a member of a military male society. Many of the survivors in the literary and cinematic texts of the time discover their Hebrew identity in the same way, by integrating, as men, into a Zionist collective endeavor depicted as masculine (in conquest of the land or in battles, for example). In this phase, they forgo their private yearnings, including memories of home and family, and become part of the new collective.[14]

Sheftel, however, fails in his first collective action. First, he loses his linguistic superiority in Israel. In comparison with the Israelis who have taken him in, his speech is halting, and his inadequate command of Hebrew seals his fate in combat. He heads for the battlefield with his comrades, but when the Arabs attack his battalion and his commander orders a retreat, he does not understand the order and spends a full night alone in the field. His incompetence in Hebrew—itself a sign of "national incompetence"—causes him to fail the first test of masculinity that should make him part of the new nation.[15] He comes across as a passive, helpless character, someone for whom others fight and die. His two failures—as a man and as a member of the new nation—are therefore fully intertwined.

He also fails the test of masculinity vis-à-vis women. Having lost his previous identity, he stops trying to find Paula and begins to ogle the young sabra women. He attempts to show them his manhood but does not succeed. They do not accept his national identity and, for this reason, they reject his masculine identity as well. From their standpoint, he is a Holocaust survivor, an exile, and an outsider. His emasculation is also connected with the loss of his previous femininity. His memories of family, daughter, and home recede, and his private, intimate encounters with Paula on the ship are replaced by collective encounters in Israel: in war, at the soldiers' hostel, and at the café. Thus, Yehudit Hendel takes apart the correlation—so clear and absolute in the other works of her time—between maleness and Israeliness and liberates masculinity from the dominion of national identity. Sheftel, unlike the other heroes, does not make the transition from a passive, feminine character to a fighting, active Hebrew. He was a man before he came to Israel, and he was able to exercise his manhood precisely because of his feminine sensitivity to family and love. Having reached Israel, he has to demonstrate his manhood in battle, and in his failure he loses both his masculine and his feminine identities.

This story also crosses the frontier between masculine and feminine in that Paula, Sheftel's friend, does not play the role that other contemporaneous works reserve for women: to help the survivor replace his Jewish identity with an Israeli one and to serve as a metaphor for this transformation—a metaphor for the transformation of the wasteland into blossoming landscape and barrenness into fertility. In Hendel's story, Paula is a three-dimensional character with whom the protagonist may be able to maintain a relationship. But the moment Sheftel is forced to take up the new Hebrew identity, she vanishes. She neither supports the change he is expected to undergo nor plays any role in it, real or metaphorical. Just as Sheftel does not fulfill the male destiny assigned him by Israeli society, Paula does not fulfill the female destiny that this society has mapped out for her. However, Paula's absence underscores the monolithic maleness of the new world into which Sheftel has been inserted—a world that has room neither for the woman he has chosen nor for his own feminine traits. In this story, Hendel analyzes a condition that recurs in other stories of hers that have women protagonists: the feminine, familial, personal essence that Israeli society lost when it became a combative male society. The films of the 1980s probe the distortion the Israeli Zionist identity inflicted on itself by repressing its Diaspora Jewish character; Hendel examines in the 1950s how the masculine Zionist identity betrayed itself by denying its own feminine character.

ORIGINAL AND COPY

On the "journey" from his old Diaspora Jewish self to an Israeli identity, Sheftel clings to a series of substitutes and reflections. In this sense, too, this story is reminiscent of the literature of its time, especially Hanoch Bartov's novel *Each Had Six Wings,* in which immigrants were led to the Zionist identity in a slow and obstacle-strewn process. The protagonists in the later stories and films follow a similar course, but in the opposite direction. They move from the Israeli-Zionist identity to acknowledgment of the past and of a Diaspora Jewish identity. Yehudit Hendel stops her protagonist halfway, at a point where he has lost one identity but has not acquired another—a phase of total vacuum.[16] She deconstructs the process the survivors underwent in the narrative of her time and shows how one survivor, by adopting the point of view of his Israeli hosts, becomes estranged from the sources of his old identity without gaining the ability to acquire and assimilate a new one. The survivor becomes a shadow and a parable of his hosts.

In his fragmentary recollections, Sheftel drifts back not only to the events of the war and the Holocaust, as do contemporary protagonists in other works, but also to what preceded the war: home, family, the photograph of his daughter that rests in his pocket, memories of a gift he bought her, a white tablecloth, everything he lost in the Holocaust. Recollections of devastation and exile usually determine the identity of Holocaust survivors. Sheftel's identity emerges through remembrances of his pre-Holocaust home and family as well.

On the ship with Paula, Sheftel recalls his daughter, his friend who has died, and his family. During his voyage Paula becomes a substitute of sorts for all this baggage, which he has lost. Later, in the army camp, Leizer asks him to show him a photograph of his beloved Paula. Leizer does not know that the picture in Sheftel's pocket belongs to the "original," his daughter, and not the "copy," Paula.

In Israel, Sheftel distances himself from both the original and the substitute, and turns toward a different original, the Israeli one. However, unless he repudiates his prior identity, which he cannot do, he will fail to acquire a new woman. At first, he tries to elude his original self by disengaging from the other, who remains on the outside, that is, from Leizer. He contemplates his comrade and observes in him, as in a mirror, the Diaspora traits that he has been asked to shed, such as his hooked nose, his ashen pallor, his dirty rucksack. Contemptuously he attempts to erect a barrier between himself and Leizer. "Leizer, a creature consumed by hardships, whose face has darkened—what has he got to do with all of that? Sheftel—different." The more strongly he adopts the Israeli point of view, the more he tends to reject Leizer's identity, which in fact is his own.

Sheftel acknowledges this at the end of the story by observing his crumpled shadow on the sidewalk and pinning his look on a stranger circulating in the street. The feeling that he has become a stranger to and a shadow of himself—like all his feelings—is projected onto and reflected in his environment. Thus it predicts the feelings of survivors in the works of the 1970s and thereafter.

REBELLION AGAINST THE DOMINANT NORM: THE PLOT

Although Sheftel leaves with nothing, he does not give up. In fact, he exacts his revenge, albeit only on the symbolic plane. The storyline escorts him in a poetic rebellion against the literary canon of the time, which becomes a prophecy of the new norms of the 1970s and subsequent years.

He exacts revenge by refusing to accept the new family that the Israelis ostensibly try to give him. In contemporary fiction, Holocaust survivors reach Israel as children or teenagers. In the course of events, they must forget their real parents, who have perished in the Holocaust, and adopt new parents who will usher them through a symbolic rebirth and remake them as Israelis.[17] Hendel's story contains such a plot in metaphorical form only, in the persona of the revered commander who serves Sheftel as a father figure, and in the manager of the soldiers' club who contemplates Sheftel and his comrade with a "motherly look" and treats them like children (p. 49). However, Sheftel refuses to play the child's role in this plot and rebels against his metaphorical parents. He refuses to treat the housemother at the soldiers' hostel like a mother figure and murders his symbolic father by causing the commander's death. Sheftel, like Appelfeld's protagonists years later, is orphaned and estranged from the collective identity into which he should symbolically be born. In contrast to Appelfeld's protagonists, Sheftel is also distanced from his prior identity, the one he has tried to escape.

However, in the final episode, as he loiters outside the café he expresses a wish to see Paula again and to return to Leizer. Beyond his despair, he may again yearn for the solidarity of those who have been alienated, and by so doing, he may also be rebelling against the process that aims to rank and dichotomize others along lines of those left out and those marked for inclusion. This may mark the beginning of a path toward the acceptance of both identities — Diaspora Jew and Israeli.

REBELLION AGAINST THE DOMINANT NORM: POETICS OF SPACE AND TIME

Along with the rebellion that occurs in the hero's actions, Hendel's story concurrently wages a poetic rebellion against the male ideological and literary canon of its time, even as it respects and embodies it. The story preserves the optimistic linear time progression that dominates the literature of that generation and the Zionist narrative and leads the Jewish survivor to an Israeli identity. It also sabotages this progression. Time in Hendel's short story does advance and lead the protagonist from Europe to Israel, but its continuity is neither steady nor stable. It is usually a static time, devoid of meaningful occurrences, leaping from event to event or creating a tapestry of random events with a proliferation of bland, meaningless details that, in contrast to those in contemporaneous stories, play no role in the plot or in the Zionist endeavor and do not create a narrative of progress.

Time seems to stand still throughout Sheftel's journey aboard the vessel. Nothing happens: "It's another two hours until dinner" (p. 17); "Look how quickly they ring for dinner" (p. 18). Sheftel himself makes no plans and sets nothing in motion. He just sits there, contemplating: "Sheftel sat for a lengthy time, watching the shore recede" (p. 18). In Israel, where Sheftel is forced to act, the ordinary progression of time does not resume; it remains fractured and truncated. Only two events are reported during this time: the battle and the furlough, with a void in between. Although the conventional continuum, known from other stories of the time, is preserved in familiar events—the voyage at sea, the act of immigration, setting out for battle, and so on—the story sabotages it throughout.

In other contemporaneous texts, space is subordinated to Zionist time and plays a didactic role in communicating Zionist ideology.[18] By means of their gaze and actions (combat, work, and an outing in the countryside), the protagonists control this space and propel events in time in a dynamic, causal plot.[19] Thus both dimensions—space and time—express the male, Zionist dominion over the country and over history.

In works dealing with Holocaust survivors, this merging of time and space is effected in plots of a special type. In the beginning of each story, the survivors are incapable of contemplating and circulating freely in the country they have reached. In this context, the ability to contemplate space and circulate in it expresses knowledge and command, given only to those who manifest and accept Zionist ideology. After survivors explore the country's landscapes and become familiar with them—after working in them and struggling and fighting for them—they acquire an Israeli identity and knowledge of Hebrew culture and adopt the Israeli point of view.

Yehudit Hendel's story liberates space from the Zionist time progression described here, just as it releases the look from the dominion of Zionist knowledge. The story concentrates on the protagonist's contemplation more than on his actions. This contemplation reveals a non-Zionist space, devoid of ideological purpose, which expresses—at the most—the protagonist's inner feelings. However, ideology is not totally excluded from this space. It exists there, albeit in a parodic, distorted form. Thus one may say that the survivor-hero, by means of his look, liberates the landscape from the dominion of the Zionist ideology that still shapes it and strives to give it autonomy.

By choosing to organize her story around space instead of time, in a poetics based on mapping instead of action, on sensory reception of colors and hues instead of ideological generalizations, Yehudit Hendel has undermined the dominant poetics in the literature of her generation. Her writing rests on an existing model in Hebrew literature that traces back to Gnessin, continues in the fiction of the 1930s, and is consummated in the fiction of S. Yizhar, another author who both expresses and subverts the norms of the era.[20] By choosing to liberate the description of space from the progression of time and to liberate look from action, Hendel also follows in the wake of a poetics that feminist theories typify as female, as a "semiotic language[21] — based on rebellion against the male point of view, which, in Western civilization, is supposed to define and control women.[22] Hendel's choice also befits the contents of the story, because it makes a statement of sorts against what history has done to the hero: "dragged along for many years and not dead." The depiction of space immediately follows this biographical summary of time as a response and an answer: "Now the sea is tranquil and singing a light breeze-song" (p. 11). Thus the choice of space over time, and of look over action, is chosen by Hendel from a subversive literary stock and is used in order to protest against history by those relegated out of it or forced to its margins: the protagonist as a Jewish survivor and the author as a woman in a male society. In other stories by Hendel, her writing articulates the protest of other outsiders: women, Sephardi Jews, other immigrants.

In many ways, accounts of space are substitutes in the story for temporal unfoldings of events and accounts of action. The fact that the day has ended and evening is approaching is reported in an account of the changing colors of the sky and the sea: "The sinking daylight turned violet. . . . Meanwhile, the sea turned red" (p. 11). The fact that the recruits are being driven to their camp is described not with appropriate verbs but rather by means of an account of the "mountain crests roasting in yellow" (p. 34). The soldiers' disembarking from the vehicle and readiness for battle is not reported at all;

instead, these are communicated in the account of how Sheftel snags his hands on the tip of a rock.

These depictions of space, used to characterize a protagonist who has exchanged action for contemplation, are metaphorical tools that express his feelings, emotions, and attitudes. Like other components, they communicate the ambivalence of his personality and his world—and shatter the familiar contours of the Zionist narrative, which they also follow. In the Zionist narrative as constructed by the films and books of the time, the move from Europe to Israel represents a transition from death to resurrection, from a dying continent to a blossoming land. The same transition exists in Hendel's story but is much more complicated. Hendel's story concurrently monitors and shatters this transition because both of these locations are perceived ambivalently.

Sheftel's attitude toward Europe, which he is about to leave, emerges from the account of the poverty he observes around him: the "bleary-eyed beggar woman" who tugs at his robe (p. 9), the polluted water in the harbor, and the sunset over the sea, which looks to him like flames "spreading over a burning field." However, the accounts of poverty, pollution, and flame merge into the beckoning colorfulness of the surroundings, which, bursting upon him in hues of white, violet, and blue, clashes with his explicit feeling: "His eyes gazed at the port in revulsion" (p. 10). Sheftel's revulsion expresses the Zionist attitude of one who is about to leave Europe and resettle in Israel. However, the depiction of this continent's beauty evades and contradicts this attitude.

When they reach Israel, survivors in other texts take a cross-country "field trip," during which they learn to dominate the landscape with their gaze, in combat, and through labor. Hendel's short story awards the landscape a different task but does not overlook its intended Zionist role. When Sheftel reaches Israel, he resembles his fictional peers. He sees nothing; the narrator describes the landscape in his place: "If there were room he would have looked out and seen Haifa." Even when he looks out, he sees nothing but a "web of houses rushing past the window" (p. 23).

Generally, the beginning of the story invokes the metaphor of blindness to typify Sheftel, following the convention in other typical texts of defining Holocaust survivors as people who neither observe nor see.[23] Sheftel, like

Bartov's protagonists, travels in the beginning of the story with eyes that are teary, glazed, or closed. He peers at the world as would a man who is either blind or blinded by the magnitude of his anguish and suffering. The blindness stereotype, however, is fractured at the very beginning of the plot when we discover, in contrast to the convention in the other texts, that the point of view of this story is usually Sheftel's. As the plot continues, he again contemplates his surroundings, and his gaze pits his knowledge against that of Israeli society.

In contemporary narratives, survivors move about at first in a wasteland and are depicted as its metaphor. The wasteland in these works, however, is a point of departure for the metaphorical change that these characters experience as it is replaced by a blossoming garden.

In Hendel's story, the wasteland incompletely serves as a metaphor. The Israeli landscape does not lead Sheftel to the classic Zionist moral. He relates to the Israeli desolation with the same ambivalence that he feels toward the country he has left. He does notice "yellow-gray hills" and "riven mountains exposed to the sun" (p. 24). However, he likens the hills to mounds of wheat and sees green through the dryness. Like the other protagonists, he bonds with this landscape in the course of battle. Unlike them, however, he does not see at this time the blossoming landscape into which he will merge after the victory. He observes a primeval, fissured, scarred landscape. Overhead, the sky resembles "transparent crystal," and "an immense gray silence descends as far as the eye can behold" (pp. 33, 34). This landscape eludes Zionist knowledge—a desert not meant to be greened.

Thus, the landscape portrayed during the protagonist's first steps in Israel resembles the one described in other texts, only its significance differs. Hendel's account attempts to restore its familiar meaning by inserting the landscape into a recognizable metaphorical pattern of transition from wasteland to efflorescence—first during the battle, when for the first time it arouses Sheftel's amazement, and later during his outing to Haifa.

This outing is structured in the form of a field trip, much like similar accounts in other texts. It takes place as an ironic conquest of the mountaintop, a typical Zionist metaphorical endeavor described in so many songs, poems, and stories of the time. At first, the landscape is still bleak, the grapevines gray and bent. The autumn birds are black and gray, and Sheftel, like other typical protagonists at this stage, is homesick. As the outing continues, Sheftel displays some activism. For the first time in the story, his movements in climbing the mountain are described with action verbs and not by reports of changing scenery. As he ascends Mount Carmel, he finds a different landscape, green and blooming, and discovers the mint-green crests of the Carmel range and the violet sky. This account, too, is ambivalent—a transition from greenery to a "gaping abyss" and "clouds [that] roll in again, become dark, and turn into night" (p. 46). The dominant spectacle here, however, is not the wasteland but the efflorescence—and this dominance persists.

Ultimately, the ascent to the "mountaintop" fails. Sheftel and his friend reach the peak, where the colors become dull and then vanish. The greenery becomes "sooty-green valley-craters," replaced by "lonely electric lamps and rotten-yellow light" (p. 60). There at the top, the observers become glassy-eyed and descend in exhaustion. Thus, Sheftel has learned to contemplate the scenery through Israelis' eyes—to set out to conquer the mountain and to seek the blossoming that lies beyond the wilderness—without becoming a part of it. He has not managed to cross the metaphorical barrier, from wasteland to efflorescence, achieved by other survivor protagonists. Aware of this failure, he invokes the same metaphor of wasteland and fertility to liken sabras to "fruit trees drenched in sunlight and juices of the earth, like a wheat stalk, like an orange, like a purple grape" and to compare himself and Leizer to dried twigs: "Leizer's laugh is like a pile of twigs" (p. 45).

Sheftel thus shares the same educational rites as contemporary protagonists. He heads for battle, explores the country, and even reaches the mountaintop. Later on, he attempts to break into the circle of dancers. These rites, which Holocaust survivors routinely use to confirm their passage into Israeli society, fail in Sheftel's case. Instead of being reborn as an Israeli, he remains an outsider—neither an Israeli nor a Diaspora Jew, endowed with neither past nor present. Despite his failure, he retains the "territory" that he has removed from Zionist culture: that of landscapes that preceded Zionism and sights that no longer serve it as metaphors and illuminate nothing but his ambivalent inner world. These sights—personal, not collective—are positioned at the margins of the national narrative; although they do not shatter this narrative totally, they infringe on its generality and absoluteness.

Years later, Israeli literature, films, and other texts invoked these formerly marginal devices to shatter this type of narrative altogether.

SUMMARY

Over the past fifty years, many works in Israeli literature and cinema have created a clear dichotomy between Holocaust survivors and the Israeli society that adopted them, thus expressing the dichotomy that the Israeli culture posited between the native Israeli and the Diaspora Jew.

In the works of the 1950s, the survivors' Jewish identity is obliterated in favor of the new Israeli identity, and in later works the opposite occurs: the Israeli identity is judged, silenced, and made to yield to the preferable identity, culture, and past of the survivor. These later works "rebel" against Zionist hegemony and award a central position to the erstwhile outsider. In so doing, however, they reestablish a homogeneous culture in which only one voice is audible and other voices (in this case, those of Zionist culture and history) are stifled.

In her short story "They Are Others" Yehudit Hendel shatters both poles of the dichotomy and attempts to present a new possibility: an ambivalent identity that embraces Diaspora and Israel, male and female, Israeli and Jewish, time and space. This identity is not realized in the story, nor could it be realized credibly in view of the options of the time. Therefore, it is presented as something that is missing, as a possibility. The very revelation of this lacuna, however, expresses the story's rebellion against its contemporary culture. It presents the narrative that had dominated other works, indicating its failure and liberating "territories" that the narrative had annexed in contemporaneous texts. It dismantles the time that articulated Zionist ideology, creates a space not connected to it, and entitles the protagonist to contemplate this space without Zionist knowledge. However, this story does not carry its hero from the one extreme of the Jewish-Israeli dichotomy to the other. Instead, it examines how the elimination of one of its poles in turn eliminates an ambivalent, inclusive, complex identity in both poles: how erasing femininity also erases masculinity, and how eradicating the identity of the Diaspora and Jewish past also eradicates a Hebrew-Israeli identity. In so doing, Hendel's story rejects the negation-of-Diaspora attitude that dominated the Israeli culture of the time, even as it rules out the rejection of Zionism that many recent texts have proposed as a response.

NOTES

1. Examples are Moshe Shamir, *He Walked in the Fields,* Abba Kovner, *Face to Face,* and films such as *My Father's House,* and *Tomorrow Is a Wonderful Day.* These films are analyzed in Nurith Gertz, "The 'Others' in Israeli Films of the 1940s and 1950s: Holocaust Survivors, Arabs, Women," in Nurith Gertz, Orly Lubin, and Judd Ne'eman, eds., *Fictive Looks—on Israeli Cinema* (Tel Aviv, 1998), pp. 381–403 (in Hebrew); and "Holocaust and Holocaust Survivors in Israeli Cinema in the 1950s," in Mordechai Bar-On, ed., *Creative and Intellectual Endeavor in Israel's First Decade,* forthcoming.

2. See Nurith Gertz, "Zionism, Kibbutz, and Town: The Struggle for the Souls of Recent Immigrants in Hanoch Bartov's Novel *Each Had Six Wings,*" in *Iunim Bitkumat Israel,* vol. 8, pp. 498–522. For example, see Aharon Appelfeld's *Searing Light* and films such as *Wooden Gun, New Land, Avia's Summer,* and *Tel Aviv Berlin.* On Appelfeld's novel, see Nurith Gertz, "From Jew to Hebrew: The Zionist Narrative in *Searing Light,*" in Iris Parouche and Yitzhak Ben-Mordechai, eds., *Between Frost and Smoke* (Beersheva, 1997), pp. 124–45.

3. Following Homi Bhabha, *Nation and Narration* (London, 1990), p. 305, one may say that the added element of the survivor's point of view shatters the totality of the national account.

4. Yury Lotman, "The Dynamic Model of a Semiotic System," *Semiotica* 21 (1977), 3–210.

5. Lucien Goldmann, *Pour une Sociologie du Roman* (Paris, 1966).

6. Homi Bhabha, "The Other Question: Difference, Discrimination and the Discourse of Colonialism," in Russell Ferguson et al., eds., *Out There* (New York, 1990), p. 6.

7. Bhabha, *Nation and Narration,* p. 12. See also Elisabeth Bronfen, *Over Her Dead Body* (New York, 1992), p. 190, James Clifford and George Marcus, eds., *Writing Culture* (Berkeley, 1986); Stuart Hall, "Cultural Identity and Diaspora," in Jonathan Rutherford, ed., *Identity, Community and Cultural Difference* (London, 1990); and Toril Moi, *The Kristeva Reader* (Oxford, 1986), pp. 210, 296.

8. As Bhabha puts it in *Nation and Narrative,* p. 317, they adopt the Israeli narrative by way of mimicry, incomplete imitation. Homi Bhabha, *The Location of Culture* (London, 1994), pp. 88–89 describes how the other uses the language in

an alien fashion, creates a void in it, and adopts the dominant point of view by way of mimicry that dismantles it and makes it look ridiculous.

9. Clifford (p. 18) defines identity as a mobile site of contradictions, a capsule containing different types of discourse. See also Hall (p. 22) and Jonathan Boyarin and Daniel Boyarin, "No Homeland for Israelis in the place of the Jews," *Theory and Criticism* 5 (Autumn 1994), p. 93, who describe such a type of identity as an exile's identity, the definitions of which vary according to categories of gender, language, and territory. Hendel strives to describe this capsule of which the survivor's identity is composed.

10. The discussion of the femininity of the Jew is well-known. Here it is based on Daniel Boyarin, *Unheroic Conduct: The Rise of Heterosexuality and the Invention of the Jewish Man* (Berkeley, 1997). See also Gertz, "The 'Other' in Israeli Films," and Rhonda Cobham, "Misgendering the Nation: African Nationalist Fiction and Nuruddin Farah's Maps," in Andrew Parker et al., eds., *Nationalisms and Sexualities* (New York, 1992), p. 47, on the fashioning of the other's femininity.

11. Concerning the house as a private space controlled by woman, see, for example, Margaret Higonnet, "Suicide: Representations of the Feminine in the Nineteenth Century," *Poetics Today* 6 (1985), 108.

12. For the distinction between the look and the gaze, see Kaya Silverman, *The Threshold of the Visible World* (London, 1996). See also Orly Lubin, "The Woman as Other in Israeli Cinema," in Lawrence Silberstein and Robert Cohn, eds., *The Other in Jewish Thought and History* (New York, 1994); Lily Ratok, "Two Responses," *Theory and Criticism* 5 (Autumn), 165–77 (in Hebrew).

13. It is the silence of the various others—the lack of language—that allows Hendel to describe one in terms of another.

14. See Y. Raz, *The Image of Masculinity in Israeli Cinema,* M.A. thesis, Tel Aviv University (in Hebrew) and Amnon Raz-Krokotzkin, "Exile amid Sovereignty: A Critique of Diaspora Repudiation in Israeli Culture," *Theory and Criticism* 5 (Autumn 1994), 113–30 (in Hebrew).

15. He underscores the barrenness of the language and thereby deterritorializes it, to use Deleuze and Guattari's term. Gilles Deleuse and Felix Guattari, "What Is Minor Literature," in Russell Ferguson, et al., eds., *Out There* (New York, 1990), p. 61. On negation of the Jewish identity and the search for alternatives to it, and on the role of language in this step, see Benjamin Harshav, *Language in a Time of Revolution* (Berkeley, 1993). The story reconstructs the event of the battle at Latrun, in which recent immigrants—Holocaust survivors—fought and were

killed after just having debarked. If one describes the myths that Israeli culture manufactured regarding this battle, one may say that the story gives shape to several conflicting accounts of the event.

16. From this standpoint, Hendel analyzes and articulates the process described by Edward Said, *Orientalism* (New York, 1977), in which the native is made to regard and experience himself as an "other." Bhabha, "The Other Question," p. 81, describes the same situation, in which, dominated by the white man's point of view, the black child dissociates from himself and his race and identifies totally with the white man, whom he perceives as the epitome of perfection.

17. The film *My Father's House* has the most obvious example of such a plot.

18. For an analysis of the dimensions of time and space, see Inderpal Grewel, *Home and Harem* (Durham, 1996), esp. p. 24.

19. See also my book, *Hirbet Hiza'a and the Morning After*.

20. See the account of this phenomenon in my book *Captive of a Dream*.

21. Julia Kristeva, *Desire in Language: A Semiotic Approach to Literature and Art*, ed. Leon S. Roudiez, trans. Thomas Gora, Alice Jardine, and Leon S. Roudiez (New York, 1980). See Caren Kaplan, *Questions of Travel* (Durham, 1996), pp. 25, 31.

22. This was the poetics of Virginia Woolf, adopted in the 1960s and thereafter by the author Amalia Kahana Karmon. See in particular Simone de Beauvoir, *Le Duexieme Sexe* (Paris, 1949). Concerning the masculine point of view, see Laura Mulvey, "Visual Pleasure and Narrative Cinema," *Screen* 16:3 (1975); and Silverman, *The Threshold of the Visible World*.

23. Boyarin, *Unheroic Conduct*, considers this an indication of emasculation. According to this construction, the trait of blindness ties into the other feminine traits of the Jewish survivor.

TEN

"A Drastically Bifurcated Legacy": Homeland and Jewish Identity in Contemporary Jewish American Literature

TRESA GRAUER

In a telling scene in Philip Roth's novel *The Counterlife,* the protagonist, Nathan Zuckerman, detects what he describes as a familiar "American-Jewish inferiority complex" in a fellow passenger on the plane leaving Tel Aviv.[1] Having been overwhelmed by Israeli attempts to persuade him that "the one place in the world that's really Jewish and only Jewish is Israel," his seatmate asks him anxiously, "Why *do* Jews persist in living in the Diaspora? . . . After everything I've seen, I don't know what to say. Does anybody know? Can *anyone* answer?" With characteristic flippancy, Zuckerman dismisses him with a short reply: "Because they like it," and gets up to change his seat (p. 161).

In the context of the novel, the unnamed man on the plane is the mouthpiece for a cliché: that American Jews are vaguely confused and defensively silent about their ongoing American existence when confronted with the reality of Israel. However, it is Zuckerman's throwaway response that may actually tell us something more significant: Jews continue to live in the

Diaspora *because they like it*. As trivial as this response might seem, it is important to recognize the unapologetic conviction with which Zuckerman makes clear that *America*—and not Israel—is the homeland of American Jews. As he has done throughout his career, Roth here calls attention to—and resists—the uncritical nature of conventional stories of American Jewish beliefs and behavior. In his two novels about Israel—*The Counterlife* and *Operation Shylock*—Roth suggests that the oft-heard question "Why live in the Diaspora?" is not, in fact, the right question for contemporary American Jews: it is neither contemporary nor American. Indeed, the question relies on inherited spatial imagery that assumes an original "center" and a corresponding exilic "periphery," notions that, for Roth, preemptively obviate any real consideration of America as a Jewish homeland. Nearly fifty years after the creation of the State of Israel, Roth proposes that we stop arguing about whether there *can* be authentic Jewish life in the Diaspora, and focus instead on the fact that there *is*. By providing us with a rich variety of narratives of Jewish experiences—and sometimes going to absurd lengths to do so—he forces a serious reconsideration of the stories of Jewish life and home that many have come to accept as normative. In other words, he asks, are American narratives about Israel and the Diaspora still meaningful? Do they represent, as the character of Philip Roth suggests in *Operation Shylock,* a "drastically bifurcated legacy" of Jewish life?[2] How does the existence of Israel challenge our understanding of what it means to be a Jew?

This chapter uses a discussion of Philip Roth's two Israel novels as the framework for a larger concern; more specifically, I am interested in what happens to representations of "home" and "homeland" in American Jewish literature when "Zion" becomes—once again—an actual as well as a metaphoric place. It is an obvious but nonetheless crucial point that the establishment of the State increased the tension between the traditionally religious view of Israel as the homeland of Jewish liturgy, and the largely secular outlook that considered how—and whether—Jews could actually be "at home" in the modern political entity. While the relationship between collective memory and place continues to be important to the construction of Jewish identity, archetypal images of exile and return are being reconsidered. Rather than figuring primarily as a metaphysical condition, or what Arnold Eisen describes as "a function of our brief sojourn as human beings on God's earth," *galut* (exile) has come to refer, for many, to a geographical location, and the decision to live outside the State of Israel.[3] Thus, the terminology has fundamentally different meanings depending on where one (literally) stands—that is, whether one speaks as a Diaspora Jew or as an Israeli.

For a Zionist polemicist like the Israeli novelist, A. B. Yehoshua, for example, the original religious context for *galut* has been abandoned in order to characterize "diaspora" as a "neurotic, painful, and compulsive choice," a decision to live a distorted, tenuous life as a Jew.[4] The ideological argument for *aliyah* (immigration to Israel) that arises out of this position thus depends on traditional spatial imagery (center/periphery) while fundamentally altering its significance: from a classical Zionist perspective, Jewish identity is determined through the acceptance of the physical land of Israel both as one's *moledet* (national homeland) *and* as one's home. However, while many American Jews—like many Israelis—may conceive of galut in principally geographic terms, the notion of "homeland" in America tends to be conflated with "home." Rather than figuring as the source of a collective identity tied essentially to the land, "homeland" signifies first the familiar comforts and potential opportunities of America, and only then, and more ambiguously, a fixed and particular place within that cultural construct. Indeed, America rather than Israel has served as the metaphoric Promised Land in much of American Jewish literary representation—the land of milk and honey for immigrants at the end of a long journey rather than the Israel that has remained defined in largely mythic terms. (The most notable example of this is Mary Antin's immigrant autobiography, *The Promised Land,* which relies on the redemptive language of the Exodus story to depict the passage from Russia to America.) Despite the fact that Israel has received such consistent and passionate support from organized American Jewry that it has been called, cynically, their new religion, generous political and philanthropic contributions have not changed the fact that most American Jews do not view their diasporic community as even remotely "exilic." The received wisdom that places Israel as "central" to American Jewish identity is not our primary story of home. Nor, short of the Messiah, is Israel the place to which most of us imagine we will "return" in a kind of unidirectional trajectory that takes us directly from "here" to "there."

Rather, if we turn to contemporary American Jewish literature, we find Israel represented according to very different imagery—if we find it represented at all. As I see it, American Jewish novels of the 1980s and 1990s challenge what James Clifford calls the "teleology of origin/return" by replacing it instead with the trope of pilgrimage. In other words, when Israel appears in the literature at all, it is not as the end of the journey for American Jews—not as the culmination or climax of the story—but as a temporary sojourn on the way back home. (Thus, we get titles like Marcia Freedman's *Exile in the Promised Land,* or Saul Bellow's *To Jerusalem and Back.*) In some ways, then, the traditional imagery is inverted: Israel can now be read as a kind of temporary "exile" from the "true" homeland that is America. Accepting the narrative of Israel as the site of Jewish origin does not necessarily mean accepting the corresponding notion of eventual return. While shared narratives of Jewish history may be constitutive elements of what we call Jewish identity, these elements are also dynamic, and subject to contemporary readings and revisions. Thus, in recent texts by American Jews, one travels to Israel—and back—and then moves on. (We can contrast this circular movement, perhaps, with the language of *aliyah* and *yeridah*—going up and going down.) What marks this story as particularly American, of course, is that there is actually a home to which one can return.[5]

This travel to Israel takes a number of forms when it appears in contemporary literature. It can be a performative ritual—or rite-of-passage—that provides a kind of cultural literacy and marks the character as Jewish within the American Jewish community at large. We see an example of this in Joanna Spiro's short story "Three Thousand Years of Your History . . . Take One Year for Yourself." Here, while her friends take a year off to "lose themselves" in Bangkok and Beijing, Rachel, the protagonist, goes to Israel seeking what she calls "initiation" and hoping "to decipher the code that might lead the way on, or back, or on." For Rachel, the way back *is* the way on; although she learns Hebrew, works on a kibbutz, and travels the country, the more she is mistaken for Israeli, the more she realizes that Israel is not her real home. Travel to Israel can also be a spiritual pilgrimage, undertaken in the hope of finding religious coherence and meaning in a place where nation and religion are often too easily conflated. We see *this* kind of travel in Nessa Rapoport's novel *Preparing for Sabbath,* in which the main character, Judith, goes in search of what she calls "the new Jewish life she wanted, pure and only possible in Israel." However, while she continues to believe that "the holiest people is Israel and the holiest land, Israel" (p. 280), she also realizes that her life and her family are elsewhere, and the novel ends with her decision that "after Shabbat, she was leaving for dailiness" (p. 287). "Dailiness," as a physical destination, becomes a more meaningful definition of home for Judith than the spiritual space that is Israel. Each of these examples of travel can also be read as a broader kind of exploratory quest, in which the voyage out into the unknown is part of a continuously unfolding narrative of self-discovery. This last, and broadest, formulation is the most relevant for Philip Roth, equating as it does the exploration of territory and of individual identity, but we see it also in many other accounts of Israel—especially in memoir.[6] Conceiving of a temporary destination, then, functions as a device to pull a character forward into more and more retellings of the self.[7]

Indeed, *however* the story is cast, the experience of Israel in these texts is not *anti*-climactic but rather *non*-climactic; in narrative terms, it does not provide closure. Instead, it functions as simply *one way* among many to organize American Jewish identity. Experiencing, perhaps for the first time, membership in a cultural, religious, and political majority, American Jews in Israel measure themselves against images of otherness in order to come to terms with the nature of "home." In other words, even when contemporary American Jewish novels take place almost *entirely* in Israel, they are still—and perhaps not surprisingly—very much about America, and American Jews. As both a "real place" and a "mythic space," Israel allows for a wide range of contesting narratives of Jewish identity. Homeland shifts between the actual and the metaphoric: the Jewish self is defined varyingly in relation to birthplace, country of familial origin, spiritual heritage, and what George Steiner calls the "dwelling-place of the script"—or an ostensible "at-homeness" in the book. Israel—the modern political entity—becomes the site of self-transformation and textual reinventions, serving as what one character in Roth's *The Counterlife* calls the "laboratory for Jewish self-experiment" (p. 167).[8]

Before I discuss Roth's Israel novels specifically, it's worth taking a step back to reiterate the fact that he is one of a very small number of contemporary authors who is addressing the subject of Israel at all. Apart from a few popular novels that continue to depict Israel—and Israelis—in stereotypically romanticized terms, Israel appears with surprising infrequency in fiction. This is despite the fact that, along with the many sociological surveys, literary critics such as Ted Solotaroff continue to espouse the story of Israel's centrality, claiming that Israel has now become the most promising preoccupation of American Jewish writers. In 1988, and again in 1993, Solotaroff argued that "the American writer doesn't have to leave home or the immediate realities to tackle this theme, so strongly does the fate of Israel affect and shape the consciousness of American Jews, so firmly is it lodged at the top of the national community's agenda." Moreover, and somewhat surprisingly, he goes on to say that "since the Palestinian uprising and the government's response, Israel has moved even *closer* as a subject; it looms now not only as the hero of our illusions but as the victim of its own." So why might it be that this claim of Israel's centrality is not borne out by representation in the literature? If Israel is ostensibly so fundamental to formulations of American Jewish identity, why doesn't it appear more in the imaginative texts?[9]

In her essay on representations of Israel in Roth's *The Counterlife* and Anne Roiphe's *Lovingkindness,* Naomi Sokoloff offers a number of possible answers to these questions: perhaps a too-attractive depiction of Israel would threaten American Jewish complacency about a comfortable material existence; perhaps American Jewish writers are wary of accusations of parochialism; perhaps writers are concerned that they will not find a sympathetic audience for a portrait of Israel that includes both good and bad.[10] This last hypothesis is reflected in the attitude of Zuckerman's seatmate on the plane—the "American Jewish inferiority complex" that says we as Americans have no authority to speak about Israel if we don't live there. As this argument goes, discussion of Israel from the safety of distance is both presumptuous and potentially dangerous, as anything less than full support of Israel may be used by its enemies against it. However, this position reflects an Israeli political perspective more than an American Jewish cultural viewpoint and, to my mind, is unlikely to carry the weight for most fiction writers that it once might have. If we accept, for argument's sake, that Americans *do* turn to Israel to give meaning to their identity as Jews, then a more viable answer might sound something like this: the narratives of Israeli heroism and Jewish righteousness that were popular in the 50s and 60s — like Leon Uris's *Exodus* — simply cannot function as they once did. In other words, even if these stories had always been understood to be mythic — to tell us more about American illusions than about Israeli reality — American Jews can no longer "identify" with an unequivocally triumphant Israel. However appealing it may be to tell stories of idealized values that we see as both Jewish and American — like democracy, and pluralism, and civil rights — it may be difficult to reconcile them with the "reality" of Israel today. If this is the case, then Jewish American writers may not be writing about Israel now because to do so would be to say something uncomfortable about Jewish identity, that is, to confront the possibility that Jews, too, could assume the identity of the oppressor.

There are, of course, several contemporary texts that, like Uris's *Exodus*, depict characters who go to Israel to stay — those who accept the "teleology of return" that is so well-suited to an idealized vision of Israel. However, almost without exception, these characters are now portrayed as fanatics. Whereas, as Deborah Dash Moore has written, American Jews once drew upon American myths of the wilderness to represent Israel as a kind of geographical frontier, these romantic images of building a country as pioneers no longer resonate. Instead, the current political situation has transformed the terms of the frontier for a certain segment of religious Americans who see the territories as a kind of *spiritual* frontier in the war against Judaism. Thus, we get satirical novels like Tova Reich's *The Jewish War*, in which Yehudi HaGoel, formerly Jerry Goldberg of Brooklyn, declares himself king of the secessionist nation of Judea and Samaria and claims that this nation is, "in important respects, a working out and maturation of diverse summer camp themes" developed when he was a counselor at Camp Ziona in Liberty, New York. Even here, where the Land of Israel is essential to the story, the primary reference points are still American.[11]

Thus, there may be another explanation for why Israel appears so infrequently in contemporary American fiction — one both simpler and more complicated than the other alternatives. As I have been suggesting, it is clearly *America* that is the homeland of American Jews — the native land that is also the emotional center. That is, even when Israel *is* considered in the literature, it almost never appears as a real place: not as an actual, physical landscape or an identifiable location or even as a set of complex, three-dimensional Israeli characters. Instead, it tends to be invoked in mythic terms — as a state of mind that tells us more about particularly *American* Jewish narratives of identity than about Israel — or Israelis — per se. Israel remains unreal, at least to some degree, to American Jewish writers, and thus, if they come to represent it, they do so in particularly American terms.

With the exception of a brief episode in *Portnoy's Complaint,* Philip Roth did not direct his literary attention toward the subject of Israel prior to *The Counterlife*. Indeed, *America,* however localized, has always been, emphatically, the "homeland" of his fiction; although physical landscape is not foregrounded in his work, there is no mistaking his cultural context or the symbolic import of place. To a 1981 interview question "What does America mean to you?" Roth gave the following response: "America is the place I know best in the world. It's the *only* place I know in the world. My consciousness and my language were shaped by America. I'm an American writer in ways that a plumber isn't an American plumber or a miner an American miner or a cardiologist an American cardiologist. Rather, what the heart is to the cardiologist, the coal to the miner, the kitchen sink to the plumber, America is to me."[12]

"American," here, does not simply designate Roth's nationality in a way that is incidental to his work; rather, it names the material that he works *upon:* Roth is a writer of the subject matter that is America. If home, as Michael Seidel writes, "is locus, custom, memory, familiarity, ease, security, sanctuary," then the "home" that resonates in Roth's fiction is quite clearly the metonymic "kitchen table in Newark" that Zuckerman invokes in *The Counterlife* to offset the mythic narratives of Israel (p. 155).[13]

Thus, even Roth, as one of the few American Jewish authors who has written about Israel, does so always with one eye turned back toward America. As he makes clear first in *The Counterlife,* and then more fully in *Operation Shylock,* America and Israel can be seen as alternative responses — or counternarratives — to the exigencies of Jewish history, and thus to Jewish identity. To return to the character we began with, Nathan Zuckerman explains *his* understanding of the particular story that was Zionism by saying: "I was the American-born son of simple Galician tradesmen who, at the end of the last century, had on their own reached the same prophetic conclusion as Theodor Herzl—that there was no future for them in Christian Europe. . . . Insomuch as Zionism meant taking upon oneself, rather than leaving for others, responsibility for one's survival as a Jew, this was their brand of Zionism. And it worked" (p. 59).

In other words, Jews who came to America chose a different destination for their life stories; a different "Zion" in which to improve their experience of living as Jews. In response to a burst of Israeli Zionist pride in the land ("See that tree? . . . That's a Jewish tree. See that bird? That's a Jewish bird"), Nathan provides a ringing defense of diaspora "at-homeness" in America that is worth quoting at length:

> To be the Jew that I was . . . which was neither more nor less than the Jew I wished to be, I didn't need to live in a Jewish nation. . . . My landscape wasn't the Negev wilderness, or the Galilean hills, or the coast plain of ancient Philistia; it was industrial, immigrant America. . . . My sacred text wasn't the Bible but novels translated from Russian, German, and French into the language in which I was beginning to write and publish my own fiction—not the semantic range of classical Hebrew but the jumpy beat of American English was what excited me. I was not a Jewish survivor of a Nazi death camp in search of a safe and welcoming refuge, or a Jewish socialist for whom the primary source of injustice was the evil of capital, or a nationalist for whom cohesiveness was a Jewish political necessity, nor was I a believing Jew, a scholarly Jew, or a Jewish xenophobe who couldn't bear the proximity of goyim. (pp. 58–59)

Israel may be the logical conclusion to the life stories of Jews with many different kinds of beliefs, Nathan thinks, but *his* Jewish imagination is activated by America, and his paean to his homeland is full of references to himself. Individual responsibility and opportunity was at the heart of the "unpolitical, unideological 'family Zionism'" of his forebears, and this legacy is far more potent for him than what he calls the "tribal epic" of the distant past (p. 60).

As Nathan sees it, Zionism itself originated not only in a consensus of opinion about what was best for the survival of the Jewish people, but also in a deeply personal desire for metamorphosis. It was an individual as well as a collective desire "to reverse the very form of Jewish existence," he explains. "The construction of a counterlife that is one's own antimyth was at its very core. . . . A Jew could be a new person if he wanted to" (p. 167). The creation of counterlives, or "anti-myths," thus serves for Roth both as a familiar *American* trope — a means of reinventing oneself as "a new person" (in this case, moving to America, or to Israel, in order to rewrite oneself as a Jew) and, simultaneously, as a way of providing new readings of traditional narratives of *Jewish* identity (e.g., Zionism is a matter of personal transformation as much as it is a collective escape from social injustice).

In depicting two very different paths for Jews as he does in *The Counterlife* — one that led to America, the other to Israel — Roth explicitly challenges the traditional imagery of exile and return that locates "authentic" Jewish identity only in the Land of Israel.[14] Presenting *two* territorial options, or *two* poles of the Jewish imagination, Roth provides a series of counterlives that demonstrate what he calls the "and / and / and / and / and" of possibilities for Jewish identity. Nathan explains, "The burden isn't either / or, consciously choosing from possibilities equally difficult and regrettable — it's and / and / and / and / and as well. Life *is* and . . . all the multiplying realities, entangled, overlapping, colliding, [and] conjoined" (p. 350). Jewish identity in Roth's Israel novels is thus not simply *either* "here" *or* "there"; instead, it can be known only through a multiplicity of places and voices.

By the time we get to his 1993 novel, *Operation Shylock,* Roth has complicated the meaning of Jewish homeland still further. Where, in *The Counterlife,* Israel is only one of a number of possible destinies that Roth invents for the American Jew, *Operation Shylock* presents Israel *itself* as subject to reinvention, denied all sacred status as it is posed against the Diaspora as just one possible place for Jews to live. Instead of *two* territorial possibilities — Israel and America — we get three, as here Roth speculates about Eastern Europe as a viable option. And, rather than presenting a coherent "story" of Israel, this novel reflects the tensions and multiplicities of the contemporary state through wildly contradictory interpretations of its significance. We hear the voices of American, Israeli, and Palestinian characters — each of whom speculates about what place means to identity, and each of whom emphasizes again and again that the current struggles in Israel are over contested *stories* — or histories — as well as territory. While these characters' stories are very different from one another, they are neither mutually exclusive nor reconciled. Rather, for Roth, any understanding of the very complex question of what it means to be an American Jew in relation to Israel must — somehow — acknowledge *all* the stories.

There are far too many different storylines in this novel to explain here, but perhaps a few examples will suffice. With his reputation established as an outspoken advocate of the vitality of Jewish life in the Diaspora, Roth parodies himself in *Operation Shylock* by creating a character who also calls himself "Philip Roth," and who travels to Israel to preach a doctrine that he calls Diasporism. (For the sake of clarity in this chapter, I will call the author Roth, the narrator Philip, and the imposter Moishe Pipik, Philip's derisive nickname for him.[15]) Trading on Roth's name, Pipik seeks support for the transfer of all Ashkenazi Israelis *out* of the unsafe homeland that is Israel and *into* Eastern Europe as, what he calls, "the Only Solution to the Jewish Problem" (p. 18). Although he is aware that Palestinians are among those endangered in the Israeli state, Pipik is concerned primarily with Jews, whom he sees as in danger not only of physical destruction from Arab hostility, but also of moral dissolution as a consequence of their own sovereignty. Israel, "with its all-embracing Jewish totalism has replaced the goyim as the greatest intimidator of Jews in the world," he argues, capable "in many, many terrible ways [of] deforming and disfiguring Jews as only our anti-Semitic enemies once had the power to do" (p. 81). Moreover, "Israel has been an exile and no more" from "the most authentic Jewish homeland there has ever been" (pp. 42, 32). If "homeland" *here* means origins and history and nostalgia, then, as Pipik explains, "The roots of American Jewry are not in the Middle East but in Europe." Or, with Roth's comedic verve: "Grandpa did not hail from Haifa — Grandpa came from Minsk" (p. 47). Mocking an American Jewish obsession with their own identities, Pipik believes that playing on these strong personal associations with European culture will make it easy to untie their merely "abstractly sentimental connection" to Israel. If homeland refers primarily to origin rather than to sacred destination, then Israel is far from central to American Jewish identity; instead, their style, their words, and their *families* come from elsewhere.

The fictional conceit of the doppelgänger—especially a doppelgänger who bears the author's name—allows Roth to articulate radically different ideological positions while also linking them to the obsessions about identity and authorship that have haunted his literary career: What is the relationship between the author and his protagonist? What is the responsibility of the author to his reading audience? And, finally, what does it mean to be a good Jew? The notion of the double—or the counterlife—does not imply a duality that is resolved or reconciled; it indicates multiplicity rather than binarism, and the impossibility of a stable identity. The confrontation that evolves between Philip and Pipik is concerned principally with establishing what is "real," at once a literary question of identity construction (which of them tells the more convincing story of Philip Roth?) and a reflection of a larger question of historical counternarratives (what is the most convincing interpretation of Jewish survival?). Although both the self and the nation by necessity have physical boundaries, the narratives that surround them are not so clearly delineated. *Operation Shylock* suggests that the myth of a nation should be considered according to the same interpretive strategies as the myth of the self. In this view, "place" is no more stable or monological than individual identity; the "territory" of the nation, like the "territory" of the self, can be best comprehended as a conversation of voices—in relation, in interaction, in contradiction.

By putting the idea of Diasporism into the mouth of an impersonator and exaggerating it to the point of the ridiculous, Roth is able to ask the irreverent question, "What is Israel if NOT the true Jewish homeland?" while ostensibly deflecting attention from his own personal position on Israel. However, as he has done since the early days of his career, Roth also relies here on public interest in the scandalous conduct of his alter ego, and the potentially titillating confusion that arises between the "real life" of the author and that of his character. In *Operation Shylock,* Roth—as both the character and the author—can be simultaneously the good Jew, defending Israel, and the deplorable Jew, questioning it. No one *really* believes that the Jews should be resettled in Poland; as Ted Solotaroff points out, the cover of satire allows Roth to make even more audacious claims without being held accountable.[16] For not only is Israel *not* the Jewish homeland, according to the principles of Diasporism, but it is actively "bad for the Jews." In this view, Israel can no longer be the idealized Zion (if it ever could), nor can it serve as the site of an "authentic" Jewish identity. Rather, as Pipik explains, "[Israel] only confuses everyone, Jews and gentiles alike. I repeat: Israel only *endangers* everyone" (p. 81). Even if we, as readers, do not accept the radical solution of Jewish resettlement—and we are not expected to—we are forced here to think about whether Israel actually *has* succeeded as a safe haven for Jews, and what kind of Jewish identities are emerging there.

According to another exaggerated figure in the novel, the Palestinian, George Ziad, Israel is not only unsafe for the Jews but bad for their character as well. Indeed, even the novel's Palestinian characters define "Jew" and "Jewish history," more readily than they do "Palestinian," which serves to flesh out the novel's presentation of Jewish identity while also acknowledging Roth's lack of authority on potentially unfamiliar ground. Ziad is far more vocal about the deformations wrought by Israel upon the Jewish "character" than he is in articulating Palestinian claims to statehood, or in outlining Israeli brutalities against the Arabs. The political violence is situationally evident in the novel, but the characters' narratives are grounded in the mythologies of Israel rather than the policies, and the construction of Jew rather than the construction of Palestinian. Thus, although Ziad is fighting for his father's confiscated home in Jerusalem, his passionate support of Pipik's Diasporism is due not only to his rejection of Israel as the Jewish homeland but also to his romanticized representations of Diasporic Jewry.

The oppositions that Ziad establishes are striking in both their displacement and their irony: rather than setting the "bad" Israeli against the "good" Palestinian, Ziad sets the "bad" Israeli Jew against the "good" American Jew. His years of living with "*real* Jews" in America have left him outraged by the chutzpah with which Israelis espouse their own superiority. "These victorious Jews are terrible people," he cries:

> Jews who make military brutes out of their sons—and how superior they feel to you Jews who know nothing of guns! Jews who use clubs to break the hands of Arab children—and how superior they feel to you Jews incapable of such violence! . . . Superior to people who know in their bones the meaning of give-and-take? Who live with success, like

> tolerant human beings, in the great world of crosscurrents and human differences? Here they are *authentic,* here, locked up in their Jewish ghetto and armed to the teeth? And you there, *you* are "unauthentic," living freely in contact with all of mankind? . . . Oh, what an impoverished Jew this arrogant Israeli is! . . . This is their great Jewish achievement—to make Jews into jailers and jet-bomber pilots! (pp. 124–25)

Ziad's invective mocks the debate over Jewish authenticity by challenging the terms of the argument: "real" Jews for him are defined neither by the land (as Yehoshua would argue) nor by the text (as George Steiner would have it), nor by nostalgia (as Roth's double insists), but, rather, by the tolerance and conscience that he believes comes with freedom. By establishing and defending their own small enclave in the midst of hostile neighbors, Ziad explains, the State of Israel has warped the Jew beyond recognition, while the pluralism and opportunities of America have far surpassed Zionist expectations for the viability of Diaspora Jewry. "Zionists are inferior by every measure of civilization," he insists, "If you want to talk about culture, there is absolutely no comparison. Dismal painting and sculpture, no musical composition, and a very minor literature—that is what all their arrogance has produced. Compare this to American Jewish culture and it is pitiable, it is laughable" (p. 122). Moreover, he adds, "[Zionists] have advertised this state for forty years as essential to the existence of Jewish culture, people, heritage; they have tried with all their cunning to advertise Israel as a no-choice reality when, in fact, it is an *option,* to be examined in terms of *quality* and *value* . . . 'The Law of the Return'? [sic] As if any self-respecting civilized Jew would *want* to 'return' to a place like this! 'The Ingathering of the Exiles'? As if 'exile' from Jewishness begins to describe the Jewish condition anywhere but *here?*" (p. 135). For Ziad, the belief that Jews should "return" to Israel has thus been negated for any "self-respecting, civilized Jew" who should, to his mind, choose the more logical option of the advantages of the American homeland.

Of course, Ziad's stereotypes are intended to be absurd; as are many of the other positions expressed in the novel. However, the fact that these words come from the mouth of a Palestinian character, who might be expected to want the Jews to leave Israel, does not lessen their significance. Although they may perpetuate some overdetermined and essentializing narratives of identity, they also contain elements of truth. Moreover, they also serve to acknowledge the fact that *each* of Roth's counterbalancing narratives of Jewish identity is fundamentally essentializing, and simultaneously true and false.

In *Operation Shylock,* there can be no single narrative of Israel: it is depicted simultaneously as the cultural antithesis of America; as the unsafe alternative, or counternarrative, to radical Diasporism; as the site of the conflicting "ethnic mythologies" of Jews and Palestinians (p. 161). Despite the irreconcilability of these stories as a whole, each interpretation is represented as a plausible reading of the "facts" as understood from a wide range of perspectives. Even though Ziad's position is presented as that of someone whose perspective has been "corroded" by circumstances, he is hardly alone *either* in his belief that his own homeland was taken unjustly, *or* in his argument that America has become an alternative center of Jewish life and culture.[17] "There is more Jewish spirit and Jewish laughter and Jewish intelligence on the Upper West Side of Manhattan than in this entire country," he exclaims, and indeed, despite the exaggeration, the novel concludes with the character of Roth returning home after his struggles with his double in Israel (p. 122). "I am back in America," he explains, as he sits eating whitefish salad in a dairy restaurant on the Upper West Side, trying to understand what his experiences in Israel have meant to him as a Jewish writer (p. 383). Although he offers himself many possible readings of the situation, the answer ultimately remains ambiguous, as Roth makes clear that Israel cannot provide closure to American Jewish questions of identity. Whether, in relation to Israel, he is a good Jew or a bad Jew must remain unresolved. Instead, having returned from this "laboratory of Jewish self-experiment" to the familiar comforts of home, he declares, with no small measure of accomplishment, "I'm myself again, solidly back on my own ground" (p. 383).

NOTES

1. Philip Roth, *The Counterlife* (New York, 1986), p. 160. All further citations from this novel are noted in parentheses in the body of the text.

2. Philip Roth, *Operation Shylock: A Confession* (New York, 1993), p. 201. All further citations from this novel are noted in parentheses in the body of the text.

3. Arnold M. Eisen, *Galut: Modern Jewish Reflection on Homelessness and Homecoming* (Bloomington, IN, 1986), p. xviii.

4. A. B. Yehoshua, *Between Right and Right,* trans. Arnold Schwartz (Garden City, NY, 1981), p. 73. In his work on ethnicity, nationalism, and the politics of space, Oren Yiftachel provides a valuable discussion of "homeland ethnicity." See especially "Between Two Nations: Regionalism among Palestinian-Arabs in Israel," where he explains that "[h]omeland ethnicity characterises groups who reside in the territory they believe to be the source of their identity" (unpublished paper in possession of author, April 1997), p. 3. Arthur Hertzberg, *Being Jewish in America: The Modern Experience* (New York, 1979), p. 223.

5. James Clifford, "Diasporas," *Cultural Anthropology* 9:3 (1994), 306. For example, in a recent essay grappling with Jewish identity, Nancy K. Miller makes a quintessentially diasporic statement: "In my family history . . . at the origin are only stories, no places." "Hadassah Arms," in Jeffrey Rubin-Dorsky and Shelley Fisher Fishkin, eds., *People of the Book: Thirty Writers Reflect on Their Jewish Identity* (Madison, WI, 1996), p. 167.

6. See, for example, Marcia Freedman, *Exile in the Promised Land: A Memoir* (Ithaca, NY, 1990). It may also be interesting to consider other accounts of Israel that weave together personal experience, cultural analysis, and anecdotal travelogue while not qualifying as memoir per se. Although the explicit intent of many such texts is not to establish a coherent narrative of the author's life—or even to focus on the author at all—these texts do rely on the authority of the truth claims of personal testimony in order to make a larger political or cultural argument about Israel. See, for example, Jonathan Boyarin's verbatim inclusion of his fieldwork diary (entitled "My Trip to Israel") in *Palestine and Jewish History: Criticism at the Borders of Ethnography* (Minneapolis, 1996).

7. Joanna Spiro, "Three Thousand Years of Your History . . . Take One Year for Yourself," in Ted Solotaroff and Nessa Rapoport, eds., *Writing Our Way Home: Contemporary Stories by American Jewish Writers* (New York, 1992), pp. 347–49. Nessa Rapoport, *Preparing for Sabbath* (Sunnyside, 1981), p. 242. All further citations from this novel will be noted in parentheses in the body of the text.

8. For her valuable discussions of literary constructions of Jewish space, see Sidra DeKoven Ezrahi, "Our Homeland, the Text . . . Our Text the Homeland: Exile and Homecoming in the Modern Jewish Imagination," *Michigan Quarterly Review* 31:4 (Fall 1992), 463–97; "State and Real Estate: Territoriality and the

Modern Jewish Imagination," *Studies in Contemporary Jewry* 8 (New York, 1992), pp. 50–67; and "The Grapes of Roth: 'Diasporism' Between Portnoy and Shylock," *Studies in Contemporary Jewry,* 12 (New York, 1996), 148–58. Steiner explains, "Writing has been the indestructible guarantor, the 'underwriter', of the identity of the Jew: across the frontiers of his harrying, across the centuries, across the languages. . . . Like a snail, his antennae towards menace, the Jew has carried the house of the text on his back. What other domicile has been allowed him?" "Our Homeland, the Text," *Salmagundi* 66 (Winter/Spring 1985), 5.

9. In "The Rambowitz Syndrome," Paul Breines points to "roughly 50" thrillers, mysteries, and political fantasies that have as their prototype Leon Uris's *Exodus,* and are "linked by their idealized representation of Jewish warriors, tough guys, gangsters, Mossad agents, and Jews of all ages and sexes who fight back against their tormentors," *Tikkun* 5:6 (November/December 1990), 17. Naomi Sokoloff makes this point in "Imagining Israel in American Jewish Fiction: Anne Roiphe's *Lovingkindness* and Philip Roth's *The Counterlife,*" arguing that while these two texts provide some of the fullest examinations of Israel to date, their treatments are nonetheless partial and inconclusive. *Studies in American Jewish Literature* 10:1 (Spring 1991), 65–80. Ted Solotaroff, "American-Jewish Writers: On Edge Once More," *New York Times Book Review* (Dec. 19, 1988), p. 33. Revised and expanded in Richard Siegel and Tamar Sofer, eds., *The Writer in the Jewish Community: An Israeli-North American Dialogue* (Rutherford, NJ, 1993), p. 65.

10. Sokoloff, pp. 72–73.

11. See, for example, the character of Henry in the "Judea" section of Roth's *The Counterlife;* the character of Andrea/Sarai in Anne Roiphe's *Lovingkindness* (New York, 1987); and most of the characters in Tova Reich's *Master of the Return* (San Diego, 1985) and *The Jewish War* (New York, 1995). Deborah Dash Moore, "Israel as Frontier," *To the Golden Cities: Pursuing the American Jewish Dream in Miami and L.A.* (New York, 1994): see especially 235–36, 260–61. Quote from Reich, *The Jewish War,* p. 16.

12. Israel is notable in *Portnoy's Complaint* primarily as the site of Portnoy's impotence. After two hundred and fifty pages of being obsessed with shiksas (non-Jewish women), Portnoy arrives "in Wonderland"—a country "full of Jews"—where "the dream thing happens: '*I couldn't get it up in the State of Israel!* How's *that* for symbolism, *bubi?*'" (New York, 1967), p. 257. This is true for his fictional protagonists as well: in *The Anatomy Lesson* (1983), Nathan Zuckerman refuses to write an op-ed piece supporting Israel, explaining, "Look, I obviously don't want to see Jews destroyed. That wouldn't make too much sense. But I am not an

authority on Israel. I'm an authority on Newark. Not even on Newark. On the Weequahic section of Newark." In *Zuckerman Bound* (New York, 1986), pp. 303–4. "The Ghosts of Roth," interview with Alain Finkielkraut, *Esquire,* September 1981, pp. 92–97. Reprinted in George J. Searles, ed., *Conversations with Philip Roth,* Literary Conversations Series (Jackson, 1992), p. 130.

13. Michael Seidel, *Exile and the Narrative Imagination* (New Haven, CT, 1986), p. 10.

14. In the final chapter of *The Counterlife,* Roth invents yet another destiny for Natan Zuckerman: marriage to a Christian woman and residence in England. However, England is never considered as a possible Jewish homeland; in Nathan's mind, it is too suffused with anti-Semitism.

15. "Moishe Pipik" is a Yiddishism, "the derogatory, joking, nonsense name that translates literally to Moses Bellybutton" and is used to refer to "the little guy who wants to be a big shot" (p. 116).

16. Ted Solotaroff, "The Diasporist," Review of *Operation Shylock, The Nation,* June 7, 1993, p. 781. "The European component [as opposed to a perhaps more defensible American destination] provides a satirical cover for Pipik's points against Israel. These go largely unanswered while the novel takes potshots at Pipik's idea of resettling the Jews in their European graveyard."

17. See, for example, George Steiner: "Judaism has drawn its uncanny vitality from dispersal, from the adaptive demands made on it by dispersal. Ironically, the threat of that 'final solution' might prove to be the greatest yet if the Jews were now to be compacted in Israel" (Steiner, p. 23). Arguing that the sensibility engendered by "exile" is ultimately the most creative and free, Ziad parodies Steiner's outlook even as he parrots it. Steiner's belief that Jewish genius is born in wandering well serves his argument that Israel is not in the best interest of the Jews; however, the fact that it also works perfectly in the service of the Palestinian cause is not lost on Roth.

ELEVEN

Impact of Statehood on the Hebrew Literary Imagination: Haim Hazaz and the Zionist Narrative

ARNOLD J. BAND

The intimate relation between modern Hebrew literature and the development of the Jewish community in Eretz Yisrael, first in the Yishuv (the Jewish community in Palestine) and then in the sovereign State of Israel, is one of the fundamental, intriguing phenomena of modern Jewish history. During the pre-state period, the Hebrew literary establishment was one of the salient components of "ha-medinah baderekh," the crystallization of interlocking institutions which grew from the First Aliya onward and were in place and operative when the state was declared. In fact, most of the Hebrew literary establishment—writers, publishers, booksellers—had settled in mandatory Palestine by the early 1930s. To use current discourse, we can say that the Hebrew literary establishment was a major agent in the formation of "the Zionist narrative," that is, the system of narratives, symbols, and attitudes which the Zionist movement generated, wittingly or unwittingly, in its attempt to mobilize the Jewish population in both the Yishuv and the Diaspora, for actions leading to the creation of a Jewish sovereign state in the ancestral homeland. In turn, the establishment of a sovereign state has generated a host of new circumstances that have contributed to the burgeoning of Hebrew literature in Israel over the past two generations.

While this story has often been told, the parallel between the growth of the state and the development of Israeli literature has distorted the historiographic perspective on the period. The model has been fundamentally biological: both the state and Israeli literature are described as twins growing up together. Recognition is accorded to the pre-state writing of such figures as S. Yizhar, Aharon Meged, and Moshe Shamir, for instance, but little attention is devoted to the impact of the establishment of a sovereign Jewish state upon more established writers such as S. Y. Agnon and Haim Hazaz, in prose, or Avraham Shlonsky, Natan Alterman, and Amir Gilboa, in poetry. While it is understandable to focus upon what seems to be the new voices that gave expression to the emerging reality of statehood, the resulting picture is incomplete.

Even when writing a literary history at a distance of a generation or two, most critics choose to cluster the writers of a literary generation together and then treat writers and works separately, tracing their development from period to period in their lives. This is probably the most coherent way to present the variety and flux of artistic productivity. Ultimately, diachronicity dominates over synchronicity, because that is how we comprehend history. But if we want to understand the synchronic status of a literature in a specific decade—how writers and audiences of different ages interact in "real time," how political and social conditions might have affected them as a group—we rarely find a synchronic marshaling of material.

These preliminary observations on the tension between the diachronic and synchronic axes in the historiography of Israel literature provide a necessary framework for the main project of this chapter: a consideration of how the Israeli prose writer Haim Hazaz contributed to the shaping of the Zionist narrative. While much has been written on Hazaz and the Zionist narrative, I have not found an adequate assessment of his central role in this crucial project. Mention is often made of his story/essay "HaDerashah" (The Sermon) (1943), but the persistent presence of Hazaz in the center of the literary stage as the normative, admired writer of the Labor Party, the central political, hence cultural, force of the Yishuv and the state in its first twenty-five years has not been appreciated.[1] This failure stems logically from the normative historiographic bias which stresses the cutting edge in each generation or decade to the neglect of the total picture of literary production in any period. Writers are situated in the period when they first make a significant impact.

Take the most obvious example relevant to our topic: Israeli literature in its first decade. If we ask who were the leading prose writers of the 1950s, we would probably agree upon three names: Agnon, Hazaz, and Yizhar. When we study what Gershon Shaked, the leading literary historian of the period, has to say about these writers in his *HaSipporet ha'ivrit (1880–1980)* (Hebrew fiction), we will find Agnon in volume 2, Hazaz in volume 3, and Yizhar in volume 4.[2] This diffusion is inevitable, given the need to select and organize, to lend coherent shape to the chaos of history. The loss, nevertheless, is regrettable. Our consciousness of the loss of historical specificity becomes more acute when we peruse a study, however inchoate, like that of Reuven Kritz. In attempting to survey the prose productivity of the "Struggle for Independence Era," during roughly the decade before Israeli independence in his *HaSipporet ha'ivrit shel dor hama'avak le'atsma'ut* (Hebrew fiction of the generation of struggle for independence) (1978), we discover scores of names and hundreds of stories which were not mentioned by Shaked, certainly because the latter did not consider them of equal importance to those he did present.[3]

To further focus the historiographic problem which affects not only the literary historian, I ask a very specific question: How did the creation of a sovereign Jewish state in 1948—certainly a major event in modern Jewish history—affect the literary imaginations of such established writers as Agnon and Hazaz, Alterman and Shlonsky, writers in their prime years of creativity in 1948? By doing so, I hope to call attention to the problem described above and help rectify a distorted picture. In the process, I shall ask other questions, such as: How did writers whose imaginative and metaphorical coordinates were shaped by non-state or exilic or diasporan existence adapt to the new social, psychological, and philosophical realities of political sovereignty and all that they imply? Can one detect in their work an imaginative confrontation with this new phenomenon in Jewish history?

Did they assimilate these changes successfully? More generally, what happens to firmly held perspectives and ideologies when they are rendered obsolete by historical events? What happens to the "Zionist narrative"?

It should be obvious that these literary preoccupations are by no means indifferent to the historical debate precipitated by the Israeli "New Historians" and "Critical Sociologists" over the past decade.[4] While I agree that the decisions made by the founders of the state were motivated primarily by the exigencies of the period, these leaders were abundantly aware that they were involved in a momentous event in Jewish history. Furthermore, they were often shaped by the same cultural experiences as the writers who interest me in this project. All Hebrew writers of the period were deeply involved in and committed to the basic principles of classical Zionism, and their reaction to the realization of the Zionist dream is of cardinal importance.

I have chosen for my initial study the figure of Haim Hazaz (1898–1973), not that he is the best writer of the period, but because his literary career offers the richest opportunities for an examination of the questions detailed above. More than any respected writer of the first decade of Israeli sovereignty, Hazaz resembles most closely the profile of the leadership of the new state: mostly Russian or Polish Jews born about the turn of the century, those clustered under the rubric of the Third Aliyah, which, in many ways, absorbed the more prominent leaders of the Second Aliyah like Ben Gurion and Berl Katznelson. Born in Ukraine in 1898, reared in a pious home, Hazaz was old enough to comprehend the violent upheavals of the Great War and the October Revolution. Never distant from the sweep of armies and marauding bands during the civil war in Ukraine, he witnessed the uprooting and brutality which became part of the fabric of human experience in the twentieth century. As a Jew, furthermore, he experienced firsthand the ever-accelerating disintegration of the once clearly defined forms of Eastern European Jewish society. The years between the Bolshevik Revolution and his escape in 1921 to Istanbul were the formative experiences of his creative life to which he devoted all his fiction through 1931, when he moved from Paris, where he had lived for eight years, to Palestine. He returned obsessively to themes of the revolution even in the 1940s and the early 1950s, the first years of Israeli statehood. While brutality and force are never far from the scene of action, Hazaz is more interested in the phenomenon of historic upheavals and their implications for both individuals and Jewry as a historic entity.

Like other writers who had experienced the Russian Revolution, Hazaz was obsessed with the dialectics of history. For him, however, the dialectics of history do not involve Hegelian or Marxist notions regarding the swings of universal history; rather, they are limited to the history of Jews. Within this framework, he often vacillates between two radical attitudes. On the one hand, Jewish history is history par excellence because its major theme is the striving for redemption, the transcendence of history in a messianic period free of the agonies and contingencies of history. On the other hand, Jewish history does not exist, for history implies action, extension in space, whereas Jews, after their loss of political sovereignty, have been passive and bereft of space. The first view derives mostly from traditional Jewish, perhaps kabbalistic sources; the second, from modern themes of nationalism. Given the pressure of political and social events in Russia from 1914 on, Hazaz had to confront these two complementary but radically different vectors. His personal experience led him to conceive of history not as evolving processes but as a series of radical ruptures. This tension lends an intensity to his stories, to his Hebrew style in which rhythms are jagged and the individual words are frequently thrust forward in unexpected verbal, nominal, or adjectival modes, vibrating with an excitement on the verge of the apocalyptic. The kinship to the various offshoots of expressionism is clear. And while Zionism is an option of action in these "stories of the Revolution," it is by no means the dominant, driving option. Hazaz himself apparently did not feel compelled in the 1920s to seek the Zionist solution of aliyah (settlement in the ancestral homeland), but rather spent some eight years, from 1923 to 1931 in Paris—writing about the post-revolutionary experiences of Russian Jews.

Highly regarded even before his immigration to Jerusalem, Hazaz quickly joined the literary establishment once he did settle there. The leading figures in the dominant Labor Party, MAPAI, embraced him, and he published most of his stories in their newspaper, *Davar*, and his books in their publishing house, Am Oved. He garnered many honors throughout his career: the Bialik Prize twice (1942, 1971); the first Israel Prize for Literature in 1954;

membership in the Hebrew Language Academy (1953); the presidency of Agudat Hasoferim (the Writer's Association) (1970); several honorary doctorates, including one, bestowed posthumously, from the Hebrew University. The writer was repeatedly invited to deliver what were considered significant cultural policy statements.[5] For some fifteen years, between the late 1950s and the early 1970s, he was Labor's senior cultural spokesperson, constantly lecturing, eulogizing, commenting on cultural issues, responding to audiences who assembled to honor him, especially upon the publication of the second edition of his collected works in 1968. He was also called upon to comment on the significance of the victory of the Six-Day War and joined the Eretz Yisrael Hashelemah (the whole land of Israel) movement together with Natan Alterman and Moshe Shamir. In many senses he was the quintessential establishment prose writer for over forty years.

And yet, so radical have tastes changed in the past two decades that even in Shaked's history Hazaz is accorded only twenty-four pages (vol. 3, 1993), in contrast to eighty for Agnon (vol. 2, 1983), and Hazaz is known today by younger readers only for several anthologized stories in textbooks and mostly for "HaDerashah." (Ironically, though a natural object of attack by the literary critics associated with the New Historians, he has almost been ignored by them.) Hazaz, I argue, has lost his potential readers since the mid-1970s for the same reason that he captivated his contemporaries during his lifetime: his fiction was shaped by meditations on Jewish history and, after his aliyah in 1931, by meditations on Zionism. Inevitably, he intuitively envisages each situation as a point in a broad historical framework. Even when he was not writing what we might call "historical fiction" he focused upon moments or aspects of the dynamic process of Jewish history, primarily in the twentieth century. And even when he was focusing on the past, for example, when he dealt with Shabbetai Zevi in his play, *Bekets hayamim* (In the end of days), or in his many chapters on the life of Jesus, he tried to embody in his fiction the essence or meaning of Jewish suffering, of yearning for redemption, for the Messiah.[6] This characteristic is at once both his strongest and weakest point. When the historical resonance increases the body and depth of the realistic situation, the story vibrates with a certain excitement and scope which transcend that of ordinary realistic writing. This is fairly characteristic of Hazaz's work in the 1920s. But when the historical import outweighs the situation itself, realistic contours are so flattened that the result is embarrassingly (to today's reader) sermonic and tendentious. This is how Hazaz developed after his aliyah in 1931. Actually, this is precisely what his audience wanted then: a literature not only engaged with contemporary issues, but offering ideological discussion and suggesting direction.

His four "Zionist" stories—"Harat Olam" (Creation of the world) (1937), "Havit Akhura" (1937), "Drabkin" (1938), and "HaDerashah" (1942)—are a case in point. In these stories he creates characters—Moroshke in the first two, Drabkin in the third, and Yudka in the fourth—who are more expositors of various Zionist positions under discussion in those turbulent years than fictive characters. In fact, these stories are major constituents of the "Zionist narrative" and are still quoted as such. Even his "Yemenite novel," *HaYoshevet baganim* (1944), finds its positive solution when Rumiyeh, the lovely granddaughter of the pious hero, Mori Sa'id, settles in a kibbutz to work the soil in a paradigmatic Zionist gesture. These stories and the novel have supported the elevation of Hazaz the writer to an iconic status in the "Zionist narrative," a status reinforced by the loss of his son in the battles for the defense of Jerusalem in 1948. A comparison with Agnon's literary output of the same period is illuminating, for in those years Agnon published: "Sippur Pashut" (A simple story) (1935), *Ore'ah nata lalun* (A guest for the night) (1938–39), many of the stories of "Sefer hama'asim" (The book of deed) (1941), "Shevuat emunim" (Betrothed) (1943), and *Temol Shilshom* (Only yesterday) (1945). Even the last two of these fictions can hardly be considered supportive elements of the "Zionist narrative" although they are set in Palestine of the Second Aliyah.

It was only logical, therefore, that with the rapid loss in the 1970s of the hegemony of the Labor Party, which was for all practical purposes the major political and cultural establishment of Israel, its icons would also topple, among them Haim Hazaz. Though Hazaz was honored with his second Bialik Prize in 1971 and the presidency of the Writers Association in 1970, by then the shift in interest had raised such writers as Amos Oz and A. B. Yehoshua to critical acclaim. They, in turn, had replaced the first generation of Israeli writers—for example, Yizhar, Meged, and N. Shaham. In 1965 Aharon Meged published his *HaHay al hamet* (The living on the dead), the most open and forceful novelistic attack on the halutzic leadership of the Third Aliyah, Hazaz's contemporaries and admirers. I have suggested since the beginning of this chapter that a more synchronic view of literary history presents a picture closer to the real time existence of the literature, its production, and its reception. By adding a few dates to those we have just given, the complexity of the picture begins to emerge: in 1963, A. B. Yehoshua's "Mul haya'arot" (Facing the forests) is published; two years later, Aharon Meged publishes *HaHay ʿal hamet;* in 1966, S. Y. Agnon receives the Nobel Prize for Literature; in 1968 Amos Oz's *Mikhael sheli* (My Michael) and Hayim Hazaz's *Kol Kitvei* (Collected writings) (second, revised edition) are published. This list, spanning five years, notes significant publications in the careers of three generations of Israeli writers. The interaction of these generations is illuminating: for instance, the attitude of the younger generations toward their seniors may be one of emulation, of rejection, of parody.

Hazaz is thus the logical candidate for the question I have posed: How did the founding of the state influence already established writers? However, a list of his works of the first decade of the state demonstrates scholarly problems that are truly formidable.

1948: "Hupah vetaba'at"
1950: *Bekets hayamim* (End of days)
1952: *Ya'ish* III, IV
1955: "Nahar Shotef"
1956: *Daltot nehoshet* (Gates of bronze)
1958: "Ofek Natuy" (Extended horizon) in *Hagorat mazalot,* pp. 7–135

Of these six works, only the first and the last were written in the period under discussion.

Bekets hayamim, the only play Hazaz wrote, was first published in serial form in late 1933–1934 but was not produced on stage until 1950, when it was also published for the first time as a complete work. A historic drama set in the period of the Sabbatean messianic upheavals of the seventeenth century, it affords abundant opportunities for monologues on the agony of exile and the glory of redemption, two of the author's favorite themes. While the play certainly fits the euphoric, almost apocalyptic mood of 1950, the year of its production, it had been conceived and written in the months after the accession of Hitler to power in Germany. Because the differences between the early and later versions are relatively insignificant, they certainly do not warrant our characterizing this powerful play as a work written under the influence of the establishment of the state. We have, furthermore, no way to compare the reception of the play in 1934 (only as a read document), with its reception as a stage production in 1950.

One of Hazaz's two "Yemenite novels," *Ya'ish,* has an intricate publication history. The first of its four volumes was published serially in 1940–1941 under the Yemenite-sounding pseudonym "Zekhariah Uzali." The novel was then published in four parts, the first in 1947 as volume 4 of Hazaz's *Ketavim* (Writings), the second in 1948 as volume 5 of *Ketavim,* the third in 1952 as volume 6 of *Ketavim,* and the fourth in 1952 as volume 8 of *Ketavim*. Clearly, this novel was long in the works, and at least half of it had been published before the establishment of the state. It is a rambling Bildungsroman tracing the spiritual and sensual development of a young Yemenite boy, Ya'ish, beginning in his home in Yemen and ending, in the later volumes, in the Land of Israel. The book parallels Hazaz's other Yemenite novel, *HaYoshevet baganim* (1944), in that it was partially composed at the same time and follows the same broad developmental stages: the premodern world of religious piety suffused with fantasies of messianism; the dissipation of that world of faith and the concomitant dissolution of the hero's moral stature; a type of redemption through settlement in the Land of Israel. Because settlement in Israel is already posited as a novelistic solution in *HaYoshevet baganim,* published five years before the establishment of the state, it is impossible to attribute any of the Zionist motifs of the latter two parts of *Ya'ish* to the impact of the new reality: Jewish political sovereignty.

During the first five years of Israeli sovereignty, Hazaz invested much of his energies in rewriting two of his stories dealing with the period following the October Revolution. "Nahar shotef"(1955) is a radical recast of his first published story, "Mizeh umizeh" (1923) while *Daltot nehoshet* (1956) is a massive expansion of "Pirkei mahapekha" (1923). Although any connection between these stories and the impact of the new political reality must be speculative because both stories are detailed efforts to re-create the realities of the immediate post-revolutionary period in the Soviet Union, two suggestions can be made. First, it is productive to develop a suggestion made by Warren Bargad regarding the question: Why did Hazaz choose, at this point in his career, to rework his early stories on the Revolution? "It may well be that certain socio-political issues of the early fifties had influenced Hazaz in this regard. Israel itself was going through the early stages of a political revisionism; it was beginning to turn away from the Soviet Union (particularly in response the U.S.S.R.'s embracing of the Arab cause) and gradually moving towards western spheres of influence."[7]

While Israel was, indeed, shifting toward a more western orientation in the early 1950s, Hazaz, it should be remembered, had fled from the Soviet Union in 1921, had lived in Paris for eight years, had never written in support of Communism, and regarded the revolution as a catastrophe for Russian Jewry. While closely associated with the hegemonic MAPAI Party of the Labor block throughout his days in Palestine, then Israel, he was more interested in Zionism than in Socialism as the redemptive solution to the Jewish problem. In the early 1950s, the Labor block was embroiled in a vicious internecine battle over this issue. The catalyst was Stalin's anti-Semitism as manifested in the "doctors' trial" and the murder of the last Yiddish writers in the Soviet Union. When one reads both "Nahar shotef" and *Daltot nehoshet* against this background, one sees how the political controversy of the years 1951–1953 energized many aspects of these texts. Unfortunately, Hazaz is so interested in recreating the realistic milieu of the revolutionary period that plot, character, and even ideology are obscured by the detail.

Second, Hazaz's concept of history, of narrative, was shaped by the ruptures of World War I, the October Revolution, and the turmoils following the revolution: civil wars and pogroms. In trying to comprehend the momentous changes in Jewish history wrought by the creation of a sovereign Jewish state, he probably found his "objective correlative" in the post-revolutionary milieu, which he knew well and which was distant enough for fictional manipulation. The daily events of the new Israel might have been too difficult for him to handle artistically.

Of the two works first created after the establishment of the state, "Hupah vetaba'at" (1948) was well received probably because it was published only several months after the declaration of the state and the death of the author's son in battle, both in May 1948. Because it seemed to give expression to the emotions evoked by the momentous events of those months—the struggle for the defense of the state and the arrival of many refugees from Europe bringing tangible evidence of the ravages of the Holocaust—it answered the needs of the reading audience. The story focuses upon the thoughts and actions of one desolate widow, Mrs. Porat, who ruminates relentlessly about the death of her children in the Holocaust. The slow flow of the plot from one mournful situation to another is barely—and somewhat ironically—relieved when we hear outside her bedroom the jubilant noise of the crowd celebrating the declaration of the state. Hazaz thus fuses the two epochal events, devoting most of the attention to mourning rather than jubilation. The reader is forced to connect the two events and to dwell upon the agony and death that preceded and accompanied the public joy of the realization of the Zionist dream. The story gains additional poignancy when seen as a personal statement of the author's continued mourning for the loss of his only son who fell in the battle for Jerusalem twelve days before the official declaration of Israeli statehood.

The short novel "Ofek Natuy" (Extended horizon) (1958) deserves more detailed attention, not because it is an artistic triumph—it is far from that—but because it is the author's most transparent attempt to deal with the overwhelming historical events of the decade in novelistic form. Read today with our heightened sensitivity to both the elitist prejudices of the Labor Party and Haim Hazaz as an occasional spokesperson for its ideology, its biases are glaring and illustrative. The shift to the first-person narrative from his more customary third-person distancing makes the ideological positions even more transparent than usual. Always verging on a travelogue, "Ofek Natuy" is the account of the author's trip to the Lachish sector of the Israeli coastal plain to visit the new settlements composed mostly of Oriental immigrants. The given situation is most felicitous: the sophisticated urbanite European plunges himself into the midst of a society supposedly free from western contamination. That these Orientals are also Galut Jews, invariably so backward that they require instruction and constant surveillance by their modern, western brethren does not deflect Hazaz from his quest. And a quest it is. Superficially, the author is inspecting the material progress of the new settlements; actually, he is searching for a new hero-type with the virtues of the imaginary pristine Hebrew. As the story progresses, however, these virtues prove to be insufficient.

The author is engulfed by Oriental Jews from the moment he boards the bus for Lachish. They are gentle but raucous in their endless bickering, their childish naivete literally charming the narrator. The vignettes depicting the new immigrants at work and at play are posed, picturesque snapshots taken by a paternalistic tourist who is always conscious of the gulf between himself and the quaint primitives. They constantly remind him of Assyrian bas-reliefs, of sphinxes, or of primitive cave paintings. Their daily activity forms the background for the experiences and reflections of the narrator and endow the novel with whatever unity it has. All the primary characters are calculated to represent various sentiments or traits which serve to shape the image of the new hero. The author's first hosts are Shimon and Miriam Zayit (Olive), the administrative heads of the area. Though middle-aged and middle-class, they had abandoned the settled life of public officials in Jerusalem to guide and educate the recent immigrants. Imbued with a sense of mission and haunted by the past, Shimon constantly quotes biblical verses. (The author, too, always carried his pocket Bible with him.) In their conversations, the degenerate complexity of city life is continually contrasted with the salutary simplicity of life on the land; the whipping boy of their jests is the public official or orator. In educating the Orientals, they and their staff of teachers who join the conversation feel a sense of personal fulfillment; they are doing a constructive act in a disintegrating world. Premonitions of the very real danger of Levantinism, which was threatening Israel, are voiced by Uri, a teacher: "in several years the children of the Oriental groups will comprise a majority in the country. And immigration continues to come from the East. Ultimately we will turn into an Oriental nation. . . . All the traits which have rooted themselves in us during the 2000 years of exile in Europe and by which we have become a European entity [will disappear]. The question is: Is it possible to deposit in the hands of an Oriental the destiny of the Hebrew nation, Hebrew history, and, more than this, the destiny of the country? . . . The East is indifferent, sunk in the routine of generations upon generations . . . anarchic, individualistic, fanatic, lazy. . . . One can't rely upon education. Primal traits and tendencies always return, and return precisely at crucial, decisive moments."[8] Because the harsh realism of these views is not consistent with Hazaz's romantic vision of the Orientals, he refutes Uri's case by depicting its pleader as a student of sociology, a neurotic intellectual. One may wonder, in passing, why this exilic stereotype had not been redeemed by his contact with the soil—or, for that mater, what Hazaz's personal position really is.

The antithesis of Uri is present in Yuval, the regional supervisor who is rarely seen without his jeep. Youthful and vigorous, efficient and businesslike, he possesses a reserve that bespeaks stability and, technically, allows the author to indulge in interim mystical reveries on the broad fields they are passing: reflections upon the freshness and force of raw nature, the distant Israelite past, the bond between the ancient Israelite and the modern Israeli farmer. In several remarkable passages the author describes his exhaustion after hours in the open fields at the mercy of the crushing desert sun. The terrain, itself, assumes symbolic value: the "outstretched horizon" (ofek natuy) reaches back to the past and forward to the future. The naked force of nature is identified with the natural past when the Hebrew was a farmer and closer to nature. This is a specifically Zionist category of naturalism, for coupled with the adoration of naked natural forces and a flight from civilized sophistication is a yearning for an imaginary preexilic Hebrew past and a possible future.

At a second encounter several months later, the taciturn Yuval is discovered to be effusive, even sentimental concerning the education of the immigrants and the dignity of farm labor. Similar sentiments are expressed even more emphatically by the rabbi of Mesharim (rightness or directness), one of the villages in the sector: "We have at our disposal three cures which are effective for every disease and plague—and they are: Torah, loyal citizenship, and tilling the soil" (p. 88). The reader will perhaps find it a bit disingenuous that the rabbi holds a law degree from the Sorbonne and is an expert marksman with a pistol. His talk of missionary work and universal religion coupled with his earthly bearing preclude any possibility of identifying him with a rabbi of the Galut.

The narrator becomes personally involved in his story upon meeting Rehela, a fiery Moroccan maiden whose desert beauty enchants him. Embarrassed at his infatuation with an adolescent yet unable to resist her charms, he lingers in the sunbaked fields to catch a glimpse of his beloved. In his mind she obviously symbolizes the legendary Hebrew beauty who seems to be at home in a primitive setting. Her name, in fact, is a derivative of Rachel—a name which her literary cousins often bear. And though she spurns him, he cannot forget her.

In his wandering through the fields, the narrator meets Binyamin Oppenheim. Binyamin's characterization is a realization of the views he represents. Tall and handsome, Binyamin is a young American rabbi who has come to tour Israel. But he cannot simply be an American: actually, Binyamin, the last of a long line of distinguished European Jews, has survived the concentration camps and spent four years in Israel before migrating to America. He looks and acts like an Israeli. Though a product of the Galut, he has already been partly redeemed. In their conversation Binyamin verbalizes many of the leitmotivs of Hazaz's literary creations with the significant exception that here the Galut is evaluated more objectively.

Although it is posited that the Galut is drawing to a close because of its inability to sustain itself, Binyamin regards its passing ruefully because "it was a mighty deed, one of the greatest things that happened in the world" (p. 124). The Jewish people accepted Galut voluntarily, even proudly: the ancestral land was not of prime significance; God was. God was the center of the universe and his adoration, the sublime purpose of all life. The Galut, therefore, was the peculiar ennobling characteristic of Jewish experience. In its transcendence of temporal interests and its devotion to God, it pointed the way to the salvation of mankind; "in it was hidden the secret of the redemption of humanity" (p. 126). But now that the Galut is drawing to a close, all that is left is a national state. "The land of Israel is a decline, a submission, bankruptcy and despair. It is not for this that we have struggled among the nations for two thousand years from one end of the world to the other and have borne all kind of harsh and evil afflictions, and have been killed in all kinds of harsh deaths, and have suffered for the sins of all of them—so that finally we will return to the Land of Israel. Folly! Absurdity! A thing which makes no sense. This is as if . . . as if . . . Jesus, let us say, after they lowered him from the cross and he rose from the dead, returns to Nazareth and works at his carpentry" (p. 125).

As the discussion ends, Binyamin parts with the narrator, each continuing on his own way through the fields. Had the story ended here, one might imagine that Hazaz regretted the alleged end of the Galut and feared for the future of the State of Israel. The ending of the story, though abrupt and artificial, seems to indicate, however, that Hazaz had not changed his position. Visiting a kibbutz in the Negev a year later, the narrator meets a pregnant woman who turns out to be Rehela. She rushes into the barn to summon her husband, who, of course, is none other than Binyamin. The reader is led to understand that he, too, has undergone the transition from Galut to complete redemption particularly through his love for Rehela, the primitive Hebrew beauty. Their child will naturally be the new ideal hero.

The search for a new hero-type is not a new phenomenon in modern Hebrew literature. By the 1880s authors rejected the stereotype of enlightened Jew battling the forces of darkness and sought heroism in romanticized portrayals of pious, often Hasidic types. Toward the end of the century, this type gave way to the *talush,* the uprooted, almost "superfluous man," common in late-nineteenth-century European literature. In Hebrew literature created in the Palestine of the Second Aliyah, the talush was often replaced by the *halutz,* the pioneer rebuilding the ancestral homeland. (The many deracinated heroes of Yosef Hayyim Brenner are perfect examples of talushim even when they seek to root themselves in the ancestral soil.[9]) The highly idealized swamp-drainer and desert-reclaimer always volunteered—as some did in real life—to undergo severe hardship and danger to realize the dream of Zionist redemption. He felt fulfillment through self-sacrifice and an unflagging devotion to this vision of personal and national salvation. But by the 1950s the halutz, too, had outlived his capacity to focus and personify the moral issues of the day. The creation of the State of Israel predicated the realization and hence the dissipation of an inspiring dream; and the formation of an organized policy based on prescribed duties and rights robbed pioneering and volunteerism of their appeal.

Since the creation of the state, therefore, the Israeli novelist has confronted a new cultural and artistic problem. Ordinarily, the individuality of a created character, his decisions and actions, should bear some relationship to an accepted set of values and an identifiable social group—but the coordinates of Israeli society became more and more tenuous. The identifiable outlines of the Palestinian community on the eve of statehood were blurred by the successive waves of immigrants of diverse ethnic backgrounds. The much discussed "return to normalcy" precipitated a moral crisis among writers not habituated to "normalcy." To what society or set of values could a hero be related either as a reflector or a rebel?

Although this quandary was shared by writers of fiction in many western countries throughout the postwar world, historical circumstances particularized the experience of the Hebrew writer. The disintegration of the mold of western society during the past two centuries was exacerbated in the instance of the Jewish community by extraordinary circumstances: violent geographical displacements, partial extermination, and the shift from a unique situation and concept of exile to landed statehood. However, the situation was temporarily assuaged by the application of interim ideologies, most of which proved fruitless. The astounding material success of political Zionism both de-energized it as a moving ideology and, now that the uniqueness of the exilic situation had been eliminated, confronted the Hebrew writer in Israel more squarely with the problems which had been besetting his colleagues in other countries. He now had to face the enraging fact that the "normalcy" which he had been taught to equate with social health—even with salvation—often implied precisely the opposite in the twentieth century. Problems of the spirit are not necessarily solved by the valiant reclamation of barren wastes or even the creation of a welfare state. The Israeli writer, indeed, had to return to the universally human questions which had obsessed those of his predecessors who did not succumb to the temptation to reduce all human situations to an obvious personification of the plight of Jewry in the Galut—for example, Agnon. His quest to redefine the human condition, furthermore, must necessarily be conditioned by the wealth of the historic associations which his language constantly evokes. He had to decide, for instance, whether the redemption he often writes of is that of normative Judaism or of Herzen and Bakunin.

Hazaz's shift from the third to the first person, I have noted, both uncovered and unleashed the obsession with ideology which was always present in his previous works. But this alone does not explain the grotesquerie of "Ofek Natuy." The ideology of his earlier stories was less verbalized than felt, emerging, as it did, from actual situations in a definable society. But in "Ofek Natuy" everything is invented, even prefabricated. The new hero, as yet unborn, is a product of will and not of the imagination—an artificial harlequinade of disparate elements. Born of Binyamin and Rehela, educated and trained by the likes of the Zayits, Yuval, and the rabbi, the future hero will stand entrenched in the ancestral soil of Lachish and scan the "outstretched horizon" beckoning towards the future. Bereft of truly imaginative creations, the story disintegrates into a secular morality play from which God is absent, Satan is the decadent Galut, and Everyman is the unwritten result of an ideological equation.

In December 1955, probably shortly before he began work on "Ofek Natuy," Hazaz wrote one of his first major articles on the mission of Hebrew literature in the newly created sovereign state of Israel.[10] He lamented the failure of Hebrew writers to capture and express in their fictions the majesty of the momentous events of the period viewed from a broad historical perspective. After centuries of exile, the Jewish people had returned to their ancestral homeland and created there a viable sovereign state. The descriptions of these events are always couched in messianic rhetoric, however secularized Hazaz might have been. One of the aspects of the Jewish messianic dream has always been the ingathering of exiles, the return of Jews from all the corners of their exile to their homeland.

In "Ofek Natuy," Hazaz is clearly attempting, however feebly, to realize this authorial aspiration. He yearned to write the great Israeli novel. In order to fully appreciate the ambitions and failures of the novel, however, one must view it not only as a late novel in the author's career but also as an integral part of the literary effort of the decade, a proposal I made at the beginning of this chapter. At about the same time, Yizhar, a generation younger than Hazaz, was deep into his expansive novel on the Israeli War of Independence, *Yeme Tsiklag* (Days of Tsiklag) (1957), certainly the most impressive novel of Israel's first decade, and A. B. Yehoshua, a generation younger than Yizhar, published his first short story, "Mot Hazaken" (The death of the old man) (1957), an ironic elegy on the death of a Zionist hero. While Hazaz's "Ofek Natuy" is a paean to the Zionist achievement, Yizar's novel and Yehoshua's short story both raise questions about this grand human project and suggest areas of failure or disappointment. Although I do not claim that any of these writers, however talented, has succeeded in meeting the high demands that Hazaz established in his essay on the mission of Israeli literature — Yizhar and Yehoshua would question whether Israeli literature should have any such mission — I do suggest that a synchronic comparison of these three more or less contemporary works would open new, extensive horizons in our understanding of the dynamics of literary change in the first decade of Israel's existence. We would also learn that many of the ideas that find articulation among the "New Historians" and "Critical Sociologists" of the 1980s and 1990s were already evident in the fiction of the younger writers of the 1950s. The disenchantment with the myths and ideals of Zionism and declared Israeli public norms was already present in the late 1950s and early 1960s in the work of such influential writers as Yehoshua and Oz in prose, and in Yehuda Amichai and Natan Zach in poetry. The student of Hebrew literature often wonders why this realization has come to political scientists and sociologists so belatedly.

NOTES

1. Haim Hazaz, "The Sermon," *Israeli Stories* (New York, 1965), pp. 65–86, reprints the *Partisan Review* translation.

2. Gershon Shaked, *HaSipporet ha'ivrit: 1880–1980* (Tel Aviv), vol. 2, 1983; vol. 3, 1988; vol. 4, 1993 (in Hebrew).

3. Reuven Kritz, *HaSipporet ha'ivrit shel dor hama'avak le'atsma'ut* (Kiryat Motzkin, 1978) (in Hebrew).

4. The emergence of the "New Historians" and the "Critical Sociologists" in Israel over the past decade has generated a broad literature in both books and periodicals. For a tentative summary and bibliographies see *History and Memory* 7:1 (Spring–Summer 1995) and *Te'oria uvikoret* (Summer 1996). For literary criticism in the light of the "New Historians," see Yitzhak Laor's *Anu kotevim otkha moledet* (Tel Aviv, 1995). This collection of essays has been critiqued by Gerson Shaked, "Aher — al '*Anu kotevim otkha moledet*' (1995) me'et Yithak Laor," *Alpayim* 12 (1996), 1–72. See also Hannah Hever, *Paytanim uviryonim* (Jerusalem, 1994).

5. For a listing of Hazaz's articles and speeches see Rafael Weiser, *Annotated Bibliography of the Writing of Haim Hazaz* (Jerusalem, 1992), items 250 ff. (in Hebrew). All these items were collected by his widow, Aviva Hazaz, in *Mishpat hage'ula* (Tel Aviv, 1977). In general, Weiser's bibliography is an indispensable source for the study of Hazaz's writings because it organizes in coherent form one

of the most chaotic publication careers imaginable. Many of Hazaz's publications were revised and republished or were parts of novels, many unfinished, and published serially. During the 1940s, Hazaz was writing some six novels simultaneously and published at least two items per month in *Davar.* For a less complete, yet eminently serviceable English bibliography see Warren Bargad, *Ideas in Fiction: The Works of Hayim Hazaz* (Providence, 1982), 133–36. For the sake of clarity, I have simplified the bibliographic complexity.

6. As indicated in Weiser, *Bekets hayamim* was first published serially in 1933 ff, but was actually finished in early 1932. The full play, adapted for theater production, was revised in 1950 and published as a separate volume that year. Many chapters of Hazaz's novel on the life of Jesus were published in the late 1940s but were never collected.

7. Warren Bargad, *Ideas in Fiction: The Works of Hayim Hazaz* (Providence, 1982), p. 117. The obvious, often contradictory ideological statements which I and Bargad find so troubling are justified by Nurith Gertz in an article dealing with Hazaz's fiction of the 1930s: "Ideology versus Literature in the Stories of Hazaz," *Prooftexts* 8:2 (May 1988). Gertz claims that this ideological confusion is deliberate, actually the result of a "poetics of contradictions" which is the author's response to the "heavy pressure exerted upon writers to express a political ideology and be mobilized in the Zionist national struggle" (p. 194).

8. All translations of "Ofek Natuy" are mine. The Hebrew text of "Ofek Natuy" used is the original 1958 edition, published in *Hagorat mazalot* (Tel Aviv, 1958); quotation on p. 29. All future citations from this work are noted in parentheses in the body of the text.

9. See Joseph Hayyim Brenner, *Breakdown and Bereavement,* trans. Hillel Halkin (Philadelphia, 1971), and *Out of the Depths,* trans. David Patterson (Boulder, 1992).

10. "HaSifrut ha'ivrit bazeman hazeh," *HaBoker,* Dec. 16, 1955. Republished in *Davar,* Dec. 23, 1955; and in *Lamerhav,* Dec. 23, 1955; and in *Daf,* vol. 11, pp. 3–5.

PART III

Political Cultures

TWELVE

Becoming Ethnic, Becoming American: Different Patterns and Configurations of the Assimilation of Eastern European Jews, 1890–1940

EWA MORAWSKA

Few historians would question today the diversity of the ways in which Jewish immigrants and their offspring incorporated themselves into the local societies in which they settled. Most historical studies of different American Jewish communities that have accumulated over the past two decades—obviously important contributions to our knowledge of American Jewish history—are community or case investigations, focused exclusively on one place. Enough material now exists to take a comparative approach and examine the specific situations that generated and sustained (or weakened) particular patterns of Jews' adaptation to the host American society in various localities. This chapter is intended to open an investigation rather than to pronounce its results.

I have selected for consideration one aspect of this adaptation, namely, the nature of and the general direction of change in the collective (group) ethnic identity. Specifically, I refer to Eastern European Jews in America, with a primary focus on the interwar period in the context of a longer-term perspective. Collective ethnic identity is understood here as a shared sense of we-ness and perceptions of group boundaries based on the recognition of common origin, history, and culture and/or current experience among group members.

Adaptation of immigrants and their descendants to the dominant society is a multidimensional process. In addition to an identificational or psychological component, it includes structural integration and extrinsic and intrinsic cultural elements. Structural integration involves incorporation into mainstream economic, political, and social institutions. These subprocesses are interdependent, but, according to Milton Yinger, they "vary in distinctive ways propelled by somewhat different sets of circumstances; they change at different rates and in different sequences."[1] My agreement with Yinger's interpretation of the complexities of assimilation also justifies separate treatment of ethnic identity.

Two models of adaptation to the dominant society by immigrants and subsequent generations have been most common in American immigration and ethnic studies, including studies on American Jews. The assimilation model, which dates back to the beginning of the twentieth century and is still widely used by social scientists despite recurrent critical barrages, posits the progressive dislodgement by mainstream society of ethnic customs, social bonds, and identities. In this model, the disappearance of group ethnic identity constitutes one of the final stages of the assimilation process, preceded chronologically by sustained participation of ethnic actors in mainstream society's civic-political organizations and activities and by their involvement in primary social relations with members of the dominant group(s). Following the demise of ethnic group identity comes the extinction of individual or subjective ethnic identification. This concludes the assimilation process.

The more recent "ethnicization" model assumes that ethnic lifestyles and identities emerge in the interplay between newcomer-actors and the host environment.[2] In this approach, the specific "contents" and pace of ethnicization are viewed not as linear, progressive developments but as contingent on time- and place-specific circumstances. In the case considered here, the issues involve attenuation or enhancement of collective group identity, and its character as accommodating or "confrontational," as well as its outward or inward orientation. This chapter employs this newer approach, which allows also for the configuration of historical circumstances that facilitate assimilation as defined. Put differently, the approach encompasses the *historicized* assimilation model, albeit made time- and place-specific and embedded in plural contexts.[3] Specifically, this chapter treats ethnic identification as a variable rather than an attribute and therefore as potentially "reversible."

Drawing from the available historical studies and censuses of general and Jewish populations in six selected American cities, content analysis of local community studies and the available autobiographies and memoirs of former residents of these Jewish communities, and information obtained from old-time residents and/or students of these localities whom I contacted by telephone, I have identified specific configurations of factors most likely to have shaped the collective ethnic identity of Eastern European members of local Jewish communities. I want to demonstrate two things: first, that the dilution of collective ethnic identity did not occur, as the assimilation model predicts, in a set linear sequence, but, rather, that it has been contingent on circumstances surrounding and within concrete American Jewish communities; and second that, depending on various configurations of factors within and outside of these communities, this group ethnic identity assumed different characteristics.

I have selected for discussion six localities (in order of general population size): New York (treated here summarily mainly for comparative purposes; it has been studied enough as the "master pattern" of American Jewish life); Cleveland; Boston; San Francisco; Charleston, South Carolina; and Greensboro, North Carolina. From the sources pertaining to Jewish communities in these localities during the period considered here and the available histories of Jewish communities elsewhere in the country—about thirty-odd studies—I have compiled twenty-six factors that were either identified by authors/informants or evaluated by me as having influenced, individually or in clusters, local Jews' collective self-perceptions or self-representations.

As table 1 indicates, these contributing factors include both structural and cultural elements of immigrants' adaptation whose interdependence with their collective identity has already been noted. One must also assume interactive relationships between some causal circumstances and the enhancement or attenuation of the collective ethnic identity of American Jews. The

TABLE 1

FACTORS AFFECTING GROUP ETHNIC IDENTITY OF AMERICAN JEWS, 1920–1940

I. Characteristics of the Surrounding Environment:

1. Size of the city
2. Presence of economic opportunities and channels for upward occupational mobility
3. Fluidity of local social structure
4. Ethnic residential segregation
5. Civic-political climate and practice concerning outsiders / newcomers (exclusive or inclusive)

5a. Public recognition of the presence and merits of Jewish group members among the city's pioneer settlers

5b. Incidents of anti-Semitism

6. Competitive ethnic relations / politics
7. Degree of social distance (separatism) of the dominant group vis-à-vis the outsiders / newcomers, and specifically Jews
8. Social relevance of race

II. Characteristics of the Local Jewish Group:

9. Size of the Jewish group

9a. Share of the Jewish population in city total

9b. Huge size of the Jewish group

10. Fit of the Jewish group's "collective human capital," particularly educational and occupational skills, into the profile and dynamics of the local economy

10a. Approximate parity between economic positions of the Jewish group and the dominant class-ethnic strata

11. Sense of the shared local past with high-status groups in the city
12. Participation in local civic-political organizations / affairs

12a. Participation in private social activities of the dominant group(s)

13. Residential concentration
14. Residential stability of the group core
15. Presence of absorbing intragroup social-institutional networks and activities

16. Degree of religious/sociocultural (self-)separatism of the Jewish group
17. Presence of the outstanding group leaders and their (inward or outward) orientation
18. Proportion of native-born American (second-generation) Jews in the group
19. Presence of the enduring "unfriendly" separation between the earlier established German Jews and their Eastern European counterparts
20. Acknowledged influence of local, national, or international events involving the Jewish group in a positive (integrative) or threatening (disintegrative) fashion

theoretical model of *structuration* as proposed by Anthony Giddens accounts for this complex interrelationship and encompasses at the same time the ethnicization approach. Giddens posits reciprocity between social environment and purposeful social actors.[4]

I discuss three major types and, within each of them, subtypes of ethnic collective identity of foreign stock (immigrant and second-generation) Eastern European Jews in six American cities during the interwar period. At one end of the spectrum is the "ethnic identity enhancement" type, represented in different ways by New York, San Francisco, and Boston, and at the opposite end of the spectrum is the "ethnic identity attenuation" type, represented in different varieties by Greensboro and Charleston. The in-between category is exemplified by Cleveland.

Two important points are worth noting before examining particular localities. First, the vistas presented here are "bird's-eye views." In each case and at the cost of unavoidable simplifications, the dominant or ascending trends and characteristics noted during the interwar period are treated as representative of the entire group. And second, because of the lack of necessary information (beyond the enumeration of "famous women" among local Jews) in most available studies, the effects of gender on the collective ethnic identities of Eastern European Jews in specific cities are not included in the discussion (I consider in my conclusion to this chapter, however, some questions in this matter that could be pursued in a comparative-historical research).

ENHANCED GROUP ETHNIC IDENTITY: NEW YORK, SAN FRANCISCO, AND BOSTON

The most salient case in this category is New York, where the entire constellation of mutually reinforcing external and intra-group factors effectively enhanced a collective ethnic identity among local Jews and gave it a distinctly assertive tone. A combination of factors seems to have been primarily responsible. These include, first, immense size and tight residential concentration of the Jewish population and a "complete" ethnic community so that in entire sections of the city, Jews—Eastern European Jews in particular—simply *were* "America," ethnically dominating local public institutions. Second, New York Jews' collective ascent into the city's expanding white-collar occupations and the accompanying modernization or Americanization of their synagogues/religious life facilitated entry into mainstream civic-political institutions in which New York Jews became "ardent participants" by the interwar period.[5] Third, Jews entered en masse a traditionally pluralist, but distinctly ethnic-conscious and competitive New York civic-political process, taking advantage of a variety of political outlets in the city's public arena. Fourth, publicly expressed anti-Semitism and social exclusion on the part of the city's Anglo-Protestant upper strata increased in reaction to the perceived status threat from upwardly mobile Jews, especially those of Eastern European origin. Finally, local, national, and international events during the interwar period brought into yet sharper relief ethnic boundaries and divisions. Thus, as table 2 shows, enhanced from several sides, feelings of we-ness and perceptions of group boundaries among New York Jews intensified, in turn, their preference for residence in ethnic neighborhoods (see table 1, factor 13), participation in ethnic life (factor 15), and a sense of sociocultural distinctiveness (factor 16). These, in turn, strengthened social distance toward them on the part of the dominant group(s) (factor 7) which, again, sustained New York Jews' collective ethnic identity.

In comparison with New York Jews, the collective ethnic identity of Eastern European Jews in San Francisco, although also enhanced, was decidedly nonassertive and sustained by a quite different configuration of factors. As table 3 shows, San Francisco had a general population of 640,000

TABLE 2

FACTORS CONTRIBUTING TO AN "ASSERTIVE" ETHNIC IDENTITY OF NEW YORK JEWS

In the surrounding environment:

—The city's dynamic economy and rapid growth of the white-collar sector (see table 1, factor 2)

—Competitive ethnic politics and accessibility of many and diverse outlets for civic-political activity (factors 6, 5)

—Incidents of anti-Semitism (especially at workplaces) (factor 5b)

Within the Jewish community:

—Huge size of the Jewish group, its residential concentration, and presence of the "total," absorbing ethnic community (factors 9b, 13, 15)

—Good fit of Jews' educational and occupational skills into the profile and dynamics of local economy/collective entry into the middle class (factor 10)

—Active participation in local civic-political affairs and presence of outstanding group leaders and public-minded individuals (factors 12, 17)

—"Mobilizing" influence of local, national, and international events involving the Jewish group (factor 20)

Note: New York: general population 6.5 million; Jewish 1.8 million, or 30% (1930)

Sources: American Jewish Year Books, "Statistics of Jews" and "Local Organizations": New York City, 1919/1920, 1927/1928, 1929/1930, 1938/1939, 1941/1942; *U.S. Bureau of the Census,* Population: New York City, 1920, 1930, 1940; *U.S. Census of Religious Bodies,* New York City, 1916, 1926, 1936; Ronald Bayor, *Neighboros in Conflict: The Irish, Germans, Jews, and Italians of New York City, 1929–1941* (Urbana, IL, 1988); Nathan Glazer and Daniel Moynihan, *Beyond the Melting Pot: The Negroes, Puerto Ricans, Jews, Italians, and Irish of New York City* (Cambridge, MA, 1970); Deborah Dash Moore, *At Home in America: Second Generation New York Jews* (New York, 1981); Oscar Janowsky, *The JWB Survey* (New York, 1948); Nettie McGill, "Some Characteristics of Jewish Youth in New York City," *Jewish Social Service Quarterly* 14 (June 1937), 251–72; the author's telephone conversations with Ronald Bayor, Deborah Dash Moore, Moses Rischin, and Selma Berrol.

TABLE 3

FACTORS CONTRIBUTING TO A "RESENTFUL" ETHNIC IDENTITY OF SAN FRANCISCO JEWS

In the surrounding environment:

– Pronounced social-economic distance of the dominant groups vis-à-vis Eastern European Jews (see table 1, factor 7)

Within the Jewish community:

– Enduring "unfriendly" separation between Eastern European and German Jews (factor 19) who were numerically much larger and, as the city's recognized pioneer-founders (factor 5a) and staunch advocates of radical Reform in Judaism (thus, low factor 16), well integrated into its economic, political and social elite (factors 10a, 12, 12a)
– Residential stability and concentration of Eastern European Jews, and presence of the absorbing, largely Orthodox (and thus separatist) ethnic community (factors 13, 14, 15, 16)
– Lack of participation in local civic-political organizations/affairs (low factor 12)

Note: San Francisco: general population 650,000, Jewish 40,000, or 6% (1930)
Sources: *American Jewish Year Books,* "Statistics of Jews" and "Local Organizations": San Francisco, 1919/1920, 1927/1928, 1929/1930, 1938/1939, 1941/1942; *U.S. Bureau of the Census,* Population: San Francisco, 1920, 1930, 1940; *U.S. Census of Religious Bodies,* San Francisco, 1916, 1926, 1936; Peter Decker, "Jewish Merchants in San Francisco: Social Mobility on the Urban Frontier," in Moses Rischin, ed., *The Jews of the West: The Metropolitan Years* (Waltham, MA, 1979), pp. 12–23; Irene Nadell, *Our City: The Jews of San Francisco* (San Francisco, 1981); William Issel and Robert Cherny, *San Francisco, 1865–1932. Politics, Power, and Urban Development* (Berkeley, CA, 1986); Earl Raab, "There's No City Like San Francisco," *Commentary* 10 (1950), 369–78; Fred Rosenbaum, *Architects of Reform: Congregational and Community Leadership, Emanu-El of San Francisco, 1849–1980* (Berkeley, CA, 1980); Raab, "Zionism versus Anti-Zionism: The State of Israel Comes to San Francisco," in Moses Rischin and John Livingston, eds., *Jews of the American West* (Detroit, 1994), 116–35; Michael Zarchin, *Glimpses of Jewish Life in San Francisco* (San Francisco, 1952); San Francisco congregational

(*sources continue on facing page*)

in 1930, of which 40,000, or 6 percent, were Jewish. The San Francisco case is interesting because several external and intragroup circumstances facilitated attenuation rather than sharpened group ethnic identity. A healthy, if not especially dynamic, city economy provided channels for the attainment of middle-class status. The civic culture was traditionally "open," or tolerant, regarding white groups because the primary social divider was race and, specifically, anti-Orientalism, and there was very little anti-Semitism. Finally, the city's conservative Republican politics did not rest on the competitive ethnic base but on the largely uncontested collaboration among four main ethnic contender groups that were about equal in size: Irish, Germans, Italians, and Yankees.[6]

In San Francisco, nearly two-thirds of the Jews of Eastern European descent were native-born and employed in the city's mainstream white-collar sector. There was no postwar influx of Orthodox immigrants from the East Coast such as had occurred in Los Angeles, where newcomers had created a visible and "vocal" group within the general Jewish community. In addition, Zionism, which effectively enhanced group identity, did not gain popularity in the local Jewish community until after World War II.

All these combined factors should have, and probably did, contribute to attenuate the perception of sharp ethnic group boundaries among San Francisco's Eastern European Jews, yet all available sources indicate the enduring "alert" sense of a separate group identity. Among the factors that apparently overrode the impact of attenuating circumstances, the most important had been a cluster of closely related elements. These include the great numerical (more than 70 percent), economic, and political dominance of German Jews over Eastern European Jews, combined with the enduring

---

(*sources continued from previous page*)
histories —see Alexandra Shecket Korros and Jonathan Sarna, eds., *American Synagogue History: A Bibliography and State of the Field Survey* (New York, 1988), pp. 75–77; the author's telephone conversations with Moses Rischin and Fred Rosenbaum. *Note:* Neither of the two histories of San Francisco Jewry (by Nadell and Zarchin), both introduced by their authors as representative of the city's Jewish community, contains more than a couple of passing references to local Eastern European institutions and personalities.

deep religious-cultural and social division between these two groups. German Jews, who had settled in San Francisco at a time when the local economic structure was still fluid and "in the making," had been recognized as founders of the city and members of the most affluent upper economic stratum, instrumental in turning San Francisco into a powerful trade and banking center. Not surprisingly in this context, they were an integral part of the city's civic-political and social elite.

The powerful position of German Jews in San Francisco's economy and civic affairs, coupled with their "unfriendly distance" from Eastern Europeans, had been reinforced by German Jews' extensive and close contacts with the city's large and influential Protestant German community. German Jews' resolute support of unreconstructed "Reform-Reform" Judaism which they had maintained through the interwar period strengthened their bonds with German Protestants and increased the separation from the Eastern European Jews. In this situation, rather than facilitating their entry into and integration with the local society, German Jews had actually been an obstacle to Eastern Europeans' involvement in San Francisco's affairs and had been perceived as such by the Eastern Europeans.

Eastern Europeans' group ethnic identity, enhanced by the internal split and resentment, was reinforced by their residential stability and concentration, by their cultural-religious traditionalism (most of them, although "not particularly observant," considered themselves Orthodox; the first Conservative synagogue was established in San Francisco only after World War II), and by the existence of the organized ethnic community, which, although incomparably less diversified and vibrant than that enjoyed by New Yorkers, nevertheless provided the support networks and opportunities for social life and cultural participation. From the outside, this ethnic involvement and thus group ethnic identity of Eastern European Jews had been sustained by the tolerance for (white) ethnic groups in the San Francisco local society that minimized the stigma attached to ethnic membership.

Enhanced primarily by circumstances within the Jewish group, a resentful sense of separateness among Eastern Europeans intensified, in turn, their involvement with each other and with their Orthodox synagogues (see table 1, contributing factors 15 and 16). This then sustained the division between San Francisco Eastern European and German Jews (factor 19) and, thus, further alienated the former from participation in the city's social and civic-political institutions (factor 12). The gatekeeping role of the German Jews protecting these institutions strengthened Eastern Europeans' shared sense of resentment and otherness.

Boston Jews represented another type of the enhanced group ethnic identity. I call it "defensive" because it was fueled by the group members' acute awareness of their minority status. As table 4 shows, the latter numbered no less than 90,000, or more than 11 percent, of the city's population of 780,000, which made a defensive character of this identity rather ironic. But several circumstances particular to Boston's ethnic-religious makeup and its civic-political life combined to make it so.

Unlike San Francisco, Boston had never attracted many German settlers, Gentile or Jewish, primarily because of the very large number of Irish Catholics in that city. In the interwar period, Boston's Irish numbered about 600,000, or well over two-thirds of the city's population, and they controlled and dominated city politics and Boston's powerful labor unions. Other outlets for civic participation, in particular social service-charity organizations—the traditional area of Jewish mainstream involvement in American cities—were dominated by Boston's Brahmins or upper-class Anglo-Protestants who constituted an impermeable socio-cultural elite. Less than 10 percent of the total Jewish group and outside the city's ruling elite, German Jews had been in no position to either hinder or facilitate Eastern Europeans' entry into public institutions. Confronted with well-established and interconnected "green power," on the one hand, and, on the other with a caste-like Brahmin elite, local Jews had not been able to secure more than a few lower-level positions in the city's civic-political establishment.

Boston's Jews found themselves even more, or more acutely, "on the outside" as a religious minority. Interwar Boston was overwhelmingly and assertively a Catholic city: 600,000 Irish together with 100,000 Italians and smaller ethnic groups added up to a population of nearly 85 percent Catholics. This dominant Catholicism was not ecumenical but, on the contrary, was intolerant and aggressive. It not only tacitly approved but also actively promulgated open anti-Semitism in public life by the clergy (such as the Christian Front of the notorious Father Coughlin) and by Irish politicians and public school teachers, and through physical attacks on

TABLE 4

FACTORS CONTRIBUTING TO A "DEFENSIVE" ETHNIC IDENTITY OF BOSTON JEWS

In the surrounding environment:

—Civic-political climate and practice unfriendly toward outsiders/newcomers or the pervasive domination of the city's public affairs by the Irish "green power" (see table 1, factor 5/exclusive)

—Pronounced social distance of the elite (Boston's "Brahmins") vis-à-vis the outsiders/newcomers, and specifically Jews (high factor 7)

—Absence of (German) Jews among the city's pioneers/early leaders (factor 5a absent)

—Frequent incidents of anti-Semitism in public life and in the neighborhoods (factor 5b)

Within the Jewish community:

—Limited participation in local civic-political organizations/affairs (low factor 12)

—Residential concentration and presence of the absorbing ethnic community with a large Orthodox (thus separatist) component (factors 13, 15, 16)

—"Mobilizing" influence of national and international events involving the Jewish group (factor 20)

Note: Boston: general population: 780,000; Jewish 90,000, or 11% (1930)

Sources: American Jewish Year Books, "Statistics of Jews" and "Local Organizations": Boston, 1919/1920, 1927/1928, 1929/1930, 1938/1939, 1941/1942; *U.S. Bureau of the Census,* Population: Boston, 1920, 1930, 1940; *U.S. Census of Religious Bodies,* Boston, 1916, 1926, 1936; Jonathan Sarna and Ellen Smith, eds., *The Jews of Boston* (Boston, 1995); *On Common Ground: The Boston Jewish Experience, 1649–1980* (Waltham, MA, 1981); Boston congregational histories—see Alexandra Shecket Korros and Jonathan Sarna, eds., *American Synagogue History: A Bibliography and State-of-the Field Survey* (New York, 1988), pp. 124–26; Hillel Levine and Lawrence Harmon, *The Death of an American Jewish Community* (New York, 1992), esp. pp. 11–43, "Blue Hill Avenue: The Glory Years"; Barbara Miller

(*sources continue on facing page*)

Jews by Irish Catholic youths in the neighborhoods. In the absence of an established German Jewish elite with long-time connections among the Boston Brahmins, no intervention against Catholic excesses could have been expected. Indeed, none came from the city's "self-distanced" Protestant establishment.

Concentrated in two city wards, the Boston Jewish community was well organized, with nearly one hundred synagogues (including a number of semiprivate, *shtibleh*-like Orthodox *minyanim,* or prayer quorums), numerous charitable organizations, educational institutions, mutual insurance and loan associations, social clubs, a theater, and its own press. Largely of Polish origin, the German Jewish minority did not differ significantly from Eastern Europeans in outlooks and life styles and was well integrated into the ethnic community. These organizations served as a center for social and cultural activities of the city's Jews as well as a "safety valve" against the outside environment. By the same token, they enhanced the collective ethnic identity of the participants. Zionism, strongly supported by the great majority of Boston's Jews, had been another positive reinforcement and a counterbalance for their generally insecure group identity. Rather unusual for the times, this widespread commitment to Zionism resulted partly from its advocacy by Louis Brandeis, who was greatly admired by Boston's Jews and considered their "local" leader. Zionism was strengthened by the absence of influential German/Reform Jews who opposed this ideology, and by the local example of Irish nationalism.[7]

Unlike in New York, in Boston it was impossible to live enclosed in a "complete" ethnic community. Local Jews were daily exposed to inimical "boundary making" expressed in words and practiced by citizens from more powerful groups. Because they had no political or economic resources for

---

(*sources continued from previous page*)
Solomon, *Ancestors and Immigrants: A Changing New England Tradition* (Cambridge, MA, 1956); Oscar Handlin, *Boston's Immigrants* (Cambridge, MA, 1941); Thomas O'Connor, *The Boston Irish: A Political History* (Evanston, IL, 1995); Charles Trout, *Boston: The Great Depression and the New Deal* (New York, 1977); Yona Ginsberg, *Jews in a Changing Neighborhood: The Study of Mattapan* (New York, 1975).

the effective public (counter)action, the "alert" group ethnic identity of Boston's Jews had an unavoidably defensive undertone.

Enhanced by a combination of specific external and intragroup circumstances, this identity intensified, in turn, the preference among Boston's Jews to reside among their fellow Jews and to be involved in Jewish communal life (see table 1, contributing factors 13 and 15), and it limited their participation in the city's civic-political affairs (factor 12). This posture, in turn, sustained the social distance of the local dominant group vis-à-vis the Jewish population (factor 7), which, again, strengthened a sense of we-ness and clear-cut group boundaries among Boston's Jews.

ATTENUATED GROUP ETHNIC IDENTITY: GREENSBORO AND CHARLESTON

At the other end of the spectrum of group ethnic identity types found in American Jewish communities of the interwar period, I placed the "attenuated" type represented (again in different subtypes) in Greensboro and Charleston, located, respectively, in North and South Carolina.

As table 5 indicates, Greensboro, with a general population of 55,000 in 1930 and a Jewish population of about 500, or 1 percent, had grown since the turn of the twentieth century into a thriving center of textile manufacturing and wholesale trade. As in San Francisco, Greensboro Jews had been instrumental in this development, but unlike in the former, both German (with larger capital) *and* Eastern European (on a smaller scale) Jewish merchants and investors were involved in this process. By 1920, representatives of both groups (although Germans were in a majority) were members of the city's economic elite. An industry owned by one Jewish family employed more than one-tenth of Greensboro's working population; the rest of the Jewish families occupied solidly middle-class positions. City government closely cooperated with the town's economic elite, which gave Jews access to political positions.

The long-time presence and influence of the Quakers on Greensboro public affairs sustained the tradition of tolerance. There was practically no anti-Semitism. The same tradition also made the whites' attitudes toward and treatment of local blacks much more open-minded than had been the norm in Southern society. The town's pride—local colleges, especially the University of North Carolina branch and Guilford College—also contributed to Greensboro's enlightened and liberal civic climate.

Greensboro's Jews were residentially dispersed, and from the turn of the twentieth century until World War II, one Reform congregation gathered in most of them, both Germans and Eastern Europeans.[8] Uncommon at that time, this "religious symbiosis" between the two groups—they were about equal in size—can be explained, on the one hand, by the fact that most Eastern Europeans were old-time residents of Greensboro and two-thirds of them in 1930 were already second-generation and, on the other hand, by close economic ties and shared participation in city civic-political and social life. Besides the temple, there were just a few other Jewish organizations in town, mainly of practical-instrumental rather than social-cultural or ideological (e.g., Zionism) character that could have reinforced the group ethnic identity of their member-participants. Instead, the local rabbi and his wife were actively engaged in organizing social and cultural events that would bring together the Gentile and Jewish communities. As old-time established residents and pillars of the city's economic well-being, Greensboro's Jews also belonged to local country clubs and other high-status associations. In these combined circumstances, their group ethnic identity, although not extinguished, had been exiguous as not particularly relevant except for special religious occasions as either a cultural or social boundary marker in everyday life.

Attenuated by a set of conditions in the local society and in the Jewish group, the "thin" ethnic identity of Greensboro's Jews weakened, in turn, their need to associate with their fellow Jews and Jewish institutions (see table 1, factor 15) and increased their readiness to participate with members and organizations of the mainstream local society (factors 12 and 12a). All these conditions then reciprocally contributed to the attenuation of a sense of commonality and separateness among city Jews.

Unlike in Greensboro a high social position and integration in the local society of Jews in Charleston did not derive from their economic might. As shown in table 6, Charleston, an old Southern city, had a general population of 62,000 in 1930, of which 2,300, or about 3 percent, were Jews. Largely unaffected by the rapid industrialization of the late nineteenth century,

TABLE 5

FACTORS CONTRIBUTING TO AN "EXIGUOUS" ETHNIC IDENTITY OF GREENSBORO JEWS

In the surrounding environment:

—Open/inclusive civic-political climate and practice concerning outsiders/newcomers, and the significance of race as the main social divider facilitating integration of white residents (see table 1, factors 5, 8)

—Public recognition of the merits of Jewish group members among the city's pioneer settlers (factor 5a) and of their current economic and political leadership

—Minimal anti-Semitism and social distance of the dominant group vis-a-vis Jews (low factors 5b and 7)

Within the Jewish group:

—Residential stability of Jewish residents and high proportion of native-born Americans in the group (including Eastern Europeans) (factor 14; high factor 18)

—Social and cultural integration between German and East European segments of the Jewish group (factor 19 absent)

—Parity between the economic positions of Jews and the dominant class-ethnic upper strata (factors 10, 10a)

—Active participation of Jews in local civic-political affairs and private/informal social activities of the dominant group (factors 12, 12a)

—No residential concentration, organizationally weak Jewish community, and low level of in-group religious/sociocultural separatism (factor 13 absent; low factors 15, 16)

Note: Greensboro, North Carolina: general population 55,000; Jewish 500, or 1% (1930)

Sources: American Jewish Year Books, "Statistics of Jews" and "Local Organizations": Greensboro, North Carolina, 1919/1920, 1927/1928, 1929/1930, 1938/1939, 1941/1942; *U.S. Bureau of the Census,* Population: Greensboro, North Carolina, 1920, 1930, 1940; *U.S. Census of Religious Bodies,* Greensboro, North

(*sources continue on facing page*)

Charleston's economy had stagnated. The town had neither a super-wealthy class (the white population was distributed between the upper and lower middle strata) nor the tough competition for socioeconomic success characteristic of contemporary American urban centers in the Northeast that stimulated perceptions of "parvenu" Jews as a status threat. In a distinctly Southern, pre-modern status system, this elevated position of local Jews had its source in the illustrious pedigree of the city's Jewish residents. Charleston's Jews dated back to colonial times, and Sephardic Jews, who had arrived in Charleston in the late 1660s, were among the city's recognized founders. Their presence among the revered patriot-heroes of the American Revolution enhanced Jewish prestige, as did their participation as devoted soldiers of the Confederacy, to which both old-time Sephardi and more recent Ashkenazi German Charlestonians pledged allegiance. Jews' integration into the local society had been further facilitated by the significance of race as the single main social divider; blacks constituted about one half of Charleston's population.

Although most Eastern Europeans had arrived later and without comparable achievements, because of the long-term influence of the honorific status of their predecessor co-religionists, and, perhaps more important, in the absence of resistance or social distancing on the part of the latter (the

---

(*sources continued from previous page*)
Carolina, 1916, 1926, 1936; Harry Golden, *Jewish Roots in the Carolinas: A Pattern of American Philosemitism* (Greensboro, NC, 1955); Greensboro congregational histories — see Alexandra Shecket Korros and Jonathan Sarna, eds., *American Synagogue History: A Bibliography and State-of-the-Field Survey* (New York, 1988), p. 179; Jack Fleer, *North Carolina Government and Politics* (Lincoln, NE, 1994); Seth Hinshaw, *The Carolina Quaker Experience, 1665–1985* (Greensboro, NC, 1985); Richard Zweigenhaft, *Jews in the Protestant Establishment* (New York, 1982), esp. pp. 71–88, "Southern Jews in the Corporate and Social Elites"; Zweigenhaft, "Two Cities in North Carolina: A Comparative Study of Jews in the Upper Class," *Jewish Social Studies* 10 (Summer–Fall 1979), 291–300; Zweigenhaft, "The Jews of Greensboro: In or Out of the Upper Class," *Contemporary Jewry* (Spring–Summer 1978), 60–76; Samuel Kipp, "Old Notables and Newcomers: The Economic and Political Elite in Greensboro, 1880–1920," *Journal of Southern History* 3:12 (1977), pp. 372–94; the author's telephone conversations with Richard Zweigenhaft.

TABLE 6

FACTORS CONTRIBUTING TO A "DE-ETHNICIZED RELIGIOUS" IDENTITY OF CHARLESTON JEWS

In the surrounding environment:

– Public recognition of the presence and merits of Jews among the city's pioneer settlers, war heroes, and current leaders (see table 1, factor 5a)
– Primary significance of race as the main social divider facilitating integration of white residents (factor 8)
– Minimal anti-Semitism and social distance of the dominant group vis-à-vis Jews (low factors 5b, 7)

Within the Jewish group:

– Social/cultural integration between German and Eastern European Jews (factor 19 absent)
– Residential stability of Jewish residents, high proportion of native-born Americans, and a sense of the shared past with high-status groups in the city (factor 14, high factors 18, 11)
– Approximate parity between the economic positions of Jews and the dominant (middle-class) group (factor 10a)
– Participation in local civic-political affairs and private social activities of the dominant group (factors 12, 12a)

Note: Charleston, South Carolina: general population: 62,000; Jewish 2,500, or 3% (1930)

Sources: American Jewish Year Books, "Statistics of Jews" and "Local Organizations": Charleston, South Carolina, 1919/1920, 1927/1928, 1929/1930, 1938/1939, 1941/1942; *U.S. Bureau of the Census,* Population: Charleston, South Carolina, 1920, 1930, 1940; *U.S. Census of Religious Bodies,* Charleston, South Carolina, 1916, 1926, 1936; Elzas Barnett, *The Jews of South Carolina* (New York, 1941); Charles Reznikoff, *The Jews of Charleston* (Philadelphia, 1950); C. Bezalel Sherman, "Charleston, S.C. 1750–1950," *Jewish Frontier* 18 (1951), 14–16; Harry Golden, *Our Southern Landsman* (New York, 1974), especially pp. 213–36, "Charleston"; Uriah Zevi Engelman, "The Jewish Population of Charleston," *Jewish Social Studies* 13 (July 1951), 195–210; Nathan Kaganoff and Melvin Urofsky,

(*sources continue on facing page*)

oldest Sephardi families were already assimilated into Charleston's gentile elite and were out of the fold), Eastern European Jews were accepted, too, as good American and Charlestonian citizens. They benefited from the civic-political and social advantages of this recognized citizenship.

Several factors contributed to this unproblematic integration of Eastern Europeans into the earlier established Jewish group. The absence of sharp economic divisions among the latter has already been noted, and Jews were not residentially concentrated by class and/or origins. Perhaps more important, however, was the religious orientation of Charleston's Jewry. Peculiar to the place, it can be best called "Orthodox Reform," wherein both components of this bizarre mix were practiced, as it were, with the laid-back approach characteristic of Southern culture.

Reform in name but loosely Orthodox in practice was the oldest congregation, Beth Elohim. Established around 1750, one century later it considered itself Reform, but, as indicated in the preserved evidence of members' religious practice, it was "an old wine in a new bottle." When they arrived in Charleston in the nineteenth century and erected a synagogue, German Jews—the majority of them from Polish lands—had retained the Sephardi rite of their predecessors because of its elevated status in the local society and decorum. The Brith Shalom, or "Polish synagogue," as it was called, did not have daily services and its members did not observe the Sabbath, but men wore hats during services and their wives kept kosher homes. By the interwar period, however, elements of Orthodox practice devolved further, and the number of "Reform" Jews increased.

The Orthodox synagogue, Beth Israel, established by Eastern Europeans at the beginning of the twentieth century to make observance stricter than

---

(*sources continued from previous page*)
"Turn to the South": Essays on Southern Jewry (Charlottesville, VA, 1979); Leonard Dinnerstein and Mary Dale Palsson, eds., *Jews in the South* (Baton Rouge, LA, 1973), pt. 4, "Life in the Twentieth-Century South"; Charleston congregational histories—see Alexandra Shecket Korros and Jonathan Sarna, eds., *American Synagogue History: A Bibliography and State-of the-Field-Survey* (New York, 1988), pp. 209–11; the author's telephone conversations with Salomon Breibart of Charleston.

that practiced at Brith Shalom, by the 1920s had become similarly "pluralistic" and tolerant of deviation. A high—nearly 70 percent—proportion of native-born Americans in the local Jewish population also affected the "loosening up" and permissiveness in matters of religious observance in these two synagogues.[9] That a considerable number of congregants, Germans and Eastern Europeans alike, either held multiple memberships in these synagogues or circulated among them further contributed to the blurring of religious and social boundaries among the Jews. About eight other local Jewish organizations—such as B'nai B'rith, Hakhnosses Orchim, Hebrew Ladies Society, Young Men's Hebrew Club (there were no Zionist groups)—were also "shared" by the entire group. Interestingly, even a small group of Orthodox immigrants from Kalushin in Poland who had come to Charleston after World War I, as if "overcome" by the city's mild Southern climate and by local Jews' catholic spirit, soon opened their Kalushiner Society to all Jews in town.

Contacts between Charleston's Jews and other members of local society were frequent and cordial. The Jews actively participated in city civic affairs and Gentile social clubs, and, what was much more unusual, invited and welcomed Gentiles to participate in Jewish celebrations. The annual Purim Ball was anxiously anticipated and eagerly attended by Charleston business and professional classes. "Rarely [have Jews] attained so high a degree of integration in the general life of a town," noted a contemporary observer.[10]

I located Charleston's Jews in the "attenuated ethnicity" category because, as in Greensboro, for the majority of them their ethnic membership did not have a felt relevance in their everyday lives as Charlestonians. Nevertheless, unlike Greensboro Jews, those in Charleston considered themselves—as did all residents of this traditional town—"religious," however lax their observance. Historians of Jewish American life in big urban centers in the prewar era have pointed to the progressive severing of the traditionally inseparable ethnic and religious components of Judaism, as the ethnic sphere gained social and cultural autonomy and, gradually, primacy over the religious dimension. Thus the transformation of synagogues into synagogue-centers and then into social centers with synagogue attachments are probably the most cited illustration of this process. In a different set of circumstances, a reverse development seems to have taken place in prewar

Charleston: an attenuation of the ethnic and maintenance of the religious elements of Jewishness. It could then be that the (once celebrated and later discarded as unfounded) thesis of Will Herberg from his book *Protestant Catholic Jew* (1955) — namely, that the ethnic identities of Americans were being replaced by the religious ones — is correct when and if *historicized* like the assimilation model. Charleston in this particular time period represented one context in which such development was taking place.

Shaped by a combination of circumstances in the local society and within the Jewish group, the de-ethnicized religious identity of Charleston's Jews contributed, in turn — in the interaction of two facilitating conditions, namely, the high-status position of Jews in the city (see table 1, factors 5a, 8, 10a) and the unusually large proportion among them of native-born Americans (factor 18) — to increased participation in the local civic-political process and informal social activities (factors 12 and 12a). These circumstances, then, sustained such de-ethnicized collective identification.

"IN-BETWEEN" GROUP ETHNIC IDENTITY: CLEVELAND

As table 7 indicates, Cleveland, a strong manufacturing and commercial center, had an ethnically diverse population of over 900,000 in 1930, of which Jews constituted about 90,000, or 10 percent. The majority of Cleveland's Jews, including those of Eastern European origins, were middle-class and employed in mainstream sectors of the city's economy, especially the clothing industry, trade, and professions.

The city's civic-political spirit and practice, informed by the inclusive and integrative Republican tradition maintained since the Social Reform era, aimed at minimizing ethnic divisiveness and stressing intergroup cooperation. The active and recognized involvement of Jews of German Reform background in this dialogue and cooperation with members of the dominant Anglo-Protestant group in diverse matters of public interest since the nineteenth century, and their similarly "dialogic" and cooperative attitude toward later-arriving Eastern European immigrants, facilitated subsequent entry of those immigrants into Cleveland's mainstream institutions where they continued the same tradition. For example, one of the widely acclaimed leaders who widened and "multiplied" communication

TABLE 7

FACTORS CONTRIBUTING TO A "MILD" ETHNIC IDENTITY OF CLEVELAND JEWS

In the surrounding environment:

— Open civil-political climate and practice concerning nondominant ethnic groups and noncompetitive ethnic relations in the public forum (factor 5/inclusive; factor 6 absent)
— Public recognition of the contributions of the early and current Jewish leaders/personalities (factor 5a)
— Limited anti-Semitism/public demonstrations against it (low factor 5b)
— Limited social distance (separatism) of the dominant group(s) vis-à-vis Jews (low factor 7)

Within the Jewish community:

— Close cooperation between German and Eastern European Jews (factor 19 absent)
— Good fit of Jews' collective educational and occupational skills to the profile and dynamics of local economy (quick-pace mobility into the mainstream middle class (factor 10)
— Participation in local civic-political organizations/affairs and in (most) private social clubs of the dominant group (factors 12, 12b)
— Presence of the outstanding/public-minded leaders (factor 17) and, at the same time,
— Residential concentration and presence of the absorbing ethnic community (factors 13, 15)
— Mobilizing influence of national and international events involving Jews (factor 20)

Note: Cleveland: general population 900,000; Jewish 90,000, or 10% (1930)

Sources: American Jewish Year Books, "Statistics of Jews" and "Local Organizations": Cleveland, 1919/1920, 1927/1928, 1929/1930, 1938/1939, 1941/1942; *U.S. Bureau of the Census,* Population: Cleveland, 1920, 1930, 1940; *U.S. Census of Religious Bodies,* Cleveland, 1916, 1926, 1936; Lloyd Gartner, *History of the Jews of*

(*sources continue on facing page*)

channels between the Jewish and other "new" ethnic groups and the dominant society during the 1920s was a devoted Republican, attorney Maurice Mashke, an American-born son of Hungarian parents. A tolerant civic climate and "public familiarity" between Jews and members of the dominant group had contributed, according to local reports, to a diminution of status anxiety felt by middle-class native-born Americans in view of a rapid upward mobility of Jews, especially Eastern Europeans, during the first decades of the twentieth century.

At the same time, German Jews' recognized influence in city public life and their friendly "inclusive" approach toward their Eastern European counterparts, along with a relatively rapid acceptance of Conservative Judaism by the majority of Eastern European congregations, helped to avoid the intragroup division à la San Francisco and made Eastern Europeans recognize German Jews' strong organizational influence and representative legitimacy within Cleveland's Jewish community at large. Of great significance in easing this Orthodox-to-Conservative transformation and in the German–Eastern European rapprochement had been the charismatic leadership of a Lithuanian-born Orthodox-later-Reform, committed Zionist rabbi Abba Hillel Silver.[11]

As a result of all these circumstances, Cleveland's Jews, including those of Eastern European origin, had been accepted in most fraternal lodges and private clubs of the dominant group, except a couple of "the very best," as my informants put it. Such integrative rather than divisive Jewish-Gentile relations made possible, unique to my knowledge, two public events symbolically expressing intergroup civic solidarity during periods of intensified

---

(*sources continued from previous page*)

Cleveland (Cleveland, 1978); Cleveland congregational histories—see Alexandra Shecket Korros and Jonathan Sarna, eds., *American Synagogue History: A Bibliography and State-of-the Field Survey* (New York, 1988), pp. 183–84; Kenneth Finegold, *Experts and Politicians: Reform Challenges to Machine Politics in New York, Cleveland, and Chicago* (Princeton, 1995); David Van Tassel and John Grabowski, eds., *Cleveland: A Tradition of Reform* (Kent, OH, 1986); Thomas Campbll and Edward Miggins, eds., *The Birth of Modern Cleveland, 1865–1930* (Cleveland, 1988); the author's telephone conversations with Yehuda Rubinstein, Lois Sharf, Scott Cline, Thomas Campbell, and John Grabowski.

anti-Semitic sentiments and actions across the country. In 1920, a mass rally was held against the anti-Semitic propaganda of Henry Ford's *Dearborn Independent,* and in 1938 a mass demonstration protested Nazi persecution of German Jews.[12] (No such events, by the way, took place in New York.)

Why, then, not place the Cleveland case in the "attenuated ethnic identity" category? According to the classical assimilation theory, involvement of ethnic group members in private clubs and, generally, integrative social relations with the dominant group, leads to the weakening and eventual disappearance of their collective ethnic identity. Despite their long-term social involvement with members of the dominant group, no such weakening occurred, however, among Jews in Cleveland. It was prevented by two factors, neither of which has been considered in the assimilation model. One of them was the presence of a vibrant ethnic community with a variety of social and cultural activities, including several Zionist organizations. Cleveland's Jews had remained involved in these organizations despite, or *parallel to,* their participation in mainstream local affairs. The other factor, apparently quite common among Jews who frequented Gentile social clubs and informal social events in prewar Cleveland, was a personal sense of a "psychological-cultural distance" possibly originating from Jews themselves that informed these otherwise cordial relations. Shared with their fellow Jews, this sensation sustained group ethnic identity rather than intensifying it, because there was no sense of threat.

CONCLUSION

The examination of just a few historical cases over a limited period and one particular aspect of the adaptation process of Jewish immigrants and their children clearly demonstrates that different historical configurations of circumstances within and outside of American Jewish communities had generated differently "textured" group ethnic identities. But it also raises more questions that could be fruitfully investigated in further research conducted in a similar comparative-configurational mode. I would like to suggest some possible directions of such study.

One could pursue further what has been done here by adding and examining more city cases. I located about thirty-odd historical studies of Eastern

European Jewish communities during the pre–World War II era that contain information about one or more specific aspects of their members' assimilation/ethnicization. The purpose of this analysis would be to identify some *historical patterns* or sets of factors that had been both necessary and sufficient conditions for the enhancement or the attenuation of those group boundary-making attachments. Comparisons across time of such identified patterns would be interesting.[13]

Another important path of research lies in the opposite direction, not toward historical generalizations but in search of greater diversity than that presented here, namely, by "breaking down" city cases into smaller units composed of subsegments/areas of local society and subgroups of Jews with different characteristics and comparing them across space. Once accomplished, such a project would lend itself to pattern analysis.

One such differentiating characteristic to be investigated could be—*should be,* really, because despite the accumulation of research on American Jewish women, there is a dearth of comparative information on gender effects as the element of both sides of the relationship—Jewish ethnic identity (and other aspects of the adaptation process) and its macro- and micro-level contexts. Other possible questions for study could be: Did participation in ethnic-competitive civic-political affairs, ethnic-divisive social distance, and incidents of anti-Semitism at work and in other public institutions sharpen a sense of group boundaries and membership more among middle-class men than among middle-class women regardless of other conditions? Did anti-Semitic incidents in the neighborhood affect, across cases, women's sense of group identity more, or more readily, than that of men to the extent that women were homebound middle-class housewives? How did other conditions in the local society and within the Jewish group mediate this effect?

And did the opposite circumstances—namely, the civic-political and work-institutional situations that underplayed ethnic divisiveness and were not marked by anti-Semitism—affect ethnic collective identities of Jewish (middle-class) women mainly through attenuated identities of the men occupied "out in the world," or was it necessary for such attenuation of women's identity that they themselves experienced the openness of mainstream society in everyday encounters in local neighborhoods and associations?

What was the mediating impact of different contextual conditions? Did the absence of a dense and absorbing ethnic community have similar differential effects on men's and women's identities across city cases or were they contingent on other (which?) external and group circumstances?

NOTES

1. Milton Yinger, *Ethnicity* (Albany, NY, 1994), pp. 40–41.

2. The concept of "ethnicization" was coined by Victor Greene in his book *For God and Country: The Rise of Polish and Lithuanian Consciousness in America* (Madison, WI, 1975), and elaborated by Jonathan Sarna in "From Immigrants to Ethnics: Toward a New Theory of Ethnicization," *Ethnicity* 5 (December 1978), 73–78. The third and most recent interpretation, the so-called invented ethnicity model, centering on ethnic actors who "construct" their group identity and institutions, can be, in my view, subsumed under the ethnicization approach, in which actors actively and purposefully interact with their environment, creating in this process new sociocultural phenomena. On invented ethnicity, see Werner Sollors, ed., *The Invention of Ethnicity* (New York, 1989). For a review of different conceptualizations of ethnicity and (im)migrants' adaptation to the host society, see Werner Sollors, ed., *Theories of Ethnicity* (New York, 1996), and John Hutchinson and Anthony Smith, eds., *Ethnicity* (New York, 1996).

3. Ewa Morawska, "In Defense of the Assimilation Model," *Journal of American Ethnic History* 13 (1994), 76–87.

4. Anthony Giddens, *The Constitution of Society* (Berkeley, CA, 1984); William Sewell, "A Theory of Structure: Duality, Agency, and Transformation," *American Journal of Sociology* 98 (1992), 1–29.

5. Deborah Dash Moore, *At Home in America: Second Generation New York Jews* (New York, 1981), p. 201.

6. Some historians have suggested that the most important factor in San Francisco's politics and civic affairs in the interwar period was a "Darwinian competition" among West Coast cities, especially with the meteorically rising Los Angeles, which created a civic-political unity that transcended intraurban divisions. See William Issel and Robert Cherny, *San Francisco, 1865–1932: Politics, Power, and Urban Development* (Berkeley, CA, 1986), chap. 9.

7. The history of Boston's Jews has thus far not attracted much research; one study points to an additional positive reinforcement of their ethnic group identity, namely, the presence (however limited by entry quotas) at Harvard University of

Jewish students and faculty, who, although social outcasts among the dominant groups, brought honor to the entire group by their outstanding performance—see Jonathan Sarna and Ellen Smith, eds., *The Jews of Boston* (Boston, 1995).

8. After World War I some Jews arrived from the East, a small number of whom established a "private" Orthodox *minyan*. (Telephone conversation with Richard Zweigenhaft, Mar. 16, 1997.)

9. The first Conservative synagogue was established in Charleston only in 1947.

10. C. Bezalel Sherman, "Charleston, S.C. 1750–1950," *Jewish Frontier* 18 (1951), 14.

11. Lloyd Gartner, *History of the Jews of Cleveland* (Cleveland, 1978).

12. Personal communications from Edward Miggins, Thomas Campbell, and John Grabowski. See also David Van Tassel and John Grabowski, eds., *Cleveland: A Tradition of Reform* (Kent, OH, 1986).

13. Historical sociologists have worked out good methods of such analysis across space and time. See, e.g., Larry Isaac, ed. "Research in Historical Sociology," *Historical Methods* 30 (1997); Charles Ragin, *The Comparative Method: Moving Beyond Qualitative and Quantitative Strategies* (Berkeley, CA, 1987); Theda Skocpol, "Emergent Agendas and Recurrent Strategies in Historical Sociology," in Theda Skocpol, ed., *Vision and Method in Historical Sociology* (New York, 1984), pp. 368–91.

THIRTEEN

Strangers No Longer: Jews and Postwar American Political Culture

IRA KATZNELSON

My subject is a radical shift in the standing and self-consciousness of Jews in the United States during and just after the Second World War. What Arthur Hertzberg has called "four centuries of an uneasy encounter" became far less watchful. During the 1930s, he noted, the morale of America's Jewish community had touched bottom. The Depression, resurgent anti-Semitism, a decline in immigrant, primarily Yiddish, cultural institutions, and the grim news from Palestine and especially from the heartland of Europe diminished Jewish confidence. By the middle 1950s, by contrast, when the tercentenary of Jewish life in America was being commemorated, the contributors to a landmark empirical volume were able to focus instead on the community's successful integration, remarkable social mobility, high measures of participation in American life, and robust political incorporation. Anti-Semitism had become unfashionable, at least its open expression. University barriers to entry became more permeable. Intergenerational mobility accelerated as access to formerly closed occupations quickened. Housing choices multiplied. Jews entered mass culture on vastly more favorable terms. Manifestly, Jews felt themselves to be more securely American. By the conclusion of the "Golden Decade" spanning 1945 to 1955, Arthur Goren observes, "one could confidently point to a baseline that demarcated American Jewry from what had existed prior to 1945 and that would hold, for the most part, during the decades ahead." How shall we understand this radical change in situation and perception?[1]

From a more distant perspective, of course, it is the continuities in the circumstances of American Jewry, especially when assessed comparatively, that are more prominent than these puzzling shifts. "In early America," as John Higham famously put it, "virtually from the beginning, there was no Jewish question."[2] From the country's founding, the United States was the only nation in the Diaspora where Jews were legally and politically emancipated simply by the act of entry. Once inside, they faced no official barriers to choice about where to live, how to work, or whether to participate in politics. Relatively secure and open to its Jews, the United States (episodes of anti-Semitism notwithstanding) thus represented the Enlightenment's and liberalism's "best case" on offer.

Nonetheless, as the difficult decade of the 1930s attests, simple success narratives of American Jewry based on its post-Emancipation status are too linear. In making this argument about the history of American Jewry from the early years of the Republic to the eve of the Second World War, I concluded a recent essay with the following paragraph:

> Writing in 1934, one of the country's leading rabbis observed that American Jews had left one world in which they could no longer live only to go to another they could not fully enter. "Only a people of acrobats could preserve a semblance of poise on a footing so unstable." It was not Father Coughlin but *The Christian Century,* the leading organ of liberal Protestantism, that asked in 1937, "Can democracy suffer a hereditary minority to perpetuate itself as a permanent minority, with its own distinctive culture, sanctioned by its own distinctive cult form?" It was not just Hitler's rise to power that confirmed for Jews the cherished qualities of their American home, while reminding

them how much they remained strangers at home, at the margins of American liberalism.[3]

Jews in the United States before the Second World War were more integrated than anywhere else in the West, but not on fully equal terms. Compared to native Protestants and, arguably, to Catholic ethnic immigrants (who like Jews confronted considerable prejudice and discrimination), they faced varied, if at times quite subtle, barriers to entry and they received multiple signals—ranging from their representation as tools of Wall Street and of left-wing, un-American, radicalism—which confirmed their liminality. On the threshold of the country's entry into the war, Jews still faced quotas on admission to leading universities, especially to professional schools, and a more widespread restrictive system of anti-Semitic practices which forced Jews to establish parallel networks of hotels, country clubs, and other social institutions. Though there had been only modest economic discrimination before the First World War, since Jews did not seek to enter crowded labor markets outside their areas of economic specialization, especially in the garment trades, their more recent quest for mobility disclosed high walls to employment, especially in banking, insurance, and engineering. Public opinion polls revealed a great deal of skepticism and popular myth about Jews. Anti-Semitic expression often was unguarded and unashamed. As in Europe, albeit more mildly, Gentile hostility toward Jews, especially among agrarian radicals, upper-crust intellectuals, and the urban working class, peaked in the late 1880s and 1890s, after the First World War, and again during the Great Depression.[4]

As both Hannah Arendt and Zygmunt Bauman, among others, have underscored, Jews in the West after the American and French Revolutions were offered exit visas out of their traditional enclosed communities without being extended full entry tickets into the wider society.[5] There was no linear path to redemption through universality. Broadly speaking, what varied in the inclusionary experiences of Jews in the West was the orientation of Jews to exit and entry and the rules, both formal and informal, which defined how entry tickets might be purchased, by whom and at what cost.

Bauman's treatment (following Ernest Gellner and Frederick Barth) of these issues underscored, as Barth famously put it, that "it is the ethnic *boundary* that defines the group, not the cultural stuff it encloses." Seen this way, members of an ethnic minority can choose from a small number of strategies, which are not mutually exclusive, in pursuit of wider participation: (a) As individuals, they can seek to pass. For Jews, this most often entailed intermarriage and/or conversion. (b) They can accept their minority status, encapsulate their differentiating cultural characteristics in a zone that does not articulate with the wider society, and participate selectively in the wider politics and society. (c) They can mobilize their ethnic/cultural identity to enter these wider spheres and engage them with collective resources. Or, (d) they can mount a frontal assault on ethnic discrimination aimed at de-legitimating practices of discrimination and separate treatment.[6]

Each of these strategic orientations has been present in the United States, but the dominant response has been the second, entailing the creation of distinctive spatial, occupational, and institutional locations from which Jews have been able to engage the wider society. The complex history of American Jewish identity formation, institutions, housing and occupational patterns, and encounters with political life thus can be understood as aspects of an overarching strategy of "city niches," an approach Jews adopted to the wider society characterized by a high, if varying, degree of spatial and institutional enclosure marked by the creation of zones with significant communal autonomy and insularity. "This particular solution," I have noted, "resembled that of other ethnic immigrants, but with differences. . . . One of these was the relatively intense urban character of the Jewish stance. Jews connected with American politics, economics, and society from the atypical locations of a small number of dense city neighborhoods and from a limited selection of occupations and places of work. Launched into America from these bounded sites, Jews fashioned dispositions and patterns of individual and collective behavior, combining gratitude and wariness, which made sense as a coherent repertoire."[7]

This pattern of cautious, edgy vigilance was exacerbated during the Great Depression when the group's considerable successes at advancement and incorporation based on a combination of enclosure and engagement was placed in jeopardy. Confidence about the ground on which Jews could stand in America was shaken not only by financial and economic insecurity but by the sometimes raw and sometimes sophisticated signals proffered by the wider society at home, and in more dangerous and humiliating ways from abroad, admonishing that the absence of menace could not be taken for granted. On the threshold of the Second World War, "Jews were not so confident of their prospects in America."[8] Enhanced Jewish visibility in economic and civic life often went hand in hand with heightened apprehension and nervous efforts to limit Jewish prominence, as in the case of the unsuccessful effort in 1938 by the Jewish Secretary of the Treasury and the Jewish publisher of the *New York Times* to persuade President Roosevelt not to appoint a second Jew to the Supreme Court.[9] In postwar America, Jews came to be far less apprehensive, strangers no longer. Their condition and repertoire altered radically. Indeed, what was so striking about postwar America as the mix of apprehension and security among American Jewry adjusted in favor of the latter was the growing availability and legitimacy of each of the four orientations to the wider society Bauman identified.

It is the shift in macroscopic conditions underpinning these changes to the strategic orientations of the country's Jews that I wish to address. The war itself provides the leading explanation. The 1940s did mark the key moment of transition. In 1942, the mass circulation *Saturday Evening Post* argued "The Case Against the Jew"; just eight years later, Oscar Handlin was able to take note of the genuine pluralism Jews had experienced since the Second World War while writing in *Commentary,* a new and proudly Jewish periodical. As fascism, especially Nazism, was discredited, so, too, was its anti-Jewish ideology, now associated with murderous practices. Moreover, as active patriots during the war, Jews visibly had earned their right to incorporation in all spheres of American life. The Second World War thus marked a turning point concerning the place of Jews in American life. The war proved a great engine of incorporation. Jews served as officers as well as enlisted men in higher proportions than their numbers in the population. They became citizens in a full sense at just the moment when Jewish citizens were being extruded virtually everywhere in Europe. Under the impact of the war, Jews seized opportunities to enter economic and academic locations from which they had been kept out, taking advantage of a new balance in supply and demand. If, for blacks, the war was the last moment they were excluded from citizenship on equal terms by the federal government, for Jews it marked the first moment of full inclusion into citizenship's most visible and demanding institution. The war had been defined as a battle against fascism, with the result that Jews, fascism's primary target, were held in the symbolic embrace of America in a manner they had previously not experienced.[10]

But a focus on the war is incomplete, for its impact cannot be considered in isolation as a single, congested cause; nor, given the impact of total war elsewhere, can its positive impact on American Jewry be taken for granted. For we need to understand not just why Jewish participation in the war effort marked an effective end of one era and the start of another, but also which conditions preceding the war transformed its meaning and effects and which conditions following the war reinforced its consequences (after all, the First World War did not have nearly the same effect on Jewish integration, even considering its different scale from an American perspective).

I am not prepared to make a strong causal argument claiming that this or that factor distinctively stands out from the rest; nor am I prepared to array the elements I address below in a crisp hierarchy of causes. But I do think it possible to delineate a constellation of demographic and spatial elements, institutional transformations, and broadly political conditions which shaped the increasingly robust incorporation of Jews into the domain of citizenship during the war and altered the patterning of Jewish group formation. These include: the closure of the immigration gate in 1924; the transformation of urban living space and its meaning; the erosion of exclusionary practices in higher education; participation at all levels in the New Deal; and the contribution Israel made to the standardization of Jewish ethnicity. These transformations to the station of America's Jews, I argue, did more than alter the balance between the available strategies of how to be Jewish in America. They modified the content of each, so much so that during the heyday of McCarthyism and even when Ethel and Julius Rosenberg were executed after having been convicted as Soviet spies, most American Jews, in spite of the disproportionate presence of their brethren in the Communist Party, remained unaffected and secure.

Until 1924, patterns of immigration had the effect of reproducing the phenomenon of the first generation, a situation made unusually stark for Jews because of the shift in population flows from the Sephardic sources of early American Jewry to newcomers from German-speaking Europe (by the mid-nineteenth century four in five congregations in the United States had been founded by German Jews) to the post-1881 mammoth population movement from Russia and Eastern Europe. The re-creation of first generations effectively reinforced Jewish particularity and visibility, especially given the press of numbers and the pace of arrival.[11] Initially, German Jewish immigration after 1815 was tied closely to more general German population movements and associational life; as German Gentiles dispersed, so did German Jews. But after 1848, as the rate of Jewish immigration from Germany increased some fivefold, the new first generation constituted a much more defined and visible group, with far greater institutional independence from the larger group of German newcomers. The separateness of the country's Jews was massively reinforced by the late-nineteenth and early-twentieth-century immigration from the Pale, which lacked organic links to non-Jewish population movements. This episodic reinforcement of first-generation status effectively reinforced the remarkable spatial concentration and propinquity of America's Jews, their strong linguistic differentiation, and a wry wariness of Christian America, itself the product of firsthand experiences with (often violent) European economic, social, and political anti-Semitism.

By the start of the Second World War, with the exception of refugees from Germany, a first generation hardly existed. Protectionist immigration legislation in 1924 stopped the external replenishment of the country's Jewish population (thus inadvertently aiding the destruction of the excluded under Nazi auspices). Earlier, immigration restrictionists had had to be content with the regulation of individual rather than group entry; now, with exclusions based on group categories, the near impossibility of Jewish entry from Europe effectively sheltered the population in place from human reinforcements of their difference. To the contrary, without the pressures exercised by the recurrent arrival of newcomers, Jews already in the United States began to accelerate their engagement with the larger society while reducing the degree of enclosure of their niches. There were many markers of this transformation: large-scale shifts in residential and occupational patterns, with a stepping up of the pace of movement out of crowded, tenement districts; the palpable decline of Yiddish as the home language and as the medium for intracommunal culture and communication; and a diminution of the social and occupational gaps distinguishing the primarily German Jews who had come before 1881 from the Eastern European and Russian Jews who had arrived in massive numbers in the subsequent four decades. Under the impact of legislated exclusion, the valence of Jewishness altered decisively. Jews, though still identifiably different from Gentile America and from each other, now were less so.

An important part of this transformation included changes to the links between city space and ethnicity. Although city neighborhood space and ethnicity did not become decoupled, the concentration, multiclass character, and unidimensional qualities of tenement housing all changed. Jewish residence space became more dispersed, as the confining relation between the garment industry and tenement districts was broken. Jews now were more likely to share their neighborhoods with other groups. Their areas of settlement were defined more by class (understood both in weberian and marxist senses of the term) than by ethnicity alone, were more divorced and distant from places of work, and were more homogeneous with regard to specific class traits and the religious preferences of specific groups of Jews. Jewish institutions, especially synagogues, became more various and dispersed. No longer in any given big city was there a single central place for Jews to live and utilize specialized services. Jews largely still lived adjacent to other Jews, but in increasingly dispersed locales.[12]

The linkages between space and ethnicity thus began to alter. The segregation in Jewish areas of first-generation settlement such as the densely packed Lower East Side of Manhattan, Philadelphia's West Side, and Chicago's West Side had been the result not just of the desire of the newcomers to live together but of migration chains, common occupations, affordable housing, and the concentrated location of communal institutions, especially synagogues and religious schools. Even more than other immigrant ethnic groups, first-generation Jews were highly concentrated in ethnic areas of tenement settlement because of the interspersed qualities of work and off-work in the needle trades. Alone among white newcomers in the late nineteenth and early twentieth centuries, Jewish residential segregation approached in degree the levels experienced in northern cities by African Americans.[13]

Following the new restrictions on immigration, the linkages between Jewish ethnic and residential patterns became more plural as the movement from first-generation sites of settlement accelerated. Some residents of the new, more middle-class, neighborhoods re-created patterns of living near ethnic shops and institutions, but other Jews began to decouple ethnicity from space, treating issues of identity in more symbolic and cultural terms.[14] By the time the Second World War began, Jewish institutional, representational, and spatial distance from other immigrant groups and from the wider society had diminished significantly as a result of the end of mass immigration, powerful impulses to occupational and residential mobility, and the emergence of new forms of biculturalism which allowed Jews to change and in some respects strengthen their Jewish affiliations while enlarging their "American" commitments and practices.

Among the many relevant institutional changes affecting the situation and prospects of America's Jews—including the growth in urban civil service occupations and large-scale changes to the occupational profile of the country—the most important was the simultaneous growth and openness of higher education. Certainly, by the end of the Second World War Jews still faced important barriers to entry, but these were lower, even in the heart of the Ivy League, than they had been before. Moreover, the number of places in public as opposed to elite private institutions was growing and the financial cost of higher education for veterans was being subsidized. The prewar trend of a movement by Jews from the working class to the middle class and the liberal professions thus was vastly accelerated by this new access, including openness at the professional-school level.

From the Civil War to the First World War, the university gained ascendancy in the United States over other organized forms devoted to the disclosure, invention, and circulation of knowledge. Modern university structures and quasi-independent disciplines consolidated in the interwar period that followed. In these periods, a tiny preprofessional university equipped to train the country's homogeneous elite was transformed into a more variegated, increasingly middle-class and professional institution to produce and disseminate knowledge. In spite of many barriers to entry, Jews pushed with a fair degree of success against the obstacles to admission put in place to reduce their numbers. As knowledge professionals inside distinctive if overlapping disciplinary scholarly communities began to replace gentlemen scholars and theologians at the heart of the university, Jews were able to advance.

Albeit instruments of the country's decentralized and intensely local civil society, the country's private and public universities developed strong ties to national institutions and the federal government during the 1920s, the New Deal, and especially during the Second World War and its immediate aftermath. The ligatures of the relationship between the academy and the rectifying reform impulse were institutionalized by countrywide networks of professionals and scholars, by the activities of foundations (Rockefeller, Carnegie, among others) which funded such interstitial organizations as the Social Science Research Council, and by a host of governmental agencies determined to end the depression, win a global war, and, later, confront a Communist foe. The post-war university was underpinned by the big, more social government convened mainly by the Democratic party and its liberal wing and by the institutions it created, including the GI Bill and the National Science Foundation. If the doors to liberal arts colleges and research universities had cracked open to Jews before the Second World War, they now swung free. The timing of this access was particularly fortuitous because it coincided with the earliest moments of the shift from manufacturing to services as the core of America's economy. Jews who found new opportunities requiring advanced learning in the burgeoning sectors of the postwar economy were poised as a result to take advantage of larger economic trends as the country entered an unprecedented period of uninterrupted economic growth.

These demographic, spatial, educational, and economic changes for American Jews were accompanied and propelled by their unprecedented entry into the heart of the country's political and policymaking life. During the New Deal, Jews (as well as immigrant Catholics) became political insiders for the first time in the higher reaches of the Roosevelt administration, the Democratic party, and the labor movement. Like women, blacks, and Catholics, but more so in proportion to their numbers in the population,

Jews secured unprecedented positions inside the heights of America's national state, including key positions in Washington's burgeoning bureaucracies. Indeed, at a time when discrimination was still rampant in private law firms, the New Deal functioned as a meritocracy. Jewish lawyers found fabulous opportunities in the Justice Department, the Department of Labor, the National Labor Relations Board, the Securities and Exchange Commission, and the Agricultural Adjustment Administration, among other agencies, so much so that Adlai Stevenson, then at the AAA, complained, "There is a little feeling that the Jews are getting too prominent." In the Department of the Interior alone, Nathan Margold was solicitor-general, Abe Fortas, later to serve on the Supreme Court during the Johnson presidency, was director of the Division of Manpower and then became undersecretary, Saul Padover was a key assistant to Secretary Harold Ickes, Michael Straus directed the War Resources Council, and Ernest Gruening, later his state's senator, was designated governor of Alaska. For the first time, an American president had visibly incorporated Jews at the center of his political circle of advisors: Supreme Court Justices Louis Brandeis and Felix Frankfurter; economist Isador Lubin; the labor leader Sidney Hillman; Secretary of the Treasury Henry Morgenthau; and political operatives Ben Cohen and Sam Rosenman. Jews also massively realigned as Democratic voters and, because they lived in pivotal cities and states, became critical voters. Moreover, much New Deal policy was consistent with the broadly social democratic values of most Jews, whose political preferences stood well to the left of those of most Americans.[15]

The resonant interposition of Jews and the New Deal was reinforced by the organizational and personal networks connecting the often vibrant political life in Jewish neighborhoods upward through city and state Democratic party organizations to Washington. The New Deal recognized the legitimacy of ethnic subcultures and constructed its broad-gauged political coalition based in part on intensely local patterns of group activity and participation. In this context, Jewish neighborhoods took on a political cast as among the country's strongest bastions of support for the Democratic party and its new social liberalism.[16]

Not surprisingly, Roosevelt was venerated by most American Jews, notwithstanding his combination of caution and inaction with respect to immigration issues and the rescue of Jews threatened by Hitler. With respect to these issues, he was confronted with very little organized pressure by a still insecure Jewish community torn between loyalty to their European sisters and brothers and their concern that they not be seen to be parochial special pleaders.

In contrast, by the close of the Second World War, the Jewish mainstream had no hesitation in openly expressing support for the Zionist project in Palestine. The shock of the Holocaust, made worse by the dramatically insufficient refugee policies of the Roosevelt and Truman administrations, in large measure was externalized by a new mobilization of American Zionism.[17] Reciprocally, the quick recognition of Israel by the United States, contrasting with the country's continuing sluggishness with respect to the admission of displaced persons, legitimated the focus on Israel as the best solution to post-Holocaust traumas. During the Second World War, the Zionist, later the Israeli, flag began to make a routine appearance alongside the American flag in the country's synagogues and in secular Jewish settings. Figures like Rabbi Stephen Wise, who had been reluctant to pressure the Roosevelt administration to legislate emergency exceptions to the immigration restrictions of the 1920s, now felt no compunction about lobbying the Truman administration on behalf of Israel.

The establishment of the State of Israel in 1948 effectively normalized Jewish ethnicity, making it comparable to Catholic ethnicities. Jews now possessed a recognized political homeland comparable to Ireland, Poland, and Italy. If, in a world of nation-states, Jews now had one, and if, in America, it had become legitimate more broadly to be defined in hyphenated terms as an ethnic-American, Jews now had access to a more common pattern. Advantageously, such access required no affirmative action by, or for, them.

These various changes to the condition of America's Jews are best understood as aspects of a mutually reinforcing configuration of elements rather than as isolated from one another. Shifts to the demographic composition and spatial locations of Jews contributed to lowering existing barriers to incorporation within higher education, the occupational structure, and political life. In turn, the acceleration of inclusion in these domains of American life further hastened changes to Jewish demography and space.

These conjoint revisions to the terms of linkage with American institutional life radically altered the manner in which Jews could comprehend and grip the most fateful events of their modern history during the 1940s. Soon, the main problems of American Jewry shifted from those of exclusion, anti-Semitism, and threat to those posed by integration and incorporation: quandaries of assimilation, intermarriage, and the sustenance of identity in the absence of jeopardy.

Put differently, the macroscopic shifts I have noted altered the mix of strategies Bauman identified which Jews effectively could pursue. These large-scale changes to the condition of American Jewry, and especially their entwined interconnection, changed both the content of each of these orientations to the wider society and the security with which Jews could attempt them. Individual-level "exit" solutions became more prevalent, but they no longer necessarily required conversion (indeed, over time, the balance of conversion altered). Jewish residential and institutional niches further diversified (simultaneously encompassing new forms of urban concentration and suburban dispersal; the recrudescence of orthodoxy and the regeneration of reform) and the robustness of engagement with the wider society from these more secure bases deepened and accelerated. Identity-based Jewish claims of multiple sorts proliferated; so, too, did the participation of Jews in civil rights causes of all kinds. In these ways, it was not just Jewish political culture that was remade; for Jews now became stalwart participants in remaking the larger political culture of the United States.

NOTES

1. Arthur Hertzberg, *The Jews in America: Four Centuries of an Uneasy Encounter* (New York, 1990), pp. 279–81; Marshall Sklare, ed., *The Jews: Social Patterns of an American Group* (Glencoe, IL,1957). For an overview, see Edward S. Shapiro, *A Time for Healing: American Jewry Since World War II* (Baltimore, 1992). Arthur A. Goren, *The Politics and Public Culture of American Jews* (Bloomington, Indiana, 1999), p. 203.

2. John Higham, "American Anti-Semitism Historically Reconsidered," in Charles Stember, ed., *Jews in the American Mind* (New York, 1966), p. 243.

3. Ira Katznelson, "Between Separation and Disappearance: Jews on the Mar-

gins of American Liberalism," in Pierre Birnbaum and Ira Katznelson, eds., *Paths of Emancipation: Jews, States, and Citizenship* (Princeton, 1995), p. 205. The quotations are from Milton Steinberg, "First Principles for American Jews," *Contemporary Jewish Record* (December 1941), and "Jewry and Democracy," *The Christian Century*, June 9, 1937; both are cited in Arnold M. Eisen, *The Chosen People in America* (Bloomington, IN, 1983).

4. On colleges, see Harold S. Wechsler, *The Qualified Student: A History of Selective College Admissions in America* (New York, 1977); Susanne Klingenstein, *Jews in the American Academy, 1900–1940: The Dynamics of Cultural Assimilation* (New Haven, CT, 1991); and Marcia Graham Synnott, *The Half-Opened Door: Discrimination and Admissions at Harvard, Yale, and Princeton, 1900–1970* (Westport, CT, 1979). For a useful overview, see Edward S. Shapiro, "World War II and American Jewish Identity," *Modern Judaism* 10 (February 1990). Shapiro cites estimates to the effect that in the early 1940s, nearly one in three job categories in the United States was restricted to Christians. Other discussions of the period's anti-Semitic upsurge include Donald Strong, *Organized Anti-Semitism in America: The Rise of Group Prejudice During the Decade 1930–1940* (Washington, DC, 1941); Alan Brinkley, *Voices of Protest: Huey Long, Father Coughlin and the Great Depression* (New York, 1982); and Ronald H. Bayor, *Neighbors in Conflict: The Irish, Germans, Jews, and Italians of New York City, 1929–1941* (Baltimore, 1978); John Higham, *Send These to Me: Jews and Other Immigrants to Urban America* (New York, 1975), pp. 128–35.

5. Hannah Arendt, *The Origins of Totalitarianism* (New York, 1951); Zygmunt Bauman, "Exit Visas and Entry Tickets: Paradoxes of Jewish Assimilation," *Telos* 77 (Fall 1988).

6. Ernest Gellner, "Ethnicity, Culture, Class, and Power," in Peter F. Singer, ed., *Ethnic Diversity and Conflict in East Europe* (Santa Barbara, CA, 1980); Frederick Barth, *Ethnic Groups and Boundaries: The Social Organization of Cultural Difference* (Bergen, 1969), p. 15.

7. Katznelson, "Between Separation and Disappearance," p. 160.

8. Beth S. Wenger, *New York Jews and the Great Depression: Uncertain Promise* (New Haven, CT, 1996), p. 2.

9. These figures are Arthur Hayes Sulzberger, Henry Morgenthau, Jr., and Felix Frankfurter. For a discussion, see Leonard Dinnerstein, *Anti-Semitism in America* (New York, 1994), p. 125.

10. Both are cited in Shapiro, "World War II," pp. 71, 80. This is the argument plausibly made by Shapiro, "World War II."

11. For an influential argument that American exceptionalism can best be understood in terms of the recurrent phenomenon of first generations, see Herbert J. Gutman, "Work, Culture, and Society in Industrializing America, 1815–1819," *American Historical Review* (June 1973).

12. For a discussion, see Olivier Zunz, *The Changing Face of Inequality: Urbanization, Industrial Development, and Immigrants in Detroit, 1880–1920* (Chicago, 1982). See Deborah Dash Moore, "The Construction of Community: Jewish Migration and Ethnicity in the United States," in Moses Rischin, ed., *The Jews of North America* (Detroit, 1987), pp. 110–15. Also see, Deborah Dash Moore, *To the Golden Cities: Pursuing the American Jewish Dream in Miami and L.A.* (New York, 1994).

13. Douglas S. Massey and Nancy A. Denton, *American Apartheid: Segregation and the Making of the Underclass* (Cambridge, MA, 1993).

14. A useful discussion of cognate changes among German immigrants is Kathleen Neils Conzen, "Immigrants, Immigrant Neighborhoods, and Ethnic Identity: Historical Issues," *The Journal of American History* 66 (December 1979); also see Deborah Dash Moore, *At Home in America: Second-Generation New York Jews* (New York, 1981).

15. Leonard Dinnerstein, "Franklin D. Roosevelt, American Jewry, and the New Deal," in Wilbur J. Cohen, ed., *The Roosevelt New Deal* (Austin, TX, 1986), p. 24. For discussions, see Dinnerstein, "Jews in the New Deal"; Lloyd Gartner, "The Midpassage of American Jewry," in Jonathan D. Sarna, ed., *The American Jewish Experience* (New York, 1986); Lawrence H. Fuchs, *The Political Behavior of American Jews* (Glencoe, IL, 1956); and Gerald Gamm, *The Making of New Deal Democrats: Voting Behavior and Realignment in Boston, 1920–1940* (Chicago, 1989).

16. For a useful discussion, see Wenger, *New York Jews,* chapter 5.

17. See "The Zionization of American Jewry," in Howard M. Sachar, *A History of the Jews in America* (New York, 1992), pp. 563–92.

FOURTEEN

Changing Places, Changing Cultures: Divergent Jewish Political Cultures

DANIEL J. ELAZAR

This chapter starts by posing a question that cannot help but fascinate students of human culture and behavior—in our particular case, Jewish culture and behavior. How is it that Jews from the same communities in the Old World—in Western Europe, Eastern Europe, or the Mediterranean world—within a relatively short time after their emigration to the new worlds of the United States and Israel came to manifest significant political cultural differences, at least overtly? How do we account for those political cultural transformations or shifts? This question poses a problem both in the study of culture, particularly political culture, and in the study of Jewry, particularly contemporary Jewry.

The modern epoch from the mid-seventeenth century onward has been one of migration for almost all people, but especially Europeans and among them, more particularly for Jews. From 1880 onward, Jews from Eastern Europe and the eastern Mediterranean came to the United States in large numbers and trickled to Israel in considerably smaller ones. Migrants went to either place from the same regions, towns, and even families. In their places of origin, most had lived their lives as had their forebears in substantially self-contained Jewish communities with a clearly Jewish political culture. Indeed, many of the basic characteristics of that political culture could be traced back to the earliest history of the Jewish people.[1] These included constitutionalism, in the form of a commitment to Torah as a constitution in the ancient sense, law-abidingness, and a sense of covenantal commitment and the equality among Jews implied in that commitment. In addition, Jewish political culture accepted the division of governing powers among the three separate but connected domains—*malkhut* (civil rule or, literally, kingship), *kehunah* (priesthood), and *Torah*—each with its own leaders and tasks.

For our purposes here we can identify four dimensions of Jewish political culture shared by virtually all emigrants, no matter where they emigrated to: social justice, solidarity, universalism, and particularism. Jewish political culture scores high on commitment to social justice, to the idea of a just society, and to the development of society in a just and righteous manner, the definition which is derived in some significant way from the definition embedded in the Bible.

The close connections and sense of mutual responsibility that Jews have for one another, what might be called solidarity, also seems to be a constant in Jewish political culture. Jewish solidarity is legendary, found wherever Jews exist.

Ideologically, at least, a strong streak of universalism runs through Jewish political culture. It is paralleled by an equally strong streak of particularism, even parochialism. On one hand, Jews seek to save the world and have messianic expectations of the degree to which human camaraderie can be achieved within a framework of justice. On the other hand, Jews have a sense of separation from other people, equally strong and widespread, embodied ideologically in the Jewish sense of chosenness and sociologically in the Jewish sense of differentness. The particular combination of these four tendencies shapes the direction of the political culture of the Jews of any particular land or community. What follows is an informal speculation on the differences in political culture that developed between those Jews who went to the United States and those who settled in Israel and how that differentiation came about out of the same background.

It is fair to assume that Jews from the same environments who reached either country brought the same particular synthesis of these four elements with them (allowing for individual references) and that the divergences occurred in their respective new environments. Upon arrival, each group of Jews began to adapt to its new environment or, more accurately, to its perceptions of that new environment.

JEWISH PLURALISM IN THE UNITED STATES

Jewish immigrants who settled in the United States confronted two major tasks. Because they had come to the United States to stay (a smaller percentage of Jews "returned" to their countries of origin or migrated elsewhere than any other major group that had emigrated to the United States at that time), with few exceptions they wholeheartedly threw themselves into the task of becoming American and accepted as equals in the United States. This meant that they soon became leaders in the battle for equal rights in their new country, a path that was rendered more difficult for them than for other native European groups because of the additional problem of anti-Semitism. While their position unquestionably was not as difficult as that of the African Americans—who had a history of being enslaved in America and who continued to experience racism following their emancipation—the vast majority of Jewish immigrants arrived at the height of American and worldwide anti-Semitism, between the mid-1870s and the end of World War II, the time when efforts were being made to exclude Jews in unprecedented ways.[2]

Furthermore, Jews were the major immigrant group that differed religiously in a fundamental way from the American majority. Catholic immigrants also had to confront a predominantly Protestant society but in the last analysis they were Christians and could fit into the Christian character of American society. Jews, however, could not do that and remain Jewish, and, although they wanted to be fully integrated into the United States in every other way, most Jews wished to retain their Jewishness and Jewish attachment in some way. In the American context, this meant holding on to

Jewish religious behavior. As President Theodore Roosevelt pointed out at the height of the mass migration from Eastern and Southern Europe, although "hyphenated Americans"—those who wished to retain their original ethnic cultures—were not acceptable to the American majority, religious differences were.[3] Hence, identification with Judaism was both a barrier and an opportunity for Jewish immigrants.

American Jews used their relative cultural advantages (e.g., they were literate) and talents to press for equal rights for minorities and for minority religions, leading the assault against the ethnic and racial prejudices of turn-of-the-century America and also the assault against the informally established Protestant republic. This led to American Jews' cultivation of those elements in Jewish political culture that emphasized universalism and social justice. The American Jewish manifestations of universalism soon coalesced in a well-nigh religious commitment to what one of their number, Horace M. Kallen, redefined as "pluralism," that is, a United States that was open to and encouraged every group to maintain its identity as it wished to do so within a common American mold which would no longer be that of the Anglo-Saxon or Anglo-Saxon/Northern European Protestant republic.[4] Thus, in their battle for acceptance as equals, American Jews developed a new ideology for America to counter that of the Protestant republic and committed themselves wholeheartedly—one might say uncritically—to it. Pluralism could encompass messages of universal social justice for all. Kallen was its first prophet, but soon many other American Jewish intellectuals joined his chorus to articulate a comprehensive ideology which was rapidly embraced by working-class American Jews.

While doing research in the Frederick Jackson Turner papers at the Huntington Library in San Marino, California, in the early 1960s, this writer came across Kallen's first articulation (in the years during World War I) of his idea of cultural pluralism in a two-part article in *The Nation* which Turner had removed from the journal and had obviously read diligently and carefully, judging from his extensive underlinings. Turner, of course, was one of the capstone articulators of the older vision of the Protestant republic in its secular dimensions. Kallen, among the first to enunciate the vision of pluralism, also emphasized its secular dimensions.

However, on the American scene the secular dimensions played less well than the religious argument for pluralism and its religious expression. So while Jews frequently meant cultural pluralism, they presented their case within the context of religious pluralism. That case reached its apogee just after World War II in Will Herberg's formulation of the triple melting pot—Protestant, Catholic, and Jewish.[5] Herberg, a repentant Communist who rediscovered Judaism and moved from a secular to a religious identification in his own life, provided the capstone synthesis for an American Jewry as it moved out of its immigrant experience and into full-fledged membership in American society.

The social justice dimensions of this American Jewish ideology of pluralism were no less important than the universalist ones. Most Jews had always advocated social justice, even in the earliest days of the republic. Not only did Jews remain partisans of social justice through the various redefinitions of what constituted social justice during the nineteenth century, but the mass immigration after 1880 brought many Jews who had become socialists in the Old World to the New.

Most rather quickly discovered that Old World socialism was not transplantable to the New World, where advocates of social justice took a different approach. As they abandoned their more rigidly socialist ideas, they became social democrats, supporters of the New Deal and the welfare state to achieve their social justice goals, just as they opposed racism and other forms of discrimination. That synthesis was essentially completed in the years immediately prior to World War II, inspired by the presidency and program of Franklin Delano Roosevelt, who had become a great hero to American Jews (a judgment later modified after his equivocal role, or worse, in the rescue of Jews from Europe was revealed after the war).

For American Jews, then, the combination of universalism and social justice meant that social justice could be achieved only if it were achieved for all in such a way that respected the identities of everyone. This has been and remains the American Jewish creed. Jews found an American "hook" to hang it on in the individualism and free market–oriented character of the United States. The traditional American commitment to freedom of religion and separation of church and state was especially important in this regard. The formal rejection of an established religion by the United States gave Jews the opportunity to argue for equal recognition of Judaism among

America's various religious communities. That world of separation between church and state became a cardinal principle of American Jewish ideology, one of the rocks upon which it was built.

ISRAELI JEWISH SOLIDARITY

Very different principles came to the fore among those Jews who emigrated to the Land of Israel. The environment they encountered differed from that encountered by their co-religionists who had emigrated to the United States. In the Middle East a deeply anchored ethnic-religious identity defined populations. Indeed, Jews who chose the Land of Israel came because they wished to "join the system," that is, to rebuild the land as the national home of the Jewish people. First believing that the land was empty, they soon discovered that it did have an indigenous population who strongly identified as Arabs, who were, for the most part, Islamic, and had their own agenda for the land. Prior to World War I, those who had political control over the land, although sharing the same religion with the Arab inhabitants, had a different national definition as Turks and opposed Jewish aspirations for both national and religious reasons. So Jews engaged in a struggle not simply to be accepted as individuals who happened to be of the Jewish faith but also to be recognized as members of a group that had its own designs as a people on the land. This meant that the first need of the Jewish settlers was solidarity, a need so great that it even overcame the strong ideological divisions within the Yishuv (Jewish community in Palestine) in Palestine between Ashkenazim and Sephardim, between the old Yishuv and the Zionist *halutzim* (pioneers), between the halutzim of the First Aliya and the intensely socialist halutzim of the Second Aliya, and between the utopian and Marxian socialists of the Second and Third aliyot. These ideologically based differences were intense and far transcended any other differences of custom or country of origin which Jews also brought with them. But whatever the degree of intensity of these new citizens, basic Jewish solidarity was cultivated devoutly.

Although Jews were a minority in the land that after World War I became Palestine, they did not seek assimilation into the majority as in the United

States but rather sought to become the majority. For that, solidarity was necessary, and the institutions of the Yishuv were designed to foster solidarity at every critical turn. In consequence, Jews turned inward. For example, the Jews who came to Palestine and indeed the socialists among them had particularly strong commitments to fighting for social justice, but that fight was directed primarily within the Jewish community. Not that lip service was not paid to social justice for Arabs as well, but the real effort was with regard to the Jews.

For example, the socialist Zionist struggle for Jewish labor had different implications for Jews and Arabs. One of the cardinal principles of socialist Zionism was that Jews should become productive in their own land and not simply members of the petty bourgeoisie, as they had been in Europe. Earlier settlers, including those of the First Aliya, hired Arabs when they needed farm laborers. It was cheaper, and the Arabs were more experienced. The socialist Zionists fought bitterly to force those Arab workers out and to replace them with Jewish laborers on the grounds that this was necessary to turn the Jews into a productive people and thereby advance socialist goals. Apparently, no one had thought about how the Arabs perceived that effort —as foreign Jews coming onto their land and taking employment from them to advance Jewish interests. One cannot doubt the good intentions of the halutzim in this regard, but neither can one doubt the consequences. (Ironically, the liberals, denounced as reactionaries by the Zionist socialists, sought to include the Arabs in Jewish plans for development of the land. True, they aimed to do so on the basis of a Jewish majority, but their vision was broad enough to include non-Jews as well.)

This turning inward characterized every Jewish subgroup. Today we see it in everything from ultra-Orthodox claims to religious exclusivism to ultranationalist claims to the whole Land of Israel regardless of the existence of a very large Arab population in the disputed territories, to the ultra-peacenik claims that Israel must not only grant the Palestinians their own state but totally separate Israel from it if Israel is to preserve its Jewish character. While universalism has remained a lip-service theme, in fact it is parochialism along with solidarity that has become the dominant mode of the political culture of the Jews of Israel.

The intensifying Israeli-Arab conflict, the continuing struggle for first the establishment, then the consolidation, and finally the security of the Jewish state, has reinforced this combination of solidarity and parochialism to make it the dominant force in Israel's political culture.

Just as in the United States, where the Jewish emphasis on pluralism had not eliminated solidarity and parochialism, in Israel the drive for universalism and social justice acquired different meaning. Universalism today in Israel is advocated by those who reject Jewish civilization and seek to make Israel part of a European heritage. Social justice still commands considerable lip service but relatively little in the way of action. In conclusion, if the consequences of the Jews existing as a minority seeking integration into the larger society are excessive universalism and individualism, the consequences of the Jews existing as a majority seeking to preserve that majority status in every respect have led to new kinds of parochialism.

THE ROAD DIVIDES

The common political culture of the Jewish emigrants divided into two streams based upon the countries to which they emigrated. Perhaps there are alternatives for those Jews who emigrated to other countries. For example, Jews who emigrated to Britain built a community on the basis of a Jewish version of Anglicanism, an official Orthodoxy softened by modernity but "established" in the minds of most British Jews. This religious pattern differed from the development of Conservative, Reform, Reconstructionist, and now New Age and traditional Jews alongside of an ever-decreasing Orthodoxy competing in the open market that America not only provided but actually demanded. However, the relation between religious and political culture is not clear.

The record reveals how Jewish migrants, by picking and choosing from among the same ingredients, forged new syntheses based upon choices perceived to be required by their environmental conditions. A common political culture became two different ones. Nor is this unusual. History is replete with similar situations where a particular system of thought or behavior is taken from its founder(s) by subsequent generations who emphasize different points from what they have inherited and as a result develop divergent, and at times even apparently contradictory patterns. It is perhaps easiest to trace this phenomenon through the examination of schools of philosophy, when one takes a look at how different sets of a philosopher's disciples will take his philosophy in one or another direction in the name of their discipleship. It appears that much the same phenomenon occurs in cultural shifts. Both the proper study of American and Israeli Jews and the study of political culture itself requires that due attention be paid this phenomenon and the process of cultural change.

WHEN COUSINS CLASH: PRACTICAL CONSEQUENCES

Today we are witnessing the consequences of this diversion of paths in two ways: first, in the cultural expressions of each group within their respective countries and, second, in the clash of interests between the descendants in each group. These Jews not only have no recollection of the common culture of their ancestors but also have reinterpreted that culture in their own terms.

Take the issues of Jewishness and Judaism — their character and their place in polity and society. The majority of American Jews see Jewishness primarily as Judaism and see Judaism as a matter of free choice on the part of its adherents who may or may not have been born Jews. They are free to choose how they want to express their Judaism and to organize accordingly, with the same rights of recognition, whether they accept traditional *halakhic* (legal) standards and institutions, or accept the principle of halakhic standards but within new forms and institutions, or reject halakhah as authoritative and rely entirely on forms and institutions that are more or less traditional. The expectation is that these choices are voluntary but that they all must be recognized by Jews everywhere as equally legitimate and accorded respect on that basis. Most American Jews hold that there can be no established authoritative Judaism even in a Jewish state because that would violate the norms of pluralism and separation of religion and state. To the extent that there is such an establishment in Israel, Israel is less than democratic and certainly less democratic than the United States.

The majority of Israeli Jews, on the other hand, whether personally religious or not, see themselves first and foremost as part of a Jewish nation which, while outsiders can join it, is essentially organic in character—that is, people are born into it. Moreover, while one's level of religious involvement is voluntary, religion is a core dimension of Jewish nationalism. Hence Judaism must be maintained in recognizably traditional forms for the nation as a whole regardless of the behavior of its individual members. Whatever the level of personal choice individual Jews may have in how religiously observant they want to be, the religion itself cannot formally offer that choice.

Judaism remains as it was revealed and has developed, anchored in its own religious laws and traditions, an overarching edifice that exists whether it has many faithful or few. Individuals and groups cannot come along and change it to suit their tastes unless they can do so through its established procedures and institutions. True, there cannot and shall not be any compulsion of individuals to observe the religion into which they were born, but there can also be no legitimate way to force that religion to change to meet new tastes. Thus the idea of institutionalizing different approaches to Judaism that do not accept its basic halakhic framework is held to be absurd from this perspective.

While not all Israeli Jews believe this any more than all American Jews believe in the pluralistic definition set forth above, the majority accept that definition without attempting to refute it or present another one. Moreover, because this is the case, even a democratic state has a legitimate right to protect that religious framework for its adherents provided they protect all separate religious frameworks present within the state (e.g., Islam, Christianity) equally for their adherents. So here we have a clash between different conceptions of what religion is or should be and what kinds of relationships should develop among religion, the polity, and society. This struggle has reached ideological proportions. Neither side can compromise except on the most pragmatic levels when other shared elements in their political culture are endangered. To date, the common Jewish commitment to the need for solidarity has limited the conflict, but as the need for solidarity erodes, so does the commitment to limit the conflict.

THE CONSEQUENCES OF CULTURAL DIVERGENCE IN AN INTERCONNECTED WORLD

Cultural divergence, in the form of subcultures, has not been unknown to the Jewish people in the past. There were clear differences between Ashkenazim and Sephardim in their general culture and probably even in their political culture. Ashkenazim, living in a persecutory Christian environment, became far more particularistic, even isolationist, and sought to separate themselves from their non-Jewish neighbors for whom they often had contempt and even hatred. Sephardim, on the other hand, although the targets of anti-Semitism specific to environments in which they lived, did not suffer unrelenting persecution. Consequently they devised a more universalistic strategy of interaction with the peoples among whom they lived, including political participation that involved mutual recognition.

These differences rarely led to clashes between the two Jewish subgroups because they lived apart from each other and interacted infrequently. Both Ashkenazim and Sephardim used other elements in Jewish culture and political culture to maintain a solidarity. Today that kind of separation is no longer possible when telecommunications are instant and physical presence is a matter of hours of travel rather than weeks or months. Interdependence means that local solutions are no longer local. Nationwide issues previously handled locally, if only for lack of options, now must be confronted by all subgroups within the Jewish community, each of whom insists on its own legitimacy. Moreover, modernity has increased the ideological and behavioral differences between subgroups just as an earlier more homogeneous people was separated by physical and temporal distance.

Jews of all groups who are concerned about Jewish solidarity are struggling with this new reality even if they reject pluralism as an ideology through which to approach it. The intensity of the problem, however, greatly increases when issues move from the customary to the ideological to the cultural in their roots. Custom, which is more a matter of style, whatever strength it has because it is familiar, can be changed fairly rapidly when it is trumped by ideology. We see this in the way, for example, that young Sephardim, educated in Lithuanian Ashkenazi yeshivot, can view halakhah through a different ideological prism and are rapidly abandoning older customs which are no longer ideologically justifiable to them. But when ideology becomes embedded in culture, more often than not culture trumps ideology. Hence we see the revitalization of the ideology of ultra-Orthodox Judaism in ways far more extreme than those that had existed when even Orthodoxy was transmitted through a mimetic rather than a deliberately learned Judaism.[6] The latter becomes especially appealing to those whose psychological orientation is to accept that kind of absolute control, what in an earlier and different situation Erich Fromm referred to as the escape from freedom.[7] Moreover, the revolt of the modern Orthodox, often expressed through religious Zionism, has collapsed under the *haredi* (zealot) challenge in no small measure because their ideology has collapsed.

Conversely, Orthodoxy in the United States can survive only or best as haredi Orthodoxy because only those willing to accept the same isolationist-parochial and absolutist premises can resist an American ideology deeply rooted in American culture that rejects all distinctions—between groups, between genders—and fosters individualism and individual choice. In the United States that culture of individualism is heightened by an ideology allowing no distinctions, thereby making it even harder for Judaism to compete, even when the majority of American Jews have adopted radical accommodationist strategies to survive in that culture. Thus the gap between American and Israeli Judaism and hence American and Israeli Jews grows wider, modified only by the solidarity elements in Jewish culture which lead to efforts to find pragmatic solutions to these ideological and cultural problems.

NOTES

1. Daniel J. Elazar and Stuart Cohen, *The Jewish Polity: Jewish Political Organization from Biblical Times to the Present* (Bloomington, IN, 1985); Daniel J. Elazar, ed., *Kinship and Consent: The Jewish Political Tradition and Its Contemporary Uses* (Lanham, MD, 1983); Stuart Cohen, *The Three Crowns: Structures of Communal Discourse in Early Rabbinic Society* (Cambridge, 1990); and Daniel J. Elazar, *Authority, Power and Leadership in the Jewish Polity: Cases and Issues* (Lanham, MD, 1993).

2. John Higham, "Anti-Semitism in the Gilded Age," in *Mississippi Valley Historical Review* 43 (March 1957), 559–78.

3. "Straight Americanism," in Hermann Hagedorn, ed., *The Americanism of Theodore Roosevelt: Selections from His Writings and Speeches* (Boston, 1923), pp. 199–210.

4. Horace M. Kallen, "Democracy vs. the Melting Pot," in *Culture and Democracy in the United States: Studies in the Group Psychology of the American Peoples* (New York, 1924).

5. Will Herberg, *Protestant, Catholic, Jew: An Essay in American Religious Sociology* (Garden City, NY, 1960).

6. Hayim Soloveitchik, "Rupture and Reconstruction: The Transformation of Contemporary Orthodoxy," *Tradition* 28:4 (1997).

7. Erich Fromm, *Escape from Freedom: A Critical Commentary,* text by Kurt L. Shell (New York, 1967).

Epilogue: On Living in Two Cultures

ARTHUR ARYEH GOREN

As young people who have pledged ourselves to the fulfillment of our ideals in our own lives, we cannot escape the realization that it is necessary for many of us to participate directly in the task of building Israel. . . . We must go there ourselves and ourselves settle the land.

—"What We Believe," Habonim, Labor Zionist Youth, 1951

Young Jews must fight with like-minded people everywhere for the emergence of a better society. We must fight the discrimination which is practiced against a man because of his color, creed or political belief. We must work toward the elimination of economic exploitation of one man by another. . . . We must at the same time be on guard against any encroachment upon the freedom of the individual, his freedom to believe what he wants, to think as he chooses, to express himself openly without restraint. . . . Without these freedoms, security is worthless.

—"What We Believe," 1951

A crack is found in [the wall of] a building. The conscientious construction worker makes no attempt to hide it. He is not concerned with his reputation. He is concerned with the fate of the building. He fears its collapse. He does not look for a pretext. He pries out the damaged bricks and prepares the surface for new brickwork. On the other hand, he who works unscrupulously hurries and covers the crack with plaster. . . . He is satisfied. Ostensibly he succeeded. But the building will eventually collapse. Let us not be unscrupulous workers, neither in deed nor in thought. Let us have no part in smearing on plaster.
—Berl Katznelson, "In Praise of Confusion, Against the Cover Up," 1940

These recollections are grounded in those extraordinary years in the aftermath of the Second World War when American Jews mobilized their resources in support of the Yishuv's struggle for statehood. The story has been told and retold: how American Zionists spearheaded the creation of an American Jewish consensus, wrung political support from a reluctant administration, raised unprecedented sums to purchase the ships to transport displaced persons to Palestine and war materials for the Haganah, and how a remarkably disciplined organization activated the thousands who participated in the political rallies, protest marches, and picket lines. Indeed, eminent public figures once indifferent or inimical to Zionist aspirations now joined in the common cause. Overnight, American Jews embraced a new cast of heroes, discovered new sacred images, and adopted a new set of slogans: Exodus and *aliyah beth* (illegal immigration), *sabras* and *Palmach*, *halutzim* (pioneers) and the siege of Kibbutz Negba, "the ingathering of the exiles" and "operation magic carpet" (the evacuation of the Jews of Yemen). Above all, American Jews were enamored of the appurtenances of sovereignty: Ambassador Abba Eban and Foreign Minister Moshe Sharett raising the Israeli flag at the United Nations, the first delegation of young Israelis sent to the United Jewish Appeal campaign appearing in the uniform of the Israel Defense Forces, and the relays of cabinet officers culminating in the 1951 visit of Prime Minister David Ben-Gurion.

It is also well to recall the rhetoric of the times. Soon after the November 1947 UN decision on partition, the *merkaz* of Habonim, the executive committee of the Labor Zionist Youth organization to which I belonged, passed a resolution the first part of which was similar to scores of others:

> For two thousand years our people dreamed. For two thousand years Jews remembered Zion and prayed for deliverance. . . . For two thousand years Jews piously hoped that the Return would take place "quickly in our time." It has happened and is happening in *our* time; the Jewish State, *medina ivrit, b'yameinu*.

Then came the solemn summons which was different from most such declarations:

> We call upon all Jewish youth in America but upon the members of Habonim first and foremost. . . . Let us rise and accept the challenge of history! Ours is the chosen generation! We dare to believe that a new code of ethics will blaze forth from Zion, a new life based on the principles of equality and social justice. The new Eretz Israel calls upon us. Let us arise and build![1]

The call for aliyah was no mere ritualistic flourish as it was for the American Zionist establishment. For my Habonim cohort—I was twenty-one years old in 1947—we were "the chosen generation." American-born and recently discharged from the service, most of us had grown up in Zionist homes and in the youth movement. (Long before the word "movement" became synonymous with civil rights activists, Zionist youth groups declared the seriousness of their ideals and commitments by calling themselves "movements," as did the halutzim in Palestine and Poland and the youth groups of the old left.)

I joined Habonim at age thirteen. The family had recently moved to Washington from Chelsea, Massachusetts. My father, an accountant, had been attracted by the security of a civil service job. My mother, who also found government employment, immediately became active in the Labor Zionist Pioneer Women. Through this connection it wasn't long before my name reached the appropriate Habonim committee. The son of a Pioneer Woman phoned, followed by a call from an "organizer" from the national office who was on tour: would I like to invite some of my friends to the house and he would drop by to talk about the movement. We met around the Ping-Pong table in our basement, and after a bit "Moshe" (then he was "Itchie") described what it was like to be in Habonim. He emphasized the special sense of *havershaft* (comradeship) that prevailed in the movement. Branches existed across the country where the homes of Habonim members were always open to the *haverim* (comrades). There were the summer camps, camp reunions, winter seminars, and national conventions. In Palestine (Eretz Israel), Habonim graduates were building and defending the homeland.

Habonim was surely the formative experience of our lives. It influenced our choice of careers, whom we married, where we settled in Israel (many of us beginning on the kibbutz), and how we voted. Even for those who returned or never went on *aliyah*, Habonim remained the baseline or yardstick by which we measured our personal and public lives. In a word, the movement shaped our identity.

How did all this happen? Even as young teenagers we were won over by the notion that it was *our* movement. We ran it. We chose our leaders and sent delegates to the national conventions where ideology and policy were debated and the national officers were elected. Youth leads youth, we proclaimed, and we scoffed at Young Judea and B'nai B'rith Youth who paid (we were told) their club leaders and where professionals, social workers, or rabbis directed the national organization. Our full-time (seven days a week) national officers and camp directors, I would find out in time, received subsistence wages.

By fifteen I was a club leader, at best two years older than my charges. More enthusiastic than knowledgeable, I passed on to them the lore and ethos of halutzim building the homeland. Through discussions, song and dance, dramatics and handicrafts, we introduced our young members to the heroes of pioneering Palestine and then embattled Israel: the *Shomrim* (guards) A. D. Gordon, Rachel, Joseph Trumpeldor, Hannah Szenes, our own Golda Meir, the plucky, committed few against the many (the British Empire and the Arab world). We learned the subject matter and techniques of group work at leadership training seminars before or after the regular camp season and attended weekly club leaders' sessions in the city, where we discussed our pedagogical problems and received a torrent of educational material from the national office. In our own peer groups, but especially at regional conclaves and summer camps, we delved into the writings of the Socialist-Zionist thinkers and the maze of current Zionist politics: at home, *our* Hayim Greenberg versus Abba Hillel Silver; in Palestine, *our Hagana* versus *Etzel,* and *our* Ben-Gurion and MAPAI (the socialist labor party) versus Begin and the Revisionists. Most of all, we talked about the kibbutz—its history and ideology, and the complexities of kibbutz living—private aspirations and collective needs, personal gratification, and the demands of the hour. *Shlihim,* emissaries from Palestine, almost always members of kibbutzim and MAPAI, were our mentors, although we criticized them for not understanding that "America was different," and hence Habonim was different from the halutz movements they knew. We were proud of the American ingredients of our kind of halutz movement.

Our summer camps, modeled after the kibbutz as we imagined it, were the ultimate educational experience. (Habonim ran twelve camps in the United States and Canada in summer 1951.) Some of the hallmarks of this venture are worth noting. Soon after the opening of camp, a "general meeting" of campers and staff elected committees that were responsible for various aspects of camp life. A "cultural committee" planned the Friday evening pageant-like sabbath program (the "Oneg Shabbat"); another committee took charge of the weekday evening programs; a "work committee" planned and assigned "members" to the two-hour-a-day work projects; and a camp committee handled disputes and complaints. We simulated the kibbutz principles of equality and communal sharing. But first the principles of collective living and their application to our imaginary kibbutz were discussed and approved at a long general meeting where we, the senior counselors, were called upon to use our most persuasive powers. It was no easy matter convincing new campers that in the name of equality, fairness, and comradeship—the essence of the kibbutz—they were to hand over the packages of goodies from home for all to share. Naturally, the campers proceeded to elect a committee to manage the commissary of treats.

Over time, the tempo of movement life intensified, and with it the personal commitment. At sixteen I was one of three senior counselors assigned to the New York camp. By then most members over eighteen were in the armed forces. Of course, for my services on this make-believe kibbutz I received no compensation; after all, the camp was the communal property of my movement. Literally days after my discharge from the service in December 1945 the national office sent me to Detroit to help prepare the

Habonim convention. I lived with a movement family, my severance pay covering "out-of-pocket" expenses. That began five years of youth work in Habonim until my aliyah.

What was unusual about Habonim—so we believed and so I still believe—is that it enabled us to mix (not necessarily "integrate" or "blend" or "fuse") our American-ness with our Israeli-ness both before and after we settled in Israel. This was so because neither the generation of Habonim's founders nor we who followed had any need to reject America or Jewish life in America. To "make aliyah" was in principle a matter of free choice. One went from an inner compulsion, not disillusionment, although the peer pressure to conform was ever present. We rejected out of hand any intimation by the shlihim that "it could happen here" (i.e., virulent anti-Semitism) or that assimilation was inevitable. The glorification of an ideal Zion, the role models of our own "graduates" who had settled in Eretz Israel, some of whom began rotating back as shlihim, created an atmosphere where aliyah and particularly the kibbutz represented self-fulfillment combined with the loftiest form of service to one's people.

However, the presence of both regard for the individual and concern for the communal good produced tension and ambivalence. "If *we* do not settle the border lands, who will?" weighed heavy on many a conscience and spurred more than a few who, though conflicted, decided on aliyah. Nonetheless, we insisted that the decision to become a halutz was a private one, to be reached without coercion and for "positive" reasons. Some never decided. By and large this built-in ambiguity—freedom of the individual and collective responsibility—led to a pluralism of the mind. All degrees of commitment were legitimate—from going to the kibbutz to being a good Labor Zionist in America.

In short, Habonim prided itself in being an *American* halutz movement which spoke in a distinctively American voice, anomalous as this appeared in the eyes of our shlihim. We believed that our openness and latitude reflected an American democratic mentality which would be our "contribution" to Israeli life. The dense and fervid politicization that pervaded the Yishuv and its labor movement and that carried over into newly independent Israel was alien to us. To be sure, we were most influenced by MAPAI's benign democratic socialism. We were also well aware of party discipline and "party keys" in making appointments (including shlihim to Habonim) that bordered on machine politics, in our view. We were delighted when a second-generation member of a moshav family came to us as a shliha, although we sensed how the kibbutz shlihim resented her presence as a dangerous precedent. We believed that the youth movement should be exempt from imported factionalism. Naively we presumed that politics had no place in education.

Unlike Habonim, Hashomer Hatzair, a "hundred percent" halutz movement and our rival, was directly linked to the left-wing Kibbutz Artzi in Israel. Hashomer Hatzair's Marxist socialism was more rigorous, its movement discipline was more demanding, and it saw no future for Jewish life in the diaspora, including the American diaspora. When one reached the designated age, usually eighteen, a member of Hashomer Hatzair declared his or her intention to go on aliyah and went to *hakhshara* (the movement's agricultural training commune) or was expelled. Singlemindedly, the movement directed its graduates to Kibbutz Artzi settlements. Undoubtedly, Hashomer Hatzair was correct in its criticism of Habonim: in trying to reach out to broad circles of Jewish youth (which never happened), Habonim made compromises. It was too American.

In intense, personal discussions, sharing our doubts about the impending future, some also spoke of preparing themselves for a professional career (especially appealing when the GI Bill made higher education so accessible). Thus one would not only fulfill personal ambitions, but bring needed skills to Israel; or, and this too was said, remain in America, contribute to the quality of Jewish life, and participate in the political struggle for a more just society. Looking back, it is interesting to recall the career of Alexander Bickel, the influential Yale professor of constitutional law who played an important public role from the late 1950s until his death in 1974. As a young man, he belonged to a West Bronx chapter of Habonim and took an active part in campus Zionism while studying at City College. On his discharge from the army, he served as editor of the excellent Habonim monthly, *Furrows*. Bickel's public stature—his name was bandied about as a possible nominee for the Supreme Court—was exceptional among the movement's alumni. Nevertheless, it was indicative of the interests and directions some took.

No wonder that of all the Socialist-Zionist thinkers we encountered, Berl Katznelson appealed to us most, particularly the writings he addressed to the youth of the Yishuv (the Jewish community in Palestine). (One of his best-known essays of this genre was translated from the Hebrew and published as "Revolutionary Constructivism" by the Labor Zionist Organization.) His pleas for the unity of the labor movement, his despair over factional splits that stemmed from doctrinaire constructions, and his sensibility for tradition—in brief, his broad humanity—struck a responsive chord among us. We were moved by his rebuke of those participants in a Youth Aliyah leaders' seminar who had insisted that ideological conformity was a requisite for leadership. Berl's remarks appeared in print as a long, polemical essay in Hebrew that reached us in America through the mediation of the shlihim. A fairly literal translation of the title reads: "The Right to be Confused and in Condemnation of the Whitewash." Berl preferred "a bewildered and perturbed soul" to one which admitted no defects and was content with the received "'truths' especially at this time." (The talk was delivered on July 8, 1940. France had fallen in June, and Germany and the Soviet Union had divided Poland the previous September. Berl aimed his barbed words at the Hashomer Hatzair participants who insisted on socialist orthodoxy.)

When we first discussed the essay in the aftermath of the war, we were hardly aware of these circumstances. What appealed to us was his call for openmindedness and tolerance. Interestingly, at a humorous camp program the year Berl's writings occupied a prominent place in our educational program (1946), a choir lampooned MAPAI by setting Berl's famous watchword to the popular melody of "Yehuda l'olam teyshev," singing it as a round: "MAPAI shall always prevail / We will grow while other parties go / 'For we have the right to be confused.'" The ditty spread like wildfire and was sung throughout the time I was in the movement, to the discomfort of the shlihim.

This levity, too, was quite American. Much as we admired Berl and MAPAI one needed a respite from the backbiting, complicated disputations couched as authoritative pronouncements and ultimatums. We resented infallibility.

There were the prosaic ways our American-ness expressed itself. I mention them in passing before considering the more substantive question of our response to the new urgency aliyah and *halutziut* assumed as the struggle for the Jewish state escalated. We grew up reading the sports pages before reading the editorial page and knew the batting averages of our home-team starting lineup.[2] Franklin D. Roosevelt was our parents' hero and ours. We believed the United States was the leader of the free world, and we were proud of it. We also railed against racism, anti-Semitism, violations of civil liberties, and southern senators filibustering liberal bills to death. In 1948, a few of us preferred Henry Wallace over Harry Truman, despite Truman's recognition of Israel. Our conventions passed resolutions calling for equality, social justice, and support of unions.

One might say that we were profoundly bicultural. In the eighth grade, if I recall correctly, we were required to memorize the Gettysburg Address. (I was much more taken by Lincoln than by Washington; we got a day off from school for Washington's birthday, which I thought was unfair to the memory of Lincoln.) About the same time, I also memorized A. D. Gordon's "Dream of the Aliyah." With his long, white beard and sad eyes staring out from the book jacket of the one-volume translation of his works, Gordon moved me as much as Lincoln did. Working the soil of Degania, declaring that physical work—sweat and toil—would renew the Jewish people was exhilarating. The occasion for memorizing his "Dream" was the annual pageant our Washington clubs held to raise money for our camp. Our "director" prepared a tableau portraying Gordon's call to the Jews of the *Golah* (Exile) to join him in an act of self-redemption. "Hear, my Brother, and hear my Sister," it began, "and remember that you also dream like me. In my dream I come to the Land. And the Land is abandoned, and wasted, and delivered into the hands of strangers." It ended with: "When I see you both working and living here, I rejoice. . . . You will build the house of Israel; you will find the road on which we set our hearts from time immemorial . . . and your life will be renewed. This new life, like a tidal river, will go on, will renew itself, and flow onward, onward, onward."[3] We also knew by heart the album "Six Songs for Democracy," which featured Paul Robeson singing "Ballad for America" and "The Lonesome Train." Around the campfire or the city equivalent, a candle on the floor of a darkened meeting room, we mixed the songs of the *Palmach* with union songs and protest ballads we had learned from the records of Pete Seeger, Woodie Guthrie, and Josh White. Good imitators, Habonim produced its own album in 1947, *Haganah, Songs of the Jewish Underground,* an audacious undertaking intended to reach all folk music lovers who we assumed were radical, young, and Jewish. The notes on the inside cover explained: "A great struggle will produce great folk music. In our own time we have witnessed the birth of immortal songs that have sprung from the Russian revolution, the Spanish Civil War, the concentration camps of Germany, and now from the Jewish pioneers of Palestine."[4]

Even before we confronted the reality of Israel and the real kibbutz, we became aware that the mix of our American upbringing and our vision of an ideal society in the making (the "master narrative") had created stress and friction. Two true tales illustrate this point.

In May 1946 a weekend conference of the designated "directors," senior counselors, and key shlihim of the Habonim summer camps met in New York to discuss the education program and related issues for the impending season. In the midst of one session, we were informed rather abruptly that a "VIP" from Palestine had asked to meet with us and would be arriving shortly. A compact, stern-looking man of middle age, bald, wearing horn-rimmed glasses walked into the room accompanied by two young *sabra* bodyguards, or so they appeared to us. The shlihim among us obviously knew who he was and froze to attention in their chairs. Yaacov, as he was introduced to us, began talking in a clipped, British-accented English. Running ten or so camps with probably two thousand campers and counselors, he stated, was an unsurpassed opportunity to teach our youth discipline, deference for authority, and personal self-defense skills that would become useful sooner than we thought. We sat astounded. He "advised" us—it sounded more like an order—to introduce close-order drill, long hikes in formation, group calisthenics, and for the older campers and counselors, "ka-pap," the Hebrew acronym for *krav panim el panim* (hand-to-hand combat using staves). For the latter, he was prepared to supply instructors.

An uproar followed. This was militarism. We were an educational youth movement attentive to the needs of each camper, teaching our members democratic values, egalitarianism, and self-expression. We had had enough of regimentation and sergeants barking out orders in the armed forces. How could we expose our young people to authoritarianism? We had found fault with the Boy Scouts, with their uniforms, ranks, saluting, and merit badges—twelve-year-olds lockstepping in mindless uniformity—let alone Betar (the Revisionist youth movement with their semi-military organization). Habonim, a Socialist-Zionist youth movement, was at the opposite pole of all this. Our shlihim were obviously upset. Yaacov stood up and left. In the agitated conversation that followed, someone dubbed him "the bald eagle." Yaacov Dostrovsky, later Yaacov Dori, became the first chief of staff of the Israel Defense Forces. At the time of his visit to us, he commanded the underground Haganah and was on a mission to oversee the illicit purchase of arms.

The Dori incident reflected a gut response to rigidity and hierarchal authority. On second thought, which was not long in coming, we understood Dori better. We now faced the circumstances he had implied—war. In March 1948, the movement's highest body between conventions, the *moetza* (national council), gathered in Cleveland to decide how Habonim should respond. The Haganah had suffered heavy casualties, Jerusalem was under siege, the British were obstructing the Yishuv's defense forces. One item was on the agenda: the proposal to declare a national mobilization of Habonim—a *giyus*—to meet the emergency.

Thoughtful comrades argued that our primary duty was to educate: "In education emergencies don't exist." Individuals might be released from their leadership obligations, they conceded, but no more than that. In fact, the "older" generation was gone. Some from my generation—we were in our early twenties—were recruited to man the "illegal" ships sailing for European ports to load refugees in an attempt to run the British naval blockade of Palestine. Others had left for Palestine on the GI Bill ostensibly to study at the Hebrew University and the Technion or reached the country in other ways. The attrition rate of the cadre of experienced Habonim leaders was considerable. Would not this effort "to speed up aliyah" prove self-defeating, leave Habonim in shambles? Moreover, the notion of coercion inherent in "mobilization" was disturbing. Yet the movement did have an ideal and conscience. Had we not proclaimed, "Ours is the chosen generation?" Statehood was weeks away, and all might be lost.

The national council established a "mobilization committee." (We preferred the Hebrew, *va'ad giyus*.) Those who had declared their intention to go on aliyah were pressured to expedite their timetables. Younger members just out of high school were directed to the movement's training farms to hasten their preparations. Others were deemed essential for maintaining the organization. *Va'ad giyus* members and shlihim traveled the country interviewing the eligible age group, persuasion tempered by affability. We were not a draft board. Six hundred members were interviewed. By fall 1948, ninety had left for training farms, two hundred had sailed for Israel, and almost half of them had organized as a collective, the core group for a future kibbutz. I belonged to the latter. (In January 1949, Garin Alef joined with members of a kibbutz evacuated in the war to establish Gesher Haziv in the western Galilee.) My aliyah was deferred for more than a year while I served as the national *mazkir* (secretary), a more plebeian term for "national director."[5]

I was not in the kibbutz long enough to offer firsthand impressions of how the Americans responded to collective life.[6] The conventional view is that in such places where there was a considerable number of us, our influence was tangible. On the debate over where the children should be housed, in a communal home or with their parents, the Americans adamantly fought for the latter. When Gesher Haziv was founded, a number of the Americans believed that the kibbutz should not affiliate with the existing kibbutz movements, which were highly politicized. Building a kibbutz, the Americans contended, was apolitical. The allocations of subsidies, loans, and technical assistance were not party matters. Soon enough we were disabused of this idyllic American notion. One needed the intervention of party people in the institutions the kibbutz depended upon — banks, the Jewish Agency, the co-op marketing organizations of the Histadrut and the kibbutz federations themselves.

One incident stands out as emblematic of the political culture as I perceived it in those early years. In September 1951, Gesher Haziv sent a truckload of its members to participate in the establishment of a new kibbutz federation. The founding conference took place in Kibbutz Kinneret, on the shore of the Sea of Galilee. It was a stormy time of political realignments on the left which split the largest and ideologically the most broad-based of the kibbutz federations, ha-Kibbutz ha-Meuchad (United Kibbutz). The new federation consisted of the breakaway MAPAI-oriented kibbutzim and the conglomerate of the smaller, more conservative communal settlements, Hever ha-Kvutzot (Association of Settlements).

One session evolved around the perennial issue of the unity of the labor movement. Speaker followed speaker until Shlomo Lavi's turn came. I knew the name and Lavi's thinking, a tribute to the intellectuals among our shlihim. Lavi had emigrated to Palestine in 1905, worked as an agricultural laborer and watchman, and formulated a plan for a large collective based not only on agriculture but industry as well, and without limitation of numbers. It was then that the term "kibbutz" was introduced in contrast to the small, agricultural *kvutza,* which stressed social cohesion, essentially an extended family. Lavi's kibbutz form, he predicted, would be economically viable and become a powerful agency for absorbing masses of immigrants. In fact, Lavi was instrumental in establishing Ein Charod, the prototype of the large kibbutz, and although he was sixty-nine years old at the time of the conference and a prolific writer, he insisted on doing physical work. Tragically, both his sons had fallen in the War of Independence. Lavi was a legend to me. Why be satisfied, he asserted, with merely joining the two federations present at the conference? Why not open the doors of the new alliance to the *moshavim* (the cooperative agricultural settlements)? It was music to my ears: his broad, inclusive vision downplayed ideological hairsplitting and sidestepped doctrinaire declarations. Suddenly, a short, enraged figure half-ran to the speaker's podium screaming at Lavi. (Was he the next speaker waiting in the wings?) How did Lavi dare suggest that the moshav movement be included within the pioneering vanguard of Socialist-Zionism? It was an affront to those present to suggest that peasant capitalists, violating even their own principles of cooperative living, be considered worthy of any alliance with the kibbutz movement. The coarseness of the attack and the absence of any protest by those present depressed me. The attitude seemed to be: this is an eccentric old man who has talked too long. A knowledgeable observer later identified the intruder as an important kibbutz functionary. Not long ago a friend from movement days and a founding member of Gesher Haziv, Moshe Kerem, who had made his mark in kibbutz circles and in education, mused over the absence of Habonim graduates in the political life of the country. None of us had "made it." According to Kerem, "We were just not tough enough, hard-fisted enough, to play that Israeli game successfully. We were products of Habonim." A prominent Israeli figure had said: "In order to play the Israeli brand of politics, one must break through the 'makhsom ha-busha'—the 'shame barrier'—to deal nastily with people, including your friends."[7] Probably the same was true in the United States, except we had no such ambitions in America.

What was it like to be an *American* immigrant in a land of many kinds of immigrants? Surely, language loomed as the enormous hurdle to overcome. Was it more painful for the Americans than for others? I think so. The German immigrants of the 1930s had similar difficulties. The fact that we were integrating well culturally in our countries of origin, benefiting from a higher education or eager to have one, essentially monolingual, and having access to the high culture of the Western world may have handicapped us in truly mastering Hebrew. I came with a fairly decent grounding in the language, that is, according to the American standards of the 1940s. I was fortunate on two other counts. Ayalah Kadman, whom I met while she was a shliha in America, studied at the university with me. I had a private tutor and, when things became difficult, a translator for my seminar papers. Marriage gave me the base of an old Tel Aviv family where Hebrew was the language of the dinner table, and a circle of Ayalah's friends where only Hebrew was spoken. I had also chosen to study Jewish history and Bible, subjects for which the course bibliographies were largely in Hebrew. For thirty-five years as a student and then a professor at the Hebrew University I lectured, read exams, wrote reports, and attended meetings where only Hebrew was used. And in the late 1960s I appeared with some frequency as an "Expert on America" on Israeli radio and television. Yet after fifty years I have remained "ha-Amerikani." The American-accented Hebrew hasn't gone away. The sharp, angular speech—the "resh," the "khet," the diphthong "o" of *kholem*—labeled me an American.

I still have to pause on occasion in lecturing or in conversation and think of the correct gender, especially when it comes to numbers. I am reminded of my immigrant grandparents. My Hebrew is better than their English was. When I was a youngster, our mode of conversation was bilingual: they spoke Yiddish and I answered in English. It was different with my children. We both spoke Hebrew but they corrected mine. And after a stint in

New York while I completed my graduate studies, they became fully bilingual. During this period they also became conversant with Jewish ritual and religious customs. Six years of Solomon Schecter Day School and two summers at Camp Ramah did that. Their great grandparents would have been pleased. (Both sons were called to the Torah at Jerusalem's proto-Reconstructionist congregation, M'vakshei Derekh, and their sons and daughter at Reform congregations in Kiryat Ono and Tel Aviv.)

Nevertheless, the immigrant experience in our family—from Eastern Europe to the United States, and from there to Israel, and the frequent American sojourns over the past four decades—has been a profound one, and not only in shaping family values and culture. At a critical moment in my studies when I decided to forgo my first love, biblical history, I searched for a field and specialty to which I might bring some insight, a field that would enhance my chances of teaching at the Hebrew University. It seemed that my own immigrant experience and that of my parents and grandparents offered such a possibility. In the one course I took at the Hebrew University in American social history before going on to Columbia, I recall being deeply moved reading Oscar Handlin's *The Uprooted* and thinking that it should be translated into Hebrew. I was fired by the idea of comparing the American and Israeli experiences. In a sense, my Columbia dissertation on the New York Kehillah (Jewish community) did that. Handlin's context of confusion and disarray is there. There is also a Zionist motif: politicking for communal fellowship and democratic governance, striving for ethnic (or nationalist) integration and a Hebraic revival. Interestingly, Judah Magnes, the founder and chairman of the Kehillah and later the first chancellor of the Hebrew University, arranged for the Kehillah archives to be sent to Jerusalem in 1945. His hope was to write its history, or at least commission someone to write it.

Living in two cultures required a personal political decision. In the early years of Israel the legal question of dual citizenship illuminated the issue of possessing dual identities. The "Law of Return," the hallmark of Jewish sovereignty, automatically gave each Jew Israeli citizenship with its rights and obligations. We could vote, and we were required to take part in defense of the country. Both acts, voluntarily entered into, were cause for losing one's U.S. citizenship. A few "opted out": they declined Israeli citizenship. Others presented themselves at American consulates and returned their U.S passports. For them, it was a matter of principle. One had to choose. Others voted, did their army reserve duty, and hoped that somehow a choice could be avoided. I belonged to the latter group and for twenty-seven years was a reservist called up periodically like everyone else. (My comprehensive examinations in Bible, which I felt unprepared for, fell on the opening day of the Suez Campaign as I was hitchhiking to my unit, not a very distinguished one. The exam was postponed of course. The war was an act of God.)

Even as late as the early 1950s an atmosphere of "burning one's bridges" was associated with aliyah, certainly halutzic aliyah. One could root oneself in Zion by not looking back, by making aliyah "unconditional." For some, I among them, America was not only our youth and an important part of our being, it was a happy part and our families were there. Yet how could one refuse to be on guard duty, refuse to be in the reserves (that is, decline Israeli citizenship), or not vote in Knesset elections?

Since that time, a remarkable transformation has occurred. Boundaries have blurred in more than one way: summer workshops for youth, a year of work-study programs, a semester or two at the university, and for academics, Fulbrights and sabbaticals are only some of the options that bring Americans for extended stays. A rising standard of living has also made it possible for American Israelis to take "home leave." (Our two sons, born in 1954 and 1955, the austerity years in Israel, met their American grandparents for the first time in 1959 when we arrived in New York so that I could complete my graduate studies.)

No less important than these developments was the removal of the original legal difficulty. Supreme Court decisions invoking "due process" have steadily rolled back automatic loss of citizenship. Today, in what is tantamount to a reverse "Law of Return," American Jews can be full-fledged Israelis and American Israelis can be full-fledged Americans. Consider the case of the former prime minister, Binyamin Netanyahu.

In one sphere, living in two cultures neither mixes nor relates: when sons, in particular, reach army age and are mobilized. I emigrated to Israel of my own free will, accepting the duties of an Israeli citizen. My sons, Avner and Amos, born in Israel, had no choice. They and their peers bore the brunt of defending the country, as my grandchildren will. Some months after my sons were mobilized, I recall, I was on a brief lecture tour to a number of American campuses. (With children in the army, parents do not take sabbaticals.) I watched the eighteen- and nineteen-year-olds walking across the campus, sitting in classes, attending my lectures, and I thought: what a wonderful transition to adulthood despite the fierce competition to get into elite schools. At home my sons were making their transition to adulthood in the army, competing to get into elite combat units and, once accepted, striving to remain. Grades of a different sort were required for that.

When Avner, the oldest, became bar mitzvah two months after the Six Day War, the euphoria we felt stemmed from our hope that by the time his turn would come for army service the mandatory time period would be greatly reduced. Perhaps a volunteer professional army would be sufficient. Now our oldest grandson, Avner's son, is about to be drafted.

Not only is this a line of demarcation between my Israeli self and American Jews. It has also opened an abyss at home in Israel: I on one side and the Haredim, the ultra-Orthodox Jews whose sons do not serve in the army, on the other, and whose authoritarian political parties manipulate fragile democratic system for their self-aggrandizement. Ingrained American notions of separation of church and state—and I am aware that they are not readily transferable—and norms of political behavior were implanted in us as we grew up in America and were reinforced because we were liberal American Jews. Agonizing, too, is the vexatious problem of those Jewish settlements in Hebron and on the outskirts of Gaza, Ramallah, and Nablus, whose presence is a perpetual incitement to conflict. On this score, I and my kind are often maligned as *y'fey nefesh* (bleeding hearts), who as naive Americans never learned the rules of a ruthless world.

Old credos don't always evaporate although they mellow with time. Once we dared believe that a "new code of ethics will blaze from Zion, a new life based on the principles of equality and social justice." Derivative as the slogan may be, my generation of American Israelis embraced it, and as Americans believed it was indivisible. Indeed, two creative *but* problematic centers of Jewish life interact and also diverge.

NOTES

The first two epigraphs are from *Arise and Build, the Story of American Habonim* (New York, 1951), p. 5. The third epigraph is from Berl Katznelson, *Writings* (Tel Aviv, 1940), vol. 9, p. 256.

1. J. J. Goldberg and Elliot King, eds., *Builders and Dreamers: Habonim Labor Zionist Youth of North America* (New York, 1993), pp. 129–30.

2. While preparing this piece for publication, I located John Updike's magnificent account of Ted Williams's last game at Fenway Park ("Hub Fans Bid Kid Adieu," in *Assorted Prose,* New York, 1965). A good test of the geographic location of one's "essential" identity is the baseball team he or she roots for. The Red Sox remain my team. Williams was, is, and will always be my hero. I never got into Israeli soccer.

3. *A.D. Gordon: Selected Essays,* ed. Frances Burnace (New York, 1938), pp. 1, 3.

4. Arthur A. Goren, "Celebrating Zion in America," in Jeffrey Shandler and Beth Wenger, eds., *Encounter with the "Holy Land"* (Hanover, NH, 1997), p. 55.

5. David Breslau, "The Eve of Statehood: Habonim Mobilizes for War," in Goldberg and King, eds., *Builders and Dreamers,* 130–32; William Goldfarb, "To Go Against the Stream," in ibid., pp. 346–49.

6. After my first year in the kibbutz I asked for a leave of absence to study at the Hebrew University. My GI Bill would have lapsed had I not begun using the college provisions. Because it was a superb year from all points of view, I decided that I had better return to the kibbutz. A year after that I left for the university for good. Even then I was nominally "on leave" for some time. Obviously, I was torn between commitment to the kibbutz and the many with whom I had grown up, and the thirst to study.

7. Moshe Kerem (Murray Weingarten) in Goldberg and King, eds., *Builders and Dreamers,* p. 355.

Index